Retailing and E-tailing

by

Mickey Kosloski, PhD
Assistant Professor
Old Dominion University
Norfolk, Virginia

Sharon R. Davis, MS Ed
Senior Lecturer
Old Dominion University
Norfolk, Virginia

Publisher
The Goodheart-Willcox Company, Inc.
Tinley Park, Illinois
www.g-w.com

The Goodheart-Willcox Company, Inc. Brand Disclaimer: Brand names, company names, and illustrations for products and services included in this text are provided for educational purposes only and do not represent or imply endorsement or recommendation by the author or the publisher.

The Goodheart-Willcox Company, Inc. Safety Notice: The reader is expressly advised to carefully read, understand, and apply all safety precautions and warnings described in this book or that might also be indicated in undertaking the activities and exercises described herein to minimize risk of personal injury or injury to others. Common sense and good judgment should also be exercised and applied to help avoid all potential hazards. The reader should always refer to the appropriate manufacturer's technical information, directions, and recommendations; then proceed with care to follow specific equipment operating instructions. The reader should understand these notices and cautions are not exhaustive.

The publisher makes no warranty or representation whatsoever, either expressed or implied, including but not limited to equipment, procedures, and applications described or referred to herein, their quality, performance, merchantability, or fitness for a particular purpose. The publisher assumes no responsibility for any changes, errors, or omissions in this book. The publisher specifically disclaims any liability whatsoever, including any direct, indirect, incidental, consequential, special, or exemplary damages resulting, in whole or in part, from the reader's use or reliance upon the information, instructions, procedures, warnings, cautions, applications, or other matter contained in this book. The publisher assumes no responsibility for the activities of the reader.

The Goodheart-Willcox Company, Inc. Internet Disclaimer: The Internet resources and listings in this Goodheart-Willcox Publisher product are provided solely as a convenience to you. These resources and listings were reviewed at the time of publication to provide you with accurate, safe, and appropriate information. Goodheart-Willcox Publisher has no control over the referenced websites and, due to the dynamic nature of the Internet, is not responsible or liable for the content, products, or performance of links to other websites or resources. Goodheart-Willcox Publisher makes no representation, either expressed or implied, regarding the content of these websites, and such references do not constitute an endorsement or recommendation of the information or content presented. It is your responsibility to take all protective measures to guard against inappropriate content, viruses, or other destructive elements.

Introduction

In today's competitive workplace, investigating multiple career options is more challenging than ever. In *Retailing and E-tailing*, you will explore career opportunities in the traditional brick-and-mortar retail industry, as well as the online retail business of e-tailing.

One of the goals of this text is to help you understand that retailing and e-tailing share common objectives. Both businesses meet consumer needs and wants. Both businesses play a defining role in the economy. The difference is the method in which each business provides their services. To highlight this difference, two chapters of this text are dedicated to creating an e-tail site. This information will allow you to compare and contrast a brick-and-mortar business to one that is online.

Retailing and E-tailing provides multiple college and career activities to prepare you for life after graduation. Also, the DECA Coach activity at the end of each chapter guides you in preparing for DECA competitive events and your future career. A Math Skills Handbook is provided as a quick reference for basic math functions.

The QR codes in each chapter link you directly to the *Retailing and E-tailing* companion website for access to study tools, such as quizzes and e-flash cards. In addition, the G-W Learning mobile site makes it easy for you to study on the go!

About the Authors

Mickey Kosloski has been directly involved with marketing education for 16 years. Following 17 years in sales and business ownership, he began his career as a marketing education high school teacher. During this time, he developed an Internet Marketing curriculum for the City of Chesapeake, Virginia—only the second such curriculum in the nation. Mr. Kosloski became the DECA state advisor for Virginia. He served several years as the Southern Region Council Chair and received the International Outstanding Service Award from DECA, Inc. He is currently employed at Old Dominion University as an assistant professor, and is the program leader for both marketing education and business and industry training. He has consulted on several projects for organizations such as DECA, Inc., MBA Research, and Opportunity, Inc. Mr. Kosloski earned a BS degree in marketing education, an MS in career and technical education, and a PhD in education with a concentration in career and technical education.

Sharon R. Davis is a senior lecturer at Old Dominion University with an extensive background in marketing education and retail merchandising. She began her teaching career in marketing education where her students received numerous awards at the district, state, and national DECA conferences. She served as the Collegiate DECA state advisor for Virginia and has developed merchandising curriculum for fashion marketing programs through private industry grants. Ms. Davis has a broad range of entrepreneurial experience with businesses that include wholesale, retail, transportation, distribution, and restaurants. She currently serves as the program leader for fashion merchandising at Old Dominion. She earned her bachelor degree in marketing and business education and an MS Ed in secondary education with a concentration in marketing education.

Reviewers

The author and publisher would like to thank the following individuals for their valuable input in the development of *Retailing and E-tailing*.

Summer D. Basgier
Business and Marketing Teacher
McAdory High School
McCalla, AL

Margie Bowden
Marketing Co-Op Advisor
McAllen High School
McAllen, TX

Kim L. Creamer
Marketing Coordinator
Virginia Beach City Public Schools
Virginia Beach, VA

Suzanne E. Demmond
Business & Marketing
    Department Chair
Hanover Central High School,
    Hanover School Corp.
Cedar Lake, IN

Efrain Filerio
Business Teacher
Yuma High School
Yuma, AZ

Dwionne R. Freeman
Business Education Teacher
Atlanta Public Schools
Atlanta, GA

Tim Gleim
Director, Special Projects &
    Brand Integrity
Dollar Tree Stores, Inc.
Chesapeake, VA

David Graham
Merchandise Buyer & IT Manager
Village Commons Bookstore
DeKalb, IL

Delda L. Hagin
Business Education Teacher
Ware County High School
Waycross, GA

Jennifer Hair
Business Education Instructor
Shawnee Mission East High School
Prairie Village, KS

Shawn Haskell-Henry
Marketing and Fashion
    Marketing Teacher
Green Run High School
Virginia Beach, VA

Emma Hering
Apparel Manager
Worth the Wait Consignments
    and Boutique
Virginia Beach, VA

Rebecca Hopple-Cuellar
Business Educator
Oxnard High School, Oxnard
    Union High School District
Oxnard, CA

DeAna Islas
Marketing Teacher
Franklin Simpson High School
Franklin, KY

Jennifer Klein
Business Education Teacher
Alan B. Shepard High School
Palos Heights, IL

Jean Kotsiovos
Executive Director of Curriculum
Kaplan University
Chicago, IL

Nick Maier
Personal Ticket Consultant
Rockford Icehogs
Rockford, IL

Kathy McLain
Business Education Instructor
Belleview High School
Belleview, FL

Cindy Miller
Marketing Education Teacher
Floyd E. Kellam High School
Virginia Beach, VA

Maurine Monteith
Business and Marketing Teacher,
    NBCT
Clover High School
Clover, SC

Heather Palasota
Business Education and
    Marketing Teacher
CTE Department Chair
Cypress Lakes High School
Katy, TX

Brian Rodriguez
Senior Programmer
Huron Consulting Group
Chicago, IL

Jo Rossman, LEED AP ID+C
Design Editor
Planning and Visual Education
    (PAVE), managed by A.R.E.
Hollywood, FL

Sean Segal
Chief Operating Officer
Urban Alliance
Washington, DC

Brenda Vines
Marketing Educator and DECA
    Sponsor
Klein Collins High School
Spring, TX

Lynne P. Williams
Hotel Marketing Instructor
Virginia Beach City Public
    Schools
Virginia Beach, VA

Contents in Brief

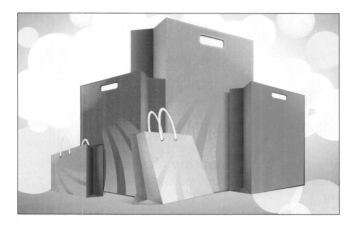

Expanded Table of Contents

Unit 1
Retailing 2

Chapter 3
Nonstore Retail Operations . . 50

Unit 2
Marketplace Strategy 70

Chapter 4
Marketing Research. 72

Chapter 5
Targeting the Market 96

Unit 7
Retail Careers 434

Chapter 19
Preparing for a Career 436

Chapter 20
Job Applications and Interviews 456

Student Focused

Retail is all around us. It influences what we buy, how we live, and the careers we choose. *Retailing and E-tailing* will help guide you in understanding how this industry affects your decisions as a consumer, as well as the career you might choose.

One of the goals of a retailing and e-tailing textbook is to show how these businesses share fundamental retail practices. Both businesses sell to customers and apply similar marketing concepts. The obvious difference is that one is a brick-and-mortar model and the other is an online model. As basic theory is presented, the application to both is discussed. To highlight the e-tail model, two chapters are dedicated to creating an e-tail website.

It is all about getting ready for college and career. College and Career Readiness activities address literacy skills to help prepare you for the real world. Standards for English Language Arts for reading, writing, speaking, and listening are incorporated in a **Reading Prep** activity as well as end-of-chapter activities. Common Career Technical Core Career Ready Practices are also addressed.

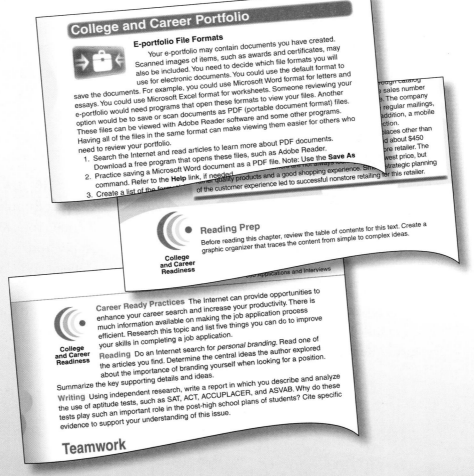

Content Connected

Ever wonder how the world of retail connects with your life? Practical activities relate everyday learning to enable you to experience real-life retailing and e-tailing.

- **Exploring Retail Careers** features present information about retail career opportunities. Retail and e-tail are a part of the marketing career cluster. By studying these features, you can learn more about career possibilities for your future.
- **College and Career Portfolio** activities enable you to create a personal portfolio for use when exploring volunteer, education and training, and career opportunities.
- **Case Study** features at the beginning of each chapter highlights a retail or e-tail business. These case studies will help you understand the connection between theory and real application.

Exploring Retail Careers

Store Manager

A store manager is responsible for the daily operations of a retail store. Depending on the size of the store and how it is structured, the tasks for this position may vary. Human resource duties, managing finances, and customer relations are some of the tasks of a store manager. Human resource duties may include hiring new workers as well as training and scheduling employees. Managing finances may entail monitoring prices and

College and Career Portfolio

Clubs and Organizations

Employers and colleges review candidates for various positions. They are interested in people who impress them as being professional or serious about a position. Being involved in academic clubs or professional organizations will help you make a good

Case Study

Nikon USA

Nikon USA makes some of the most technologically advanced digital imaging equipment in the world. Sometimes, having the best products is not enough. The company believed that a website face-lift would improve both online and in-store sales. A web design company overhauled the site. Some changes were more obvious to customers than others. For example, modifications that helped the site show up higher in search engine rankings were probably not apparent to customers. The file size of Nikon USA web pages was reduced so the pages displayed more quickly. Customers may have noticed pages that originally took ten seconds to load could be viewed in less than one second. Just these two changes increased site traffic by 214 percent.

The addition of a learning center was a very visible change to the site. Nikon products can be complex. So, a section of the website is dedicated to helping customers understand and use the equipment. The Learn & Explore section includes how-to articles, key terms, equipment recommendations, photography expert tips, and videos. After the learning center launched, sales increased in all product lines, but particularly for the most complex and expensive products. Nikon USA created a more effective and useful e-tail store that led to increased sales.

Checkpoint 3.1

1. Give three examples of nonstore retailing.
2. What are the advantages of online shopping?
3. Why do consumers use the Internet to conduct research before buying?
4. Explain how product reviews affect purchasing decisions.
5. What security and privacy concerns does e-tailing present to

Review Your Knowledge

1. How does a store's image attract specific customers? What physical components are used to portray a retailer's image?
2. Explain the use and impact of visual merchandising.
3. List and describe the different types of floor plans.
4. What factors are important to consider in the selling area?
5. Define open and closed displays and give an example of each.
6. What is the *traditional approach* to creating visual displays?
7. Describe the use of props in displays.
8. Identify and describe the three types of lighting used in a display.
9. Why are signs important for retail stores?
10. Differentiate between symmetrical and asymmetrical balance.

Apply Your Knowledge

1. Recall the purpose of merchandising in retail. Explain how merchandising and visual merchandising are related activities. How does visual merchandising

Career Ready Practices What do you think the old adage, "Necessity is the mother of invention" means? Find examples of how the need for something has led to the development of something new.

Listening Ask a classmate to give you directions on how to drive to the nearest mall. Take notes as the directions are given. Evaluate and summarize your notes. If necessary, ask the speaker to slow down or repeat a point. Use prior knowledge of the city to follow the directions that are given.

Reading Now that you have completed reading multiple chapters in this text about retailing and e-tailing, analyze the themes and structures that the author used. Create a concept map that illustrates how the themes of this text are related.

College and Career Readiness

Teamwork

Legal issues were covered in this chapter. Working with your teammates, identify five legal issues that may be of concern in a retail business. These issues could impact the consumer, employer, or retail. After you have identified the issues, list ways each of the issues could be resolved.

College and Career Portfolio

It is important to assess what you learn as you progress through the text. Multiple opportunities are provided to confirm learning as you explore the content. *Formative assessment* includes the following:

- **Checkpoint** activities at the end of each major section of the chapter provide you with an opportunity to review what you have learned before moving on to additional content.
- **Review Your Knowledge** activities cover basic concepts presented in the chapter so you can evaluate your understanding of the material.
- **Apply Your Knowledge** activities challenge you to relate what you learned in the chapter with your own experiences and goals.
- **Teamwork** activities encourage a collaborative experience to help you learn to interact with other students in a productive manner.
- **College and Career Readiness** activities provide ways for you to demonstrate the literacy and career readiness skills you have mastered.

Features Spotlighted

DECA prepares emerging leaders and entrepreneurs in the areas of marketing, finance, hospitality, and management within high schools and colleges around the globe. The **DECA Coach** activity at the end of each chapter provides a first-hand opportunity for you to explore learning activities that prepare you for DECA competitive events.

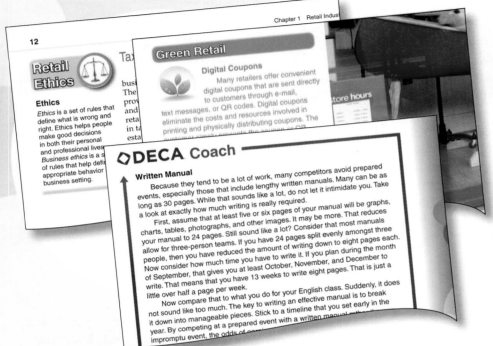

Practical information helps you prepare for your future. Special features add realism and interest to enhance learning.

- **Retail Ethics** offers insight into ethical issues that arise for retail businesses and how they make good decisions.

- **Green Retail** shares how retailers apply best business practices for the environment.

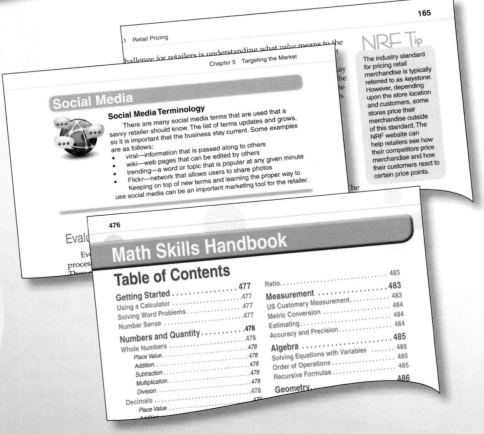

- **NRF Tips** from the National Retail Federation help you understand the value of professional organizations.

- **Social Media** features illustrate how retailers make the most of social media tools and practices to promote their businesses.

- **Math Skills Handbook** provides you with a quick reference of basic math functions. This helpful information will help clarify math applications presented in the chapters.

Technology Applied

Technology is an important part of your world. So, it should be part of your everyday learning experiences. The following technology-based resources and activities are available to support your learning:

- Chapter **pretests** and **posttests** are available on the G-W Learning companion website, as well as the G-W Learning mobile site. Taking the pretest will help activate your prior knowledge of the content. Taking the posttest will help you evaluate what you have learned about the chapter content.
- **E-flash cards** for every key term are available on the G-W Learning companion website, as well as the G-W Learning mobile site. Using the e-flash cards will reinforce what you learned in the text and allow you to study on the go.
- Research skills are critical for college and career. The **Web Connect** feature at the beginning of each section provides an opportunity to put those skills to work.

G-W Learning Companion Website

The G-W Learning companion website for *Retailing and E-tailing* is a study reference that contains e-flash cards, vocabulary exercises, and interactive quizzes.

G-W Learning companion website: www.g-wlearning.com

G-W Learning Mobile Site

The G-W Learning mobile site* is a study reference to use when you are on the go. The mobile site is easy to read, easy to use, and fine-tuned for quick access.

The G-W Learning mobile site for *Retailing and E-tailing* contains chapter pretests and posttests, as well as e-flash cards and vocabulary practice. These features can be accessed using a smartphone or other handheld device with Internet access. These features can also be accessed through an Internet browser on the G-W Learning companion website.

G-W Learning mobile site: www.m.g-wlearning.com

Scan now!

Goodheart-Willcox QR Codes

This Goodheart-Willcox product contains QR codes*, or quick response codes. These codes can be scanned with a smartphone bar code reader to access information or online features.

For more information on using QR codes and a recommended QR code reader, visit the G-W Learning companion website at www.m.g-wlearning.com.

*An Internet connection is required to access the QR code destinations. Data-transfer rates may apply. Check with your Internet service provider for information on your data-transfer rates.

Scan now!

Unit 1
Retailing

Introduction

The retail industry encompasses a wide array of options, locations, and opportunities. Regardless of the "location" of a retail business, the intent of any retailing venture is the same—offer goods and services to the customer with the goal of making a profit.

Unit 1 introduces the basic characteristics of the retail industry, including profits, supply and demand, competition, merchandising, and the supply chain. The chapters also explore various types of store-based retail locations and online retail operations, as well as options for owning a retail establishment.

Green Retail

Carbon Footprint

A carbon footprint is a measurement of how much the everyday behaviors of an individual, company, or community impact the environment. This includes the amount of carbon dioxide put into the air from the consumption of energy and fuel used in homes, for travel, and for business operations.

Online carbon footprint calculators can be used to determine areas and practices that need to change. Companies can reduce their carbon footprint by recycling, reducing waste, and using responsible energy options. For example, satellite and video communication systems can be used to hold business meetings across the country. This reduces the fossil fuel emissions for travel by automobile, train, or airplane.

In This Unit

littleny/Shutterstock.com

3

Chapter 1
Retail Industry Profile

Many factors, both economic and social, affect the success of a retail business and the retail industry as a whole. Retailers choose which goods and services to provide based on consumers' needs and wants. Consumers may consider value, store experience, and the retailer's efforts to be socially responsible when choosing where to shop. Consumers benefit from retail through competitive prices, enhanced product, unique shopping experiences, and creating or supporting a standard of living.

Successful retailers actively work within the functional areas of a retail business. They evaluate the utility of their products and business to best serve customers and increase sales.

Case Study

Zara

Zara is a worldwide leader in retail apparel sales. With more than 1,800 stores in 75 countries, this retailer has found a key to retail success. Zara stores offer trendy, unique clothing at reasonable prices. They often beat high-fashion houses to the market with up-to-the-minute, stylish products.

Zara is known for having a "fast-fashion" system. More than 200 in-house designers create and sell over 10,000 new designs per year. Customers know the products are exclusive and in fixed quantity. If Zara customers do not "act now," they know that may lose their chance to buy a special product.

Zara has achieved retail success by focusing on the customer and recognizing what is needed and wanted. Zara provides brick-and-mortar stores as well as online shopping, making it convenient to buy anywhere and at anytime. Zara also understands the importance of eco-friendly stores and a commitment to the environment.

College and Career Readiness

Reading Prep

Before reading this chapter, try to find a quiet place with no distractions. Make sure your chair is comfortable and the lighting is adequate.

Check Your Retail IQ

Before you begin the chapter, see what you already know about retail by taking the chapter pretest. If you do not have a smartphone, visit the G-W Learning companion website.

G-W Learning mobile site: www.m.g-wlearning.com

G-W Learning companion website: www.g-wlearning.com/marketing/

Sections

1.1 What Is Retail?

1.2 Industry Overview

Andresr/Shutterstock.com

Section 1.1 What Is Retail?

Objectives

After completing this section, you will be able to:
- **Describe** the characteristics of the retail industry.
- **Recognize** the ways consumers benefit from retail.
- **Describe** the economic benefits of the retail industry.
- **Explain** how the retail industry benefits society.

Key Terms

retail
goods
services
retailer
business-to-consumer (B2C)
consumer
customer
competition
standard of living
economic benefits

gross domestic product (GDP)
free-enterprise economic system
revenue
profit
supply
demand
corporate social responsibility (CSR)
philanthropy

Web Connect

How profitable is retail in the United States? Search the Internet for the top five retailers of the year. Which retail store was the most profitable? How do the numbers among the top five retailers compare to each other? What factors do you think contribute to the profitability of these retailers?

Critical Thinking

The term *retail* means different things to different people. Write a paragraph explaining the role retail plays in your life as a consumer. Include information about how various aspects of retail affect your daily life.

Retail Market

You have heard the word "retail" used many times. You visit retail stores with physical locations, as well as online retail stores. But, do you know what "retail" really means? **Retail** is the business of exchanging goods and services for personal, family, or household use. **Goods** are tangible products that can be touched, such as food and clothing. **Services** are intangible activities performed for the benefit of others, such as repairing a car or giving a manicure. **Retailers** are businesses that offer goods to or provide services for individual consumers. A retailer that sells to consumers is known as a **business-to-consumer (B2C)** business.

Consumers

A **consumer**, or *end user*, is a person who buys *and* uses products or services. Most retail stores sell to consumers. A **customer** is a person or group that makes a purchase. For example, when you buy a product or service for personal use, you are both a consumer and a customer. However, when you buy a gift for someone, you are a customer, but not a consumer.

Retailers offer products that satisfy consumers' needs and wants. A *need* is something that is necessary for survival, such as air, water, food, clothing, and shelter. A *want* is something that a person desires but can function without, such as a new cell phone or a vacation.

Consumer Goods

Retail products are categorized by how the products are purchased. The three basic categories of consumer goods are convenience goods, shopping goods, and specialty goods, as shown in Figure 1-1.

Convenience goods are products bought with little effort for immediate use. Convenience goods include grocery items, most clothing, and gasoline. The consumer market for convenience goods is broad.

Categories of Consumer Goods

Art Allianz/Shutterstock.com

grzym/Shutterstock.com

GuoZhongHua/Shutterstock.com

Convenience Goods	**Shopping Goods**	**Specialty Goods**
Groceries	Furniture	Cars
Clothing	Home electronics	Jewelry
Home decor	Household appliances	Rare antiques
Personal care products	MP3 players	Luxury home items
Gardening supplies	Cell phones	

Goodheart-Willcox Publisher

Figure 1-1 The three basic categories of retail products are convenience goods, shopping goods, and specialty goods.

Shopping goods are products usually purchased after comparing price, quality, and style in more than one store. Shopping goods are bought less often by consumers than convenience goods. They include more expensive and durable items, such as appliances and furniture.

Specialty goods are unique items that consumers are willing to spend considerable time, effort, and money to buy. Specialty goods have the fewest consumer purchases. Examples of these items include a unique sports car and rare antiques. Decisions to buy expensive specialty products are based on personal preference, brand name, or special features.

Consumer Benefits of Retail

Consumers have many different needs and wants, which create a demand for certain products. Retailers offer products to satisfy consumer demands because they cannot survive without customers. Customers compare products, quality, and prices at different stores, and choose value-added retailers or products. Many retailers offer a unique store experience that appeals to consumers seeking more than just products.

Competitive Prices

Retailers compete with each other to attract customers to buy their products. Competition is the act or process of trying to win something, such as a customer's business. Competition among retail stores helps keep prices fair. When several retailers offer the same products, each retailer is forced to price products competitively. What would happen if there were only one gas station in an area? There is a chance that station would charge whatever it wants for a gallon of gas. With more than one gas station in an area, customers can compare prices and decide which business to patronize. This type of competition forces most retailers to sell products at the lowest prices possible, yet still make a profit.

Value-Added Retailing

The term *value-added* describes any enhancement to a product or service that makes consumers want to buy. Wise consumers consider the value of different products before they purchase. They comparison shop to learn which product to buy and where to get the best values.

Low prices alone do not always mean a good value to consumers. While important, price is not always the only reason to buy at certain stores. Sometimes retailers add value through expert sales associates, bundling options, or great customer service. Many stores offer credit so customers can buy now and pay later. Some retailers even offer gift wrapping, delivery, or personal shopping services for added value.

Unique Store Experiences

Ultimately, retailers want to provide consumers with a shopping experience that cannot be duplicated anywhere else. Retailers consider a store's interior design as important as the products they sell. Color, furniture, music, lighting, and service are all part of a store's experience. Interiors are designed to welcome customers, make them want to spend more time there, and hopefully buy more. For example, Apple and Abercrombie & Fitch stores have environments that feel special. These stores appeal to consumers who want more than just merchandise.

Standard of Living

Standard of living is a level of material comfort measured by the goods, services, and luxuries available to people. In other words, it describes a lifestyle. Retail stores help to enhance standard of living in two ways: supply and influence.

Retailers supply nearly every product a consumer might want. Technology helps create large amounts of product, and consumers have vast product choices available to them.

Retailers influence the types of products people want by making consumers aware of new and better products through retail marketing efforts. Print, radio, and TV ads, as well as attractive product displays and social networking, often motivate consumers to buy. Many people do not know they want or need a product until they see it on TV or in a store display.

The uncluttered and accessible interior of an Apple store invites customers to explore its products and interact with employees.

bioB/Shutterstock.com

Economic Benefits of Retail

Economic benefits are gains that are measured in financial terms. Retailing benefits the US economy in many ways, at both national and local levels.

US retail sales totaled an estimated $4.4 trillion in 2012. Approximately two thirds of the gross domestic product (GDP) in the United States comes from retail sales. **Gross domestic product (GDP)** refers to the market value of all goods and services produced within a country during a given period of time. The GDP is one measure of a country's economic health.

Retailing works best in a free-market economy, such as the economy of the United States. A **free-enterprise economic system**, also called a *free-market*, allows businesses to compete with limited government intervention. All businesses must follow certain laws and rules, but owners may run their businesses any way they choose. While these economic concepts are often taken for granted, not every country can conduct business with such freedom. Unlike the United States, businesses in some countries are controlled more by the government than by individual business owners. This means the *four Ps of marketing*—product, price, place, and promotion—are mostly determined by the government.

The amount of money a company generates from sales during a specific period is **revenue**. The amount by which revenue from sales exceeds the costs of making and selling the product is **profit**. The free-enterprise system is the driving force that enables retailers and others to make a profit and stay in business.

All US businesses have the following rights and options.

- Anyone is allowed to open a business in a free-market system.
- Businesses can buy and sell what they want, based on the right to make a profit.
- Businesses may utilize the economic principle of *supply and demand*. **Supply** is the amount of product retailers are willing to offer. **Demand** is the amount of product consumers are willing to buy.
- Businesses have a right to compete in the marketplace, which encourages retailers to offer consistent products at fair prices.
- All companies are treated equally by the government and protected under the law.
- Businesses have the right to own property without government intervention.
- Businesses may enter into contracts with the companies they choose.

FYI

In some countries, the government controls all of the manufacturing and retailing industries so that product choices can be limited.

Consumers are also part of a free-market economic system. Retailers decide which products to sell based on consumer demand. If consumers like the products a store sells, they reward the retailer by making a purchase. If consumers do not like the products, they shop at other stores that offer exactly what they want.

Because competition is encouraged, a free market also means that consumers influence prices. For example, three stores in a town sell the same cell phones. With all other factors being equal, most consumers will choose the store with the lowest price. Therefore, all three competing stores try to keep their prices as low as possible to win more business.

Employment

An economic benefit of retail is the employment it provides. The retail industry has more than 14 million employees in the United States. This makes retail the second largest industry in the country, behind health care. According to the National Retail Federation, over 24 million people worked in retail-related jobs in 2010, or nearly one out of every five US workers. These jobs include loss prevention, accounting, supply chain logistics, e-commerce web app development, and human resources.

The local economy benefits from having citizens who are employed. Retailers hire employees who earn money and, in turn, buy more local products and services.

Exploring Retail Careers

Store Manager

A store manager is responsible for the daily operations of a retail store. Depending on the size of the store and how it is structured, the tasks for this position may vary. Human resource duties, managing finances, and customer relations are some of the tasks of a store manager. Human resource duties may include hiring new workers as well as training and scheduling employees. Managing finances may entail monitoring prices and profits. Dealing with unhappy customers is also part of the job. Ultimately, it is the store manager's task to increase sales and maintain a positive work environment. Some examples of tasks that store managers perform include:

- establish goals and objectives for the store
- assign duties to and supervise workers
- make personnel decisions such as hiring, firing, training, and promoting
- prepare budgets and other financial reports
- resolve problems with customers, employees, and the store itself

Store managers must have strong leadership, communication, and problem-solving skills. They should be able to manage and motivate employees. An understanding of the basics of finance is needed. A high school diploma and several years of retail experience are usually required for these positions. Many large retailers also require some college or a bachelor degree.

Taxes

Retailers, like other businesses, pay taxes on profits from their businesses. The larger the business' revenue, the more taxes are paid. The taxes support local, state, and federal governments, and help provide necessary civic services, such as education, law enforcement, and road repairs. According to the National Retail Federation, retailers generally pay between 30 and 40 percent of their net income in taxes. Additionally, retailers who own physical stores pay real estate taxes.

State and local sales taxes are collected by retailers on behalf of the government bodies that require those taxes. Retailers also collect their employees' state and federal income taxes for the government.

Social Benefits of Retail

Retailing also provides social benefits, which help to better society or a community. Being *socially responsible* means behaving with sensitivity to social, economic, and environmental issues. **Corporate social responsibility (CSR)** is when a business is not only concerned with its own profits, but also acts with the welfare and interests of society in mind. Socially responsible retailers give back to the communities in which they operate. Some consumers actually use social responsibility as a deciding factor in where they shop.

Retailers may want to be known as socially responsible businesses. Retailers with a high level of CSR may attract more customers who share and support similar concerns. For example, some people may be willing to pay a little more for products from companies that support their personal values, such as cancer research or saving whales. Other consumers may prefer to buy only from green businesses that recycle or sell organic products.

Retailers who are socially responsible help to build their own brand by promoting goodwill. *Goodwill* is an intangible asset a business has due to its good reputation. It is developed over time through the actions of the retailer. Goodwill helps develop a positive brand image and customer loyalty, as consumers tend to shop with retailers they like and trust. Retailers understand that people are more likely to buy from businesses that reflect their own values.

Philanthropy

Philanthropy is action that contributes to the improvement of the welfare of others. Retailers have many opportunities to be philanthropic through donations of money and property, or even by providing work to those in need. Both small and large retailers support social causes through different philanthropic efforts. Some donate to local or national charities. Others organize employees to volunteer in schools or for other community projects, such as Habitat for Humanity.

For example, Macy's has raised more than $45 million with its nationwide *Shop for a Cause* effort. Macy's gives schools and other nonprofit organizations savings passes to sell in their communities. Consumers benefit by purchasing a generous savings pass to use on products at Macy's. The nonprofit organizations keep the proceeds from the savings pass sales to fund their operations.

Environment

Direct efforts to protect the environment affect society as a whole. There are many ways for a socially responsible business to conserve natural resources and reduce pollution. Many retailers have taken action to improve our ecology to build their brand with consumers, as well as to better serve the environment. *Going green* means to take action that is good for the environment. Many consumers and businesses prefer buying from retailers that use sustainable, green business practices.

Often referred to as the three *R*s, environmentally friendly retailers attempt to *reduce, reuse,* and *recycle*. They may *reduce* the amount of natural resources used by using a paperless bookkeeping system or landscaping with plants that require less water. Retailers have many opportunities for *reuse,* such as providing customers with reusable shopping totes or bags made from recycled materials. *Recycling* is a common practice. Retailers look at everything the business uses, including paper, printer cartridges, and glass and plastic bottles.

Sustainability refers to methods that do not completely use up or destroy natural resources. Everything from raw materials to packaging and marketing can be sustainable in the retail business. Many retailers are becoming more committed to environmental protection by recycling, saving paper, and choosing green energy options. Basic activities, such as recycling, using energy-efficient lightbulbs, and turning off lights are simple ways a business can save money and conserve resources.

Many retailers offer reusable shopping totes in an effort to be environmentally friendly and support their customers' environmental priorities.

Several government resources are available to help retailers establish greener practices. A common resource is the *Environmental Protection Agency (EPA)*, which provides information about environmental compliance rules and regulations. These laws vary by business sector. The EPA (www.epa.gov) also has a vast amount of information devoted to environmental law and sustainable business practices.

Some corporations, such as Whole Foods, Patagonia, and American Apparel, are dedicated to offering green, organic products or those made from recycled materials. Some retailers offer small discounts to customers who bring reusable bags to pack their items. Most businesses advertise their green product offerings and business practices on their website, which is considered a green marketing tool.

Checkpoint 1.1

1. To whom does retail appeal?
2. Explain the difference between a *consumer* and a *customer*.
3. Explain the concept of value-added retailing.
4. What are the economic benefits of retail?
5. Describe what it means for a corporation to be socially responsible.

Build Your Vocabulary

As you progress through this course, develop a personal glossary of retailing terms and add it to your portfolio. This will help you build your vocabulary and prepare you for a career. Write a definition for each of the following terms, and add it to your personal retailing glossary.

retail	economic benefits
goods	gross domestic product (GDP)
services	free-enterprise economic system
retailer	revenue
business-to-consumer (B2C)	profit
consumer	supply
customer	demand
competition	corporate social responsibility (CSR)
standard of living	philanthropy

Section 1.2 Industry Overview

Objectives

After completing this section, you will be able to:
- **Describe** the role retail plays in the supply chain.
- **Explain** the importance of NAICS codes to the retail industry.
- **List** the functional areas of retail businesses.
- **Identify** how retailers provide utility through products.

Key Terms

supply chain
channel of distribution
supply chain
  management
manufacturer
wholesaler
intermediary
NAICS

merchandising
operations
promotion
finance
human resources
information
  technology (IT)
utility

Web Connect

Retailers are classified according to the type of product they sell. Research the development and use of NAICS codes, and write several paragraphs on your findings.

Critical Thinking

As a consumer, you shop in many types of retail establishments. What criteria do you use to classify various types of retailers? Make a list of criteria you use to distinguish different retailers.

Retail in the Supply Chain

It is important to understand how products get from the manufacturer to the customer. The **supply chain** is the businesses, people, and activities involved in creating products and delivering them to end users. The **channel of distribution** is the path that goods take through the supply chain from the *producer* (or manufacturer) to the consumer, as shown in Figure 1-2.

In a *direct channel* of distribution, the producer of a product sells it directly to the end user. For example, a farmer that grows corn may set up a roadside store and sell corn directly to anyone who wants to buy it.

A more common path is an indirect channel of distribution. An *indirect channel* of distribution uses other businesses to get products from the manufacturers to the end users. Nearly all products sold at retail stores flow through an indirect channel, as products are not actually made in the stores. For example, shoe stores sell shoes, but the shoes are not made in the shoe store.

Figure 1-2 Products may pass through one (direct) or several (indirect) channels on the way to the consumer.

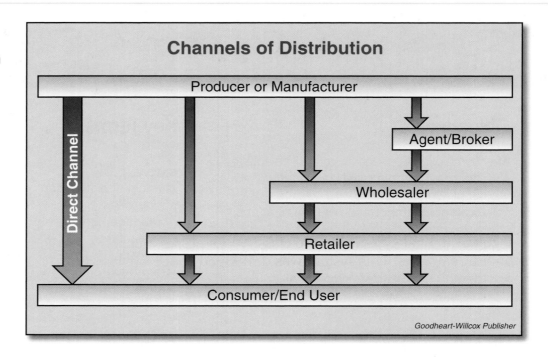

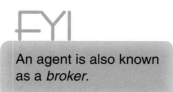

Goodheart-Willcox Publisher

Supply chain management is the process of coordinating the manufacturers, wholesalers, agents, and retailers to get products into the hands of the consumers. **Manufacturers** are the businesses or people that make the products. **Wholesalers** purchase goods in large quantities directly from manufacturers. For a fee, an *agent* helps manufacturers locate buyers for their goods and negotiates purchasing contracts. Unlike wholesalers, agents do not actually own the products.

Retailers are **intermediaries**, or *middlemen*, in the supply chain, positioned between the manufacturers and the consumers. Wholesalers may also act as intermediaries when they store products and resell them in smaller quantities to retailers and consumers.

There are specific factors that define a business as a retailer. For example, a retailer must make more than half of their sales to end users. If less than half of sales are to end users, a business is considered a wholesaler.

Certain characteristics are unique to retailers:

- Retailers are open to the public, while producers and wholesalers do not sell to the general public.
- Retailers sell in smaller quantities, while producers and wholesalers sell in bulk.
- Retailers have higher prices per unit than wholesalers or producers.
- Retailers tend to use a one-price policy, but producers and wholesalers may have variable pricing.
- Retailers create an image of the store and influence consumers through the environment they create, such as lighting, décor, or music.

FYI

An agent is also known as a *broker*.

Retailers are the primary businesses that sell to consumers. Some very small or individual producers may sell their goods directly to consumers. However, these sales are usually personal sales or online.

NAICS Codes

There are many types of retailers that provide goods and services. One way to distinguish retailers is to identify the different types of retail business NAICS codes. The North American Industry Classification System, or **NAICS** (pronounced "nākes"), is a governmental system used to classify businesses and collect economic statistics. This system was developed cooperatively by the governments of the United States, Canada, and Mexico for trade purposes. The NAICS codes help countries define industries using the same business categories. The countries can compare industry statistics with each other for economic reasons, as well as use the data internally. The retail industry has two overall classification codes: 44 and 45. Under those two industry classification codes, there are 12 category codes by business type, as shown in Figure 1-3.

Each category may have subcategories, which help to further compare and analyze specific retail business types. For example, code 448 (clothing and accessories stores) may be broken into men's, women's, infants' and children's, and family clothing stores.

NAICS Retail Codes and Categories	
Code	Category
441	Motor vehicle and parts dealers
442	Furniture and home furnishings stores
443	Electronics and appliance stores
444	Building material and garden equipment and supplies dealers
445	Food and beverage stores
446	Health and personal care stores
447	Gasoline stations
448	Clothing and clothing accessories stores
451	Sporting goods, hobby, book, musical instrument, and fabric stores
452	General merchandise stores
453	Miscellaneous store retailers
454	Nonstore retailers

Goodheart-Willcox Publisher

Figure 1-3 Retail industry category codes were developed by the North American Industry Classification System (NAICS).

Each of those subcategories may be further divided into even more product detail, such as shoes, specialty sizes, formalwear, etc. As a category gets more specific, the NAICS code becomes longer, as shown in Figure 1-4.

Functional Areas of Retail

Function is a general word for a category of activities. Each *functional area* of a retail business exists to best serve customers and increase sales. The functional areas of retail are: merchandising, operations, promotion, finance, human resources, and information technology (IT). Each of these functions is usually performed by an individual or department in the business. Some retailers may hire outside resources to assist with some functions. For example, accounting or advertising may be done by an outside firm.

Merchandising

According to the American Marketing Association, *merchandising* is "identifying the product and product line decisions of retailers." Merchandising includes selecting and buying products to be resold to customers. It also includes displaying the merchandise in appealing ways.

Operations

Operations are the day-to-day activities necessary to keep a business up and running. In a retail business, operations can include scheduling, building maintenance, inventory and warehousing, store security, and shipping.

A primary goal of the operations function is efficiency. Efficient operations lower expenses, increase profits, and help keep product prices down.

NAICS Subcategories and Codes	
4461	Health and personal care stores
44611	Pharmacies and drug stores
44612	Cosmetics, beauty supplies, and perfume stores
44613	Optical goods stores
44619	Other health and personal care stores
446191	Food supplement stores
446199	All other health and personal care stores

Goodheart-Willcox Publisher

Figure 1-4 The NAICS code number gets longer as subcategories become more focused.

Social Media

Social Media as a Tool

Social media plays an important part in your life every day of the week. You use social media to build your personal brand, develop a community, and to communicate with others. Businesses have also learned the many advantages of using social media.

Webster's dictionary defines social media as, "forms of electronic communication (such as websites for social networking and microblogging) through which users create online communities to share information, ideas, personal messages, and other content (such as videos)." Social media is one tool that can complement the strategies for a retail business when used wisely. Social media can help a business be visible. By communicating regular updates on new products, events the company is attending, or recognizing customer feedback, a retailer can help keep its brand in front of customers.

Promotion

Promotion is all of the communication techniques sellers use to inform or motivate people to buy their products. It includes advertising, sales promotions, public relations, and personal selling.

Institutional promotion is promoting a business, rather than its specific products. Promoting a company's brand or image makes consumers aware of the company. *Product promotion* is promoting specific products or services offered by the retailer. More often, promotions tend to focus on products.

Finance

Finance is activity involved in controlling and managing money and other business assets. It includes recordkeeping, payroll, accounting, taxes, budgets, and any other financial considerations. Finance also includes analyzing the financial health of a business by creating financial statements. The information on financial statements is used to make sound business decisions.

Human Resources

The **human resources** function involves managing employees and looking out for their general well-being. To operate a store, people must be recruited, hired, trained, evaluated, and sometimes fired. Other human resources tasks include managing employee benefits, setting store policies, conflict resolution, and dealing with labor unions.

Information Technology (IT)

Information technology (IT) includes all forms of technology used to create, store, exchange, and analyze various types of digital information. Retailers depend heavily on technology in the form of computers and software programs to manage their stores. IT is not a stand-alone function; it plays a role in each of the other five functions. Technology is necessary for running online stores, of course, but is important for brick-and-mortar stores as well.

Utility

Another meaning of the word *function* is "purpose." One of the purposes of retail is to provide utility for consumers looking to buy products. **Utility** is the attribute that makes a business or product capable of satisfying a need or want; it defines how or why something is useful. Retailers provide the products consumers need, when and where consumers want them. As a result, retail stores are in nearly every community. It would be useless for a retailer to sell a product that consumers would not buy—there would be no utility, or purpose, in that retail effort.

The four basic types of utility are: time, place, form, and possession.

Time Utility

Time utility is making merchandise available when it is needed. For example, many retailers are open in the evenings to accommodate working people with limited shopping time. Typical retail hours for many stores might be 10:00 a.m. to 9:00 p.m. Some retailers, such as gas stations, make an extra effort to provide additional time utility and may be open 24 hours per day.

Place Utility

Place utility means having convenient locations for consumers. The location of a store plays a big role in its success, since consumers must be willing and able to travel there. Online stores provide the ultimate in place utility. People can shop from anywhere they wish, as long as they have an Internet connection.

Form Utility

Form utility, also called *product utility*, means offering products that meet wants or needs of consumers. For example, if you needed a new coat, you would only visit stores that sell coats. In this example, stores without coats would not provide form utility.

Possession Utility

Retailers provide *possession utility* by making a purchase possible or easier. For instance, some retailers offer financing or credit options. Others may offer delivery services to make it easy for consumers to buy their products.

Checkpoint 1.2

1. Explain direct and indirect channels of distribution.
2. Describe the NAICS code system and why it is important to retail.
3. What are the functional areas of retail?
4. What is the difference between institutional promotion and product promotion?
5. What are the four basic types of utility?

Build Your Vocabulary

As you progress through this course, develop a personal glossary of retailing terms and add it to your portfolio. This will help you build your vocabulary and prepare you for a career. Write a definition for each of the following terms, and add it to your personal retailing glossary.

supply chain	merchandising
channel of distribution	operations
supply chain management	promotion
manufacturer	finance
wholesaler	human resources
intermediary	information technology (IT)
NAICS	utility

Chapter Summary

Section 1.1 What Is Retail?

- Retail provides goods and services for the end user, or consumer. Retailers provide convenience goods, shopping goods, and specialty goods to meet those needs and wants.
- Through retail, consumers reap the benefits of competitive prices, enhanced products, unique shopping experiences, and the potential of a positive standard of living.
- Economic benefits of retail for the United States include increased GDP, employment for its citizens, and taxes to run the government.
- Retailing provides social benefits, which help to better society or a community. Being socially responsible means behaving with sensitivity to social, economic, and environmental issues.

Section 1.2 Industry Overview

- Retailers are an important intermediary in the supply chain. Through direct and indirect channels, product makes its way from the manufacturer to the consumer.
- NAICS codes help distinguish retailers based on the product or services they offer.
- The functional areas of retail exist to best serve customers. The universal functional areas of retail are merchandising, operations, promotion, finance, human resources, and information technology (IT).
- Utility defines how or why something is useful. The four basic types of utility are time, place, form, and possession.

Review Your Knowledge

1. Compare and contrast goods and services.
2. What is the difference between a need and a want?
3. What are the consumer benefits of retail?
4. Explain the economic principle of supply and demand.
5. Explain why it is important for a business to have goodwill.
6. What characteristics are unique to retailers?
7. How do retailers provide time utility? Give an example.
8. How do retailers provide place utility? Give an example.
9. How do retailers provide form utility? Give an example.
10. How do retailers provide possession utility? Give an example.

Apply Your Knowledge

1. Retail is considered a B2C market. Give an example of a retailer that might also sell to businesses. What types of products does the business sell?
2. There are three basic categories of consumer goods. Create a chart with a heading for each category. Under each heading, list product examples and a retailer that sells the product.

3. One benefit of retail is competitive prices. Select a well-known retail business and explain how the retailer provides competitive pricing.
4. The gross domestic product (GDP) in the United States was approximately $15.685 trillion in 2012. Research the GDP for the previous four years and chart the changes. What economic influences do you think affected recent GDP statistics?
5. How do you think employment rates in the United States affect the retail industry? Research recent unemployment statistics and retail industry trends. Write several paragraphs to defend your opinion.
6. Identify ways that businesses contribute to their communities economically and socially.
7. Create a template for the supply chain. Select a product that you regularly purchase. Using the template, trace the product from the manufacturer to you as the buyer. What did you learn from this exercise?
8. Visit the US Census Bureau website and find a detailed chart of the NAICS codes. Describe the information the chart contains. Did you find any of the information surprising?
9. Research the American Marketing Association. Make a list of services the organization provides to the retail industry.
10. Utility is an important concept in marketing. Explain how utility serves retail.

Check Your Retail IQ

Now that you have finished the chapter, see what you learned about retail by taking the chapter posttest. If you do not have a smartphone, visit the G-W Learning companion website.
G-W Learning mobile site: www.m.g-wlearning.com
G-W Learning companion website: www.g-wlearning.com/marketing/

College and Career Readiness

Career Ready Practices Successful employees also are responsible citizens. Exceeding expectations is a way to be successful at school and in your career. Make a list of five things that you expect of yourself on a daily basis, such as being on time, completing tasks as assigned, or being courteous. Think about each of the things you expect from yourself, and then record what you could do to exceed those expectations. What effect do you think exceeding your expectations has on your success?

Writing Standard English means that word choice, sentence structure, paragraphs, and the format of communication follow standard conventions used by those who speak English. Well-written paragraphs are usually the product of editing. Research the topic of college access. Where did the concept originate? Generate ideas and gather information that might help you. Write an informative report consisting of several paragraphs to describe your findings. Edit the writing for proper syntax, tense, and voice.

Speaking The way you communicate with others will have a lot to do with the success of the relationships you build with them. There are formal and informal ways of communicating a message. Create a speech that will introduce you to a counselor at a local college. The counselor should be a person you have never met. Deliver the speech to your class. How did the style, words, phrases, and tone you used influence the way the audience responded to the speech?

Teamwork

Working with your teammates, select a product that your team uses on a regular basis. Examples may be clothing, school supplies, or computer equipment. Create a flowchart showing the supply chain. What did you learn from this exercise?

College and Career Portfolio

Portfolio Overview

When you apply for a job, for community service, or to a college, you may need to tell others about how you are qualified for the position. A portfolio is a selection of related materials that you collect and organize. These materials show your qualifications, skills, and talents. For example, a certificate that shows you have completed lifeguard and first-aid training could help you get a job at a local pool as a lifeguard. An essay you wrote about protecting native plants could show that you are serious about eco-friendly efforts and help you get a volunteer position at a park. A transcript of your school grades could help show that you are qualified for college.

Two types of portfolios are commonly used: print portfolios and electronic portfolios, or *e-portfolios*. An e-portfolio is also known as a digital portfolio.

1. Use the Internet to search for *print portfolio* and *e-portfolio*. Read articles about each type of portfolio. In your own words, briefly describe each type.
2. You will be creating a portfolio in this class. Which portfolio type would you prefer to create? Write a paragraph describing the type of portfolio you would prefer to create.

◇DECA Coach

Learn about DECA

DECA provides a wide array of opportunities to its members. From community service, to leadership, to networking, to public relations, DECA has something for everyone.

One exciting facet of DECA is its competitive events programs. DECA members have the opportunity to compete in authentic situations related to current business practices. These events are sponsored at the local, state, and international levels.

One of the most valuable resources at your disposal is the DECA website. When preparing for your competitive event, visit DECA's website early and often. Here you will find many necessary tools, such as a full description of the current competitive events, guidelines, and performance indicators. The website includes sample role plays, case studies, and written event summaries. These elements are updated frequently and will provide you with the most current information. Consider the DECA website your toolbox for competitive events.

Visit www.deca.org to learn more information about DECA.

G-W Learning Mobile Site

Visit the G-W Learning mobile site to complete the chapter pretest and posttest, and to practice vocabulary using e-flash cards. If you do not have a smartphone, visit the G-W Learning companion website to access these features.

G-W Learning mobile site: www.m.g-wlearning.com

G-W Learning companion website: www.g-wlearning.com/marketing/

Chapter 2
Brick-and-Mortar Retail

Store-based businesses have advantages over online retailers. Store-based businesses offer a face-to-face customer experience, personal service, and can create an in-store experience that appeals to customers' physical senses. These qualities make shopping a social experience and, hopefully, create loyal customers!

Brick-and-mortar businesses also distinguish themselves by the kind of products or services they offer, pricing, and business ownership type. Customers expect certain things from certain retailers—a high level of customer service, unique products, bulk pricing, or a consistent shopping environment. The business decisions made and ownership structure put in place are critical to a retailer's long-term success.

Case Study

h.h. gregg®

Henry Harold Gregg and his wife Fansy opened an 800 square-foot appliance showroom in Indiana in 1955. Their attention to good retail practices helped this small, family-owned business become a thriving chain of superstores known around the country. You know them as h.h. gregg, the appliances and electronics superstore—there may be one near you!

h.h. gregg started with one small store, which eventually grew to a 5,200 square-foot store. As the business continued to grow, h.h. gregg opened one new Indiana-based store at a time. Selecting just the right location was critical to the success of each new store. Growth was slow and strategic.

h.h. gregg understood the importance of brick-and-mortar superstores and opened their first one in 1979. With positive customer response to the superstore concept, h.h. gregg opened three more by 1984 and began expanding into markets outside of Indiana. In 2007, h.h. gregg became a publicly traded company on the New York Stock Exchange. Since that time, h.h. gregg has continued to open new superstores in select locations around the country. As of 2012, h.h. gregg has more than 220 superstores and is one of the fastest growing companies in the nation. Strategic planning and smart growth lead to real retail success for h.h. gregg.

College and Career Readiness

Reading Prep

Before reading this chapter, look at the chapter title. Write a paragraph describing what you already know about the topic. After reading the chapter, write a paragraph to summarize what you have learned. How do the two paragraphs compare?

Check Your Retail IQ

Before you begin the chapter, see what you already know about retail by taking the chapter pretest. If you do not have a smartphone, visit the G-W Learning companion website.

G-W Learning mobile site: www.m.g-wlearning.com

G-W Learning companion website: www.g-wlearning.com/marketing/

Sections

2.1 Store-Based Retail

2.2 Retail Ownership and Structure

Anton Gvozdikov/Shutterstock.com

Section 2.1 Store-Based Retail

Objectives

After completing this section, you will be able to:
- **Identify** the unique characteristics of store-based retailers and their various shopping locations.
- **Define** traditional retailers.
- **Describe** the different types of discount retailers.
- **Explain** how service retailers differ from other retailers.

Key Terms

brick-and-mortar
anchor store
town center
central business
  district (CBD)
traditional retailer
specialty store
manufacturer retail
  store
boutique
kiosk
supercenter
warehouse club
off-price retailer
factory outlet
big box store
service retailer

Web Connect

Search the Internet for retailers in your zip code and make a list of ten local retailers. For each retailer, indicate if the store is located in a shopping mall, strip mall, or central business district. Are any of the stores in a stand-alone location? What conclusions can you make about retailer locations in your area?

Critical Thinking

Americans have drastically changed their shopping habits, which has forced many retailers to change how or where they operate. Some retailers even went out of business. Have these changes affected any shopping centers or stores in your community? Describe recent changes in your community's retail environment.

Shopping Locations

Store-based businesses are brick-and-mortar retailers that have an accessible storefront. Brick-and-mortar stores have a physical location to display and sell merchandise and services. These stores offer a face-to-face customer experience, as opposed to online stores. Many consumers want to walk into a store, touch the merchandise, and interact with a salesperson.

While some retail stores may be isolated, most are conveniently located close to other stores in a shopping center or central business district.

Shopping Centers

A *shopping center* is a group of retail stores that is planned, developed, owned, and managed as a single property. Shopping centers are built to provide a one-stop-shopping place for customers. Many may have distinct features, such as parking structures, restaurant offerings, and unique architectural design. Types of shopping centers include shopping malls, strip malls, and town centers.

Shopping Malls

Traditional *shopping malls* usually have anchor stores and various other retailers under one roof. This makes it convenient for consumers to shop in any weather condition and draws a wide variety of customers. An **anchor store** is a large retail store that attracts many consumers to the mall. Sears and Macy's are examples of anchor stores. Other stores within the mall may depend on the customers drawn to the big anchor stores.

Malls can be one or more stories with stairs, elevators, or escalators to move consumers between floors, as shown in Figure 2-1. Shopping malls also typically include a number of places to eat. Restaurants can attract potential customers and encourage them to remain in the mall. Many malls include a centrally located *food court*, which is an area where a number of fast-food restaurants are located. The food court may also include a common eating area for diners to sit and eat.

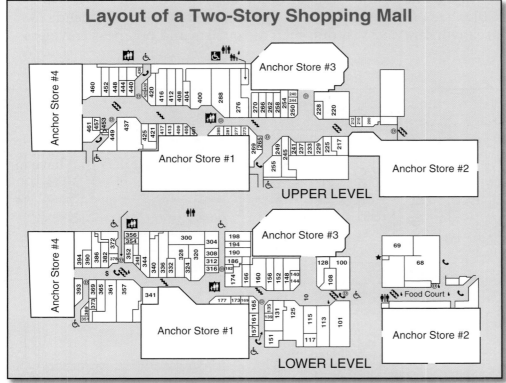

Figure 2-1 In a traditional shopping mall, the anchor stores are located at the ends of the mall to draw customers into the stores within the mall.

Goodheart-Willcox Publisher

Strip Malls

Strip malls are smaller, open-air shopping centers where the stores are attached to each other with a sidewalk in front. They may be located close to residential areas for convenience. Strip malls often target local neighborhood residents and generally have at least one place to eat. They may or may not include an anchor store.

The stores in a strip mall may be configured in several ways. All of the stores may be in a row or in *L* or *U* shapes. The outdoor walkways connecting one store to the next are typically unsheltered and open to the elements. Parking is often provided in front of the store locations, as shown in Figure 2-2.

Town Centers

Town centers are open-air shopping centers with many retailers. They are arranged more like the center of a small town with open walkways and abundant landscaping. The retail development is usually built around a main center or square. Some town centers have anchor stores, and nearly all have restaurants.

A town center is often designed to look like the neighboring area. For example, a town center near a colonial neighborhood might be made of brick and use colonial-period architecture.

Central Business Districts (CBD)

Central business districts (CBD) are central locations for retail, business, and transportation activities in a city or town. CBDs are often referred to as *downtown*. They serve the needs of area workers and visitors, such as tourists and business travelers.

Figure 2-2 In this strip mall layout, the stores are arranged in a row with parking spaces accessible from the storefronts.

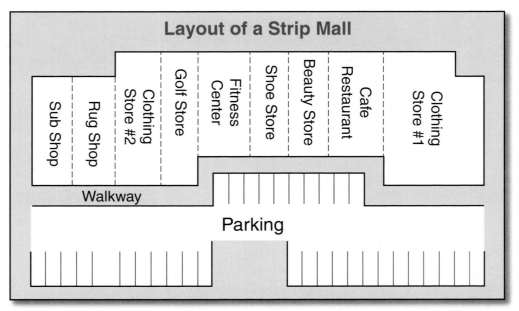

Goodheart-Willcox Publisher

Retail stores are typically clustered near each other. Hotels, restaurants, and entertainment choices bring people to the area. CBDs tend to have a wide variety of stores, offering merchandise at all price points.

Some retail businesses, especially restaurants, may choose to locate in a large downtown office building with many employees. A similar choice is to locate near an *office park*, which is an area with many commercial and office buildings. Most office parks form their own business districts and are located outside of downtown areas. Workers in office buildings or office parks offer a steady stream of potential customers. Convenience and location are key to a retailer's success in these areas.

Parking at office parks is typically free. However, most downtown parking options are fee-based and can be quite expensive. Convenient public transportation options can be important to potential customers. The higher crime rates of some downtown locations can make consumers reluctant to visit the CBD.

Traditional Retailers

In-store shopping is a social experience. Some people like to get out and browse at their local stores as much for entertainment as for shopping. **Traditional retailers** are store-based retailers that use the five senses (sight, touch, taste, smell, and hearing) to enhance the shopping experience. For example, apparel stores may use fragrance to give their store a distinctive smell. Some stores may play a certain type of music or use lighting to create a certain environment. Each traditional retailer has features that define its appeal, depending on the needs and wants of the consumer. Traditional retailers include specialty, department, and convenience stores.

Specialty Stores

Specialty stores sell a limited product line, but offer a wide variety of options within the product line, in addition to other related items. For example, a shoe store may only sell shoes and shoe accessories, but it offers many different types and sizes of shoes. The store may also sell shoe-shine kits, shoelaces, socks, and other shoe-related products. Specialty stores also include manufacturer retail stores, boutiques, supermarkets, drugstores, and kiosks.

Manufacturer Retail Stores

Manufacturer retail stores only sell the products from one manufacturer. These stores may be owned by the manufacturer or by another party. The automobile industry commonly uses manufacturer retail stores in the form of car dealerships. Some higher-end furniture stores operate this way, as well.

Retail Ethics

Customer Data

E-tail websites gather personal and confidential information from customers such as credit card numbers or phone numbers. Sharing or tampering with personal information is not only unethical, but may also be illegal. Protecting the customers' data will help protect the reputation of the business.

Specialty stores sell a wide variety of options within a limited product line.

Blend Images/Shutterstock.com

Manufacturer retail stores are often in direct competition with other stores that sell the same products. Interestingly, the *Harvard Business Review* reports that manufacturer retail stores usually charge higher prices for their own products than other retailers. Some well-known manufacturer retail stores include Apple, Ethan Allen, and Nike.

Boutiques

Boutiques are highly-specialized stores that cater to consumers seeking unique items and a high level of customer service. Exclusive apparel and personal service are two qualities that help define a boutique. Because boutiques provide extra services and unique, high-end products, their prices are higher than other stores.

Most boutiques have only one location. Some designer boutiques, however, may be found inside various upscale stores. The French design house Chanel, for example, often sells its products in special boutique areas located within larger stores. Whether visiting a stand-alone or in-store Chanel boutique, consumers find the same unique Chanel designs.

Supermarkets

Supermarkets sell fresh produce, meat, and other groceries, with a limited line of nonfood items. Supermarkets also typically have deli-style counters for sliced meats, cheeses, and premade salads and sandwiches. According to the Food Marketing Institute, a typical supermarket carries roughly 38,700 products. As a retail-industry category, supermarkets employ about 3.4 million people, with total sales of nearly $563 billion. Supermarkets offer a vast selection of grocery products conveniently located in one store.

Drugstores

The first drugstore, or pharmacy, in the United States was opened in Fredericksburg, Virginia, during the Revolutionary War. Drugstores started as places where people could buy medications. By the 1920s, drugstores expanded to include snack bars so customers waiting for prescriptions could eat or have a refreshing drink. Drugstores continued to evolve beyond just a pharmacy. While many offer other items and services, the majority of drugstore products remain health, hygiene, and beauty related.

Kiosks

Kiosks are very small structures with one or more open sides to display and sell a limited number of goods. This type of retailer is found in airports or the aisles of shopping centers. Small items are typically sold in kiosks, like souvenirs, magazines, sunglasses, or cell phone accessories. These miniature stores are a good way to start a business on a small scale. If the kiosk is successful, the retailer may expand the product lines and move into a storefront in the mall.

Department Stores

The concept of selling a wide assortment of merchandise under one roof was introduced in the mid-nineteenth century. This type of retail store is called a *department store*. At the time, a one-stop shopping experience was a new idea. Consumers were used to going to different specialty stores for their needs. Now, department stores are commonplace.

A department store is basically a group of specialty stores, called *departments*, merged into one store. The merchandise in a department store is carefully planned and organized so customers can easily find what they need. Products are arranged by categories, such as cosmetics, men's and women's apparel, shoes, and furniture. A consumer can buy clothing, shoes, cosmetics, luggage, and a sofa without ever leaving the department store. Some examples of department stores include JC Penney and Dillard's.

Convenience Stores

A *convenience store* is a small retail store that is typically open long hours for consumer convenience. The store sells a limited grocery line, snacks, and sometimes gasoline. Convenience stores offer consumers the ability to make a quick purchase without large crowds, big parking lots, and long lines. There are usually many neighborhood locations, so they are easy to find.

Because convenience stores sell fewer products than other stores, the prices are generally higher than at larger stores. Still, many

NRF Tip

NRF defines retailers as "a business that sells directly to consumers through a store or website." Service providers are defined as "a company that primarily seeks a business-to-business relationship (client, partner, distributor, etc.) with retailers." Both may join the NRF.

consumers are willing to pay higher prices so they can get what they need quickly, at any time of the day or night. For example, buying milk at a convenience store that is on your way home from work may be easier than going to the nearest supermarket. The convenient location and time savings may be worth paying a little more for your milk.

According to the Association for Convenience and Fuel Retailing, there were over 149,000 US convenience stores in 2012. These stores accounted for about $680 billion in sales. Some common convenience stores include 7-Eleven, Plaid Pantry, and Circle K.

Discount Retailers

A *discount retailer* sells items at lower prices than most other retail stores. Discount stores keep their prices low in a number of ways:
- buy merchandise in very large quantities
- buy out-of-date or slightly flawed products for very little cost
- have a very short supply chain for low shipping costs

When discount stores save money on purchasing merchandise, they can offer lower prices to consumers. Discount retail stores include supercenters, warehouse clubs, off-price retailers, factory outlet and big box stores, and dollar stores.

Exploring Retail Careers

Customer Relationship Management

Customer relationship management (CRM) professionals help create and maintain a company's image by planning and directing activities to improve the retailer's relationship with its customers. A customer relationship manager also helps others within the business to maintain good customer relationships. Typical job titles for these positions include *customer relationship manager*, *custom relations manager*, and *customer service director*.

The following are some of the tasks that CRM professionals perform:
- Listen to recordings of an individual representative's customer interactions and score the interaction based upon company criteria.
- Develop, run, and maintain customer retention programs.
- Maintain customer databases and analyze data for trends.
- Work with the IT department to keep databases current.

CRM professionals spend most of their time communicating with company executives, customers, and the sales team. Excellent communications skills are important. Good management skills and strong analytical, technical, and mathematical abilities are helpful in these positions. CRM positions require a bachelor degree, with many also asking for prior CRM experience.

Supercenters

A **supercenter**, also called a *hypermarket*, is a very large discount department store that also sells a complete line of grocery products. This type of store is the fastest growing retail category. Supercenters provide the one-stop shopping experience of a department store with the low prices of a discount store. They often carry between 40,000 and 60,000 items. Products range from groceries, hardware, sporting goods, furniture, and appliances to computers and other electronics. Examples of supercenters include Super Target, Meijer, and Walmart Supercenter.

Warehouse Clubs

Unlike other retailers, a **warehouse club** only sells merchandise in bulk. Items are packaged in large quantities to sell at less expensive unit prices. For example, a warehouse club may only offer cereal in a case of six boxes. A single box of the same cereal at a supermarket may cost $3.99. When purchased in a six-box case at a warehouse club, however, the unit price for a single box may be only $2.59.

Warehouse clubs offer a wide variety of merchandise. Within product categories, the actual items for sale change often. Categories can include food, automotive supplies, jewelry, computers, furniture, and more. Warehouse clubs make money by charging a yearly membership fee for the right to shop there. This fee is why this type of retailer is considered a club—nonmembers cannot shop there. Charging membership fees is profitable for warehouse clubs because of the large number of people who join to save money on purchases.

Target stores have always offered their customers a wide variety of merchandise. In 1995, Target added groceries to many locations to provide guests with convenient one-stop shopping

Northfoto/Shutterstock.com

Warehouse club retailers keep costs down by buying products in very large quantities. The stores are large, usually at least 100,000 to 150,000 square feet, with products stocked high on racks and shelves. The organization resembles that of a typical warehouse. Some warehouse club retailers include Costco, BJ's Wholesale Club, and Sam's Club.

Off-Price Retailers

An **off-price retailer** sells brand-name merchandise at big discounts. These retailers take advantage of manufacturer overruns and canceled orders. To make room for new products, manufacturers and large retail stores must sell their goods leftover at the end of a season for very low prices. This is how off-price retailers acquire designer labels and other brand-name products. Because off-price retailers buy products at reduced prices, the savings are passed on to customers. Off-price retail stores have become popular with value-minded consumers. Some examples of off-price retail stores are T. J. Maxx, HomeGoods, and Big Lots.

Factory Outlets

Factory outlets are retail stores in which excess or unsold merchandise is sold at a discount directly to the public by the manufacturers, designers, or specialty stores. These stores are typically found in shopping centers that only have factory outlet stores, although some are stand-alone stores. Discounts in factory outlets can be as much as 75 percent off the original prices. Many well-known designers and manufacturers have outlet stores, including Levis, Coach, Ralph Lauren, J. Crew, and Gap.

Big Box Stores

A **big box store** is a large, specialty discount store. Big box retailers can buy products at lower prices because of their size and many locations. This allows them to sell products at lower prices. Big box stores also tend to have a greater variety of items in their specialty areas. Due to their massive size and low prices, big box stores are often called *category killers*. Small, local stores that offer the same category of products can be put out of business by a big box store. Some common big box stores are Home Depot, Best Buy, and Toys "R" Us.

Some big box stores are considered *superstores*. A superstore is a large retail store that offers a wide variety of merchandise in a specific product line, such as electronics, appliances, or sporting goods.

Dollar Stores

A *dollar store* is a retailer that sells a variety of general merchandise at very low prices. Dollar store products are often lower quality and are not popular brand names. There is typically a limited assortment within product lines. Packaged foods, such as pasta and canned goods, are staples in dollar stores because they last a long time.

The term *dollar store* can be misleading. Many assume that a dollar store sells all of its products for $1. Some dollar stores, such as the national chain Dollar Tree, sell all of their products for exactly $1. However, other dollar stores may offer items that cost more or less than $1.

Service Retailers

A **service retailer** is a business that provides services for a price. Services are activities performed for the benefit of others. Services are different from physical products in four basic ways:

- A service has no physical characteristic; it is *intangible*.

- The service is unique or *variable*.

- The production of the service is used when it is performed; the production and the service are *inseparable*.

- The service is *perishable* because it cannot be stored for later use.

Services can range from providing a meal to preparing taxes or renting a movie. Some of the many forms of service retailers include: financial, hospitality, maintenance and repair, recreation and tourism, personal, food, rental, security, and transportation services. Service retailers fall into two major categories: services provided inside the business and services provided outside the business, as shown in Figure 2-3.

Two Major Categories of Service Retailers

Tyler Olsen/Shutterstock.com

Stephen Coburn/Shutterstock.com

Inside the Business	Outside the Business
Tax preparation	Towing/roadside assistance
Dry cleaners	Package delivery
Hair salons	Airport transportation
Vehicle repair	Landscaping maintenance
Hotels	Cleaning services
Medical services	Food delivery

Figure 2-3 Some services depend on the customer coming to the retailer's location. For others, customers may never see the inside of a business' location to receive their services.

Service retailing is growing rapidly. The busier people's lives become, the more they rely on outside services to perform some activities they used to do themselves. For example, home maintenance and landscaping businesses give homeowners more leisure time. Instead of mowing the lawn, weeding, and planting on weekends, someone else can do it for a fee.

Checkpoint 2.1

1. What are two common locations for brick-and-mortar retailers?
2. Describe a typical central business district (CBD).
3. Name three different categories of traditional retailers.
4. How are discount retailers able to keep prices low?
5. What are the two major categories of service retailers?

Build Your Vocabulary

As you progress through this course, develop a personal glossary of retailing terms and add it to your portfolio. This will help you build your vocabulary and prepare you for a career. Write a definition for each of the following terms, and add it to your personal retailing glossary.

brick-and-mortar
anchor store
town center
central business district (CBD)
traditional retailer
specialty store
manufacturer retail store
boutique

kiosk
supercenter
warehouse club
off-price retailer
factory outlet
big box store
service retailer

Section 2.2 Retail Ownership and Structure

Objectives

After completing this section, you will be able to:
- **Identify** the forms of retail business ownership.
- **Explain** the different types of retail ownership structures.

Key Terms

independent store	liability
chain store	partnership
franchise	corporation
franchisor	stockholders
franchisee	limited liability
leased department	company (LLC)
sole proprietorship	

Web Connect

Like other businesses, there are various options for the ownership of a retail business. Search the Internal Revenue Service website (www.irs.gov) for information on the categories of business ownership. What kind of information does the IRS offer about the types of business ownership? Write a summary of your findings.

Critical Thinking

Make a list of five local businesses that are owned by an individual person or family. What do these businesses have in common? Explain your thoughts about the pros and cons of being the sole owner of a retail business.

Retail Ownership

Retail establishments, like any other business, must position their business to compete with other retailers. A business can distinguish itself in the marketplace in the following ways:
- *product assortment*—variety of product offered
- *level of service*—ranges from self-service to full service
- *price*—follow the suggested retail price, offer discount pricing, or other pricing that attracts customers
- *ownership*—recognized as being an independent business or being part of a franchise or chain

One of the primary ways retail businesses distinguish themselves is by ownership type. Retail stores can be owned and operated in a number of different ways, including independent stores, chains, franchises, and leased departments, as shown in Figure 2-4.

Independent Stores

An **independent store** is often a small retail business with one location and is privately owned and operated. Independent stores in most communities include hair salons, restaurants, repair shops, boutiques, and many more.

The owners of independent stores are most often local residents. They are usually at the store daily and are in close contact with the customers. Because of this, independent store owners often know their customers well and quickly respond to their product and service needs.

One big disadvantage for independent retailers is the inability to purchase merchandise in large quantities. As a result, the retail selling prices at independent retailers are higher than at stores that can purchase in large quantities. Many independent retailers attempt to overcome higher-prices by providing excellent customer service.

Retail Businesses			
Type	Ownership	Location	Examples
Independent Store	Privately owned and operated	Single location	Hair salons, local restaurants, repair shops, boutiques
Chain Store	Same person or company owns all locations	Two or more locations	Walgreens, Office Max, many supermarkets
Franchise Store	Parent company owns the chain and brand	Franchisee buys the rights to use the brand and operate a location	Subway, H&R Block, RadioShack, RE/MAX
Leased Department	Larger retailer/ building owner owns space	Designer or boutique retailer leases space for their products	Sephora within JC Penney stores, souvenir shop within a hotel

Goodheart-Willcox Publisher

Figure 2-4 Popular retail ownership options include independent store, chain store, franchise store, and leased department.

Chain Stores

Chain stores are two or more retail stores owned by the same person or company. Most chains have numerous locations, the same operations, and offer similar merchandise. Chain stores began to appear in the mid 1800s as specialty stores within individual communities. If the store was successful in one area, the owner would open a second store in another location. If each store in its new region was profitable, the owner would continue opening stores in different locations.

Some department stores are chains. However, the stores tend to specialize in categories, such as food, clothing, or housewares. The owners of chain stores go to great lengths to make sure that the shopping experience is the same in each of their stores. For example, if you went to an Ace Hardware store on the east coast, it would look very much like an Ace Hardware store on the west coast. You would find a similar layout and environment, and generally the same products and services.

Consumers expect a chain store to have a certain look and feel no matter where they shop. Consumers typically shop in chain stores because they know exactly what types of products they will find. Common chains stores include Walgreens, Best Buy, Office Max, and many supermarkets.

Franchises

A **franchise** is a legal agreement granting the right to sell a company's goods or services in a particular geographic area. The **franchisor** is the parent company that owns the chain and the brand. **Franchisees** are people who buy the rights to use the brand, learn the franchisor's trade secrets, and open their own businesses.

There are many advantages to owning a franchise. The franchisor provides a successful business model, training and other support, the products or resources for services, some marketing support, and brand recognition.

There are, however, some important disadvantages. Depending on the size and brand of the business, franchises can be very expensive to purchase. Additionally, franchisors charge monthly fees to franchisees for the right to continue selling the franchise products. Franchisees must also follow the rules and regulations of the franchisor, which may be quite limiting.

Part of a franchise agreement generally requires each franchised location to look and feel the same. For example, you expect all Radio Shack stores to look a certain way, regardless of the city in which it is located. You see the same logo on the outside of the stores and similar electronics, parts, and other items for sale inside. The franchise agreement ensures that this is the case. In fact, many customers cannot tell if they are in a chain store or a franchise because of the consistency from one store to the next. Examples of other well-known franchisors include Subway, H&R Block, and Hampton Hotels.

An *entrepreneur* is someone who starts his or her own business.

Leased Departments

A **leased department** is space within a larger store that is leased to a smaller store, boutique, or designer. This creates a store within a store. For example, the cosmetics store Sephora leases space in some JC Penney stores to sell its products. This arrangement benefits both stores. Consumers looking for the leased department are brought into the larger store. The boutique or designer leasing the space benefits by increasing their retail exposure to a new set of customers as well.

The larger retailer chooses which designers or boutiques to partner with, and does not have to purchase the merchandise to resell. The larger retailer also makes money from the lease agreement, which may be paid by square foot of space or by the amount of product sold. The leased department takes advantage of preexisting retail space that it does not have to construct.

Business Ownership Structures

The types of retail ownership include independent stores, chains, franchises, and leased departments. Within these categories, the actual ownership can take different forms. Ownership may be held by one person, a number of people, or a corporation. There are advantages and disadvantages to each form of ownership. Selecting the correct form of ownership is critical to a retailer's long-term success.

As shown in Figure 2-5, the ownership of retail stores is generally structured in one of four different ways:

- sole proprietorship
- partnership
- corporation
- limited liability company

Sole Proprietorship

Proprietor means owner. A **sole proprietorship** is a business owned by one person. The owner makes all the business decisions in a sole proprietorship. Both being the boss and receiving all of the profits sounds appealing. The possible rewards of a sole proprietorship can be great. This form of ownership also offers tax benefits, since earnings are taxed at the owner's personal income tax rate. A sole proprietorship is the simplest form of business to start and own. According to the US Census Bureau, over 70 percent of all businesses in the United States are sole proprietorships.

Business Ownership		
Type	Owner	Liability
Sole Proprietorship	One person owns the business	Owner takes all legal and financial responsibility
Partnership	Two or more people create and own the business	Partners share legal and financial responsibility; may not be equal
Corporation	A separate legal entity from the owners, or investors, of the business	Owners' liability determined by amount they invested in the company
Limited Liability Company	One or more owners share profits of the business	Personal liability of owners is limited

Goodheart-Willcox Publisher

Figure 2-5 The four common structures of business ownership are sole proprietorship, partnership, corporation, and limited liability company (LLC).

However, a sole proprietor also takes all of the business risks. One of the greatest risks is the owner's personal **liability**, or legal and financial responsibility. Because the store has one owner, he or she is personally liable for any business losses. For example, a store and its inventory are worth $1.5 million, but the business lost a $2 million lawsuit. As a sole proprietor, the owner is personally responsible for paying the remaining $500,000. In addition to losing the business, the owner might have to use personal savings or sell his or her home to meet the financial obligation.

Partnership

A **partnership** is the relationship between two or more people who join to create a business. Each person contributes money, property, labor, or skill, and each shares in the profits and losses of the business. The partners share responsibility for the daily operations of the business and make all business decisions jointly.

In any partnership, it is important to clearly define the duties, responsibilities, and expectations for each partner before entering into a partnership agreement. Partnerships are not always divided equally. Partnerships depend on the roles people play in the business or the money they have invested. Like a sole proprietorship, each partner is personally liable for any debts or risks of the business. It is wise to seek legal advice before entering into any business partnership agreement.

Social Media

Mobile Social Media

Customers use social media at home on their personal computer. However, a large percentage of social media users prefer a handheld device, such as a smartphone or iPad. This is the perfect opportunity for retailers to interact with customers as they are shopping in their store. Customers benefit by downloading digital coupons and other discounts and taking advantage of offers in real time. Retailers benefit by getting immediate feedback on products and marketing ideas on the spot.

Corporation

A **corporation** is a business that is recognized as a separate legal entity from its owners. Think of a corporation like an individual person. A corporation can make a profit, own property, sue or be sued, pay taxes, and sell products just like a person can. However, the owners of a corporation are *not* personally liable for the losses or debts of the business. Their liability is limited to the amount they invested in the company. Profits earned by a corporation may or may not be spread among its owners.

Corporations are owned by people who invest money in a company through buying *stock*, or a part ownership. The owners are called **stockholders** because they own stock (shares of ownership) in the company. Stock can also be referred to as *shares*. Shares of stock can be bought or sold publicly or privately, depending on the type of corporation. Owners receive certificates stating the number of shares they own in the company. Corporate stockholders are generally not responsible for daily business operations. They can, however, be involved in making some decisions for the corporation by voting. Stockholders usually have one vote for every share of stock owned.

Setting up a company as a corporation is a popular choice due to the liability protection. However, there are also disadvantages. Corporations are difficult and more costly to establish than sole proprietorships or partnerships. There are also many legal requirements to form and maintain the *corporation* business status. Also, the tax benefits of other ownership forms do not necessarily apply to corporations. The tax benefits are determined by the type of corporation established.

Limited Liability Company

A **limited liability company (LLC)** is a form of business ownership that limits the personal liability of owners and can provide tax benefits. Like a corporation, owners of an LLC are not personally responsible for business losses or debts. However, like a partnership or proprietorship, the income from the business is passed directly to the owners. The owners, thereby, avoid being taxed twice.

An LLC may sound like the best of all worlds, but it does have some disadvantages. Owners must personally guarantee any loans taken out by the LLC. Also, if one or more of the owners leaves the company, the LLC agreement has to be restructured. For example, if one owner decides to leave the business, the others must agree to buy that owner's share of the business or a new person must buy it. A new agreement must be written stating who is responsible for the previous owner's responsibilities. This is not always easy and can lead to disagreements. If an agreement cannot be reached, the LLC is dissolved.

Checkpoint 2.2

1. How can a business distinguish itself in the marketplace?
2. List the four types of ownership of retail stores.
3. Examine the advantages and disadvantages of owning a franchise.
4. Explain the ownership structure of a corporation.
5. In a partnership, who is responsible for the liabilities of the business?

Build Your Vocabulary

As you progress through this course, develop a personal glossary of retailing terms and add it to your portfolio. This will help you build your vocabulary and prepare you for a career. Write a definition for each of the following terms, and add it to your personal retailing glossary.

independent store	sole proprietorship
chain store	liability
franchise	partnership
franchisor	corporation
franchisee	stockholders
leased department	limited liability company (LLC)

Chapter Summary

Section 2.1 Store-Based Retail

- Brick-and-mortar stores have a physical location to display and sell merchandise and services. These stores are typically located in a shopping center or central business districts (CBD). Shopping centers can be shopping malls, strip malls, or town centers. Central business districts are where people also go for work, to visit restaurants, and for entertainment.
- Traditional retailers appeal to consumers who prefer an in-store experience. Traditional retailers include specialty, department, and convenience stores.
- Some consumers seek deals when they are making purchases and choose discount retailers. Discount stores include supercenters; warehouse clubs; off-price retailers; and factory outlet, big box, and dollar stores.
- Retail is not limited to buying objects. Service retailers provide services such as accounting, lawn, and pet-sitting services. Services are unique because they are intangible, variable, inseparable, and perishable.

Section 2.2 Retail Ownership and Structure

- Retail businesses are distinguished by their type of ownership. These include independent stores, chains, franchises, and leased departments.
- Forms of retail ownership each come with unique legal responsibility. Ownership choices include sole proprietorship, partnership, corporation, and limited liability company (LLC).

Review Your Knowledge

1. Name and describe the three types of shopping centers.
2. How is a department store organized?
3. Explain why consumers are attracted to convenience stores.
4. Why are big box stores often called *category killers*?
5. How are services different from products?
6. What is a disadvantage of an independent retailer?
7. What motivates consumers to shop in chain stores?
8. Name and describe the four common business ownership structures of a retail store.
9. Explain who is liable for the risks of a sole proprietorship.
10. Compare and contrast a sole proprietorship with a limited liability company (LLC).

Apply Your Knowledge

1. If discount stores, off-price retailers, wholesale clubs, and other types of retailers have lower prices, why do so many people still shop at department stores? Compare and contrast pricing policies and strategies among different types of retail businesses.
2. While most consumers love Walmart for low prices and convenient locations, the retailer also has many critics. Create a PowerPoint presentation about the history of Walmart. Include the advantages and disadvantages of Walmart moving into a community.

3. As a consumer, you choose where you shop. When you are looking to buy clothing, which type of store do you prefer? Make a list of the reasons why you made your decision.

4. Consider the differences between product retailers and service retailers. For example, a consumer can go to the movie theater (service provided inside the business), rent a movie (service provided outside the business), or buy a movie (store-based retail). Compare the advantages and disadvantages of service and product retailing.

5. Retailers may use product assortment to distinguish themselves from the competition. Describe how product assortment affects the decisions you make about where to shop and what to purchase.

6. Visit the Federal Trade Commission website. Search the site for a franchise disclosure document. Review this document. What did you learn?

7. Consumers have many lunchtime meal options. They can make their own lunch with groceries they purchased, go to a restaurant, have a restaurant deliver food, or run into a convenience store. What are some factors consumers typically consider when deciding where to buy lunch? How do retailers compensate for these factors?

8. A retail business must have multiple licenses to operate. Research a DBA (doing business as) license. Why must a business have this license?

9. Make a list of five businesses in the community that are owned as a partnership. Identify the business type of each. Research the partners involved in each business, such as education, experience, and skills. Have these partnerships created successful businesses? Explain your findings.

10. What type of ownership structure do you think is the most beneficial when starting a new business? Defend your choice by comparing it against several other ownership structures.

Check Your Retail IQ

Now that you have finished the chapter, see what you learned about retail by taking the chapter posttest. If you do not have a smartphone, visit the G-W Learning companion website.

G-W Learning mobile site: www.m.g-wlearning.com
G-W Learning companion website: www.g-wlearning.com/marketing/

College and Career Readiness

Career Ready Practices It is important for an employee to apply both technical and academic skills in the workplace. Conduct an online search for desirable workplace skills. Then conduct another search for top academic skills. Create a Venn diagram showing the overlap between the two lists.

Reading Skimming means to quickly glance through an entire document. Skimming will give you a preview of the material to help comprehension when you read the chapter. You should notice headings, key words, phrases, and visual elements. The goal is to get the main idea of the content. Skim this chapter. Provide an overview of what you read.

Writing Interview the mayor or other government official of your city. Ask that person what he or she likes best and least about the job as well as several other questions of your own. Write a one-page paper describing what you learned from the interview.

Teamwork

In most communities, there are multiple franchise businesses, such as health clubs, restaurants, and grocery stores. Working with your team, select a local franchise business and schedule an interview with the owner.

Create a list of interview questions that include why the owner decided to buy a franchise, the cost or investment involved, and other details about owning the franchise business. Share your findings with the class. Would you be interested in owning a franchise?

College and Career Portfolio

Objective

It is helpful to have a checklist of components that should be included in your portfolio. Your instructor may provide you with a checklist. If not, create a checklist that works best for you.

Before you begin collecting information for your portfolio, you should write an objective related to creating your portfolio. An objective is a complete sentence or two that states what you want to accomplish. The language should be clear and specific. The objective should contain enough details so that you can easily judge when it is accomplished. Consider this objective: "I will try to get better grades." Such an objective is too general. A better, more detailed objective might read: "I will work with a tutor and spend at least three hours per week on math homework until my math grade has improved to a B." Creating a clear objective is a good starting point for beginning work on your portfolio.

1. Create a checklist to use as an ongoing reference as you create your portfolio throughout this class.
2. Decide on the purpose of the portfolio you are creating—temporary or short-term employment, career, and/or college application.
3. Do research on the Internet to find articles about writing objectives. Also, look for articles that contain sample objectives for creating a portfolio.
4. Write an objective for creating your portfolio that will be used in applying for a job, for volunteer work, or to a college. Include statements for both a print portfolio and an e-portfolio.

◇DECA Coach

Impromptu and Planned Events

DECA offers multiple competitive events from which to choose. A key to selecting the event that best suits you is to understand how events are categorized. DECA events are classified as either impromptu or prepared events. Knowing the differences between the two will influence your success in the event.

Impromptu events are those events that allow for limited preparation. Most of these events include a written test for which you should study. The written test is followed by one or more case studies. You will have 10 or 15 minutes to prepare a solution to the case study problem. Next, you will present your solution to the judges. As listed on the DECA website, the following categories are considered impromptu:

- Principles of Business and Administration
- Team Decision-Making Events
- Individual Series Events

All other events are prepared events. While the topics may vary, *prepared events* provide months to prepare a presentation that you will deliver in front of a judge. Most events that are prepared in advance of competition contain a written portion ranging from 10 to 40 pages. These are commonly referred to as *written manuals*.

There are multiple factors to consider when selecting an event. Some events are team events, while others are individual events. It is important to make sure the preparation time fits within your personal schedule. Are you comfortable with a written test, written paper, or a presentation? Each event has a different combination of these factors. Be honest with yourself to determine how these factors meet your needs. Then, select a topic and event that matches your interests.

Visit www.deca.org to learn more information about DECA.

G-W Learning Mobile Site

Visit the G-W Learning mobile site to complete the chapter pretest and posttest, and to practice vocabulary using e-flash cards. If you do not have a smartphone, visit the G-W Learning companion website to access these features.

G-W Learning mobile site: www.m.g-wlearning.com

G-W Learning companion website: www.g-wlearning.com/marketing/

Chapter 3
Nonstore Retail Operations

The Internet has changed the way people find and buy products and services. It has also created a whole new culture. Terms like *websites, online stores, apps, dot-coms,* and *search engines* are now common. Online shopping has become a natural way to shop and is now necessary for many retailers to remain profitable.

Some nonstore retailers do have a physical presence, such as sales through catalogs, in-home parties, and street vendors. These options are still very convenient and often involve some face-to-face interaction. Nearly every brick-and-mortar store also uses one or more nonstore retail option. Adding nonstore retail options increases how many customers the retailer can reach and potentially boosts sales.

Case Study

Omaha Steaks

At a time when very few people would consider buying groceries through phone ordering, Omaha Steaks proved to be a thriving retail food business. How did Omaha Steaks become so successful in a market that others did not dare to enter? The answer is a good product and a good system, with an excellently integrated marketing strategy. The company strives to make shopping easy for customers.

Omaha Steaks began selling its products to customers through catalog sales. It was one of the first companies to implement a toll-free sales number for ordering. Today, Omaha Steaks has an easy-to-use website. The company also has an aggressive marketing strategy. Customers receive regular mailings, telephone calls, and e-mails with specials and promotions. In addition, a mobile app is available to help customers cook their products to perfection.

Approximately 94 percent of Omaha Steaks' sales occur in places other than brick-and-mortar stores. With more than 1.5 million customers and about $450 million in annual sales, Omaha Steaks is the consummate nonstore retailer. The company proves that customers are not always looking for the lowest price, but rather quality products and a good shopping experience. Smart, strategic planning of the customer experience led to successful nonstore retailing for this retailer.

College and Career Readiness

Reading Prep

Before reading this chapter, review the table of contents for this text. Create a graphic organizer that traces the content from simple to complex ideas.

Check Your Retail IQ

Before you begin the chapter, see what you already know about retail by taking the chapter pretest. If you do not have a smartphone, visit the G-W Learning companion website.

G-W Learning mobile site: www.m.g-wlearning.com

G-W Learning companion website: www.g-wlearning.com/marketing/

Sections

3.1   Electronic Retailing

3.2   Other Nonstore Retailers

Zurijeta/Shutterstock.com

Section 3.1 Electronic Retailing

Objectives

After completing this section, you will be able to:
- **Define** nonstore retail.
- **Explain** the concept of e-tailing.
- **List** the advantages and disadvantages of online shopping for a customer.

Key Terms

off-site purchasing
e-tailing
m-commerce
mobile app
web-influenced sale
shopping bot
identity theft

Web Connect

Internet Retailer© is a company that provides business intelligence for the electronic and online retailing market. Research this company. Explain the types of information that the company provides for retailers. How does this business reach its customers?

Critical Thinking

There are several companies that compile consumer information about buying habits for both retail and e-tail businesses. How do you think businesses use this information? Do you think this information is important to consumers?

Nonstore Retail

Store-based businesses provide customers with a hands-on, face-to-face shopping experience. However, some customers do not require a hands-on experience. Some may not want to travel to a physical retail location to make a purchase. For these customers, there are nonstore retail options.

Nonstore retail is any method of selling products or services outside of a traditional brick-and-mortar store. Many retailers offer both store-based and nonstore options to their customers. Nonstore retail businesses can take many forms:
- e-tail
- home-shopping television
- direct mail and catalogs
- direct sales
- portable retailers (food trucks and street vendors)
- vending machines

When customers make a purchase from a nonstore retailer, it is known as off-site purchasing. **Off-site purchasing** is any type of sale that takes place in a location other than a brick-and-mortar store.

E-tailing

The fastest-growing form of off-site purchasing is *electronic retailing*, or e-tailing. **E-tailing** is the sale of products or services through the Internet. A subset of e-tailing is m-commerce. **M-commerce**, short for *mobile commerce*, refers to online sales that take place through smartphones or other mobile devices instead of computers.

Mobile apps are software applications developed specifically for portable digital devices, such as smartphones and tablet computers. These apps make accessing an Internet site more convenient than keying an entire web address. Retailers can both market and sell through mobile apps. According to the research company Nielsen, 40 percent of all US mobile phones are smartphones. In addition, two out of three new mobile phones purchased are now smartphones. This means that m-commerce is an important and effective component of a retail business.

E-tailing began in the 1990s on a small scale when the Internet was still gaining in popularity. However, it is no longer a trend. Figure 3-1 shows the growth of a few e-tailers in a 10 year span of time, as reported by Internet Retailer©. According to the technology and market research company Forrester Research, online retail sales are projected to grow by more than 10 percent yearly. The growth of Internet shopping is outpacing overall retail growth, which averages at 2.5 percent yearly. By 2017, Forrester believes online sales will total $370 billion, up from $231 billion in 2013.

In addition to online purchases, Forrester Research reports that about 53 percent of retail sales were influenced by the web. **Web-influenced sales** are purchases made in a brick-and-mortar store where buyers first researched the products or services on the Internet. For example, most people buy cars at dealerships or from private owners. One J.D. Powers and Associates study found that roughly 84 percent of all car buyers first researched their purchases online. Web-influenced sales are projected to continue growing.

E-tail Sales Growth

Company	2003 Sales	2012 Sales	Overall Increase
Urban Outfitters	$7.3 million	$663.3 million	9000%
Apple	$405.5 million	$8.8 billion	2078%
1-800 Contacts	$19.8 million	$392.0 million	1880%
FragranceNet.com	$10.5 million	$145.0 million	1280%

Source: Internet Retailer©
Goodheart-Willcox Publisher

Figure 3-1 Data compiled by internet RETAILER© shows a significant increase in sales over the last 10 years for online retailers.

E-tailing is an important and growing part of the retail industry because the number of consumers shopping online increases every year. Most homes in the United States have one or more computers or smartphones with Internet access. In addition, the Internet is commonly available in public libraries, Internet cafés, and other public locations that offer Wi-Fi. As a result, e-tailers can reach nearly every potential customer through the Internet.

The Internet has exposed consumers to new cultures, ideas, and products. This has created new demand for products that are available in countries all around the world. E-tailing allows consumers to shop in a global marketplace using retail methods like online stores, direct mail and catalogs, home-shopping television, and apps on smartphones, tablets, and other personal electronic devices. For example, a customer may want to buy electronics directly from an overseas manufacturer known for the quality of its electronic products. The customer may be able to shop the manufacturer's e-tail store online or request a product catalog.

Shopping Online

It is important for e-tailers to understand why people shop online. Not all online customers actually plan to make a purchase. Just as in brick-and-mortar stores, many online customers make impulse purchases. If they come across a good sale or a unique product while browsing the Internet, it is very easy to buy it on the spot. Knowing this information helps successful e-tailers design functional e-tailing websites that make both browsing and buying easy.

Some customers intend to make a purchase online. Just like buying at the mall stores, they are looking for a specific item. Another group of consumers uses the Internet primarily to research potential purchases. These consumers use the Internet to search for sales, compare prices, and collect product information. They also look for ideas, track fashion trends, and read product reviews on the Internet. However, consumers can still choose to either purchase online or at a physical store.

Advantages of Shopping Online

In general, people like to shop. There are many advantages to browsing and buying online, including convenience, easy price comparison, product pricing, and product reviews. Shopping online also offers a wide selection of products and access to retailers all over the world.

Convenience

Buying online is the most convenient way to shop. Customers can make purchases when their schedules permit because online stores never close. People can purchase from any location, at any time, and avoid crowded stores. Buying online also eliminates the time and expense of travel to a brick-and-mortar store.

Online Merchandise

When merchandising online, e-tailers should be aware of all the information the customer needs to know. Details such as fabric content, size charts, and shipping dates should all be easily accessible and visible. Withholding any information will leave the customer uninformed and untrusting of your company. This may be considered an unethical act if the customer has not been properly informed.

Price Comparison

The Internet makes comparing the prices of items easy because there is no need to visit multiple brick-and-mortar stores. Customers can also compare prices among online and physical stores. They can even use shopping bots, short for shopping robots, to compare prices. Shopping bots are online search tools that compare prices for an item on different websites. The National Retail Federation's *STORES* magazine reports that easy price comparison is the top reason people buy online.

Pricing

Online stores without physical locations may have reduced overhead costs. As a result, online stores often sell products for less than brick-and-mortar stores. Online auction sites, like e-Bay, allow customers to bid on products, which can result in even lower purchase prices.

Product Reviews

The availability of personal reviews by product owners or users is unique to Internet shopping. Summaries of personal experience, ratings, and quality evaluations can help a customer decide to make a purchase or discourage it, depending on the review comments made. Product reviews may be found on the e-tailer's website or on other sites related to the product or e-tailer.

VI.P/Shutterstock.com

Most product reviews include a rating in graphic form. From the graphic rating, the consumer immediately knows if the product review is mostly positive or negative.

Selection

E-tail stores provide access to nearly every product contained in brick-and-mortar stores, and more. Online customers can also find many unique items and better selection. Even the largest brick-and-mortar retailers lack the space to have every product available in every store.

Many crafters have their own websites to sell unique products. Or, they may join online group sites, such as Etsy, to sell their one-of-a-kind items found nowhere else.

Global Shopping

Brick-and-mortar retailers can only reach consumers who can physically visit the store. However, online customers can browse and buy from unlimited e-tailers around the world, day or night. When the US dollar is strong against foreign currency, prices in foreign countries are often very reasonable. However, one drawback to purchasing from an e-tailer in another country is potentially high shipping costs.

Disadvantages of Shopping Online

While there are many advantages to shopping online, there are some disadvantages as well, as shown in Figure 3-2. Some people will not shop online due to security and privacy concerns. Other significant drawbacks include delayed satisfaction, inability to see and touch products, and the work involved to return a product.

Security and Privacy Concerns

Some people fear that online shopping may lead to identity theft. **Identity theft** involves stealing someone's personal information, such as Social Security or credit card number, to get money or make purchases. Some customers fear that credit card information may be stolen when making online purchases. However, security protection is built into most online shopping sites. The reality is that credit card information is just as likely to be stolen by passing the card to a store salesperson. Customers may also worry about losing their privacy. E-mail addresses and other customer information can be sold to other firms for marketing purposes.

Delayed Satisfaction

In general, online shopping does not allow instant access to a purchase. Some exceptions to this include software and music downloads. For typical purchases, customers must buy first and wait for the product to arrive. Overnight shipping is costly. So, customers may wait days or weeks before the items arrive. If the product is needed right away, the wait time can be a problem. Buying something the day you need it is rarely possible when shopping online.

Cybercrime is any illegal activity that takes place using a computer or computer network.

Shopping Online	
Advantages	**Disadvantages**
Convenient	Security and privacy concerns
Easy price comparison	Delayed satisfaction
Potentially lower pricing	Cannot see and touch products
Product reviews	Hassle of product returns
Vast product selection	Lack of social interaction
Access to global shopping	

Goodheart-Willcox Publisher

Figure 3-2 Knowing what consumers think the advantages and disadvantages of shopping online are helps retailers design e-tailing websites with functionality and appeal.

Inability to See and Touch Products

Some customers prefer to see and touch merchandise before buying. Many people want to try on clothing and shoes to check the fit. Also, viewing products online may not provide an accurate representation of what the products really look like.

Product Returns

The chances of returning a product are higher when buying online. If a product is not suitable when it arrives, the customer has to repackage the product to send it back. The customer must also get it to the post office or other courier to be sent back. The cost of return shipping is often paid by the customer, as well. Returning goods this way means extra time and money for consumers.

Lack of Social Interaction

Shopping is an enjoyable social experience for many people. Going into a store, picking up products, and talking to salespeople can be socially enjoyable. However, that personal interaction and service is lost when shopping on the Internet. Questions or concerns about products or purchases online generally require a phone call or e-mail. For this reason, some customers may leave websites without making a purchase.

It is difficult to experience any social interaction when shopping online.

Monkey Business Images/Shutterstock.com

Exploring Retail Careers

Market Analyst

A profitable retailer is one that entices customers to visit and buy product. Companies rely on market analysts to find out what products or services people want and how much they are willing to pay for them. Market analysts research market conditions. Data about potential competitors and their pricing is gathered. Market analysts review current sales of similar products. They decide if a retailer can make money selling the product at current prices. This data helps retailers decide which products to offer.

Other typical job titles for market analyst include *purchase price analyst*, *market research analyst*, and *business development specialist*. Some examples of tasks that market analysts perform include:

- collect data on competitors to analyze their prices and sales
- analyze data on potential customers (including demographics, buying habits, needs, and preferences)
- detect shopping patterns in consumers
- monitor industry statistics and trends
- forecast trends in sales and marketing

Market analysts must understand how to analyze data to find trends. They must be able to communicate complex data to company executives. A strong background in statistics is necessary. The ability to use data-retrieval software is also needed. A bachelor degree is usually required. Top-level jobs often require a master degree.

Checkpoint 3.1

1. Give three examples of nonstore retailing.
2. What are the advantages of online shopping?
3. Why do consumers use the Internet to conduct research before buying?
4. Explain how product reviews affect purchasing decisions.
5. What security and privacy concerns does e-tailing present to customers?

Build Your Vocabulary

As you progress through this course, develop a personal glossary of retailing terms and add it to your portfolio. This will help you build your vocabulary and prepare you for a career. Write a definition for each of the following terms, and add it to your personal retailing glossary.

off-site purchasing	web-influenced sale
e-tailing	shopping bot
m-commerce	identity theft
mobile app	

Section 3.2 Other Nonstore Retailers

Objectives

After completing this section, you will be able to:
- **Explain** how retail channels function.
- **Identify** portable retailers.
- **Describe** how vending machines are a form of retail.

Key Terms

retail channel
multichannel retailer
home-shopping television
infomercial
direct mail
vendor
street vendor
food truck
vending machine

Web Connect

E-tailing began in the 1990s. Research the first companies to become official e-tailers. What was the name of the company you chose and what did it sell? Is it still in business today?

Critical Thinking

It is possible to shop globally without leaving your home. Make a list of 10 items that you would consider purchasing from another country. Why would you buy these items from a global retailer instead of a local retailer?

Retail Channels

Retail channels are all the different pathways through which goods or services can be sold. Brick-and-mortar stores, the Internet, mobile apps, catalogs, television, consultants, vendors, and direct mail are examples of retail channels. A **multichannel retailer** uses two or more retail channels to sell products, as shown in Figure 3-3. For example, the retailer Lands End sells products in physical stores, through catalogs, on its website, and through mobile apps.

Multichannel retailing is very important to reach every potential customer. According to research by PricewaterhouseCoopers, 40 percent of customers prefer multichannel buying options. *Multichannel customers* expect to have consistent shopping experiences regardless of the retail channel they use to make a purchase.

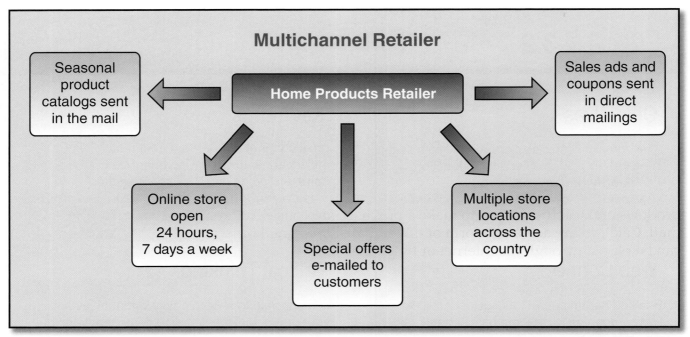

Figure 3-3 A retailer that uses multiple retail channels can reach the greatest number of potential customers.

Home-Shopping Television

Home-shopping television is television that is devoted solely to retail sales. Home-shopping television channels are a form of nonstore retailing. Items such as apparel, jewelry, housewares, and sporting goods are sold regularly, often for discounted prices. Home-shopping television appeals to customers who like unique items or are bargain hunters. Those who do not want to interact with salespeople or cannot leave the home also like home-shopping television.

Viewers see live demonstrations, learn about the features and benefits, and hear call-in testimonials about the product. Additionally, viewers may be able to call into the program and ask questions about the products. Constant updates on the television screen show product sales numbers and the quantity of products left. This encourages viewers to act quickly to make a purchase before the product is sold out. Most home-shopping channels also use a multichannel approach by selling featured products on their websites.

Infomercials are paid television commercials placed in television program time slots, usually 30 minutes. These time slots are often during less-expensive, low-viewing hours, such as late night or very early mornings. Infomercials generally feature a single product or bundle of products. The entire program is a sales tool and often features a celebrity as the spokesperson.

Infomercials focus on the fact that the products are not available in stores. To get the low prices being offered, viewers must order within a short time period. While infomercials are expensive to produce and air, they often generate very successful sales numbers.

Direct Mail and Catalogs

Direct mail is any piece of marketing communication sent to potential customers through the post office. These mailings are often thought of as *junk mail* because the product information may not have been requested. Brochures, postcards, and letters that describe products and ask the readers to make a purchase are considered direct mail. Catalogs are actually a form of direct mail. Direct mail orders can be placed through the Internet or by phone.

In 1894, Richard Sears created the first retail catalog and changed the retail industry forever. Sears advertised merchandise with catchy phrases that made products more appealing. The famous *Sears Wish Book* annual holiday catalog was more than 400 pages long at the height of its publication. While sales directly from catalogs are gradually decreasing, they still play an important role in nonstore retailing.

Most large brick-and-mortar retailers use some form of catalog in their multichannel-approach to sales. Before the computer age, catalogs were the primary source for reaching remote customers. Catalogs were mailed at peak buying times, such as back-to-school or holidays. Today, many retailers send between 20 and 30 different catalogs per year. These are often specialty catalogs, which may feature products not offered in their physical stores.

Some e-tailers provide print catalogs simply to meet customer needs. Customers can browse the catalogs at their leisure and, if they prefer, order products online. By providing both the website and print catalog, customers have more buying options.

Social Media

Social-Media Marketing (SMM)

Social-media marketing (SMM) is the use of social media as a part of the retail marketing plan to convince consumers to buy product or services. For SMM to be effective, consistent communication must take place. Traditional marketing using print brochures, catalogs, and postcards require time and commitment to create each piece. After the piece is mailed, it is hoped that customers will respond and want more information or buy the product. "Snail mail" creates lapses in time in the communication stream. However, with social media marketing, multiple daily communications must take place in order for it to be effective.

Catalogs allow customers to shop at their convenience from anywhere.

Pressmaster/Shutterstock.com

Catalogs were originally developed by retailers to reach customers who were not near one of their retail locations. While catalog sales for brick-and-mortar stores have decreased, other retailers are generating sales in record numbers. Companies such as Brookstone and Ballard Designs depend heavily on their catalogs to generate sales.

Much like shopping online, catalogs let customers buy things without physically going into a retail store. The main difference is that catalogs are printed pieces, not in electronic format. Websites may have a bigger advantage over catalogs, in that purchases can be made immediately. Catalog customers must make a phone call, mail an order form, or use a website to order. Catalog and online shopping have similar advantages and disadvantages.

Advantages of Catalog Shopping

For retailers, catalogs provide another marketing channel. Catalogs are an alternative for customers who do not want to make a purchase online or drive to a mall. For consumers who did not grow up with online shopping, catalog purchasing provides a trusted, familiar service.

Catalogs are very convenient for consumers. They arrive in the mail regularly, with little or no effort on the customer's part. Catalogs can be mailed anywhere in the world, and products can be shipped globally. Customers can look at merchandise at any time. If the retailer has a website or 24/7 customer service, customers may also buy at any time.

Like online retailers, catalog companies without stores may have reduced overhead costs. This can result in lower prices than brick-and-mortar stores. Also, catalog companies are not confined to the available space of a physical store. Catalogs can offer a wide selection of products that may not be available for sale in brick-and-mortar stores.

Disadvantages of Catalog Shopping

Catalogs are expensive for a retailer to create, print, and mail to customers. There must be enough sales made through the catalogs to justify the expense. Because the process of creating and printing catalogs can take months, product information may be out-of-date.

When catalog shopping, customers lose the hands-on and social experiences of shopping for a product in a brick-and-mortar store. Even though retailers offer toll-free customer service numbers, the service is not personal.

When a catalog order is placed, customers are usually charged for shipping and must wait for delivery. If a product needs to be returned, the customer must repackage the item, arrange for shipping, and often pay for return shipping.

Direct Sales

Direct sales is a form of nonstore retailing. The salesperson has direct communication with the customer. The sale does not take place in a store, but through a consultant or in-home parties.

Consultant Sales

A direct sale through a consultant involves a trained professional, such as a wedding planner or interior designer. The consultant helps customers make decisions about large purchases or planning an event. The consultant may bring sample products to the customer's home and make recommendations. For example, an interior designer may bring samples of carpet, fabric, and wallpaper for the client to make a selection. The consultant makes the purchases or arrangements for the customers and charges a fee for their service.

In-Home Parties

In-home parties are direct sales events. Hosts invite people to their homes for a viewing or demonstration of products presented by a company salesperson. The products are not sold in stores and can only be purchased though in-home parties or online. The salesperson earns a commission and the host receives free products based on the amount of products sold at the party. Some common in-home party retailers include The Pampered Chef® and Mary Kay®.

Portable Retailers

Another way retailers interact with customers outside of a physical location is by moving from place to place to sell to their customers. Street vendors and food trucks are nonstore, portable retail businesses.

NRF Tip

NRF recognizes the importance of e-tailing as a modern option of the retail experience. The NRF website has compiled research on consumer behavior while shopping online. The research explains the effectiveness of e-tailing as well as the downfalls to avoid.

Street vendors sell everything from food and beverages to souvenirs and flowers. Their "stores" are portable so they can move along the streets or sidewalks and encounter as many customers as possible.

Elena Rostunova/Shutterstock.com

Street Vendors

A **vendor** is a person or business that sells something. **Street vendors** are people who set up portable stores outdoors on sidewalks, in parking lots, or in open-air markets. The vendors sell products that are easy to move, such as jewelry, scarves, food, and souvenirs. Larger cities often have many street vendors. Most cities require street vendors to have a license in order to do business.

Food Trucks

Food trucks are mobile kitchens that prepare and sell different foods. There is usually a sales counter on the side of the truck. Customers walk up to the counter to order and pick up their food. The first food trucks were the popular ice cream trucks that came though neighborhoods during the summer months. Food trucks have come a long way since then. They now sell everything from sandwiches to gourmet crepes to Asian delicacies. Food truck owners need licenses to do business and often rent specific spaces from a city or a private business.

Vending Machines

Vending machines are coin, bill, or credit card machines used to sell small products. They are probably one of the most common and convenient forms of retail sales. Vending machines can be used to sell a wide variety of products, such as food, snacks, drinks, personal care items, and toys. Some vending machines provide more expensive items, such as cameras and software.

Vending machines are relatively inexpensive to own and operate. One advantage is that personnel are not required to make each sale, only to refill the machine and collect the money. Also, vending machines can be located in high-traffic areas to produce high sales volumes.

However, vending machines can sometimes be targets for vandals. Because they are unattended, vending machines are easily destroyed or robbed. Another challenge is making certain that products are always stocked. Empty vending machines do not generate revenue.

Checkpoint 3.2

1. Describe the roles of retail channels and how they relate to multichannel retailers.
2. To whom does home-shopping television appeal?
3. Why do some retailers still provide catalogs?
4. Explain how direct sales is a form of nonstore retailing.
5. Identify two types of portable retailers.

Build Your Vocabulary

As you progress through this course, develop a personal glossary of retailing terms and add it to your portfolio. This will help you build your vocabulary and prepare you for a career. Write a definition for each of the following terms, and add it to your personal retailing glossary.

retail channel
multichannel retailer
home-shopping television
infomercial
direct mail

vendor
street vendor
food truck
vending machine

Chapter Summary

Section 3.1 Electronic Retailing

- Nonstore retail is any method of selling products or services outside of a traditional brick-and-mortar store. Some types of nonstore retail may include e-tail, home-shopping television, direct mail and catalogs, direct sales, portable retailers, and vending machines.
- E-tailing is the sale of products to consumers through the Internet. E-tail has many advantages over brick-and-mortar sales, but also has disadvantages. E-tail sales continue to rise through computers, smartphones, and other mobile devices.
- It is important for e-tailers to understand why people shop online. Shopping online has many unique advantages and disadvantages.

Section 3.2 Other Nonstore Retailers

- Retail channels are all the different pathways through which goods or services can be sold. A multichannel retailer uses two or more retail channels to sell products. Multichannel retailing is important to reach every potential customer.
- Portable retailers include street vendors, or people who set up portable stores outdoors. It also includes food trucks, which are mobile kitchens that sell food product.
- Vending machines are machines used to sell products that do not require any form or personnel to make sales other than to restock the machines and collect the money.

Review Your Knowledge

1. Explain how e-tailing and m-commerce are related.
2. Summarize the disadvantages of online shopping.
3. How is shopping online convenient for customers?
4. Explain the concept of global shopping.
5. Illustrate how online shopping delays customer satisfaction.
6. What do multichannel customers expect from retailers?
7. How do infomercials generate sales?
8. What are the disadvantages of catalog sales for the retailer?
9. Describe how an in-home party is a form of direct sales.
10. Explain how vending machines are a form of retailing.

Apply Your Knowledge

1. Consider all the types of nonstore retailing discussed in this chapter. Choose five types of nonstore retailers. Prepare a PowerPoint presentation that identifies two products that are best sold with each type of nonstore retailer.
2. Search the Internet for current e-tail and m-commerce sales trends. Which one is growing faster? Explain why you believe that is the case.
3. Del Monte® is famous for selling fruits and vegetables. Even though customers probably will not buy their products online, Del Monte still maintains a website. What are some ways Del Monte's website might influence in-store purchases?

4. The number of people using the Internet as a research tool greatly outnumbers those using it as a purchasing tool. Given the advantages of shopping online, why do you think *all* people are not shopping online?

5. Perform an Internet search for "shopping bots" and select one of the sites returned in the search. Conduct a price comparison on your favorite brand of jeans. Look at the results closely, including shipping costs. How did this tool make your shopping easier? Why is it an advantage for the consumer to use shopping bots?

6. For many consumers, online product reviews are an important factor in online shopping. If there are many reviews for a product, there are likely some good reviews and some bad ones. In what ways do you believe customers allow reviews to influence their decisions? Is this an advantage to the e-tailer or customer or both?

7. One disadvantage of doing business on an e-tail site is that you cannot see or touch an item before purchasing. Search at least three different online stores for a piece of your favorite clothing. What are some of the ways that e-tailers address the fact that you cannot see and touch the products?

8. Which types of nonstore retailing would be best to sell a newly developed video game? Explain your choices.

9. Infomercials are expensive to produce and usually broadcast during hours of low viewership. Yet, they often have very successful sales rates. What are some reasons that might explain the success of infomercials?

10. Online customers are often catalog customers, as well. Provide reasons why this may be the case.

Check Your Retail IQ

Now that you have finished the chapter, see what you learned about retail by taking the chapter posttest. If you do not have a smartphone, visit the G-W Learning companion website.
G-W Learning mobile site: www.m.g-wlearning.com
G-W Learning companion website: www.g-wlearning.com/marketing/

College and Career Readiness

Career Ready Practices Maintaining a healthy lifestyle has an impact on how you function physically and mentally. Make a list of unhealthy behaviors you think could have an effect on how well you do your job. How do you think employers should deal with behaviors that affect the personal health of their employees?

Listening Active listening is fully participating as you process what others are saying. Practice active listening skills while listening to a news report on the radio, the television, or a podcast. Select a single story and prepare a report in which you analyze the following aspects of the business story: the speaker's audience, point of view, reasoning, stance, word choice, tone, points of emphasis, and organization.

Reading Affix means to add a prefix or suffix to a root word. Write a paragraph explaining how the word *e-tail* was created.

Teamwork

Culture has a direct influence on the types of products people buy. Factors such as language and customs may impact purchasing decisions. Working with your team, make a list of cultural influences that determine preferences for products that teens usually buy for personal use.

College and Career Portfolio

Organization

As you collect items for your portfolio, you will need a method to keep the items clean, safe, and organized for assembly at the appropriate time. A large manila envelope works well to keep hard copies of your documents, photos, awards, and other items. Three-ring binders with sleeves are another good way to store your information. If you have a box large enough for full-size documents, it will work also. Plan to keep like items together and label the categories. For example, store sample documents that illustrate your writing or computer skills together. Use notes clipped to the documents to identify each item and state why it is included in the portfolio. For example, a note might say, "Newsletter that illustrates desktop publishing skills."

1. Select a method for storing hard copy items you will be collecting for your portfolio. (You will decide where to keep electronic copies in a later activity.)
2. Write a paragraph that describes your plan for storing and labeling the items. Refer to this plan each time you add items to the portfolio.

◇DECA Coach

Apply Your Strengths and Weaknesses

When it comes to your schoolwork, what types of things do you like to do? What are you good at? DECA's competitive events offer you the opportunity to write, make oral presentations, take tests, make quick decisions, supervise and plan, manage your time, complete projects, and even help people out in the community.

The odds are that there are one or more things on this list that either interest you or that you are good at. There is also a possibility that the list includes something you do not particularly like to do, and that is okay. For example, if taking a test makes you nervous, look for an event that does not require you to take a test. If you are interested in an event that allows or requires you to form a team, select a teammate that has some of the talents that you do not. For example, you may prefer expressing yourself more in writing. If you select a partner who is more outgoing and good with public speaking, this opens the door for you to enter competitions that you might not otherwise be comfortable entering. Each teammate can lend his or her talents to the team.

Finally, select a topic. Many of the events let you pick your topic, so pick something that you and your teammates are interested in. Whether it is sports, fashion, cars, electronic gadgets, animals, or helping others, be interested in your topic. Combining your interests with your talents, as well as the talents of your teammates, is a winning combination.

Visit www.deca.org to learn more information about DECA.

G-W Learning Mobile Site

Visit the G-W Learning mobile site to complete the chapter pretest and posttest, and to practice vocabulary using e-flash cards. If you do not have a smartphone, visit the G-W Learning companion website to access these features.

G-W Learning mobile site: www.m.g-wlearning.com

G-W Learning companion website: www.g-wlearning.com/marketing/

Unit 2
Marketplace Strategy

Introduction

Identifying the customer is key to being successful in the marketplace. Using marketing research, retailers can gather consumer data and opinions. This information can be collected directly from consumers or by reviewing existing data and records. The data collected are analyzed and used to identify customers by common traits, such as location, age, recreation interests, and purchasing habits.

Retailers use consumer data to plan their business strategy, organize retail operations, and choose products and services that will generate a profit. Understanding what motivates their customers helps retailers achieve success in the marketplace.

Green Retail

Shades of Green

Most retailers today are environmentally conscious and make environmentally-friendly business and operations choices. Many retailers offer their customers alternatives to common plastic shopping bags. Reusable shopping bags are available in various *shades* of green.

Plastic bottles made of polyethylene terephthalate (PET) are recycled and turned into a type of polyester fiber. This fiber is used to make durable bags, sometimes called *bottle bags*. Waste cotton produced during the spinning process used to be disposed in landfills. Today, that cotton fiber is recycled and used to make reusable shopping totes.

Savvy retailers take advantage of many shades of green to help show corporate responsibility.

In This Unit

Chapter 4
Marketing Research

Retailers need to understand their customers' needs and wants in order to be successful. Marketing research allows retailers to collect information directly from consumers. Retailers typically want to know about products, promotions, the competition, and general consumer opinions. This information can be gathered through surveys, interviews, group discussions, or by reviewing internal records.

After consumer information is gathered, it has to be analyzed to be useful. Graphs or charts are created to represent the research data collected. Based on the research data, retailers may make changes to their business strategy or operations. For example, they may choose to target a certain geographic area for promotions or to improve customer service. Ultimately, marketing research is a tool to help make a retail business successful.

Case Study

California Milk Advisory Board

When you think of California, you probably think of movie stars and the ocean. But, the California Milk Advisory Board (CMAB) wants you to think of cows and fresh dairy products. In an effort to increase the sales of California dairy products, the CMAB created an aggressive marketing plan.

The first and most important step was defining who buys dairy products. Research revealed that women between the ages of 25–54 should be the primary focus of CMAB's marketing efforts. Women in this age group are more likely to make household buying decisions at the grocery store.

The CMAB developed a series of "Happy Cows" commercials that were light and happy to target their customers. Later, the CMAB developed "Make Us Part of Your Family" commercials that appealed to both 25–54 year-old women and their children. The commercials featured a cow singing pop songs and interacting with kids and teens in the family. The commercials aired more often during daytime television than in the evening.

Consumers responded positively to the CMAB commercials and marketing efforts. Production of California cheese increased by 609%. California moved into the number one spot in the country for cheese production. The California Milk Advisory Board identified their customer, analyzed marketing data, and created promotions that resulted in much higher sales.

College and Career Readiness

Reading Prep

Before reading this chapter, review the objectives for each of the sections. Keep these in mind as you read, and focus on the structure of the author's writing. Was the information presented in a way that was clear and engaging?

Check Your Retail IQ

Before you begin the chapter, see what you already know about retail by taking the chapter pretest. If you do not have a smartphone, visit the G-W Learning companion website.

G-W Learning mobile site: www.m.g-wlearning.com
G-W Learning companion website: www.g-wlearning.com/marketing/

Sections

4.1 What Is Marketing Research?

4.2 Analyzing the Data

Section 4.1 What Is Marketing Research?

Objectives

After completing this section, you will be able to:
- **Define** marketing research.
- **Describe** the research process.
- **Identify** the major sources of information used for marketing research.
- **Explain** how a sampling plan is created.

Key Terms

marketing research
actionable research
market research
research process
data
research proposal
internal record
secondary data
primary data

qualitative data
quantitative data
survey
interview
focus group
diary
test marketing
sample

Web Connect

Retailers must conduct research in order to be effective and profitable. One source of information is the US Census Bureau. Visit the website of the US Census Bureau and find information about your community. List the information you found that would be helpful to local retailers.

Critical Thinking

Sales are down at the local hardware store. Identify as many potential reasons as you can for the poor sales. For each reason you identify, explain what you think the retailer can do to address the problem.

Marketing Research

In order to be successful, retailers must understand the needs and wants of their customers. A *need* is something necessary for survival. A *want* is something that a person desires, but can function without.

Marketing research is gathering information on how to promote, sell, and distribute a product or service. Having valuable marketing information may reduce the risk of product or business failure. Marketing research can help retailers solve problems and make informed decisions by gathering information on various topics:

- Are promotional efforts working?
- What is the competition doing?
- What are consumer opinions on issues like product prices, packaging, store location, or recent advertising campaigns?
- How can a retailer anticipate future trends and customer needs?

Retailers often engage in **actionable research**, which is research intended to improve the retailer's practices. Actionable research addresses *how* to fix a problem or make it better, more than *why* something is a problem.

The terms *market research* and *marketing research* are often incorrectly used to mean the same thing. **Market research** involves gathering statistics on a specific market's size, makeup, and buying trends. *Marketing* research covers a wider range of activities than *market* research does. Most importantly, marketing research involves analyzing gathered data. It also explores areas such as new product development, advertising, promotions, and modes of distribution.

Research Process

Without research, retailers leave their success to chance. The **research process** is a set of defined steps through which marketing data are collected, analyzed, and used. **Data** are the pieces of information obtained through research.

There are five general steps to conduct effective research, as shown in Figure 4-1.

1. *Define the problem.* What is the retailer trying to discover? Defining the problem helps shape the remaining steps of the research. A *hypothesis* may be written which is a statement that can be tested and proved either true or false.

2. *Develop the research plan.* Once the problem is defined, develop a research plan that addresses the problem. A **research proposal** is usually written before the research process begins. A research proposal outlines the details of the research process and estimates the value of the research data to the business. Most businesses require this step to justify the time and expense of research.

3. *Collect the data.* There are different ways to collect data. The retailer may choose to collect data directly from customers, use internal records, or review existing data. The form of collection depends on the research problem and when the data are needed.

4. *Analyze the data.* Once collected, the data are analyzed to detect patterns. Sometimes the analysis is simple and done by hand. Other times, it requires statistical software to make complex calculations. Researchers use the process of *statistical inference* to estimate the outcome of the research from random samples of the data and review the research hypothesis.

5. *Report the findings.* The answer to the research problem is addressed using the analyzed data. Findings are reported in a *research brief*, or *summary report*, that describes the entire research process and outcomes. The report allows the process to be reviewed to spot any potential flaws in the research that may have affected the results. Then, recommendations are made based on the findings.

Note that the word *problem* in research does not mean something negative. In research, the problem is the issue being addressed by the study.

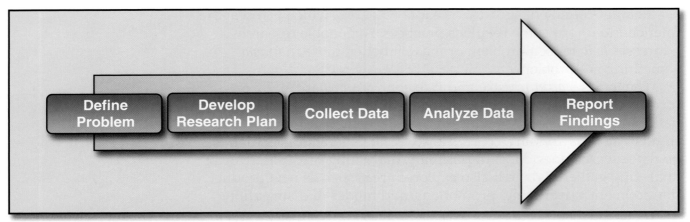

Goodheart-Willcox Publisher

Figure 4-1 Follow the steps in the research process to conduct effective research.

For example, suppose that Logan's Department Store just got its quarterly sales report. While overall sales were up, men's clothing sales dropped by 10 percent. Data revealed that men's clothing sales had dropped for three straight quarters. Using the research process, Logan's conducted research to learn why sales were dropping.

1. *Define the problem:* Logan's looked at internal reports that showed men's clothing sales had dropped for three straight quarters. They posed the question, "Why have the sales of men's clothing dropped?"

2. *Develop the research plan:* It was decided the best way to collect data was to survey Logan's Department Store customers.

3. *Collect the data:* An online survey link was sent to current customers via e-mail. The surveys were collected over a period of 30 days.

4. *Analyze the data:* The researchers discovered that both men and women enjoyed shopping at Logan's. However, neither liked shopping in the men's clothing department. Customers felt the department was too crowded with merchandise. Finding what they were looking for was difficult. It was easier to shop elsewhere for men's clothing.

5. *Report the findings:* The researchers reported the findings to department store's management team. The report explained why customers did not like to shop in men's clothing. The researchers also suggested how to reorganize the department to be more shopper-friendly.

This is only one example of how retailers and e-tailers use marketing research to solve problems. However, the process is the same regardless of the problem. It starts with identifying a research problem, and ends with reporting the findings. All steps must be completed for research to be useful.

Sources of Information

A *marketing information system (MkIS)* consists of the processes involved in collecting, analyzing, and reporting marketing research information. There are many ways to collect data for research purposes. Data can be gathered from internal store records, secondary data, or as primary data. Each data source provides a different perspective when addressing a research problem.

Internal Records

Internal records, such as sales data and shipping reports, provide information about current traits and activities of customers. Records are kept by sales, finance, shipping, production, personnel, and other departments. These records are a valuable source of data. For example, most retailers create a customer database from sales records.

Another source of data comes from the *universal product codes (UPC)*, or *bar codes*, that are scanned at checkout. Scanning UPCs allows the business to track inventory based on sales. Scanned UPC data is stored in a computer and reports are generated based on the information as needed. For example, UPC data reports can show the most effective selling price point per item or peak sales times for items.

By analyzing internal records, retailers may also find new issues. For example, why are so many goods shipped to one state or why is Saturday a slow sales day? Once identified, additional data may help the retailer determine *why* the situation exists and *how* to correct or improve it.

FYI

A *database* is an organized collection of data, most often in digital form.

Secondary Data

Secondary data are information that already exist. While some retailers do not share their data, many secondary data files are public and can be used by anyone. Data can be found through some publicly available databases, the Internet, trade journals, and public service organizations. For example, the Small Business Administration website provides new and existing businesses with a variety of statistical data, which helps the business owner to make decisions.

Scanning UPC codes is an easy way for retail stores to track sales data.

Monkey Business Images/Shutterstock.com

Exploring Retail Careers

Marketing Manager

A retailer's marketing policies play a large role in the products or services it offers. People who work in marketing identify potential customers and develop strategies to market products or services effectively to customers. In addition, marketing managers help keep the retailer on track. This is accomplished by monitoring customer wants and needs and suggesting products or services to satisfy those needs. Typical job titles for these positions also include *marketing director*, *marketing coordinator*, *brand manager*, *commercial lines manager*, and *market development manager*. Some examples of tasks that marketing managers perform include:

- coordinate marketing activities and policies to promote the retailer's products or services
- develop marketing and pricing strategies
- perform market research and analysis
- coordinate or participate in promotional activities and trade shows to showcase the retailer's products or services

Marketing managers need a strong background in sales and marketing strategy. It is also necessary to understand the principles of customer service. They need a solid knowledge of the English language, business and management principles, and media production and communication. Marketing managers must be able to think creatively and solve problems. A bachelor degree in marketing, advertising, communications, or a related field is required. Management positions generally require one to five years of experience.

It is much easier to analyze existing data than to collect and analyze new data. If relevant data exist, it can save the retailer the time and expense of collecting new data. However, data sources should be closely examined. Some data may be self-published and may not be reliable. When using secondary data, there is no control over the data collection process or the purpose of the research. As a result, retailers should only use verified data from a reputable source.

Depending on the source, secondary data can be quite expensive. If the data can help the retailer make sound business decisions, it is often worthwhile to spend the money for the information. For example, Dun & Bradstreet (D&B) is one of the most valued business data sources in the United States. The company charges retailers for access to their research and business resources. D&B currently has information on more than 50 million companies worldwide. Retailers would not be able to collect the same data on their own.

Government Sources

Local, state, and federal government agencies often collect and provide useful public data. Some of these agencies are shown in Figure 4-2. The data records are free to the public and broad in nature, such as demographic data. Local government sources can provide information about a specific neighborhood or region, which can be very helpful to a retailer. State and federal government sources collect data on a broader scope. For example, they collect data concerning income, employment rates, and buying patterns. The data can be helpful to both small and large businesses.

There are also non-government *public agencies* that perform public service. These agencies are defined by the US Government as "non-government entities that operate as a part of the government." The American Red Cross is an example of a non-government public agency. A public agency that provides valuable retail data is the US Chamber of Commerce.

Government Data Sources

Government Agency	Website	Data Provided
Small Business Administration	www.sba.gov	Statistics in various business-related areas, including: • Consumers • Employment • Demographics • Trade • Economic indicators
FedStats	www.fedstats.gov	Statistics from more than 100 government agencies, including: • Bureau of Labor Statistics • Occupational Safety and Health Administration • Census Bureau • Statistics of Income
E-Stats	www.census.gov/econ/estats	Economic statistics for the following industries: • Manufacturing • Retail trade • Merchant wholesale trade • Selected service
World Trade Organization Statistical Database (WSDB)	http://stat.wto.org	Statistical information on: • Trade profiles • Service profiles • Tariff profiles • International trade

Goodheart-Willcox Publisher

Figure 4-2 A sample of the government agencies that collect data. The data collected is available to the public.

Research Company Sources

There are many companies in the research business. These companies collect and analyze various types of data. They believe the value and quality of their data is high enough that someone else will want to buy the information. One leading source of marketing data is The Nielsen Company, the largest marketing research company in the country. Nielsen focuses on studying consumer shopping and media habits and trends. Forrester Research is a highly reputable e-tail researcher. They provide some free data on their website, but access to most data requires a membership or the purchase of a report.

Academic Sources

Places of higher education, such as universities and colleges, house as much data as possible in their libraries. The libraries typically provide directories, journals, databases, and a variety of other resources. However, a single library cannot house all existing data. Most also provide online access to the libraries of other education institutions. As a result, a well-functioning library at a university can provide access to nearly all existing secondary data. Most universities open their libraries to the public, with some restrictions. Retailers in search of data will find that academic sources are a good place to start.

Industry Association Sources

Industry associations, also known as *trade associations*, are organizations that are created and supported by the industry that they serve. These associations act to protect their industry and provide businesses with support to help them be successful. The National Retail Federation (NRF) is the world's largest retail trade association. The NRF conducts its own research and also compiles secondary research. They also publish a monthly *trade publication*, or content-oriented magazine, that covers important retail issues.

Online Sources

Various types of marketing information can be found using online sources, such as search engines, databases, blogs, and listservs. These sources are available to everyone with access to the Internet and are typically free to use. Some online sources may require registration to use all the resources on the site. Online sources can be used to identify groups of people with similar interests and opinions, research characteristics of certain geographic areas, check sales trends and economic conditions, and so many other types of data useful to retailers.

Primary Data

Primary data are the data collected directly by researchers. There are times when good, relevant secondary data may not be available or reliable. For example, consider the Logan's Department Store example. The problem was unique to Logan's. There would have been no existing data to help them determine why their men's clothing was not selling. As a result, collecting primary data was the best way to learn the answer.

Primary data can be qualitative or quantitative. **Qualitative data** provide insight into what people are thinking. **Quantitative data** provide facts and figures.

Marketing research provides critical information about the buying habits, needs, preferences, attitudes, and opinions of current and prospective customers. There are many ways to collect primary data, but most retailers use one or more of six basic research types:

- surveys
- interviews
- diaries
- observations
- test marketing
- experiments

The type of information required and the amount of money available for research determines which techniques are used.

Surveys

A **survey** is a set of questions asked to a group of people to determine how that group thinks, feels, or acts. A survey should be long enough to get the necessary responses. However, it should be short enough that respondents are willing to participate. Also, the layout, or presentation, of the survey should be uncomplicated and accessible to everyone asked to complete it.

Questions in a survey must be free of *bias*, or influencing questions. For example, asking a survey respondent "Why do you like our store?" infers that the respondent does like the store. To phrase the question without bias, ask, "Do you like our store? Why or why not?" The order, or sequencing, of survey questions is also important to consider. The sequence of questions should not influence the respondent's answers.

The survey questions and number of people in the sample may also be affected by the method of routing the survey, or how the survey will be distributed. Common methods of routing surveys include:

- **Mail.** Printed surveys may be mailed to participants with a return envelope for return of the completed survey.

Retail Ethics

Ethical Communication

Distorting information for a retailer's gain is an unethical practice. Honesty, accuracy, and truthfulness should guide all communications. Ethically, communication must be presented in an unbiased manner. Facts should be given without distortion. If the information is an opinion, it should be labeled as such.

- **Internet.** Sending surveys in e-mail or posting them on websites is an immediate way to get participation. Once participants complete the survey, they hit the Send button and the survey is immediately returned. Internet surveys save time and money.
- **Telephone.** An interviewer calls people from a database of contact information. If the individuals agree to participate in the survey, the interviewer asks them questions and records their answers. However, many people decline telephone surveys.

The wording of questions may need to be changed for delivery formats. For example, a survey that is mailed, delivered through the Internet (posted on a website or sent in an e-mail), or completed using a scanned form should have clearly worded instructions and user-friendly response options. The respondent cannot ask questions about how the survey needs to be completed with these types of surveys. The survey questions used for discussion groups or telephone and in-person interviews may be open-ended to prompt discussion and interaction with the interviewer or discussion group participants.

Interviews

Interviews are an effective way to gather qualitative data. An **interview** is a meeting or conversation where one or more persons, called interviewers, question or evaluate another person. These conversations, like questions in a survey, must also be free from bias.

Interviewers may also conduct the discussion with a small group of people called a focus group. A **focus group** is a group of six to nine people with whom an interview is conducted. An interviewer or research representative leads the group discussion.

FYI

Focus groups may also be called *consumer panels*.

Focus groups are a valuable source of primary data.

Monkey Business Images/Shutterstock.com

Participants may be asked questions about products, advertising, price, service, or other related topics. Focus group discussions are recorded for future reference. At least three focus groups are needed to get balanced results.

Diaries

A **diary** is a written record of a person's own experiences, thoughts, or observations. It produces a detailed history of the research as it unfolds. Consumers are often asked to a keep a research diary, which may have different purposes. Research participants are given instructions on the types of comments to include in their diary and how to format their entries.

Diaries are a good way to collect data that may not be easily collected in an interview or other face-to-face methods. Some participants are more open when they can write their comments privately. Also, diary participants have time to reflect on and think about their entries, while interviewees are asked to respond on the spot. Diaries can collect valuable data for research that calls for reflection and personal insight. However, analyzing diary entries to develop the research data can be time consuming and expensive.

Observations

Responses to surveys and focus groups are not always reliable because participants may tell the researcher what they think the researcher wants to hear. For example, during a survey participants may say that they will purchase a certain new product. However, when it comes down to making the purchase, they may not. By observing consumers, researchers learn about actual consumer behavior. Generally, researchers want to view consumer behavior as it happens naturally. So, they do not let shoppers know that they are conducting research. Another way retailers collect observation data is through secret shoppers. *Secret shoppers* pose as customers and make purchases. They may also be called *mystery shoppers*. Research firms hire secret shoppers and may send them to many different retailers during a day. The secret shoppers report their experiences with the store's products, employees, and service.

Keeping a research diary allows participants time to think and reflect, and provide researchers with personal insight.

auremar/Shutterstock.com

Test Marketing

Test marketing is placing a new product in selected stores to test customer response in actual selling conditions. This can help the retailer learn information about product modifications, price adjustments, or package improvements. For example, Target has twenty test market stores across the United States. The retailer "tries out" merchandise in these stores before it is placed in all stores. This helps to discover how products are perceived before investing in a product nationwide.

Experiments

Retailers may conduct experiments in their stores to collect data. Experiments can help retailers learn new information related to a research question. For example, a retailer with 100 stores may want to try out a new visual display, but cannot decide between its two best displays. To test customer response, both displays may be put in fifty different stores. After a given period of time, the retailer can evaluate which display generated the most sales. The most effective display may then be put in all the retail stores.

Sampling Plan

After deciding which primary data source to use, a *sampling plan* must be created. Among many things, a sampling plan considers:
- criteria for the sample
- size of the sample
- defined time frame
- method of collecting data
- process of analyzing data

Typically, a sample of people from the target market is asked to participate in the survey. A **sample** is a subset of the targeted population. The sample selected should match as closely as possible to the traits of the target market. For example, if a researcher wants to learn more about Macy's shoppers, the sample surveyed should be people who shop at Macy's. Otherwise, the research results will not reflect the target market.

The number of people needed in the sample depends on how many people are in the target market. To be valid, the sample must be large enough to represent the target population. There are a variety of formulas used to determine the proper sample size. The formulas are based on the size of the population and the type of research being conducted.

The sampling may be random from the target group. This is known as *probability sampling*. For example, choosing every fifth person from a list of people to invite is probability sampling. A convenience sample, known as a *nonprobability sampling*, could also be used. This sample is made up of people who are convenient to invite, like neighbors or relatives.

With the sample selected to participate, the research is executed. It is unlikely that the data collected will be 100% accurate. There are always errors that occur during research. Measurement errors and sampling errors are common. Measurement errors occur because respondents are not always truthful in their responses. This is considered a *response error*. Sampling errors develop when the survey sample does not match the target audience. This is considered a *nonresponse* error.

Checkpoint 4.1

1. What is the purpose of marketing research?
2. Identify the five steps in the research process.
3. What is a marketing information system (MkIS)?
4. Describe the types of marketing research used in retail to gather primary and secondary data.
5. Explain how researchers collect consumer data through observation.

Build Your Vocabulary

As you progress through this course, develop a personal glossary of retailing terms and add it to your portfolio. This will help you build your vocabulary and prepare you for a career. Write a definition for each of the following terms, and add it to your personal retailing glossary.

marketing research	qualitative data
actionable research	quantitative data
market research	survey
research process	interview
data	focus group
research proposal	diary
internal record	test marketing
secondary data	sample
primary data	

Section 4.2 Analyzing the Data

Objectives

After completing this section, you will be able to:
- **Discuss** the importance of using ratings scales in marketing research.
- **Explain** why retailers conduct research.

Key Terms

scale
Likert scale
behavioral intention
semantic differential
   scale
one-way labeled scale

data analysis
data mining
attitude research
competitive
   intelligence
product research

Web Connect

Search the Internet for several customer service survey templates and guidelines. Evaluate the different response and rating scales used in the survey samples. Was one type of response or rating scale used more often than other types? Explain your findings.

Critical Thinking

A local grocer gave out free reusable shopping bags to the first 200 customers of the day. In return, the customers were asked to complete a survey about the product. What information do you think the grocer wants to gather from these surveys?

Rating Scales

When collecting primary data, analyzing results is usually simple. For example, a customer's gender, age, or household income fall into specific, predetermined categories. However, retailers often want information about customer attitudes and opinions. Because attitudes and opinions are personal views, they are hard to measure. There are no definite responses.

Researchers use different response formats to measure attitudes and opinions. These formats are called scales. Scales allow researchers to assign numeric values to responses. Different types of scales are used based on the type of data needed.

Likert Scale

A **Likert scale** (pronounced "LICK-ert") is commonly used in marketing research to measure attitudes. On this type of scale, people are asked how much they agree or disagree with a given statement. Each response is assigned a number to help analyze the data. Lickert scales usually offer three, five, or seven available responses, as shown in Figure 4-3.

Statement	Extremely unlikely	Unlikely	Neither unlikely nor likely	Likely	Extremely likely
I plan to buy a new swimsuit within the next 30 days.	1	2	3	4	5
I am likely to shop at this store again.	1	2	3	4	5

Goodheart-Willcox Publisher

Figure 4-3 An example of a Likert scale used to assess behavioral intention.

One specific use of the Lickert scale in marketing research is to determine behavioral intention. **Behavioral intention** is the likelihood of engaging in a certain behavior.

Semantic Differential Scale

A **semantic differential scale** contains a range of opposite responses. Research participants describe how they feel about something by assigning a value somewhere between the opposites. For example, a retail store owner may want to know how customers feel about anything from prices to service, as shown in Figure 4-4.

One-Way Labeled Scale

A **one-way labeled scale** measures a topic's importance to the participants. One-way labeled scales are presented like semantic differential scales. However, the responses are restricted to positive options. An example is shown in Figure 4-5.

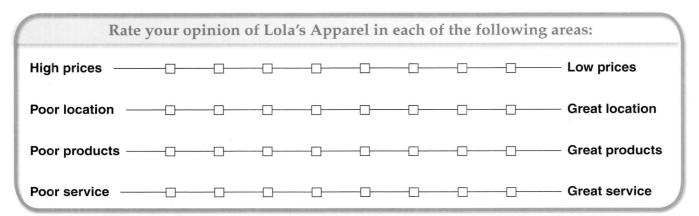

Goodheart-Willcox Publisher

Figure 4-4 On a semantic differential scale, participants indicate their feelings or reactions by marking a value on the scale.

How important is each of the following to you when buying electronics?					
Statement	Extremely important	Somewhat important	Neither important or unimportant	Not very important	Not important at all
Knowledgeable salespeople	○	○	○	○	○
Convenient store location	○	○	○	○	○
Quality products	○	○	○	○	○
Low pricing	○	○	○	○	○

Goodheart-Willcox Publisher

Figure 4-5 The response options on a one-way labeled scale are positive phrases.

Why Retailers Conduct Research

Research data are collected to identify and, ultimately, solve a problem. Once collected, data must be compiled and analyzed to be useful. **Data analysis** is the process of studying raw data and organizing the information into meaningful graphs or charts. Decisions are made using the graphs or charts that represent the data collected. **Data mining** involves searching through large amounts of data to find useful information. This process generally makes use of statistical software systems to help find patterns in the data. Web mining applies the processes of data mining on websites. Many e-tailers use web mining as a research tool to determine user website viewing patterns. This helps the retailer customize the information shown to each customer. However, some people look at web mining as invasion of privacy.

Marketing research is planned based on the goals and objectives of the business. If the research does not generate information that is helpful to the business in some way, the research is useless. There are many reasons retailers conduct research. Most retail research is conducted with one of four possible objectives:

- explore consumer attitudes
- learn more about the competition
- collect product information
- assess the success of advertising and promotion efforts

Research is constant in retail. For example, when a sales associate asks for your zip code at the checkout in a store, the retailer is collecting information about their customers. A retailer can learn a lot by knowing their customers' zip codes. By plotting customer zip codes on a map, the retailer can learn where customers live. The data may show the need for a new store location. A zip code map may also indicate where the retailer should focus promotional efforts to reach a greater number of customers.

Explore Consumer Attitudes

Attitude research, also called *opinion research*, is designed to find out how consumers think or feel about a company, their products and services, or other aspects of the business. Attitude research can be collected in-house to identify customers' opinions, or by using a marketing research company to identify the opinions of a broader group of customers.

Attitude research is generally conducted using focus groups and surveys. Researchers collect data from a sample that represents the retailer's target market so that the research findings also represent all or most of their customers.

Learn about the Competition

Competitive intelligence is data collected to analyze a particular retail industry. For example, a sporting goods retailer might collect information about the sporting goods industry, as well as information about its competitors. According to the research and consulting company Fuld & Company, nearly half of all companies use competitive intelligence.

Market research, also known as *market intelligence*, is conducted to analyze the retailer's competition, market population, target market, and the size and location of the target market. Data collected through market research allows retailers to estimate future sales and predict future economic conditions as they relate to the target market.

Often market research is conducted by analyzing existing data, such as demographics and economic indicators. Retailers may also combine existing data with their own data to get a better picture of the market. Some stores may also use internal data collected from their customers. E-tailers, in particular, often require their customers to provide a lot of personal information when making a purchase or signing up for certain online features.

Attitude research may be conducted by surveying a sample that represents the retailer's target market.

Monkey Business Images/Shutterstock.com

Collect Product Information

Product research focuses on consumer opinions of both new and existing products. It may relate to packaging, product design, or product functionality and usage. Retailers can learn if consumers have accepted a product and if not, why.

Product research is especially important for new products and is conducted before a product is launched into the market. Often, this type of research determines whether or not a product ever makes it into a store. Product research is conducted using surveys, focus groups, interviews, observations, test marketing, and experiments.

Assess Sales Promotions and Advertising

Sales promotions and advertising serve slightly different purposes. *Sales promotions*, such as coupons, are developed to motivate the consumer to act. For example, coupons are issued to urge customers to make a purchase. The number of coupons used can be counted to measure how many people responded. *Advertising* is used to get the attention of the customer. Advertising may or may not motivate them to immediate action. Unless the customer mentions that the advertisement influenced a purchase, the business would not know if this was successful. This makes measuring traditional advertising more challenging.

Review sales data gathered during a sales promotion to determine whether the promotion was successful.

Pablo Calvog /Shutterstock.com

Social Media

Social-Media Marketing (SMM) Goals

Like any other business, a retail business should identify its goals for social media pursuits. There are many reasons to use social media—communicating with customers, promoting products, or getting the name of the business in front of potential customers. By aligning social media plans with the marketing and business goals, a retailer can set priorities appropriately. Like other efforts to reach out to customers, not every social media idea will work as planned. A business could have several false starts in finding a mix of social media efforts that work well.

Checkpoint 4.2

1. List and describe three types of rating scales.
2. Describe how a research participant would respond using a semantic differential scale.
3. Why do retailers conduct marketing research?
4. Explain the role of market intelligence.
5. Explain the difference between sales promotions and advertising.

Build Your Vocabulary

As you progress through this course, develop a personal glossary of retailing terms and add it to your portfolio. This will help you build your vocabulary and prepare you for a career. Write a definition for each of the following terms, and add it to your personal retailing glossary.

scale	data analysis
Likert scale	data mining
behavioral intention	attitude research
semantic differential scale	competitive intelligence
one-way labeled scale	product research

Chapter Summary

Section 4.1 What Is Marketing Research?

- Marketing research is gathering information on how to promote, sell, and distribute a product or service. It is important for retailers to conduct marketing research.
- The research process consists of five steps. They are: define the problem, develop the research plan, collect data, analyze the data, and report the findings. All five steps must be followed for the research to be useful.
- Three major sources of marketing information are internal records, secondary data, and primary data. Internal records provide information from within the company. Secondary data are information that already exist. Primary data must be collected by the researchers.

Section 4.2 Analyzing the Data

- Researchers use rating scales to assign numeric value to responses. This makes qualitative responses easier to analyze. Three commonly used ratings scales are Likert scales, semantic differential scales, and one-way labeled scales.
- Retailers conduct research for several reasons. Research helps retailers explore consumer attitudes, learn more about the competition, collect product information, and assess the success of advertising and promotion efforts.

Review Your Knowledge

1. What is the difference between *marketing* research and *market* research?
2. Explain the purpose of a research brief.
3. How can the data from UPCs be used in marketing research?
4. Why might retailers choose to use secondary data rather than other types of data?
5. What is *bias*? Give an example of a biased survey question.
6. Why do researchers use rating scales?
7. Which scale is used to determine behavioral intention?
8. What is the difference between a semantic differential scale and a one-way labeled scale?
9. How can retailers use data mining as a research tool?
10. How is product research conducted?

Apply Your Knowledge

1. In order for research to be useful, retailers align their business goals and strategies with the results of their marketing research. Choose a local retail business and list five goals that business may have for the year. For each goal, indicate a research activity that could help the business plan for and meet the goal. Which research technique would be most effective for each research activity listed? Identify online sources that can provide marketing information to help the business meet its goals.
2. An eyewear retailer has successful sales for designer eyewear in its brick-and-mortar store. However, online sales are suffering. The retailer wants to conduct actionable research to understand how to improve online sales. Using the research process model, identify the marketing research problem and create a research proposal to

analyze why online sales have not been successful. Next, create the steps that will be necessary to write the research brief after the research concludes.

3. A clothing retailer is interested in researching the level of customer interest in reusable shopping bags. Write five survey questions that might help a clothing retailer learn what type of shopping bags interest their customers. Use the five questions you have written to create survey questions for five different research techniques.

    (a) Create a list of questions that are worded and formatted appropriately for a survey that is printed and mailed to customers.

    (b) Reword the questions for a survey to be delivered over the telephone.

    (c) Reword the questions so they can be used by a facilitator for a focus group.

    (d) Write the questions for a one-on-one interview with a customer.

    (e) Make a list of criteria you would use if you were observing customers rather than asking them questions.

    Create survey documents for each of these five survey techniques. Distribute them to your classmates for feedback. Which research technique would you recommend to the clothing retailer? Explain your choice.

4. Search the Internet for information about sampling plans and who may be selected, how many people might be selected, how to control the sample design, and how many are generally chosen for the sample. Write several paragraphs to describe your findings.

5. Errors occur regularly during the research process. Make a list of potential response errors and non-response errors that occur during primary research. Next to each, suggest how to control the sources of error.

6. Bias should be kept out of the research process. How can a researcher control sources of bias? Make a list of potential biases and how they can be avoided.

7. Design an experiment that you can conduct in your home or school. Decide what question or problem you want the experiment to answer or solve. Plan and execute your experiment. Create a report describing the goal of the experiment, how it was conducted, and the information that was gathered from the experiment.

8. A retailer is interested in how much consumers are willing to pay for an e-reader and which brand they prefer. Create a survey of ten questions to help the retailer gain this information. Consider the types of questions, question wording, sequencing, length, and layout of your survey. Use the Likert Scale, semantic differential scale, and one-way scale as the format for some of the questions on your survey. Share your surveys with the class. Which scale to you think would be most effective for this research problem?

9. Distribute the survey created in the last activity to half of your classmates. Use the survey questions to personally interview half of your classmates. Collect the survey and interview responses and tally the data. Estimate the outcome of the survey from random samples of the data collected. Evaluate the research hypothesis against the data. Present the data in a PowerPoint presentation for the class.

10. Diaries are used to gather research data. Keep a diary for one week to record all of the ways you experience retail in your life. Make notes on the various types of media you use to review products or make purchases, all of the retail ads you see and hear, and any sales associates with whom you come into contact. At the end of the week, briefly explain your thoughts and opinions on each diary entry. How do you think a market researcher might use the data from your diary? Swap diaries with a classmate and review their entries, as well. What information did you gather from the classmate's diary entries?

Check Your Retail IQ

Now that you have finished the chapter, see what you learned about retail by taking the chapter posttest. If you do not have a smartphone, visit the G-W Learning companion website.
G-W Learning mobile site: www.m.g-wlearning.com
G-W Learning companion website: www.g-wlearning.com/marketing/

College and Career Readiness

Career Ready Practices To become career ready, it is important to learn how to communicate clearly and effectively by using reason. Create an outline that includes information about trade-offs and opportunity costs. Consider your audience as you prepare the information. Using the outline, make a presentation to your class.

Listening Engage in a conversation with someone you have not spoken with before. Ask the person how he or she manages time. Actively listen to what that person is sharing. Next, summarize and retell what the person conveyed in conversation to you. Did you really hear what was being said?

Research Primary research is conducted by the writer in preparation for writing a report. The most common types of primary research are interviews, surveys, and experiments. Before research begins, questions should be formulated. Find an article on workplace safety. Take notes on what you learn and summarize in your own words.

Teamwork

Internet surveys are an efficient method of gathering consumer data and receive adequate participation from an audience. Survey Monkey® is one organization that provides this service. Each team member should research a different company that executes Internet surveys. Compare the services, formats, and delivery options available from each Internet survey company. Which company does the team recommend? How can a retailer use this service?

College and Career Portfolio

Electronic File Organization

You will create both a print portfolio and an e-portfolio in this class. You have already decided how to store hard copy items for your print portfolio. Now you need to create a plan for storing and organizing materials for your e-portfolio. Ask your instructor where to save your documents. This could be on the school's network or a flash drive of your own. Think about how to organize related files into categories. For example, school transcripts and diplomas might be one category. Awards and certificates might be another category, and so on. Next, consider how you will name the files. The names for folders and files should be descriptive but not too long.

This naming system will be for your use. You will decide in a later activity how to present your electronic files for viewers.

1. Create a folder on the network drive or flash drive on which you will save your files.
2. Write a few sentences to describe how you will name the subfolders and files for your portfolio.
3. Create the subfolders to organize the files, using the naming system you have created.

◇DECA Coach

Create an Advisory Panel

If you want to do your best in competitive events, enlist the help of others. While most of the work is yours to do, you still do not need to go it alone. Your instructor is an important "go to" person. However, those in business and industry can be an invaluable asset to you in the preparation process. If you plan to complete a prepared event, one of your first steps should be to form an advisory panel.

An advisory panel is a group of people working in business and industry in a field that can provide you with real-world understanding of your topic. To determine who to invite to be on your panel, consider the subject area. The first one or two people on your advisory panel should be currently working in the field. They can evaluate your work from a different perspective than people in education. However, your panel does not need to be limited to business and industry professionals that are familiar with your content. You may also consider enlisting the help of a public relations firm representative to help with your presentations. An editor at your local newspaper may be willing to edit or make suggestions on your writing. Invite those professionals who can help you based on what type of event you chose.

Once your panel has been formed, be sure and use it wisely. While these individuals are happy to help, remember that they also have full-time jobs. You should meet with them sparingly and only when your meeting has been organized ahead of time.

Visit www.deca.org to learn more information about DECA.

G-W Learning Mobile Site

Visit the G-W Learning mobile site to complete the chapter pretest and posttest, and to practice vocabulary using e-flash cards. If you do not have a smartphone, visit the G-W Learning companion website to access these features.

G-W Learning mobile site: www.m.g-wlearning.com
G-W Learning companion website: www.g-wlearning.com/marketing/

Chapter 5
Targeting the Market

Retailers are successful only when they sell enough products to generate profits. Successful retailers spend time and resources finding customers who are most likely to buy their products and services. Customers may be identified by common traits, such as location, age, recreation interests, and purchasing habits.

Customers buy products and services to satisfy their needs and wants. Retailers need to understand what motivates them into making purchases. Knowing this, retailers can choose products and services that will generate a profit. Understanding all the factors in how customers make decisions allows retailers to develop effective marketing strategies.

Case Study

Sports Endeavors Inc.

Creating a niche market with customers all over the world started as a high school senior project. Mike Moylan worked for a swimwear mail order company in high school. He saw a potential market for mail order soccer equipment. Mike created a business plan for the mail order company as his senior project. In 1984, the Moylan family used Mike's business plan to launch Sports Endeavors Inc. and the first Eurosport catalog. The catalog carried the best soccer products from all around the world. The first catalog was mailed to 6,000 soccer players and friends.

The company grew at a steady pace with catalog sales. In 1994, Sports Endeavors Inc. jumped on the emerging World Wide Web platform and registered the www.soccer.com URL. Since launching their e-tailing website, Sports Endeavors Inc. has acquired several of their catalog and online competitors. They have partnered with many competitive soccer organizations around the world. The Eurosport catalog is now sent to almost a million customers every month. The Moylan family and their partners saw potential in a niche market and became the largest international soccer specialty retailer.

College and Career Readiness

Reading Prep

Before reading this chapter, read the opening pages and section titles for this chapter. These can help prepare you for the topics that will be presented in the unit. What does this tell you about what you will be learning?

Check Your Retail IQ

Before you begin the chapter, see what you already know about retail by taking the chapter pretest. If you do not have a smartphone, visit the G-W Learning companion website.

G-W Learning mobile site: www.m.g-wlearning.com

G-W Learning companion website: www.g-wlearning.com/marketing/

Sections

5.1   Target Market

5.2   The Mix

5.3   Consumer Behavior

Dmitry Kalinovsky/Shutterstock.com

Section 5.1 Target Market

Objectives

After completing this section, you will be able to:
- **Discuss** the process of identifying the customer.
- **Distinguish** the four ways of segmenting the market.
- **Identify** the use of a customer profile.

Key Terms

market
mass market
target market
market segmentation
market segment
demographics
demographic
  segmentation
geographic
  segmentation
psychographic
  segmentation
attitude
values
behavioral
  segmentation
buying status
usage rate
customer profile

Web Connect

Choose one of your favorite e-tailers. Based on the type of products they sell, describe the primary customers for that specific e-tailer. What characteristics do you think the customers have in common?

Critical Thinking

It is important for businesses to identify who is most likely to buy the goods or services they offer. Make a list of the critical factors you think a business considers when identifying potential customers. Explain your reasoning for each factor.

Identifying the Customer

Successful brick-and-mortar retailers do not just open a store and wait for customers to walk in. They spend time, effort, and money to locate customers who are most likely to buy in their stores. The same applies to e-tailers—they do not create an online store and wait for customers to visit. E-tailers must be proactive in getting customers to visit their website.

There are many steps in getting the attention of customers, but the first step is to find them. One of the market strategies a retail business must address is *identifying the customer*.

Retail businesses are successful only when they sell enough products to generate profits. To sell products, they must know who its customer is. The **market** is a group of people who want a product and are able to buy it. For example, the market for a clothing retailer is anyone who needs and wants the type of clothing it sells and has

FYI

In this text, *retail business* includes both brick-and-mortar retailers and online stores operated by e-tailers.

the money to make a purchase. The entire group of people who might buy a product or service is considered the mass market. Retailers who aim their marketing efforts at the mass market maximize the exposure of their products. However, the cost of reaching that many potential customers is significant.

A target market is a specific group of customers to which retailers aim to sell their products and services. The target market is a selected section of the mass market. It is the group of people most likely to buy a retailer's products. A *niche market* is a piece of the target market that is very narrow and specific. For example, surfing gear is a niche market within the larger sporting goods retail market.

An important step in building a successful retail business is identifying the best customers. Knowing exactly who the customer is allows retailers to provide better products and services. This process is known as *targeting the customer.*

Market Segmentation

It is not logical to think that everyone who needs and wants a product or service will buy from any one particular retailer. Each retail store has its own specific product offerings and types of customers. Retailers identify prospective customers based on who is most likely to buy their products.

Dividing large markets into smaller groups is called market segmentation. Market segmentation enables retailers to create their target markets. For example, a retailer that sells skateboards may choose to segment their market by age and gender. A market segment is a group of individuals in the market who share common characteristics or interests, such as where they live, income level, age groups, opinions, and various other criteria.

Retailers build a marketing strategy based on one or more market segments. It costs money to reach people with a message. Retailers do not want to waste money trying to reach people who are not interested in their product. An advantage of market segmentation is that the process *identifies* people who may be in the market for a product or service and *eliminates* those who are not. A disadvantage to market segmentation is that it creates a limited pool of potential customers. If segmenting was not done correctly, the research will not be accurate.

Customers can be grouped into different market segments using four broad categories based on key characteristics. The four categories, shown in Figure 5-1, are demographics, geographics, psychographics, and behavioral traits. Retailers may blend together more than one of these categories to suit their needs.

Figure 5-1 The four categories of market segments.

S. john/Shutterstock.com

Demographic Segmentation

Demographics describe people in terms of personal traits, such as age, gender, education, employment, income, family status, and ethnicity. **Demographic segmentation** divides the market by customers' personal traits.

- *Age.* People within defined age groups tend to have similar characteristics, needs, and wants. One way to classify by age is by generational groups, as shown in Figure 5-2.

- *Gender.* Retailers may decide to market their products exclusively to men, to women, or to both genders.

- *Education.* Customers with similar educational backgrounds, such as number of years of education or degree earned, may have similar buying habits.

- *Occupation.* This segment includes both occupation and employment status. A customer's job may have an effect on his or her buying patterns.

- *Family size.* Family size may affect various purchases, such as the type of car needed and the amount of products regularly purchased from the grocery store.

- *Ethnicity.* People of the same ethnic background tend to have related buying habits. Retailers target their markets for cultural preferences in items like food, entertainment, and clothing.

Generational Groups	
Generation	Approximate Birth Years
Greatest Generation	1901–1925
Silent Generation	1926–1945
Baby Boomer Generation	1946–1964
Generation X	1965–1983
Generation Y	1984–1995
Generation Z	1996–2013

Goodheart-Willcox Publisher

Figure 5-2 Generations of customers.

- *Income.* Customers' income level may indicate the types of products and services that interest them, and the prices they may be willing to pay.

Every ten years, the US Census Bureau conducts a census survey that includes personal information about US citizens. Using the statistics and reports from the census survey can be useful in planning for the success of a retailer's business.

Geographic Segmentation

Geographic segmentation divides consumers based on where they live. People who live in the same geographic areas may share similar buying patterns. For example, retailers may sell more winter clothes in areas with cold weather seasons, and lighter-weight clothing in warm climates. Some variables within geographic segmentation include region, population density, and climate.

Region

A region could be a country, state, city, or zip code. The marketing plan for a business can be tailored to individual geographic areas. This allows the retailer to localize the products, advertising, and sales efforts. For example, a restaurant in the southern United States may customize its menu to reflect southern cuisine and local tastes.

Population Density

Customers may be grouped based on the population density where they live, such as urban, suburban, and rural areas. Purchasing behaviors, such as social fads and trends, may relate to specific market segments based on the population density.

Copyright Law

It is unethical to use something created or written by another person without his or her permission. Under copyright law, as soon as something is in tangible form, it is automatically copyrighted. Anything in print, including music, images on television or movie screens, or on the Internet is copyrighted. If any material is copied or used without the copyright holder's permission, a theft has occurred.

Climate

Climate is used to geographically segment customers. People in warm climates have different needs than those who live in cold climates. For example, the sale of snow boots would be targeted to people who live in climates with snowy winter seasons.

Psychographic Segmentation

Psychographic segmentation divides consumers based on personal lifestyle preferences or choices. Some factors in this type of segmentation include attitudes, activities, interests, and values. Researchers use social traits to learn more about why a group behaves as it does and how these social traits influence purchasing decisions.

Attitudes

Attitude is a person's perspective and feelings about something. Attitudes can be positive or negative, and can reflect individual likes and dislikes. For example, today's buyers tend to purchase more *green*, or eco-friendly, products. This reflects more environmentally conscious attitudes. Attitude also influences customers who want fashionable clothing. For example, some customers may seek savings while others may shop for particular brands or styles.

Activities

Consumers who share similar lifestyles form a marketing segment. For example, people who are interested in fitness make up a market segment. Product usage, interests, and leisure activities are some categories that can be used to segment lifestyle markets.

Interests

Customers may be grouped by their interests. This includes political opinions, views on the environment, and art and cultural involvement. The interests that consumers have and the activities they engage in impact the products they buy.

Values

The market can be segmented by consumer values. **Values** are beliefs about what is good or appropriate. For example, customers valuing safety are more likely to buy a car with a good crash-test rating. Customers who value the environment may choose a hybrid or electric car.

Fans of professional sport teams usually shop for products that show their team pride.

Behavioral Segmentation

The behavior of buyers is important in segmenting a market. **Behavioral segmentation** divides the market by the relationship between customers and a product or service. Some of the ways consumer behaviors can be categorized include buying status, usage rates, and benefits sought.

Buying Status

Buying status describes the timing of when a customer will buy a product or service. Buying status classifications of customers are potential, first-time, occasional, and regular customers. A *potential customer* has not purchased the product or service, but is considering it. A *first-time customer* has purchased the product for the first time. *Occasional customers* buy the product or service, but not on a regular basis. *Regular customers* buy the product all the time.

Usage Rates

Retailers may segment customers based on **usage rate**, or how often customers use or buy a product or service. Consumer usage rates are classified as heavy, moderate, light, and nonuser. Many retailers find that the *80/20 rule* applies. This means that 80 percent of a retailer's sales are attributed to 20 percent of its customers.

Benefits Sought

Customers often choose the same products, but for different individual reasons. For example, one customer may want an e-book reader that is small and easy to use. Another customer may only want an e-book reader that is inexpensive. Both of these customers are buying an e-book reader, but are seeking a different benefit.

Customer Profile

Once the target market is established, a customer profile can be created. A **customer profile** is the detailed description of a customer, based on demographic, geographic, psychographic, and behavioral data. The profile describes the type of customer likely to purchase the retailer's product. Customer profiles are updated regularly so that advertising and marketing efforts are aimed at the correct audience.

Checkpoint 5.1

1. Describe the difference between a mass market and a target market.
2. What do retailers do with market segmentation data?
3. Name the four market segments used to group customers.
4. What are some of the factors examined when segmenting a market based on psychographics?
5. Explain the purpose of a customer profile.

Build Your Vocabulary

As you progress through this course, develop a personal glossary of retailing terms and add it to your portfolio. This will help you build your vocabulary and prepare you for a career. Write a definition for each of the following terms, and add it to your personal retailing glossary.

market	psychographic segmentation
mass market	attitude
target market	values
market segmentation	behavioral segmentation
market segment	buying status
demographics	usage rate
demographic segmentation	customer profile
geographic segmentation	

Section 5.2 The Mix

Objectives

After completing this section, you will be able to:
- **Explain** how the marketing mix influences the target market.
- **Describe** the retail mix.
- **Give examples** of controllable and uncontrollable factors in the marketing environment.

Key Terms

marketing mix
product mix
service mix
price
promotional mix
place
retail mix
personnel
presentation
process

Web Connect

Research the terms *marketing mix* and *retail mix*. How are these terms similar? What characteristics differentiate the terms? Explain the impact that each has on a retailer's business.

Critical Thinking

Based on what you currently know about marketing, what do you think the marketing environment is? Write down your definition. What are some examples of influences in the marketing environment?

Marketing Mix

There are many marketing strategies a retailer must consider and address. In addition to target marketing, another important retail marketing strategy is creating a marketing mix. The **marketing mix** is the marketing strategy that considers the four *P*s of marketing—product, price, promotion, and place. Retailers can combine these elements to influence the target market to buy a product.

Product

Product is anything that can be bought or sold, such as goods or services. A good is something tangible that you can touch, like a piece of clothing. A service is intangible, like the delivery of an Internet order. The **product mix** is the range of all goods sold by the retailer. The **service mix** is the range of all services, such as delivery services, sold by a retailer.

Product strategy involves selecting the goods and services that will meet customer needs and wants. Retailers attempt to provide a combination of products that will generate greater sales together than if the products were sold by themselves. For example, most clothing stores also sell clothing accessories, hoping customers will buy accessories to go with their newly purchased outfit. Product mix is important to the profit margin of the retailer.

Price

Price is the amount of money requested or exchanged for a product or service. *Pricing strategies* include all the factors that are taken into consideration to establish a price. Profit margins, competition, and other factors are used to determine a price that is profitable for the business.

Promotion

Promotion involves communicating with potential customers in an effort to influence their purchasing decisions. The **promotional mix** is a combination of personal selling, sales promotion, advertising, and public relations used in a retailer's promotional efforts. *Promotional strategy* is deciding which elements to include in the promotional mix for the greatest success.

Place

Place, also called *distribution*, is all of the activities in getting the product to the customer. Will the business distribute the product online, in a store, in a catalog, or all three? *Place strategy* includes product warehousing, transporting product to the store location, processing orders for customers, and controlling inventory. The objective is to make sure customers get exactly what they want, at the right place, and right time.

Clicks or bricks is a phrase used to describe whether a product is sold online (clicks represents mouse clicks) or in a traditional store (bricks).

Retail Mix

The way a retailer uses the four *P*s of marketing plays a big role in the business' success. There are additional factors unique to the retail industry that must also be considered. Three additional *P*s are added to the marketing mix to create the **retail mix**:
- personnel
- presentation
- process

Personnel

The term **personnel** refers to the people who work for the retail business. Retail stores involve a great deal of person-to-person interaction.

Therefore, personnel play a large role in a retailer's success. They help to distinguish one retailer from another in areas of service, support, and communication.

Personnel strategy considers capability, level of interaction, availability, and efficiency. For example, a specialty boutique may pride itself on high levels of attentive customer service. However, a warehouse club retailer provides very little interaction between customers and personnel, other than at checkout. These types of retailers have very different personnel strategies.

Presentation

Presentation, also known as *visual merchandising*, is the way merchandise is presented in a store. Presentation includes atmosphere, lighting, fixtures, and other elements. *Presentation strategy* is the process of selecting elements that represent a retailer's brand, such as music playing in the store, uniforms for the staff, and other elements that help build a brand.

Process

Process is a series of actions that lead to an end, such as a sale or a return. Processes may be invisible to the customer, but they impact a customer's overall experience. Some of the most obvious processes are sales transactions, credit processes, and product or service delivery.

Northfoto/Shutterstock.com

The retailer Abercrombie & Fitch® is well known for their distinctive visual merchandising and the atmosphere within their retail stores.

Some processes are less obvious, but still impact the shopping experience, such as order processing, standardization from store to store, and how database information is used.

Marketing Environment

In general, the marketing mix and the retail mix are under the control of the retailer. Retailers make decisions that influence the retail mix. Decisions such as how to price and promote products are completely controlled by the retailer. These are known as *controllable factors*.

External factors that the retailer cannot control are known as *uncontrollable factors*. For example, the economy may change and people may lose their jobs. If people become unemployed, they may be unable to buy products. This is not a factor that the retail mix can change. If the competition comes out with a better product, the marketing mix cannot immediately change the loss of sales. Uncontrollable factors are beyond the control of the retailer.

To be prepared for the future, retailers must understand the marketing environment. In order to make a profit, retailers must control influences that directly impact the business. Knowing there are factors that cannot be controlled, like developments in technology, evolving consumer trends, and changes in government regulatory standards, helps retailers prepare and put safeguards in place.

Checkpoint 5.2

1. Explain the importance of the marketing mix.
2. Explain the concept of product strategy.
3. What are the three additional *P*s that make up the retail mix?
4. Explain presentation strategy, or visual merchandising, that takes place in a retail business.
5. Explain controllable and uncontrollable factors affecting the marketing environment.

Build Your Vocabulary

As you progress through this course, develop a personal glossary of retailing terms and add it to your portfolio. This will help you build your vocabulary and prepare you for a career. Write a definition for each of the following terms, and add it to your personal retailing glossary.

marketing mix	place
product mix	retail mix
service mix	personnel
price	presentation
promotional mix	process

Section 5.3 Consumer Behavior

Objectives

After completing this section, you will be able to:
- **List** the steps in the consumer decision-making process.
- **Explain** consumer buying motives.
- **Describe** the three factors that influence consumer purchasing.

Key Terms

evoked set
consumer behavior
motive
buying motive
rational buying motive
emotional buying
  motive
patronage buying
  motive

psychological
  influences
self-actualization
social influences
reference group
culture
peer pressure
word-of-mouth
  publicity
situational influences

Web Connect

There are three factors that influence consumer purchasing: psychological influences, social influences, and situational influences. Select one of these factors and research its effects on consumer behavior. Write several paragraphs to report your findings.

Critical Thinking

Explain your decision making process for purchases over $100. Do you research the product? Compare prices? Consult product reviews? Make a list of the steps you take before you actually buy an expensive product.

Consumer Decision-Making Process

Consumers buy products and services daily. How do they decide what to buy? Consumers go through a process in making decisions, similar to the five-step process shown in Figure 5-3.

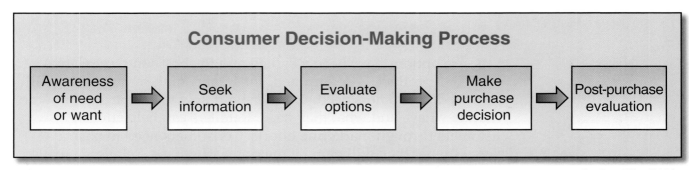

Goodheart-Willcox Publisher

Figure 5-3 The five steps in the consumer decision-making process.

Awareness of Need or Want

The first step in the decision-making process is to identify a need or want. People must be aware that they need or want something before they will make a purchase. If there is a gap between what they have and what they need or want, they will want to fill that gap. For example, Adam made the soccer team and needs cleats and shin guards. If he does not already have cleats and shin guards, he needs to buy them. Adam needs to fill that gap.

Seek Information

Once the need for a product or service is clear, consumers examine how they can fill that need. Consumers use many sources to find information. They may recall personal experiences, ask peers, search the Internet, or look through retailer promotion ads for information.

The products and retail stores that come to mind while searching for information are called the evoked set. An **evoked set** includes the choices that a consumer is aware of and thinks highly of during the search process. This set of choices may relate to the product, brand, or retail location. Retailers work hard to be part of a consumer's evoked set. For example, once Adam begins to collect information on his soccer gear, he may instantly think of a particular sporting goods retailer. He may then ask his friends where they purchased their soccer gear, what brand they bought, and how much they paid.

Evaluate Options

After collecting information, consumers weigh their options for filling the need. Consumers consider many factors at this stage, including value, price, quality, product features, and location of the retailer. Customers decide which combination of these factors best suits their needs. For example, Adam may prefer shopping at a local sports equipment shop, but their prices are a little high. The sporting goods chain store is farther away, but their prices are more affordable. Adam must decide if he wants to pay more to shop at the store he likes, or save money by driving a little farther to the sporting goods chain store.

Buying Decisions

Once options have been weighed and the best *value,* or relative worth of a product, is determined, consumers make a purchase to fill their need. Customers need to understand how to fill the gap between what they have and what they need. Retailers can help educate customers through marketing efforts. Consumers need to have a sense of what they will gain by making a purchase. Retailers can also make the buying process as easy as possible to ensure that customers complete their purchase.

Exploring Retail Careers

Usability Specialist

A usability specialist helps e-tailers to determine how people use the store's website. A person in this position typically helps the company determine what makes the e-commerce site effective by analyzing colors, fonts, navigational tools, overall page layout, and other aspects of the website. They test websites to help eliminate confusing navigational menus, error messages, missing links, and other elements that may confuse or frustrate customers. Usability specialists also help web designers direct online visitors through the e-tail site as intended. Another title for a usability specialist is *usability engineer*. Some examples of tasks that usability specialists perform include:
- use eye-tracking tools to determine what online users look at the most and in what order
- track cursor movement to determine what online users click on and in what order
- work with software engineers to combine software functionality and usability
- determine an e-tailer's best choices with regard to website layout, colors, fonts, icon style, and other design elements

This position requires ability to work in a fast-paced environment. Good oral and written communications skills are necessary. Education requirements range from a high school diploma to a master degree.

Levels of Buying Decisions

Some buying decisions require more time and research than others. The more important consumers think a decision is, the more thought they put into that decision. Expensive items are examples of products considered important when making buying decisions. Most consumers would probably do more research on buying a new smartphone than on buying a pair of socks. However, products do not need to be expensive to be important to the consumer. For example, some people may spend a lot of time choosing just the right pair of jeans. But, other consumers may simply buy any pair of jeans in their size at the first store they visit.

There are four levels of buying decisions: routine, limited, extensive, and impulse.
- *Routine buying decision.* A routine buying decision is a purchase made with very little effort or thought, like buying gas for your car.
- *Limited buying decision.* With limited buying decisions, consumers go through each step of the buying process, but do not spend a great deal of time on them.
- *Extensive buying decision.* An extensive buying decision involves significant time and effort spent on research, analysis, and purchase planning.
- *Impulse buying decision.* Impulse buying decisions are made with no research and are not planned. These purchases are usually spurred by attractively presented or conveniently located products within a store.

Once a buying decision is made, the actual purchase takes place.

Social Media

Social Media Terminology

There are many social media terms that are used that a savvy retailer should know. The list of terms updates and grows, so it is important that the business stay current. Some examples are as follows:

- viral—information that is passed along to others
- wiki—web pages that can be edited by others
- trending—a word or topic that is popular at any given minute
- Flickr—network that allows users to share photos

Keeping on top of new terms and learning the proper way to use social media can be an important marketing tool for the retailer.

Evaluate the Purchase

Even though the purchase has been made, the decision-making process does not end until consumers have evaluated their decision. They consider the pros and cons of their purchase, and sometimes question whether or not they made the right decision. Retailers do everything they can to make customers feel good about their purchase. Happy customers are much more likely to be repeat customers. This is why retailers often offer returns, discounts, upgrades, and other concessions to buyers who are not happy with their purchase.

Consumer Buying Motives

FYI

Motive comes from the Latin word *motivus*, which means "to move or caused to be moved."

Retailers study consumer behavior. **Consumer behavior** includes all the actions people take to satisfy their needs and wants, which includes what they buy. When considering shopping needs and wants, people buy products and services for different reasons. These reasons are called buying motives. A **motive** is the reason a person acts in a certain way. A **buying motive** is the reason people buy what they buy. Retailers need to understand what moves customers to action.

Why do some people buy only one particular brand of gasoline, while others buy the cheapest gas they can find? To save money? Are they concerned with the quality of the gas? Are they loyal to the retailer? The answer could be any or all of these. Discovering consumer buying motives can make the difference between having a customer browse or actually make a purchase.

Breaking down buying motives can be a complex task. Consider the following example. Kailey is a college student. She bought a popular backpack before her first semester. Why did she buy this particular backpack? She may have believed that it was a good quality backpack. She may also have thought it was trendy. Or, maybe she purchased it at a store she always shops at. It could even be a combination of all three. The reason behind Kailey's purchase explains buying motives in a most fundamental way.

Illustrated in Figure 5-4, there are three primary motives that explain why people buy:

- rational
- emotional
- patronage

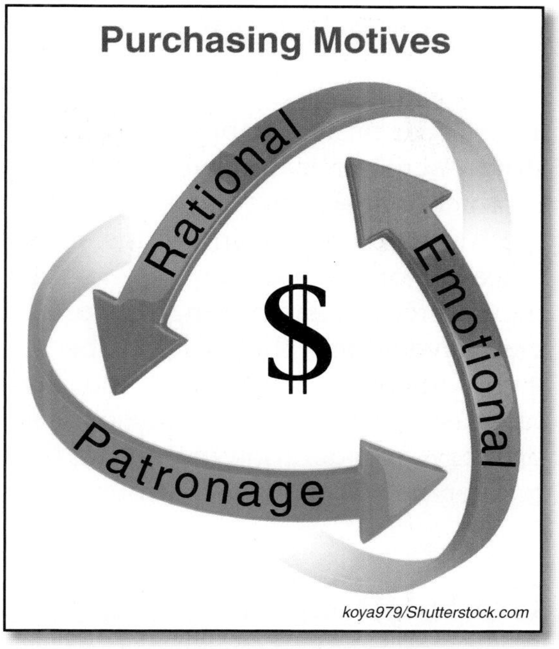

Figure 5-4 The primary motives of consumer purchasing.

Rational Motives

A **rational buying motive** means that a customer makes his or her purchase for a practical reason. Rational motives may be price, quality, durability, or any other practical reason for making a purchase. Most items are not bought based on rational buying motives alone. If Kailey bought the backpack because she felt she was buying a quality product to meet her needs, it would be based on a rational buying motive.

Emotional Motives

An **emotional buying motive** is a motive that appeals to the way a customer thinks or feels. Most purchases have some element of emotion attached. Emotional motives may include a sense of status, fear, excitement, or a desire to do the right thing. If Kailey bought the backpack because it was trendy and others might admire her for it, the purchase would be emotional.

Most purchases are, at least in part, based on emotions. Consumers do not usually buy items strictly because they are the most functional. For example, consumers buy clothing because they like it or think it is attractive. Consumers buy food because it fills the need for food and because they like the taste. These products do fill a need, but consumers consider how products make them think or feel, at least in part, when making buying decisions.

Patronage Motives

Patronage buying motives are based on loyalty and suggest that a customer prefers to buy a particular brand or from a particular store. A customer may be influenced to shop for a particular product or at a particular store by the appearance of the store, recommendations from friends, or good customer service experience. Once customers have a good experience with a product or retailer, they prefer to keep buying that product or from that store. Kailey may have bought the backpack because she *always* shops at that store. It could be because she loves the products or prices, has a favorite sales associate, or even because the store is close to her home. If her primary consideration in making the purchase was the brand or retailer, her motive was patronage.

Consumer Buying Influences

Many things can influence consumer buying behavior, especially since every consumer is different. There are three main factors that influence consumer purchasing: psychological influences, social influences, and situational influences.

Psychological Influences

Psychological influences come from within a person—why a person has specific needs and wants. In the 1950s, Abraham Maslow developed a theory explaining why people act the way they do. Maslow believed that people act to fulfill a need. *Maslow's Hierarchy of Needs* theory is still regarded today and plays an important role in retailing.

Maslow's theory states that there are five different types of needs that range in importance. These needs are divided into five categories:

- physical
- security
- love and acceptance
- esteem
- self-actualization

People take action based on their attempt to fill these needs. The needs at the bottom of the hierarchy, shown in Figure 5-5, are the most important. Physical needs *must* be met in order to survive, such as having enough air, water, and food. The next level of need is security. People need to be safe from physical harm and have financial security. The third level in the hierarchy includes the needs for love and acceptance.

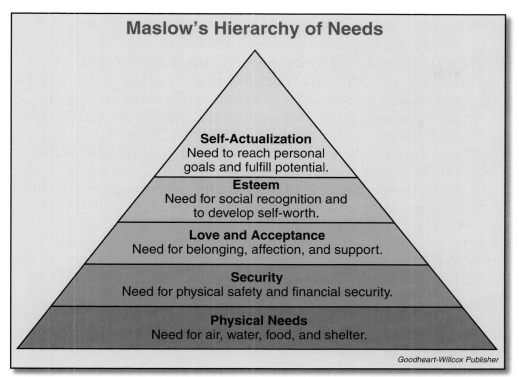

Figure 5-5 Beginning at the bottom of the hierarchy, needs progress from survival to personal growth.

Once needs at the base level are fulfilled, a person can attempt to fulfill higher-level needs. People continue to climb the levels of needs as they satisfy each one. At the top of the hierarchy is self-actualization. **Self-actualization** is the need to fulfill one's own potential through reaching personal goals and contributing to the well-being of others.

Social Influences

Social influences come from the society in which a person lives and are acquired from the people around him or her. Consumers may be influenced by friends, family, members of a club or team, or even celebrities.

People sometimes use reference groups as a basis for choices. **Reference groups** are other people whose values, beliefs, behaviors, and opinions are used by an individual as a basis for decision making. Someone does not have to be a member of a reference group to be influenced by its characteristics, either positively or negatively.

There are three types of social influences:

- culture
- family
- peers

Culture

Culture is the way a group collectively thinks, feels, and acts. Similar values are shared by most or all of the members of the group. The values are accepted and expected within the group. Culture may determine what is right or wrong, important or unimportant, and acceptable or unacceptable. These values are also passed onto other members of the group through immersion or teaching.

The culture people grow up in impacts their buying decisions. For example, people who grew up celebrating birthdays with gifts and birthday cake find that the tradition becomes important to them. These people will likely celebrate birthdays in this way for years to come. Culture influences how people dress, eat, and entertain themselves. As a result, consumer purchases are influenced by culture.

Cultural influences also come from the media. Celebrities on television, in movies, in magazines, or in other forms of media influence how consumers want to act, dress, wear their hair, etc. Retailers often hire celebrities to endorse their products, knowing that consumers will be influenced.

Family

Family members influence other family members. Children grow up watching certain buying habits of older family members, and get familiar with certain products. For example, your mother may always purchase the same brand of bread. When you start shopping for your own groceries, there is a good chance you will buy the same brand of bread because it is familiar to you. Family members generally trust other family members to be honest with them, as well. As a result, family members are often asked to recommend products and services.

Family members also pass down values, religion, and behaviors. For example, someone that grows up in a family that regularly visits the beach for vacation will probably want to take vacations at the beach as an adult. The family's behavior will be reflected in their personal buying habits.

Peers

Peer groups of friends, classmates, coworkers, and teammates have a significant influence on our buying habits. They are important reference groups because we feel the need to *conform*, or behave like others in the group, in order to be accepted. Peer pressure is the social influence, mild or strong, exerted on an individual by his or her peers. Peer pressure exists in school, in the workplace, and within other social or professional groups. For example, peer pressure may influence you to buy a certain brand of clothing because it is commonly accepted within your group of peers.

We tend to trust our peers more than strangers. When peers recommend a product with which they have experience, they influence a person's decision to buy that product when it is needed. **Word-of-mouth publicity** is when people talk casually about their experiences with a product, service, or business. These casual conversations can affect buying decisions both positively or negatively. Social media sites, such as Facebook and Twitter, have greatly expanded our peer groups, as well as our word-of-mouth circle.

Situational Influences

Situational influences come from various factors in the general marketing environment. Situational influences related to the retailer may include the store location, current sales and promotions, and store hours. The consumer's buying choices may also be affected by the weather, their mood, and the state of their finances.

Checkpoint 5.3

1. Describe the consumer decision-making process.
2. List and describe the three primary motives that explain why people buy.
3. What are the three main factors that influence consumer purchasing?
4. Summarize Maslow's Heirarchy of Needs theory.
5. What are the three types of social influences on purchases?

Build Your Vocabulary

As you progress through this course, develop a personal glossary of retailing terms and add it to your portfolio. This will help you build your vocabulary and prepare you for a career. Write a definition for each of the following terms, and add it to your personal retailing glossary.

evoked set
consumer behavior
motive
buying motive
rational buying motive
emotional buying motive
patronage buying motive
psychological influence

self-actualization
social influences
reference group
culture
peer pressure
word-of-mouth publicity
situational influences

Chapter Summary

Section 5.1 Target Market

- Identifying the customer is a marketing strategy that helps determine the success of the business. The group of people who want a product and are able to buy is known as the market. The mass market is everyone who might buy a product or service, while the target market is a specific group within the mass market.
- Segmenting the market helps the retailer focus marketing efforts. Four ways of segmenting the market include demographic, geographic, psychographic, and behavior criteria.
- A customer profile is a description of a customer, based on demographic, geographic, psychographic, and behavioral data. The customer described is often the type of customer most likely to purchase from the retailer.

Section 5.2 The Mix

- The marketing mix uses the four *P*s of marketing—product, price, promotion, and place—to influence the target market to buy a product.
- The retail mix is an extension of the marketing mix. Three additional *P*s are added: personnel, presentation, and process.
- Retailers faced controllable factors and uncontrollable factors in the market. Decisions such as pricing and product promotions are controllable factors. The economy and the competition are examples of uncontrollable factors.

Section 5.3 Consumer Behavior

- The five steps in the consumer decision-making process are: awareness of need or want, seek information, evaluate options, buying decisions, and evaluate the purchase.
- Three primary consumer buying motives are rational buying motives, emotional buying motives, and patronage buying motives.
- Three factors that influence consumer purchasing are psychological influences, social influences, and situational influences.

Review Your Knowledge

1. Describe the difference between a mass market and a target market.
2. What is a niche market? Give an example.
3. Name the four market segments used to group customers.
4. Name and describe the four buying status classifications for customers.
5. What are some activities involved in place strategy?
6. How do personnel play a large role in a retailer's success?
7. What are uncontrollable factors in the marketing environment? Give an example.
8. Explain the four levels of buying decisions that are made by most consumers.
9. Why do retailers study consumer behavior?
10. Explain how peer pressure can affect buying decisions.

Apply Your Knowledge

1. A cell phone retailer in your area plans to offer the latest smartphone models in their store. Identify the mass market for this product. Create a market segmentation plan that would be appropriate for the store. Consider the four categories of segmenting: demographics, geographics, psychographics, and behavioral traits.

2. Based on your market segmentation plan in the last activity, create a PowerPoint presentation that explains how you segmented the market. Are any potential customers in the mass market eliminated because of the market segmentation? Explain both the benefits and disadvantages of marketing to the mass market and to the selected market segment.

3. Write a customer profile detailing the ideal customer for the cell phone retailer based on your market segmenting plans and research. How can the retailer use this customer profile in planning their marketing strategy?

4. Create a sales presentation for the latest model smartphone that is aimed at the ideal customer described in your customer profile. Deliver the presentation to your class. Assess their interest in the product based on your sales presentation. Do they want to buy the smartphone? What persuaded them that they need the smartphone?

5. Niche market retailers can reach a great number of potential customers online (e-tailing). Search the Internet for three examples of niche market e-tailers. Describe the niche market for each e-tailer. Explain how e-tailing benefits the retailer. Do the niche e-tailers also have brick-and-mortar retail stores? Is the niche e-tailer part of another retail business?

6. Create a visual that illustrates the social influences that influence a person's needs and wants. Use a flowchart, images, or other media to demonstrate the influences.

7. Design a consumer decision-making process template. As you create the template, consider how a consumer might use it. Ask for feedback on your template from your family members and friends. Adjust your design based on feedback.

8. Distribute the consumer decision-making process template to your classmates. Ask them to complete the decision-making process template for purchasing a used car. Discuss the experience with your classmates.

9. Retailers cannot control all of the marketing environment changes that impact their business, including changes in technology, consumer trends, economic trends, and regulatory changes defined by the government. Select a well-known retailer. Give examples of each one of these environmental changes that has impacted the way in which the retailer conducts business. What were your findings?

10. Think about the last purchase you made for yourself. Evaluate what influenced you to make the purchase. Was the influence psychological, social, or situational? Describe the purchase and explain the influence.

Check Your Retail IQ

Now that you have finished the chapter, see what you learned about retail by taking the chapter posttest. If you do not have a smartphone, visit the G-W Learning companion website.

G-W Learning mobile site: www.m.g-wlearning.com

G-W Learning companion website: www.g-wlearning.com/marketing/

College and Career Readiness

Career Ready Practices The Internet can provide opportunities to enhance the career search process and increase your productivity. Search the Internet for information about how to make the job application process efficient. List five things you can do to improve your skills in completing a job application.

Speaking Rhetoric is the study of writing or speaking as a way of communicating information or persuading someone. It is important to be prepared when you are speaking to an individual or to an audience. Style and content influences how the listener understands your message. Make an informal presentation to your class about the importance of a positive attitude. Adjust your presentation length to fit the attention of the audience.

Research Primary research is conducted by gathering information. Research the current amount of the national debt and how it affects the economy and you as a citizen. Explore the topic. Confirm your understanding by summarizing what you read.

Teamwork

Segmenting the market was discussed in this chapter. However, some marketing people believe that mass marketing is a better alternative. Working with your team, divide into two sides. One group should defend the idea of market segmentation. The other side should defend mass marketing. Each team should describe the advantages and disadvantages for each.

College and Career Portfolio

E-portfolio File Formats

Your e-portfolio may contain documents you have created. Scanned images of items, such as awards and certificates, may also be included. You need to decide which file formats you will use for electronic documents. You could use the default format to save the documents. For example, you could use Microsoft Word format for letters and essays. You could use Microsoft Excel format for worksheets. Someone reviewing your e-portfolio would need programs that open these formats to view your files. Another option would be to save or scan documents as PDF (portable document format) files. These files can be viewed with Adobe Reader software and some other programs. Having all of the files in the same format can make viewing them easier for others who need to review your portfolio.

1. Search the Internet and read articles to learn more about PDF documents. Download a free program that opens these files, such as Adobe Reader.
2. Practice saving a Microsoft Word document as a PDF file. Note: Use the **Save As** command. Refer to the **Help** link, if needed.
3. Create a list of the format(s) you will use to store your electronic files.

◇DECA Coach

Learn How to Practice

Aside from the fear of flying, public speaking ranks at the top of the "most feared things to do" list in several studies. Yet most of DECA's competitive events require you to do some type of presentation in front of judges. Overcoming butterflies is not as difficult as you might think.

There are two things you can do to reduce presentation anxiety. The first is to be as prepared as possible. The more confident you feel about what you are going to say, the better your presentation. In addition to preparation, the second best way to be more comfortable with presenting is to practice. While the old, "practice in front of the mirror" helps, you need to do more than just that. You need to practice out loud and in front of other people.

The most common place people practice is with their friends, classmates, parents, or even instructors. This is good, but is only the first step. Your next step is to practice in front of people that you might not be so comfortable around.

Once the competition draws close, schedule a time to present in front of your guidance counselors or principals. You will not be as comfortable around them, and this will better simulate the actual competition. You should also plan to give your presentation to your advisory panel. Not only can they help you with your presentation mechanics, but also point out any content that you might have left out. Just remember, more is better.

Visit www.deca.org to learn more information about DECA.

G-W Learning Mobile Site

Visit the G-W Learning mobile site to complete the chapter pretest and posttest, and to practice vocabulary using e-flash cards. If you do not have a smartphone, visit the G-W Learning companion website to access these features.

G-W Learning mobile site: www.m.g-wlearning.com

G-W Learning companion website: www.g-wlearning.com/marketing/

Unit 3
Product, Place, and Price

Introduction

Merchandise includes all the goods a retailer purchases to be resold to customers and generate revenue for the business. A retail buyer is responsible for selecting and purchasing merchandise that meets the needs of the target market. The retailer must effectively manage and track inventory to ensure that there is enough merchandise on hand to meet customer demand. Even with the right type and quantity of merchandise, the retailer must set the right prices to actually sell the products and make a profit. Having the right products, at the right time, for the right price can make or break a retail business.

Green Retail

Green Computers

Manufacturers of computer equipment are working to make their products and packaging more environmentally-friendly. You can now find lead-free and mercury-free computers that are built using reduced amounts of BFR (brominated fire retardants) and PVC (polyvinyl chloride). Many manufacturers have phased out the use of arsenic in the production of glass panels for display screens. Some manufacturers use recycled materials in the construction of their electronic equipment.

Additionally, many electronics retailers offer recycling services for unwanted and unusable electronic equipment. These retailers most often partner with responsible recyclers who use the best environmental practices available to repair, repurpose, or recycle the equipment.

Pavel L Photo and Video/Shutterstock.com

In This Unit

SALE 40%

Chapter 6
Merchandise Planning

Having the right products, at the right price, at the right time can make or break a retail business. In order to make smart buying decisions, strategic planning is necessary. A retail buyer is responsible for understanding the retailer's target market and purchasing merchandise to meet the customers' wants and needs. Retailers must have the right amount of merchandise, the right selection of merchandise, and merchandise available at the right time to generate a profit.

Case Study

Sundance Retail

Sundance, founded by actor Robert Redford, carries high-end, artisan products with a southwestern style. Products include clothing, jewelry, and home décor items. In the early days of the company, Sundance relied on printed documents, electronic spreadsheets, and a "gut feeling" when deciding which products and how much to buy. Using this imprecise process worked when the company was small. However, the buying process did not change as the company grew. Sundance would often run out of some items, while having significant overstock of other items. Despite higher sales, the poor buying process of the business negatively impacted profits.

To correct the situation, Sundance hired Dievo Hagen to take control of Sundance's buying team. Hagen was an experienced buying manager. He reorganized how the retailer managed sales and inventory data. As a result, the company used better data to project its buying needs. Buyers used up-to-date inventory data and actual sales figures when planning and purchasing merchandise. Because of this, buyers purchased the correct amount of merchandise and backorders decreased. Better information resulted in better buying decisions, which allowed Sundance to become more efficient and profitable.

College and Career Readiness

Reading Prep

Before reading this chapter, flip through the pages and make notes of the major headings. Analyze the structure of the relationships of the headings with the objectives for each section.

Check Your Retail IQ

Before you begin the chapter, see what you already know about retail by taking the chapter pretest. If you do not have a smartphone, visit the G-W Learning companion website.

G-W Learning mobile site: www.m.g-wlearning.com

G-W Learning companion website: www.g-wlearning.com/marketing/

Sections

Tyler Olsen/Shutterstock.com

125

Section 6.1 Planning to Buy

Objectives

After completing this section, you will be able to:
- **Explain** merchandising as a functional area of retail.
- **Describe** the components of a merchandising plan.
- **Identify** the categories of merchandise assortment.
- **List** the stages of the merchandise life cycle.

Key Terms

product
merchandise
merchandise assortment
merchandise planning
merchandise plan
planned stock
planned retail purchases

model stock
product management
product life cycle
introduction
growth
maturity
decline

Web Connect

Planning is an important element of any transaction that occurs in business. Retailers create merchandise plans to help guide their product buying decisions. Research the technology options available for merchandise planning. Choose one merchandise planning service or software utility and describe its features and benefits.

Critical Thinking

Merchandising is a functional area of retail. Using your knowledge of retail, explain why merchandising is an important element for any retail business.

Merchandise

Merchandising is the process of identifying product and product lines decisions of retailers. Merchandising is one of the functional areas of retail, as shown in Figure 6-1.

Product is anything that can be bought or sold. It is the most important element of the four *P*s of marketing. Without product, there would be no reason to have the other three *P*s.

Product can include goods or services. A *good* is a tangible product that can be touched. A *service* is an activity performed for the benefit of others, usually for a fee. A service is intangible and cannot be touched.

In the retail business, product is known as *merchandise*. **Merchandise** includes all the goods a retailer purchases to be resold to customers. These goods are also known as *inventory*.

The *product mix* is all of the merchandise that the retailer carries. Having the right product, at the right price, at the right time can make or break a business. Product strategies include selecting the appropriate products and services that will meet customer needs and wants.

FYI

Digital products, such as apps, music downloads, and e-books, are considered goods, even though these items are not tangible.

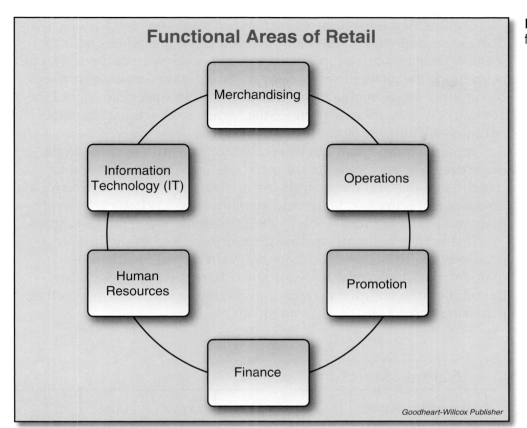

Figure 6-1 The six functional areas of retail.

Retailers typically organize merchandise by product line. A *product line* is the group of closely related products within the product mix. The *product width* is the number of product lines a company offers. For example, a sporting goods store may sell several different product lines of athletic clothing, such as women's, men's, and children's apparel. Within each product line there is an assortment, or number of items. The merchandise assortment is the number of items within the product line. For example, the children's product line may have an assortment of swimwear, ski jackets, and exercise apparel.

A *product item* is the specific model, color, or size of products within a product line. Women's petite running pants is a product item. *Product depth* is the number of product items within a product line. This is also known as *product variety*.

Merchandise Plan

In order to make smart buying decisions, strategic planning should be done. Merchandise planning is the process of deciding which products will appeal to the target audience. Market research identifies the target customer. Next, the retailer must determine which products will meet the customer needs.

The first step is to create a merchandise plan. The **merchandise plan** defines the goals and budgets for purchasing. It is sometimes called a *six-month plan* because it typically covers a 26-week span of time. The plan helps guide the retailer to meet sales goals and control stock assortments. By carefully following the merchandise plan, the retailer can control the amount of money spent to produce the highest sales without overstocking or under-stocking the store.

A merchandise plan can be created for an entire store, a single department, or each category of merchandise. The plan is used to coordinate sales and merchandising goals into a budget. An example is shown in Figure 6-2. Merchandise plans help a retailer effectively plan and evaluate sales, stock, stock reductions, and retail purchases.

Technology helps streamline the planning and evaluation processes. By using a spreadsheet program for the merchandise plan, information can be sorted many different ways. This allows the retailer to scrutinize various aspects of the plan, such as whether prices are correct and stock is adequate.

Sample Merchandise Plan								
Spring 20 __ __		February	March	April	May	June	July	Season Total
Sales Dollars	Last year sales	44,000	41,000	54,000	65,000	75,000	39,000	**318,000**
	Plan 10% increase for this year	48,400	45,100	59,400	71,500	82,500	42,900	**349,800**
	Actual							
Retail Stock BOM	Last year	132,000	131,200	172,800	182,000	172,500	117,000	
	Planned stock for this year	145,200	144,320	190,080	200,200	189,750	128,700	
	Actual							
Reductions: Markdowns, Adjustments, and Loss	Last year	2,000	2,800	4,000	2,000	8,400	12,600	**31,800**
	Planned dollars for this year	2,200	3,080	4,400	2,200	9,240	13,860	**34,980**
	Actual							
Retail Purchases	Last year	45,200	85,400	67,200	57,500	27,900	48,500	**32,870**
	Planned	49,720	93,940	73,920	63,250	30,690	53,350	**36,157**
	Actual							

Goodheart-Willcox Publisher

Figure 6-2 A merchandise plan is created for a six-month period of time.

Planned Sales

All merchandise planning begins with *planned sales*. To determine planned sales goals for a six-month period, past sales history and current trends are reviewed. Based on this information, the percent of increase or decrease in planned sales for the new six-month plan can be projected.

In Figure 6-2, the actual sales for the previous six months totaled $318,000. Assume that management determined that a 10 percent increase in sales is appropriate for the next time period. The new sales goal is calculated as follows.

sales from previous six months + 10 percent = planned sales goal

$318,000 × 10% = $31,800 planned increase

$318,000 + $31,800 = $349,800 total planned sales

The new planned sales goal for the next season is $349,800.

Planned Stock

After estimating sales, the next step in merchandise planning is to plan stock. **Planned stock** is the dollar amount of merchandise required to meet sales goals. The amount of stock at the beginning of the month (BOM) is shown in dollars. This is the amount of stock that should be on hand at the start of each month to meet established sales goals.

However, retailers should not order all of the stock needed to fulfill 100 percent of the projected sales at the beginning of the sales period. Enough stock should be on hand to meet only a percentage of projected sales. The retailer should reorder stock to maintain lower stock levels without running out. This strategy benefits retailers in case of an unexpected downturn in sales.

Social Media

Business Pages

To take advantage of social media to increase a retailer's visibility, it is important for the business to select one type of social media to use first. It is not necessary to try to use every option at one time. Research can help a business focus on which one or two vehicles make the most sense for the business. Each business social media account will include some kind of profile. Profile fields may include a business bio, company websites, blogs, locations, and an image. These pages provide an opportunity for the business to share information and communicate with customers.

Most retailers offer end-of-season markdowns to reduce their stock of season-specific merchandise.

Stephen Coburn/Shutterstock.com

Planned Stock Reductions

Reductions are any activities that decrease the selling price of merchandise. Planned reductions are important because selling discounted merchandise results in lower profits. Retailers should expect to make less money on reduced items than originally planned for when the items were purchased. For example, end-of-season markdowns are price reductions that help reduce stock. The actual quantity of stock may also be reduced due to damaged or obsolete product that cannot be sold.

Planned Retail Purchases

Planned retail purchases are the amount of merchandise that is planned for delivery during a given period. The planned retail purchases for a given month must be enough to cover the projected sales. The amount must cover any merchandise reductions made during the month. The planned retail purchases must also provide enough product to begin the next month's sales while new merchandise begins to enter the store.

Merchandise Assortment

Retailers make merchandise plans for an entire store, a specific department, or for each category of merchandise. The four categories of merchandise are staple, seasonal, fashion, and convenience.

- *Staple merchandise* includes products that are ordered without seasonal or fashion considerations, such as canned goods in a grocery store or tires at an auto parts store.
- *Seasonal merchandise* is available during a short selling period, such as swimwear and holiday decorations. This merchandise must be priced high enough to offset markdowns that will occur at the end of the selling season.
- *Fashion merchandise* may sell for one or more seasons. Some styles gain immediate success and account for significant sales. Other styles are slow to be accepted by customers.

- *Convenience merchandise* includes products that customers buy without much thought, such as magazines and newspapers that customers pick up by the cash register.

Assortment planning allows the retailer to identify how many pieces of merchandise are needed in a category at a specific price point. Style and color range may also be included in planning, depending on the item.

Planning the merchandise assortment involves the following steps:

1. Review past sales records.
2. Focus on the price points customers are most likely to pay.
3. Identify styles or trends that are most popular for the target customer.
4. Identify key colors and sizes, if relevant.
5. Break down the specific number of pieces needed to meet customer demand.

The goal in merchandise assortment planning is to create the model stock. **Model stock** is the optimum amount of merchandise needed on hand from each category to meet customer demands.

Product Life Cycle

All products have a life cycle. **Product management** is the process of managing a product across its complete life cycle. The **product life cycle** is the customers' acceptance levels and buying levels of a product. A product life cycle may last a few months or be decades long. The demand for and sale of all products moves in cycles. Products go through four stages in a life cycle, as shown in Figure 6-3. These stages are introduction, growth, maturity, and decline.

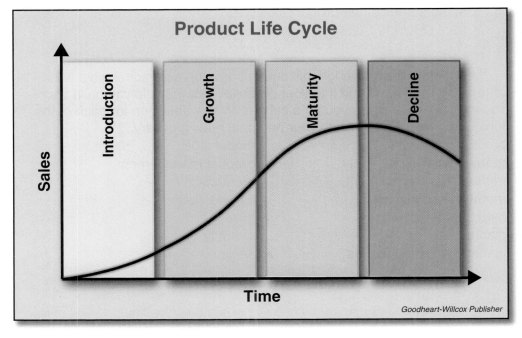

Figure 6-3 A product life cycle may last a few months or several decades.

Goodheart-Willcox Publisher

The first stage of the product life cycle is *introduction*. **Introduction** is the stage when a limited number of customers buy the product. Retailers purchase limited quantities until customer acceptance is verified. If customers reject a product, retailers must clear out the merchandise as quickly as possible.

The second stage of the product life cycle is *growth*. **Growth** is the stage when there is evidence that sales of this product are increasing. Retailers may feel more at ease buying larger quantities.

The third stage of the product life cycle is *maturity*. **Maturity** is the stage when the greatest number of customers buy the product. During this stage, retailers should be looking for early signs of declining sales.

The final stage of the product life cycle is *decline*. **Decline** is when retailers see a drop in sales as the product gradually loses customer appeal. Once a product reaches this stage, retailers may need to mark down the item.

To improve forecasting skills, retailers must understand the life cycle of each product they purchase and its impact on sales. Products move through the cycle at various rates. The faster a product moves through the life cycle, the higher the retailer's risk for fast sales and earning high profits. Knowing what stage a product is in helps retailers judge its sales potential. Each stage of the life cycle suggests different retailing strategies to retailers planning the merchandise assortment.

Checkpoint 6.1

1.   Describe merchandising as a functional area of retail.
2.   Define *product line* and *product item*. How do they relate?
3.   Explain how retailers use a merchandise plan.
4.   Identify and describe the four categories of retail merchandise.
5.   List the stages of the product life cycle.

Build Your Vocabulary

As you progress through this course, develop a personal glossary of retailing terms and add it to your portfolio. This will help you build your vocabulary and prepare you for a career. Write a definition for each of the following terms, and add it to your personal retail glossary.

product	model stock
merchandise	product management
merchandise assortment	product life cycle
merchandise planning	introduction
merchandise plan	growth
planned stock	maturity
planned retail purchases	decline

Section 6.2 Retail Buyers

Objectives

After completing this section, you will be able to:
- **Describe** the role of the retail buyer.
- **List** the basic responsibilities of the buyer.

Key Terms

retail buyer
trend research
vendor
trade publication
purchasing
  management
open-to-buy
market week
negotiating

trade discount
manufacturer's
  suggested retail
  price (MSRP)
closeout
free on board (FOB)
lead time
buffer stock

Web Connect

There are many career opportunities in retail. Search the Internet for information on a retail buyer career. List the educational and personal requirements of the position. What are the typical travel requirements, salary, and work hours of this position? What is the career forecast for this position?

Critical Thinking

Finding a reputable vendor that meets a retailer's needs can be a challenge. What qualities do you think are important in a retail vendor? Create guidelines to use when interviewing potential vendors.

Retail Buyer

A **retail buyer** selects and purchases merchandise for resale. The buyer is responsible for ensuring that the store has the right amount of inventory, the right selection of inventory, and that the inventory generates a profit. Competition for retail customers is intense. For the retail buyer, this competition makes selecting merchandise very challenging. Buyers must know and understand their target market. Selecting the right merchandise is critical to attracting customers. Buyers must know what to buy and where to purchase the merchandise.

Deciding What to Buy

Buyers must place the right merchandise in stores to make sure customers are happy with the products they find each time they return to the store. Buyers must purchase the right amount of merchandise for the sales volume of the store. Buyers also ensure that merchandise is delivered at the right time—when the customers want it.

Merchandise bought too early will sit on shelves and runs the risk of becoming damaged or shopworn. Old and shopworn merchandise can result in lost profits. If merchandise is bought too late, customers may buy from the competition instead. Knowing when to place merchandise on the store shelves ensures that customers have the best selection of merchandise when they are ready to buy.

To make the correct purchasing decisions, buyers study past sales records to forecast future inventory needs. They may use market research and trend research to anticipate the business' needs for new or different products. **Trend research** is research that shows what has happened in the past and is an indicator of the future. Trends constantly change, rising or declining in popularity. Trend research helps retailers understand what, where, and why consumers are buying. This research also helps the buyer identify quickly growing product categories.

Buyers may get assistance from industry professionals, such as fashion forecasters, reporting service specialists, trade publications, and consumer magazines, to predict the type of inventory needed for upcoming seasons. A **trade publication** is a publication, usually a magazine, geared toward people who work in a specific industry. There are trade publications for almost every merchandise category, from fancy pet clothes to stationery.

Deciding Where to Buy

A **vendor** is a company from which a buyer purchases merchandise. Vendors are also known as *suppliers*. Most major retail vendors have locations in large metropolitan areas, such as New York, Chicago, Los Angeles, Atlanta, and Dallas.

Having the right merchandise available to meet customers' needs is important to the success of any retail business.

Dmitry Kalinovsky/Shutterstock.com

A buyer must compare all of the available options and determine which products have the potential to generate the most profits. The quantity and variety of products makes the retail industry very diverse. Customers have more product choices from many domestic and international businesses at a variety of prices.

Buyers are always looking for new vendors. They may look for lower prices, goods that are not available in domestic markets, or prestigious fashion collections. While many vendors have catalogs in print and online, a trip to the vendor location may be necessary to view merchandise. Occasionally manufacturers' representatives may travel to the buyer's location to show merchandise. Buyers may also visit trade shows, such as the MAGIC Market Week in Las Vegas, to see the latest products and make purchases.

A list of trade shows can be found in trade publications, like *Women's Wear Daily* and *Daily News Record*.

Responsibilities of the Buyer

Large retail businesses generally have multiple buyers. Each merchandising department, such as children's shoes and small electrics, has its own buyer. In a smaller business, the owner or manager may perform all of the buying functions in addition to operating the business.

In general, most retail buyers have the same defined responsibilities. Specific duties may vary depending on the size or type of business. However, all buyers share a common set of job responsibilities.

- Budget the money available for new purchases.
- Review past sales records to identify purchasing trends.
- Select merchandise assortments that will best serve customers and earn a profit.
- Shop the competition to compare merchandise and prices.
- Research and select the vendors for each item to be bought.
- Negotiate the best terms and discounts for each purchase.
- Time the deliveries.

A buyer's job is much more complex than just purchasing merchandise. Buyers must have a total understanding of the retailer's target market and of the customers' wants and needs. **Purchasing management** involves ordering the necessary goods, receiving them into stock on arrival, and paying the vendor for the order.

Budget the Money Available

The money available to purchase new merchandise is determined by the merchandise plan. Most retailers use a six-month merchandise plan to determine the amount of merchandise needed to reach their sales goals. It is a tool to help retailers control the amount of money spent on inventory. A merchandise plan can be used for an entire department or for one classification of merchandise, like men's casual shirts.

NRF Tip

The NRF website provides retailers with a detailed overview of the retail industry. Retailers can access current and reliable information about sales forecasts and records. The *Retail Sales Outlook* is released quarterly. This allows retailers to gain insight into the current market climate as well as future projections for the sales year.

Open-to-buy is the amount of money available for purchasing new merchandise after all other purchases have been deducted. A buyer must know how much money is available for new purchases. It is important for the retailer to have just enough inventory to support projected sales indicated on the six-month merchandise plan. Using the open-to-buy figures from the plan, buyers determine the amount of money they have to spend for new merchandise.

Review Sales Records

An important part of the buyer's job is to study the business' past sales records. Past performance is an indicator of future sales. Records of past customer purchases may reveal patterns or trends in the sales figures. Buyers may review past sales information based on product price, color, and size. Current sales are compared with sales from the previous month, as well as sales from the same period in the previous year. This comparison helps buyers estimate possible changes in the coming year. Buyers also look for national and local economic trends.

Once the sales information has been reviewed, buyers ask the following questions:

- Are there any important sales patterns over the last few years?
- Does the pattern represent an increase or decrease in sales?
- What is the percent of increase or decrease in sales?
- Do recent sales records continue to support these trends?

Once these questions have been reviewed, the buyer develops a sales forecast. Sales forecasting is not a precise process, but it provides the best starting point to plan future sales.

Select the Assortment

Once sales are forecasted, buyers must plan how much inventory is needed to support the forecast. The selection of merchandise is important to any retail business regardless of its size. Buyers must purchase a merchandise assortment that meets customers' needs. Price, quality, and the personal preferences of customers are factors to consider. Buyers must also carefully select merchandise that has the most potential for resale and profit.

Shop the Competition

Buyers visit stores that compete with business they service. Shopping the competition can help when making decisions about what customers want. It also allows buyers to gauge how the merchandise in their store compares to other retailers.

Buyers carefully look at the competition's merchandise. They compare styles, quantities, and prices. It is also important to look for merchandise the competition carries that the buyer's store does not. Knowledge about the competition helps in making good planning and pricing decisions.

Exploring Retail Careers

Merchandise Buyer

Many retail stores, such as department stores and electronics superstores, offer a large variety of products. The goods for sale in these stores are selected by a merchandise buyer. A merchandise buyer determines which products will satisfy customer needs and wants. These selections are based on past buying trends and the prediction of future buying trends associated with his or her research. The buyer then works with manufacturers or vendors to purchase these products for the store. This position is usually focused on one type of merchandise, such as furniture or shoes. Other typical titles for the position include *purchasing agent*, *retail buyer*, *product manager*, and *purchasing manager*. Some examples of tasks that buyers perform include:

- select and purchase appropriate amounts of products that are in line with the retailer's image
- suggest purchase prices for products, as well as mark-up and mark-down rates
- negotiate contracts and product prices with manufacturers and vendors
- communicate with market analysts and sales associates to assist in determining customer needs and wants

Buyers must be skilled in logic and reasoning. Forecasting skills are necessary to predict buying trends. They should also have good negotiation skills. The position requires a high school diploma and on-the-job training. Many retail stores require some college or a bachelor degree.

Select Vendors

Once buyers decide on the merchandise to purchase and how much money can be spent, they must select vendors. Buyers research many vendors before deciding from which they will purchase merchandise. This gives them the opportunity to establish relationships and build strong partnerships. Buyers may use vendors close to home or located around the world. To find merchandise that is unique and profitable, some buyers look across the globe.

When selecting vendors, buyers should ask the following questions:

- Does the merchandise and prices offered reflect the retailer's image?
- What are the vendor's distribution policies?
- Does the vendor have merchandising and display criteria for stores carrying their line?
- Is the vendor reliable?
- What are the discount and credit terms offered? Who pays for shipping?
- Does the vendor offer services such as cooperative advertising, return and exchange privileges, pre-ticketing of merchandise, and sales training?

Buyers meet with vendors at trade shows to see the products offered and establish business relationships.

pio3/Shutterstock.com

Armed with all of the preplanned buying information (what to buy and how much to spend), the buyer chooses the best merchandise and vendors. Buyers may visit the selected vendors during merchandise market week. **Market week** is an event where many designers or manufacturers display and sell their latest products. This gives both buyers and the media an opportunity to take a look at the latest trends from fashion to electronics. Most importantly, these events let the industry know what's "in" and what's new for the season.

An important factor in purchasing is timing purchases to maintain a balance between inventory and sales throughout the season. This keeps the product assortment in the store fresh and new. New inventory keeps customers interested, even if they do not make a purchase at each visit.

Mutual respect, trust, and cooperation between the vendor and buyer are necessary to ensure fair treatment and dependability. The majority of buyers limit their purchases to a few vendors. But, they save some of their open-to-buy for new vendors with products that will benefit the retailer's profitability. When purchasing from new vendors, the buyer should ask the following questions:

- Will the vendor produce merchandise without changes in style and quality?
- Will the quality and price reflect the store image?
- Will merchandise be delivered on time?
- Will the merchandise serve the needs of our customers?

If the answer to these questions is "yes," there is a good chance the retailer will earn the expected profits.

Buyers look for vendors who ship the merchandise that was ordered in the right quantities and at the time specified. Vendors want to do business with buyers who pay bills promptly, accept the goods they order, and only return merchandise that has been authorized. To achieve these goals, buyers and sellers need to act as partners.

Negotiate

It is the buyer's job to purchase goods at the best price that will earn the best profits. In order to do this, the buyer negotiates with vendors. **Negotiating** is a mutual discussion and planning of the terms of a transaction or agreement. The buyer and vendor negotiate the best terms possible. This is known as *terms and conditions of sale*.

The vendor prepares a *product specification sheet* that provides product information, including sizes, colors, materials, and other details. This is used to summarize the product assortment.

Price

The price is the amount of money the buyer pays for the purchase from the vendor. The price of the merchandise may be reduced if the vendor applies discounts.

A **trade discount** is the amount that a vendor reduces the list price, or manufacturer's suggested retail price (MSRP). The **manufacturer's suggested retail price (MSRP)** is the list price for merchandise as recommended by the manufacturer. The trade discount allows retailers to resell the merchandise at MSRP to their customers.

A *quantity discount* is given for purchasing in large quantities. A *seasonal discount* is given for merchandise purchased prior to the regular buying season or after the traditional selling season.

The buyer must negotiate the terms of the purchase transaction, including price, shipping terms, and delivery time.

Dean Drobot/Shutterstock.com

Retail Ethics

Sourcing

Ethical retailers purchase merchandise from reputable suppliers where products are created in safe conditions. Factories in which products are created should be clean and safe for its workers. Manufacturers in other countries may have different work safety standards than the United States. Purchasing products at the expense of others to save money is unethical.

Some vendors give advertising and promotional discounts during certain promotion periods. During this time, the merchandise is promoted directly to consumers. In addition to the reduced merchandise cost, taking advantage of advertising and promotional discounts may reduce the amount retailers spend on marketing.

A cash discount is usually a percentage removed from the total invoice amount. *Cash discounts* are given as an incentive for the retailer to pay a bill promptly. Typical terms are "2/10, *net* 30." This means if the bill is paid within 10 days of the invoice date, the retailer can deduct a two percent cash discount for paying early. If the retailer does not take advantage of the cash discount, then the entire bill is due in 30 days.

The price that is quoted by vendors may be negotiable by using trade, quantity, or seasonal discounts. However, vendors are generally prohibited from giving retailers special individual price considerations due to the *Robinson-Patman Act*. This federal legislation was passed to limit price discrimination and to protect small businesses from the retail giants who would otherwise be charged lower prices. However, there are two exceptions to this rule. Vendors can offer discounts when the price reduction is made to meet competition. Vendors can also offer discounts when the merchandise is damaged or is part of a closeout. A **closeout** is end-of-the-season merchandise sold at reduced prices.

Remember that all buyers may negotiate a better price for their merchandise through discounts for prompt payment, buying in quantities, accepting the merchandise early in the season, buying closeouts, and advertising and promotional assistance. Any discounts negotiated by the buyer reduce the cost of the merchandise and increase the profit earned on the merchandise.

Shipping Terms

After negotiating the best price and determining when the merchandise will be received, the next step is to discuss who pays the shipping charges, or the *shipping terms*. Most shipping terms are *FOB*. **Free on board (FOB)** means that the manufacturer owns the merchandise until it is received by the retailer. This type of shipping arrangement protects the retailer from expenses related to lost goods and damage that occurs during shipping.

Moving product across the country or around the world costs money. Knowing the shipping cost is very important because shipping adds to the cost of the merchandise. Whoever owns the merchandise while in transit must also pay insurance to cover possible loss or damage while in transit. If there are shipping problems, the owner of the merchandise must file any claims of loss or damage by the shipping company.

Delivery Time

After buyers make their buying plans, they select the best dates for merchandise to arrive. Timing is critical in merchandise planning. For example, merchandise that arrives after the determined date may create a problem. The retailer may plan a store promotion that requires the merchandise to be on hand, or maybe the merchandise is needed for a major selling season. Merchandise must be available at the right time to meet customers' needs.

The buyer must also be aware of lead time. **Lead time** is the total time it takes from placing an order until it is received. It may not be possible to order merchandise and receive it immediately. Scheduling the delivery of products made overseas can be more complex because international shipping is not always reliable. To compensate for timing issues, some retailers have buffer stock on hand. **Buffer stock** is additional stock kept above the minimum required to meet anticipated needs.

Timing the delivery of merchandise is crucial for the retailer to make a profit.

Kzenon/Shutterstock.com

Merchandise must be available when the customer is ready to buy or the sale is lost. There is often a beginning and ending delivery period. If delivery is not made by the promised date, the buyer may refuse delivery of the late shipment. Of course, this reduces inventory and lost sales is most likely the result.

Checkpoint 6.2

1. Describe the role of the retail buyer.
2. How do buyers use trend research?
3. List the common responsibilities that all retail buyers share.
4. How do buyers determine the amount of money available to purchase new merchandise?
5. What questions should buyers ask when selecting vendors?

Build Your Vocabulary

As you progress through this course, develop a personal glossary of retailing terms and add it to your portfolio. This will help you build your vocabulary and prepare you for a career. Write a definition for each of the following terms, and add it to your personal retailing glossary.

retail buyer
trend research
trade publication
vendor
purchasing management
open-to-buy
market week
negotiating

trade discount
manufacturer's suggested retail price (MSRP)
closeout
free on board (FOB)
lead time
buffer stock

Chapter Summary

Section 6.1 Planning to Buy

- Merchandising is identifying the product and product line decisions of retailers. Merchandise consists of goods purchased with the intent of reselling to customers. Creating the product mix and the merchandise assortment are parts of merchandising.
- The merchandise plan coordinates sales and merchandising goals along with a budget. Merchandise plans help retailers plan and evaluate sales, stock, stock reductions, and retail purchases.
- The merchandise assortment is achieved by combining different amounts of the four categories of merchandise: staple, fashion, seasonal, and convenience. The merchandise assortment must be carefully planned.
- There are four stages to the product life cycle: introduction, growth, maturity, and decline. Product management takes into account how the product life cycle will affect profit.

Section 6.2 Retail Buyers

- A retail buyer selects and purchases merchandise for resale.
- The buyer is responsible for ensuring that the store has the right amount of inventory, the right selection of inventory, that merchandise is delivered at the right time, and that the inventory generates a profit.
- In general, most retail buyers have the same defined responsibilities: determine money available, review past sales records, select merchandise assortments, shop the competition, choose vendors, negotiate terms and prices, and time deliveries.

Review Your Knowledge

1. Compare and contrast products and services. List the characteristics of each.
2. Describe product depth.
3. State the formula for calculating planned sales for a merchandise plan.
4. Identify and describe the four categories of merchandise.
5. What are the stages in a product life cycle?
6. How do buyers decide what merchandise to buy?
7. Explain the role that past sales records play in making future buying decisions.
8. Explain the buyer's task of selecting the assortment of merchandise.
9. Discuss the negotiation process.
10. Explain the importance of delivery time in merchandise planning.

Apply Your Knowledge

1. Using the Internet, research merchandising practices in the global market place. How are they similar to merchandise practices in the United States? How are they different?
2. *Product mix* is the merchandise that is carried by a retailer. Conduct an Internet search for examples of product mix. Based on the information that you find, list the steps for product mix planning. Turn this list into a flowchart. Explain the product mix planning process to your class.

3. Technology helps to streamline the process of creating a merchandise plan. A spreadsheet allows the buyer to sort information in a variety of ways to scrutinize the plan. Search the Internet for an example of a merchandise plan. Print the example and highlight the various sections of the plan. Next to each section, describe its purpose.

4. The first step in creating a merchandise plan is to calculate planned sales for the time period. A skateboard retailer is planning for the next six months. Sales in the previous six months were $404,000. Instead of an increase in sales, the retailer estimates a decrease of 15 percent in sales during the next time period. Calculate the new planned sales figure for the period. Show your calculations. What factors do you think would cause a decrease in sales for this type of retailer?

5. There are four categories of merchandise: staple merchandise, fashion merchandise, seasonal merchandise, and convenience merchandise. Create a chart with four columns. Assign one of the categories to each column. In each column, give five examples of products or services that fit the merchandise category.

6. Locate three job listings for retail buyer positions. Compare and contrast the jobs described in the listings, including necessary education and experience, as well as the responsibilities of the job. Create a career plan to become qualified for these positions.

7. One of the important responsibilities of a buyer is to shop the competition. Select two competing retailers or e-tailers that offer a similar product mix. Visit their stores or websites. Look at the merchandise to compare styles, quantities, and prices. Write several paragraphs that summarize the similarities and differences between the two competitors.

8. Fashion trends come and go. Think of a trend that recently became popular. Research the history and sales of the trend. Use related trade publications in your research. Write several paragraphs about your research that answers the following questions: When did the trend begin? How did it start? Has it ended or is it projected to end? Relate the effects of fashion trends to retail sales.

9. Choose a line of merchandise that you use or purchase regularly, such as clothing, shoes, electronics, athletic equipment, or hobby merchandise. Use the Internet to search for trade shows related to the merchandise you selected. Choose two of the trade shows and review the vendors that will be there and the events planned during the show. Which trade show is best suited for a buyer looking for merchandise to stock a local, independent retail shop? Explain your reasoning.

10. Research the Robinson-Patman Act. Create a presentation that summarizes the history and details of the Robinson-Patman Act. Include any noteworthy legal cases that involve the Robinson-Patman Act.

Check Your Retail IQ

Now that you have finished the chapter, see what you learned about retail by taking the chapter posttest. If you do not have a smartphone, visit the G-W Learning companion website.

G-W Learning mobile site: www.m.g-wlearning.com

G-W Learning companion website: www.g-wlearning.com/marketing/

College and Career Readiness

Career Ready Practices A successful employee demonstrates creativity and innovation. Whether you see problems as challenges or opportunities, they often require creative thinking to solve them. Many new inventions are the result of attempting to solve a problem. Describe a competitive situation for a business where the solution led to the creation of a new way of doing things or a new invention.

Speaking Etiquette is the art of using good manners in any situation. Etiquette is especially important when making phone calls because the two parties cannot interact face-to-face. Create a script for a telephone conversation to request assistance from a loan officer asking for support for a student loan. Make a list of the important facts that support why you should be granted a loan. Say "please" and "thank you" when appropriate. Ask a classmate to assume the role of the loan officer to practice your telephone conversation. How would you rate your use of good manners? How does your classmate rate your speech?

Research Primary research is conducted by gathering information. Research the current amount of the national debt and how it affects the economy and you as a citizen. Demonstrate your understanding of the information and formulate a research topic based on the information you find.

Teamwork

Working with your teammates, select a product that is no longer produced. Research the life cycle of the product. Why did the product become obsolete? How long was its product life cycle?

College and Career Portfolio

Certificates

You have identified the types of items you might place in your portfolio. You will begin adding items in this activity and add other items as you continue this class. Locate certificates you have received. For example, a certificate might show that you have completed a training class. Another certificate might show that you can keyboard at a certain speed. You might have a certificate that you received for taking part in a community project. Include any certificates that show tasks completed or your skills or talents. Also, create a document that lists each certificate along with when you received it. Briefly describe your activities, skills, or talents related to each certificate.

1. Scan these documents to include in your e-portfolio. Use the file format you selected earlier.
2. Use the naming system you created earlier. Give each document an appropriate name. Place each certificate and the list in an appropriate subfolder for your e-portfolio.
3. Place the hard-copy certificates and list in the container for your print portfolio.

◇DECA. Coach

Avoid Distracting Habits

Now you understand the importance of being confident in your presentation and the importance of practicing. You should also understand that practicing means more than just saying the words in front of other people. Your words are important, but your mannerisms are every bit as important as the words you use. It is critical that you appear poised, confident, and professional.

Many of us have habits that take away from our presentations. You have likely heard a speech or presentation during which the speaker said "um" every few seconds. This is an unintentional pause that allows the speaker to think about what to say next. Listening to yourself saying "um" during practice can help you to reduce or eliminate the habit. The same holds true for other bad habits, such as twirling your hair, fidgeting and shifting, or putting your hands in your pockets. All of these bad habits can attract the focus of your judges and detract from what you are saying. During practice, have your audience point out your presentation habits. Then work on eliminating them.

Understand that when you are presenting, you *will* make mistakes. Do not apologize or draw attention to your mistakes, such as by saying "I forgot my line." Just keep going as if you never made the mistake. This is difficult for many to do and requires a lot of practice. However, focusing on your habits during practice will make you a much better presenter.

Visit www.deca.org to learn more information about DECA.

G-W Learning Mobile Site

Visit the G-W Learning mobile site to complete the chapter pretest and posttest, and to practice vocabulary using e-flash cards. If you do not have a smartphone, visit the G-W Learning companion website to access these features.

G-W Learning mobile site: www.m.g-wlearning.com

G-W Learning companion website: www.g-wlearning.com/marketing/

Chapter 7
Purchasing and Inventory Control

Merchandise is purchased to generate revenue for a business. The purchasing process involves placing the purchase order, transporting the order, and receiving the order. Merchandise moves through the supply chain and is received by the retailer. Typically, retailers must plan to store merchandise until they are ready to place the products in the store.

Managing inventory is necessary for a business to be successful. There must be enough merchandise on hand to meet customer demand. Effective inventory management requires reliable tracking. As retailers track inventory, they collect data used to schedule purchases, calculate turnover rate, and plan merchandise and marketing decisions. All of these activities impact the profits of the retailer and reflect the effectiveness of the buyer.

Case Study

Macy's

Macy's began using an RFID (radio frequency identification) tagging system for their merchandise several years ago. Today, that tagging system is being used to meet their customers' needs. The RFID system integrates Macy's store locations, the Internet, and mobile devices to make every item in inventory available to fulfill customer purchases, no matter where the items are located. Sales associates at brick-and-mortar stores can sell a product that is not available at their location by accessing merchandise at other Macy's locations or on the retailer's website. The merchandise is then shipped directly to the customer. Purchases made through Macy's website may also be fulfilled by a brick-and-mortar location if the distribution center does not have merchandise on hand.

In addition to fulfilling customer purchases, Macy's uses RFID tags to track merchandise, replenish inventory, and regularly monitor inventory. Taking advantage of this technology has produced more accurate merchandise data and created greater customer satisfaction. Both of these are important factors in a business' profitability.

College and Career Readiness

Reading Prep

Before reading this chapter, review the highlighted terms within the body. Determine the meaning of each term.

Check Your Retail IQ

Before you begin the chapter, see what you already know about retail by taking the chapter pretest. If you do not have a smartphone, visit the G-W Learning companion website.

G-W Learning mobile site: www.m.g-wlearning.com

G-W Learning companion website: www.g-wlearning.com/marketing/

G-W Mobile

Sections

7.1   Inventory

7.2   Inventory Management

bikeriderlondon/Shutterstock.com

Section 7.1 Inventory

Objectives

- **Summarize** the activities involved in purchasing inventory.
- **Explain** the retailer's process of receiving orders.
- **Describe** the retailer's options for storing inventory.

Key Terms

purchase order
packing slip
receiving record
quality control

marking
invoice
distribution center

Web Connect

Use the Internet to research storage options available for a grocery retailer. What criteria must be considered when selecting a facility to store merchandise until it is needed in the retailer's store?

Critical Thinking

Businesses use purchase orders when they buy merchandise from a vendor. Why do you think a purchase order is necessary? Would a receipt for the purchase be sufficient instead of using a purchase order?

Purchasing Inventory

Once the buyer selects the vendors that best represent their image, the vendor's lines of merchandise are viewed and evaluated. Then, it is time to purchase inventory. Purchasing inventory involves placing the purchase order, transporting the order, and receiving the order.

Purchasing merchandise should not be confused with purchasing supplies or other assets used within the business. Goods and services used for the operation of the business, like paper, computers, and janitorial services, are classified as *operations*. Merchandise is purchased to resell to customers and generate revenue for the business. It is important to keep merchandise and operations accounts separate.

Placing the Purchase Order

The process of actually purchasing inventory begins with writing a purchase order. A **purchase order** is the form a buyer sends to a vendor to officially place an order. Purchase orders identify merchandise quantities, costs, and shipping details that were agreed upon by the buyer and vendor. Purchase orders are legal contracts that outline these agreed upon details.

Once the purchase order has been signed, both parties must honor the agreement. An example of a purchase order is shown in Figure 7-1. A purchase order typically states:

- contact information for buyer and seller
- purchase order number
- shipping information
- delivery dates and payment terms
- style numbers and brief descriptions of the items purchased
- quantities purchased
- unit prices and total dollars spent

A return-to-vendor policy should also be noted on the purchase form. If the order is not fulfilled as stated, the buyer can cancel or refuse the shipment. However, the buyer cannot cancel or return merchandise without cause.

NRF Tip

Retailers can access facts about their store location through the NRF website. This information includes the market climate for their current or future location, how similar businesses are doing in the surrounding area, and can assist in pinpointing a target market for that location.

Cell Phone Style

123 Main Street
Tampa, FL 33601
Phone: (813) 555-1234
Fax: (813) 555-1235

PURCHASE ORDER
PO #: 003725
Date: 03/31/2014

Vendor Name/Address:	Vendor ID:	Customer ID:
Salt Lake Wholesale 9807 Second Avenue Atlanta, GA 30060 (678) 555-1236	24	1068A

SHIPPING METHOD	SHIPPING TERMS	DELIVERY DATE
Ground	Received by 05/01/2014	05/01/2014

Item	Job	Description	Qty	Unit Price	Line Total
013188	12	Car charger	24	14.95	358.80
011088	12	Black armband case	60	7.95	477.00
012488	12	Blue gel case	48	9.50	456.00

1. Please send two copies of your invoice.
2. Enter this order in accordance with the prices, terms, delivery method, and specifications listed above.
3. Please notify us immediately if you are unable to ship as specified.
4. Send all correspondence to:
   Cell phone style
   E-mail: tgreen@cellphonestyle.com
   Fax: (813) 555-1235

Subtotal		1,291.80
For resale? Yes / No	Tax ID: 12-3456789	Sales Tax —
	Shipping	126.95
Total Net 30 days		**$1,418.75**

Authorized by: *Tyler green*

Date: 3/31/2014

Image credit: beboy/Shutterstock.com; Goodheart-Willcox Publisher

Figure 7-1 Purchase orders contain detailed information about the vendor, the buyer, and the merchandise being purchased.

Various modes of transportation may be used to move products move through the channel of distribution.

Franck Boston/Shutterstock.com

Transporting the Order

The *supply chain* includes businesses and people involved in creating products and delivering them to end users. *Place* refers to all the activities involved in getting a product to the end user. Place is one of the four *P*s of marketing. Place is also known as *distribution*. A *channel of distribution* is the path that the goods take through the supply chain. Place includes order processing, transportation, and storage. All of these activities add to the retailer's cost of doing business.

After the vendor processes the order, it is shipped to the retailer. *Transportation* is the physical movement of product through the channel of distribution. Faster transportation options often costs more money, while slower transportation may cost less. Depending on the merchandise, transportation options available to retailers may include:

- road
- rail
- air
- water
- pipeline
- digital

Transporting merchandise also involves ownership. The merchandise becomes the responsibility of each business in the channel of distribution as it is transported. Each business also assumes the risks involved in handling the merchandise. For example, when a vendor sends product on an airplane, the airline takes ownership of the merchandise until it hands off the merchandise to the next business in the supply chain. The airline also assumes the risk for any lost or damaged merchandise. It is important for the retailer to know who has ownership at each step in the channel of distribution and that proof of insurance is provided.

A *freight forwarder* is a company that organizes shipments and acts as an agent.

Receiving the Order

Most retailers have a receiving dock where trucks unload merchandise. When the merchandise arrives, each piece must be compared to the packing slip. A **packing slip** is a form that lists the contents of the box or container. The retailer, or an employee, needs to verify that each item on the packing slip has arrived. As each item is accounted for, it is recorded on the receiving record. A **receiving record** is the form on which all merchandise received is listed as it comes into the business.

While the merchandise is being checked in, it is also evaluated for damage and quality. **Quality control** is the actions involved in checking goods as they are received to ensure the quality meets expectations. The person confirming the inventory received should also verify that the merchandise is correct as ordered. If merchandise is incorrect or damaged, it needs to be returned to the vendor.

Merchandise is marked for resale once all the items are received and verified. **Marking** is recording the selling price on each item that will be sold to customers. Items are usually marked with *Universal Product Codes (UPC)*. The merchandise is then placed into stock to be sold.

After the vendor ships the order, an invoice is sent to the retailer. An **invoice** is the vendor bill requesting payment for the goods shipped or services provided. The invoice shows the items shipped, amount owed, and payment terms. The retailer compares the invoice to the receiving record to make sure all items have arrived and are correct. The person paying the invoice also compares the invoice to the purchase order for accuracy.

Storing the Inventory

When merchandise is purchased, it must be stored and protected until needed. Elements, such as the weather, can damage products that are not stored correctly. Merchandise is also subject to theft, fire, and other hazards.

The type of merchandise dictates the type of storage that is used. For example, fruits and vegetables require refrigeration and reams of paper require low humidity. The type of storage needed affects the price retailers must pay.

Social Media

Social Media Analytics

Metrics are ways to measure the effectiveness of marketing activities. Social media analytics is the gathering of information from social media activities. It is important for a retailer to measure the returns from using social media as a tool. There are many programs available that measure how many responses are received from an activity, how many dollars are being generated, and other important information that helps determine if the investment of time and money has been productive. Retail marketing should include plans for analyzing the effectiveness of the social media marketing that is used for the business.

Retailers often keep merchandise in a warehouse until it is needed in the store.

wong yu liang/Shutterstock.com

Storage for merchandise may be available within the store, such as in the basement of the facility, or in the retailer's warehouse. Sometimes merchandise is stored at a distribution center. A **distribution center** is a warehouse that receives merchandise from multiple vendors and distributes it to multiple store locations. A distribution center may also price the merchandise and divide it into smaller quantities for individual stores.

Checkpoint 7.1

1. What are the three activities involved when purchasing inventory?
2. Describe how a purchase order is used when ordering inventory.
3. Explain how *place*, one of the four *P*s of marketing, relates to transporting an order.
4. Describe the retailer's process of receiving an order.
5. What is the role of a distribution center?

Build Your Vocabulary

As you progress through this course, develop a personal glossary of retailing terms and add it to your portfolio. This will help you build your vocabulary and prepare you for a career. Write a definition for each of the following terms, and add it to your personal retail glossary.

purchase order   marking
packing slip   invoice
receiving record   distribution center
quality control

Section 7.2 Inventory Management

Objectives

- **Summarize** the importance of inventory management.
- **Describe** different methods of tracking inventory.
- **Explain** the significance of stock turnover.

Key Terms

inventory management
perpetual inventory control system
manual tag system
point-of-sale software
Universal Product Code (UPC)
radio frequency identification (RFID)
periodic inventory control system
stock shrinkage
loss prevention
stock turnover rate

Web Connect

Using the Internet, conduct a search for "perpetual inventory control software." Write a summary describing what the software is and the functions it performs. Explain why this software could be useful and important to retailers.

Critical Thinking

Think about your favorite retailer. How do you think the store keeps track of inventory? Do you think it is computerized? Do you think the employees count every item? Explain your thoughts on the ways retailers manage inventory.

Managing the Inventory

The retailer must manage inventory effectively in order for the store to be successful. There must be enough merchandise on hand to meet customer demand. When merchandise is *out of stock*, sales are lost and store loyalty is reduced due to customer dissatisfaction. The end result is lower profits for the retailer.

Having too much merchandise in inventory at one time can be costly because it ties up cash. A business is *overstocked* when there is too much inventory compared to what is needed to cover estimated sales. The excess merchandise is at risk of becoming damaged, lost, shopworn, or obsolete. This merchandise must eventually be marked down. Too many unplanned markdowns will negatively impact the retailer's profit.

Inventory management involves ordering merchandise, receiving it into stock on arrival, and paying the vendor. Inventory management also includes shipping, storage, and controlling expenses. It is important to monitor stock so that there are no out-of-stock or overstock conditions.

FYI

In the retail business, out of stock is also known as a *stock out*.

Some retailers use an *automatic store replenishment system* to avoid out-of-stock situations. This system uses software and the UPCs or other electronic markings on pieces of merchandise to track inventory electronically. An automatic store replenishment system automatically records when stock comes into and out of inventory. This software detects low stock and automatically triggers the reorder process.

Inventory Systems

Successful inventory management requires a reliable inventory system. There are two methods of tracking inventory that retailers generally use: perpetual and periodic.

Perpetual Inventory Control System

A **perpetual inventory control system** shows the quantity of items on hand at all times. This system tracks all purchases and returns as they happen. This method of tracking can be done manually or using software.

Using a **manual tag system**, sales are tracked by removing the price tags when products are sold. Price tags show information about the vendor, date of receipt, department, product classification, color, size, and style. The tags are tabulated and the information is manually recorded.

A computerized inventory control system is commonly used in both big and small retail businesses. *Electronic data interchange (EDI)* is the standard transfer of electronic data for business transactions between organizations. The EDI system eliminates paper transactions, which makes it easier for customers or distributors to place orders. The system also leaves less room for errors. EDI is an important part of computerized inventory control systems. EDI software tracks sales, inventory, and other details needed for accurately recording inventory.

UPCs can be scanned to automatically record stock information.

Kzenon/Shutterstock.com

Point-of-sale software electronically records each sale when it happens using scanned product bar codes. Cash registers are equipped with optical scanner software, such as lasers or light pens, to record sales transaction data directly from the **Universal Product Codes (UPCs)**. The UPC is a bar code containing a 13-digit code. When a transaction is recorded, the code is read by an optical scanner at the cash register or computer. The code includes information on the item, such as the manufacturer, a description of the item, type of packaging, and other information. This information is translated into data. The computer system uses the item data to track sales and inventory.

Radio frequency identification (RFID) is a system that uses radio frequency receivers and computer chips attached to inventory items to track inventory. Many clothing retailers use the RFID chips to track merchandise.

The sales and inventory data gathered are also used for market research. Retailers can track type of products, number of items purchased, time of year, and other consumer buying habits from the scanned product codes. Although there is no personal information about the customer, the buying data helps retailers plan merchandise decisions.

Periodic Inventory Control System

A **periodic inventory control system** involves manually counting merchandise at regular periods, such as weekly or monthly. An accurate number can be obtained by visually inspecting or counting the merchandise on hand. It is a good practice to physically count inventory at least once a year. Even when perpetual inventory systems are used, physical inventories are still conducted.

A physical inventory will help expose stock shrinkage. **Stock shrinkage** is the difference between perpetual inventory and the actual inventory on hand. Several factors may cause stock shrinkage:

- employee theft
- shoplifting
- administrative error
- vendor fraud

Loss prevention is a plan and actions designed to prevent the loss of company assets. Security and employee training programs may help prevent loss.

Retailers should physically count inventory at least once a year.

Golden Pixels LLC/Shutterstock.com

Stock Turnover

The most effective and commonly used measurement in controlling inventory is the stock turnover rate. **Stock turnover rate** is the number of times merchandise is sold during a given period of time. The stock turnover rate is usually based on the merchandise (six-month) buying plan. Inventory levels should be balanced between stock and anticipated sales.

Stock turnover may show how efficiently a store or department is being operated. High turnover means sales are high in relation to the dollars invested in inventory. The buyer has met consumer need by stocking the right merchandise at the right time and at the right price. If goods move fast, they are less likely to become shopworn. This means that fewer items will be marked down. Also, if the customer knows merchandise in the store moves fast, they are less likely to wait for markdowns before making purchases.

Turnover can also be *too* high. A turnover rate that is too high may indicate poor ordering habits. Too much reordering can increase shipping costs, which adds to the cost of the merchandise. It may also prevent the company from earning quantity discounts.

Low turnover means that merchandise is not selling. This could indicate that the buyer purchased merchandise that customers do not want. Inventory that does not sell takes up space in a brick-and-mortar store. The retailer's money is tied up in merchandise that is not making a profit for the business. When this happens, markdowns may be necessary to sell the products and make room for product that will sell.

Turnover rate is calculated by dividing the cost of merchandise that has been sold by the value of the average quantity of inventory on hand.

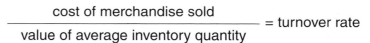

$$\frac{\text{cost of merchandise sold}}{\text{value of average inventory quantity}} = \text{turnover rate}$$

Retail Ethics

Collusion

It is unethical and illegal for a retailer to participate in acts of collusion. *Collusion* occurs when competing businesses work together to eliminate competition by misleading customers, fixing prices, or other fraudulent practices. Unethical retailers sometimes collude with other businesses so they can dominate the marketplace. Collusion is not only unethical—it is illegal.

For example, the cost of merchandise that a retail business has sold is $250,000. The value of the average amount of inventory on hand is $125,000. When calculated, the turnover rate is 2, or 2 times per year.

$$\frac{\$250,000}{\$125,000} = 2 \text{ (turnover rate)}$$

Is a turnover rate of 2 times per year good? Deciding this depends on the specific retailer and the industry standard.

Large retailers calculate the turnover rate per department. Many buyers are evaluated by the markups they achieve and the stock turnover rate for their department. If the rate is above the industry standard, the buyer is doing an excellent job. If the turnover rate is below the industry standard, the buyer needs to determine the problem and make corrections.

Exploring Retail Careers

Retail Stock Clerk

Having items available for sale when customers are ready to purchase them can be important to the success of e-tailers and retailers. When merchandise is received, the retail stock clerk receives and unpacks the merchandise. Each item must be compared with the packing slip for accuracy. If any items are damaged or missing, the clerk reports the information. After items are received, the clerk enters them into inventory. As items leave the inventory for orders or to be placed in the store, the clerk tracks each item. Other typical job titles for retail stock clerk include *retail stocker*, *order filler*, and *recording clerk*. Some examples of tasks that retail stock clerks perform include:

- record items shipped, received, or transferred to another location
- find, sort, or move merchandise between different parts of the store
- report changes in inventory or received merchandise
- check records for accuracy

A high school diploma and basic computer skills are required for the position. Attention to detail and good communication skills are necessary. Most retail stock clerk positions include on-the-job training.

Checkpoint 7.2

1. Describe the importance of inventory management.
2. Identify and describe two methods of tracking inventory.
3. How do UPCs aid in inventory control?
4. Explain the importance of stock turnover rate to retailers.
5. State the formula for calculating turnover rate.

Build Your Vocabulary

As you progress through this course, develop a personal glossary of retailing terms and add it to your portfolio. This will help you build your vocabulary and prepare you for a career. Write a definition for each of the following terms, and add it to your personal retail glossary.

inventory management
perpetual inventory control system
manual tag system
point-of-sale software
Universal Product Code (UPC)

radio frequency identification (RFID)
periodic inventory control system
stock shrinkage
loss prevention
stock turnover rate

Chapter Summary

Section 7.1 Inventory

- Purchasing inventory involves placing the purchase order, transporting the order, and receiving the order.
- Inventory storage is an expense for all retailers. The type of merchandise dictates the type of storage that is used. Some businesses use a distribution center for storing inventory.

Section 7.2 Inventory Management

- Retailers must manage inventory effectively for the business to be successful. There must be enough merchandise to meet customer demands.
- Effective inventory management requires reliable inventory tracking. Two methods of tracking inventory are perpetual inventory control and periodic inventory control.
- Stock turnover rate is an effective measurement in controlling inventory. High turnover means that inventory is meeting customer demands. When stock turnover is too high, it indicates poor planning by the business. Low turnover means that the customer is not buying the product.

Review Your Knowledge

1. What information is typically stated on a purchase order?
2. Explain the concept of ownership in merchandise transportation.
3. What does it mean to mark merchandise?
4. Describe how an invoice is used.
5. Where can a retailer find storage for its inventory?
6. Explain the difference between *out-of-stock* and *overstocked*. How can both situations have negative outcomes for a retailer?
7. How does the manual tag system work?
8. What are some of the causes of stock shrinkage?
9. How are sales and inventory data used for market research?
10. Explain why the stock turnover rate is a significant measure when planning inventory.

Apply Your Knowledge

1. A purchase order contains many types of detailed information. Review the list of information that is typically stated on a purchase order. Research purchase order forms online. Print several examples that you find. Compare and contrast each purchase order form. Which do you think is the better form? Write a paragraph to support your opinion.
2. Transporting is an important step in the channel of distribution. Categorize each mode of transportation by creating a list of shipping options available to businesses such as rail, air, etc. Next to each category of transportation, indicate which type of merchandise is best suited for that category. Next, consider storage as a step in the channel of distribution. Make a list of storage categories a retailer may select to protect merchandise until it is ready to be placed in the store. How many categories did you come up with? Are there any products that demand specific storage?

3. Universal Product Codes (UPC) are commonly referred to as "bar codes." Look at the bar code on an item in your home or classroom. Using the Internet, identify the type of bar code used. What transactional data is collected using this type of bar code? How would this information be used for market research? Present your findings to your class.

4. Research automatic store replenishment systems used by retailers to avoid out-of-stock situations. Make a list of the activities that the software performs. Summarize the advantages and disadvantages of using this software. Does this system conflict with or complement inventory control systems that may be used in the business?

5. What type of retail business would be most likely to use a manual tag system? In today's technological environment, why would a business use a manual system? Write a paragraph explaining your opinion.

6. Electronic data interchange, or EDI, is the standard transfer of electronic data for business transactions. Research the role of EDI in retail. Write several paragraphs identifying the transactional data that is tracked using this system.

7. Optical scanners play an important role in retail inventory tracking. Use the Internet to research the various types of optical scanners retailers use for data collection. List and describe the types of scanners that are available and how a retailer might use them in a business.

8. Periodic inventories are conducted by most retailers. Research the topic and make a checklist of the general steps retailers take to conduct a periodic inventory. Write a paragraph explaining how retailers use the results of a periodic inventory and the importance of this process.

9. Turnover rate can be *too* high or *too* low. Research the implications of having an incorrect turnover rate for a retail business. Write several paragraphs on your findings.

10. The cost of merchandise sold by a retailer during one year is $63,000. The retailer has an average inventory value of $42,000. Calculate the stock turnover rate. State the formula you used and show your work.

Check Your Retail IQ

Now that you have finished the chapter, see what you learned about retail by taking the chapter posttest. If you do not have a smartphone, visit the G-W Learning companion website.

G-W Learning mobile site: www.m.g-wlearning.com

G-W Learning companion website: www.g-wlearning.com/marketing/

College and Career Readiness

Career Ready Practices Through the use of reliable and valid research strategies, you will be able to tackle challenges that you confront. Do an Internet search on the decision-making process. Create a flow chart showing the steps that you can use to solve problems logically.

Listening Active listeners know when to comment and when to remain silent. Practice your listening skills while your instructor presents this chapter. Participate when appropriate and build on his or her ideas. Respond appropriately to the presentation.

Speaking There will be many instances when you will be required to persuade the listener, such as when retail buyers negotiate with vendors. When you persuade, you convince a person to take a course of action, which you propose. Prepare for a conversation with your principal about the importance of having severe weather days. Request the principal's assistance in rewriting the severe weather day policy for your school. Plan and deliver a focused presentation that argues your case and shows solid reasoning.

Teamwork

Working in teams, select a familiar retail business. Focus on one product that you may buy at that store. Create a flow chart that depicts the retailer's purchasing process to get that product on the shelf. Share your findings with the class.

College and Career Portfolio

Community Service

Community service is an important quality that interviewers expect in a candidate. Serving the community shows that the candidate is well rounded and socially aware. In this activity, you will create a list of your contributions to nonprofit organizations. Many opportunities are available for young people to serve the community. You might volunteer for a community clean-up project. Perhaps you might enjoy reading to residents in a senior-living facility. Maybe raising money for a pet shelter appeals to you. Whatever your interests, there is sure to be a related service project.

In this activity, you will create a list of your community service activities. Remember that this is an ongoing project. Plan to update this list when you have new activities to add.

1. List the service projects or volunteer activities in which you have taken part. Give the organization or person's name, the dates, and the activities that you performed. If you received a certificate or award related to this service, mention it here.
2. Give the document an appropriate name using the naming system you created earlier. Place the file in your e-portfolio.
3. Place a copy of the list in the container for your print portfolio.

◇DECA Coach

Study Performance Indicators

If you are competing in an impromptu event, you will be handed a case study with instructions and given 10 or 15 minutes to prepare. Because you do not have much time, your natural tendency is to go straight to the case study to start analyzing it. However, your first step should be to read and analyze the first page that describes your "performance indicators." It is important to understand what performance indicators are and how they will impact your overall score.

Performance indicators are skills and knowledge that you have learned in the classroom. These are the measures by which you will be judged. Here is a tip: the performance indicators are a mirror image of the judge's evaluation sheet. When you read the performance indicators, you will know exactly what the judges will evaluate when they give you a score. For example, a performance indicator reads, "Identify types of advertising activities." The judges will score you based on your ability to identify types of advertising activities in your solution. While your presentation might be clever, unless it directly addresses the performance indicators, you will not score well. If you are able to address all performance indicators, you will be on the right track. Visit DECA's website to download a sample event in your category. Pay close attention to the performance indicators.

Visit www.deca.org to learn more information about DECA.

G-W Learning Mobile Site

Visit the G-W Learning mobile site to complete the chapter pretest and posttest, and to practice vocabulary using e-flash cards. If you do not have a smartphone, visit the G-W Learning companion website to access these features.

G-W Learning mobile site: www.m.g-wlearning.com

G-W Learning companion website: www.g-wlearning.com/marketing/

Chapter 8
Pricing Strategies

In order to make profits, retailers must set appropriate prices for the products they sell. Retailers do not randomly assign product prices; there are many factors that influence pricing. Each retailer has its own pricing strategies based on factors such as competition, the economy, and supply and demand. Pricing objectives are developed to maximize either sales or profits.

Before sales can be made, the base price must be established for each product. The base price is the price at which a retailer expects to sell the product before discounts. Demand-based pricing, competition-based pricing, and cost-based pricing are the three common methods of determining a base price. Retailers may adjust the base price of products using psychological or discount pricing techniques to attract customers.

Case Study

Apple Inc.

When Apple Inc. introduced the iPhone in June 2007, the retailer used a price skimming technique. Price skimming is when a company first sets a high price for a product and plans to reduce the price over time. Once the initial demand of the iPhone was met, Apple planned to reduce the price. During the first two months after the product launch, Apple sold 1,400,000 iPhones at the $599.00 price. This made the iPhone one of the most successful products in history.

In keeping with the price skimming strategy, Apple dropped the price of the iPhone to $399.00 in September 2007. The drastic price reduction angered many of the original buyers of the iPhone. However, the lower price opened the market to include new customers. People who would not have paid the higher price were now purchasing the iPhone. Dropping the price in the fall also benefited iPhone sales during the holiday season when competing products were introduced into the marketplace. Using the right pricing strategy allowed Apple Inc. to maximize both the sales of and profits from the iPhone.

Reading Prep

Before reading this chapter, skim the photographs and their captions. As you read, determine how these concepts contribute to the ideas presented in the text.

College and Career Readiness

Check Your Retail IQ

Before you begin the chapter, see what you already know about retail by taking the chapter pretest. If you do not have a smartphone, visit the G-W Learning companion website.

G-W Learning mobile site: www.m.g-wlearning.com

G-W Learning companion website: www.g-wlearning.com/marketing/

Sections

8.1   Retail Pricing

8.2   Determining Prices

Section 8.1 Retail Pricing

Objectives

After completing this section, you will be able to:
- **Explain** the role of price in the success of a retailer.
- **Discuss** factors that affect price.

Key Terms

price
value
list price
selling price
unit pricing
operating expenses
fixed expense

variable expense
early adopter
price competition
nonprice competition
supply
demand

Web Connect

Choose an electronics item you would like to buy. Find four e-tailing websites that sell the item and compare the prices. Which e-tailer would you choose to make the purchase? Why?

Critical Thinking

Retailers use various methods to price products. One method is to price products by the manufacturer's suggested retail price (MSRP). Car advertisements often mention *MSRP*. How do you think MSRP is different from a selling price?

Price

Price is the amount of money requested or exchanged for a product. It is one of the four *P*s of marketing.

Pricing products correctly plays a major role in retail success. Setting the correct price for a product can result in many sales of that product. Incorrect pricing may lead to lost sales and possible business failure. If a price is too high, customers may not buy it. If a price is too low, the business may not make a profit.

Retailers do not set prices at random. There are several basic factors that are considered when setting a price. Retailers must ensure that the price accomplishes the following:
- covers the cost of the product
- covers the cost of operating and other expenses
- generates the necessary profit
- is an amount customers are willing to pay

Customers use price to establish value. Value is the relative worth of a product. Each individual customer uses personal criteria to determine value. Some customers may be willing to pay more for a product if they believe the value is high. However, if the perceived value is low, the customer will probably expect a lower price.

A challenge for retailers is understanding what *value* means to the customer. Every individual customer may evaluate the same product in different ways. For example, some consumers may think that paying $300 for a smartphone is a poor decision. However, others may be willing to pay that amount because of the advanced features on the phone. Those consumers may feel $300 is a good value because of the features. In this case, differences in values affect the price consumers are willing to pay for a smartphone.

Market research helps retailers define how customers perceive value. Through research, information can be gathered to help determine appropriate product pricing.

Pricing Levels

Most retailers have several levels of pricing. The **list price** is the established price expected to be paid for a product. The list price is usually stated on a label, tag, sticker, or other type of price display. The list price is often subject to discounts.

The **selling price** is the price customers actually pay for the product after discounts and coupons. Discounts may be shown as a dollar amount, such as *$5 off,* or as a percentage, such as *10 percent off all items.* For example, the list price of a hat is $30. The retailer is offering a 10 percent off sale. As a result, the selling price is $27. If there had been no sale event, both the list price and the selling price would have been $30.

Another type of price is the manufacturer's suggested retail price (MSRP). The *manufacturer's suggested retail price (MSRP)* is the list price recommended by the manufacturer. MSRP is often associated with big-ticket items, such as cars and furniture. It is common for retailers to advertise an item at MSRP, but discount the price to show that the customer is getting a good buy. For example, a piece of jewelry may be displayed with a $1,000 MSRP. However, the retailer offers a discount that brings the price down to $599. Customers immediately see a good product at a reduced price.

Some manufacturers require retailers to sell their products at MSRP. Some high-end product manufacturers do not allow retailers to discount the MSRP. This practice helps the manufacturer preserve its image of quality.

Unit Pricing

Unit pricing is the practice of pricing goods based on a standard unit of measure, such as an ounce or a pound. It allows customers to compare the per unit price between different products or different quantities of the same product. Some states require certain industries to provide unit pricing for their products.

Grocers and drug stores commonly display unit pricing. Grocery stores usually display the total price and the unit price of products. For example, the total price of a 32-ounce can of beans may cost $2.56.

NRF Tip

The industry standard for pricing retail merchandise is typically referred to as *keystone*. However, depending upon the store location and customers, some stores price their merchandise outside of this standard. The NRF website can help retailers see how their competitors price merchandise and how their customers react to certain price points.

FYI

The selling price may also be referred to as the *market price*.

Unit pricing helps customers
easily compare similar
products.

Tyler Olsen/Shutterstock.com

The unit price of 8 cents per ounce is also displayed. By comparing
the unit price of one can of beans to other brands and sizes, the
customer can determine which one he or she prefers to purchase.

Consumers commonly use unit pricing to find volume discounts.
For example, a 30-count bottle of vitamins may cost 10 cents per unit
while a 100-count bottle of the identical product may cost only 8 cents
per unit. The customer can decide whether or not the amount of
per-unit savings is worth buying more of the item. Unit pricing also
helps retailers sell in larger volume.

Pricing Policies

Retail pricing is influenced by both controllable and
uncontrollable variables. *Controllable variables* are those that the
retailer can influence, such as company goals, expenses, and product
life cycle. *Uncontrollable variables* are those that the retailer cannot
control. These include competition, the economy, and fluctuations in
supply and demand. A retailer's pricing policies must consider all of
these factors.

Company Goals

Retailers establish prices that will help meet company goals.
Company image is one factor that influences how products are priced.
Some retailers position their stores as low-priced or bargain stores.
Prices in these stores should be low. Other stores project an image of
luxury and often price products much higher.

Setting prices according to the projected company image can affect the success of the business. If a low-priced store sets high prices, customers will not buy and the business will not sell enough products to reach its sales goals. However, if that business prices its products to meet the company image, the retailer has a chance of meeting their sales goals.

Operating Expenses

Products must be priced to cover the operating expenses of a business, as well as the cost of the product. **Operating expenses** are ongoing expenses that keep a business functioning. Retailers only make a profit after expenses have been paid.

There are two basic types of expenses: fixed and variable. **Fixed expenses** do not change and are not affected by the number of products sold. For example, rent and insurance cost the same every month. **Variable expenses** change based on the activities of the business. For example, the cost of advertising or office supplies may vary from month to month. Examples of both fixed and variable expenses are shown in Figure 8-1. In order to make a profit, a retailer must make enough money to cover fixed and variable expenses, as well as the cost of goods.

Product Life Cycle

The price of a product can vary depending on the product life cycle stage. If new products in the market are priced high, it may be because the retailer has a limited supply. The pricing needs to remain high for the retailer to recover costs. However, the price may be artificially high only because some people will pay the higher price.

Types of Expenses	
Fixed Expenses	**Variable Expenses**
Equipment rental	Advertising and promotion
Insurance	Bonuses
Interest	Credit card payments
Licenses	Hourly wages
Loan payments	Office supplies
Mortgage	Packaging
Rent	Sales commissions
Salaries	Shipping and handling
Service payments (cell phone, Internet, subscription TV)	Utilities

Goodheart-Willcox Publisher

Figure 8-1 Fixed expenses do not change, while variable expenses change often.

Retail Ethics

Advertised Merchandise

It is a deceptive practice for a retailer to advertise merchandise that it does not have available in its store. Advertising merchandise to draw customers into the store without sufficient stock or a plan to fulfill the consumer's request for merchandise is unethical.

This type of customer is called an early adopter. An **early adopter** is a person who wants to be the first to own the newest products and is willing to pay more to do so.

When new products are priced very low, it may be because the retailer does not know if the public will accept or want the new product. Setting a low price for a new product increases the odds that customers will be willing to try it. If the product begins to become widely accepted, the price may increase. As the demand for a product grows, the price typically levels off. New products that were initially priced high begin to decrease. Products that were initially priced low begin to increase. Widely accepted products will encounter competition, which may result in a price decrease.

Competition

Retailers must be knowledgeable about their competition. Many stores and products are often similar to each other. These stores compete for the same customers. Price becomes very important when competing with another retailer.

Smart retailers know what the competition is offering and how their products are priced. For example, if a competitor stocks new products or suddenly lowers its prices, it could take business away. To help learn about the competition, retailers often use *secret shoppers*. Secret shoppers visit several competing stores and note competitors' prices. The retailer analyzes the pricing notes and compares the data with its own research.

Price competition occurs when lower pricing is the main reason customers buy from one retailer over another. Retailers may or may not choose to adjust prices based on competition. If price is the primary factor, the retailer may have to lower prices to match the competition. However, reducing price also reduces the profit margin.

Competitive advantage based on factors other than price is called **nonprice competition**. Rather than lowering a price to meet competition, a retailer may choose to offer higher levels of customer service. Some customers are loyal to a product or a retailer, and are willing to pay more to buy their favorite product regardless of price.

Economy

The economic cycle in the United States varies over time. In positive cycles, employment rates and consumer spending are high. During these times, prices tend to be higher. When people have jobs and money, they tend to spend more freely. In negative cycles, both employment and consumer spending decrease. When spending is low, retailers must try harder to entice customers to buy. One way to do this is to reduce prices. When prices are reduced by one retailer, the competition may feel forced to lower prices, as well. This can create a cycle of price reductions, which can ultimately result in businesses being forced to close.

Not all products and retailers are negatively impacted by bad economic times. For example, during the Great Recession that began in 2008, auto sales significantly decreased. People could not afford to buy new cars. Because of this, they had to service the cars they already owned. As a result, the sale of auto parts increased drastically and lasted for several years. Therefore, auto parts retailers did not feel the need to reduce prices.

Supply and Demand

Supply is the quantity of merchandise available. **Demand** is the quantity of merchandise required to satisfy customers' buying needs. The *law of supply and demand* states that if supply is plentiful, prices are lower. When supply is limited, customers are willing to pay more. For example, the supply of fresh fruit during off-season is limited and may be harder to find. Customers may be willing to pay higher prices because they want fresh fruit. As a result, grocers are able to charge higher prices for fruit when it is off-season.

Not all products are greatly impacted by supply and demand. For example, milk is a product that most people need to buy. The sale of milk does not necessarily increase if prices go down. There is only so much milk a family can drink, and milk has a short shelf life. If prices go up, consumers will probably still buy milk because it is a product that is needed. However, if the prices get too high, consumers may seek alternatives to milk. Gasoline is another example of a product that is not impacted by supply and demand. For example, a person who needs to drive a car to get to work is probably willing to pay high prices because gas is necessary.

During off-season, customers are usually willing to pay higher prices for fresh produce.

bikeriderlondon/Shutterstock.com

Checkpoint 8.1

1. What role does price play in the success of a retailer?
2. Name the three levels of pricing.
3. Define *controllable variables* in retail pricing. Give examples.
4. Name two reasons a retailer would set the price for a new product very high.
5. Explain how supply and demand affect pricing.

Build Your Vocabulary

As you progress through this course, develop a personal glossary of retailing terms and add it to your portfolio. This will help you build your vocabulary and prepare you for a career. Write a definition for each of the following terms, and add it to your personal retailing glossary.

price
value
list price
selling price
unit pricing
operating expenses
fixed expense

variable expense
early adopter
price competition
nonprice competition
supply
demand

Section 8.2 Determining Prices

Objectives

After completing this section, you will be able to:
- **Identify** two retail pricing objectives.
- **Describe** how base price is determined.
- **Compare** price adjustment methods.

Key Terms

pricing objective
volume pricing
break-even point
base price
demand-based pricing
competition-based
  pricing
cost-based pricing

keystone pricing
psychological pricing
odd pricing
even pricing
prestige pricing
price lining
promotional pricing
discount pricing

Web Connect

Conduct an Internet search for examples of pricing strategies. What types of strategies did you find? Summarize the information and share your findings with the class.

Critical Thinking

Think about the last visit to one of your favorite retail stores. What types of sales did you see? Were there end-of-season sales? Buy one, get one sales? Give an example of the type of sale that was in progress and explain why you think the retailer had that type of sale.

Pricing Objectives

The retailer must set prices that meet company revenue goals. **Pricing objectives** are the goals defined in the business plan for the overall pricing policies of the company. Pricing objectives and strategies vary among retail establishments. Most businesses establish objectives that include both short- and long-term goals. However, most retailers set pricing objectives with the intention of maximizing either sales or profit.

Maximize Sales

One pricing objective is to maximize sales. Sales grow when there is an increase in market share. *Market share* is the percentage of total sales in a market produced by one business. Market share can be increased by increasing the number of customers *or* increasing the sales volume per customer.

Retailers can maximize sales by increasing the number of items each customer purchases from their store.

Andresr/Shutterstock.com

Increase the Number of Customers

Retailers can increase the number of their customers by taking customers away from the competition. Product pricing can attract customers away from the competition. Low pricing may not be the only factor consumers consider before making a buying decision, but it is a major consideration.

Finding new customers is another way to increase the number of a retailer's customers. A new customer is a first-time buyer of the product. However, the process of finding new customers can be very difficult and expensive because it involves market research. Generally the more expensive an item, the more likely a customer is to compare prices. Retailers may reduce prices or offer coupons or discounts to attract customers. Some retailers offer one-time discounts to new customers.

Increase Sales Volume

Increasing the sales volume per customer can be accomplished using volume pricing. With **volume pricing**, the per-unit price of products is lower when a greater number of units are purchased at one time. Lower per-unit pricing gives customers an incentive to buy more than one item. For example, two AAA batteries may cost $4. If retailers package eight AAA batteries for $10, the cost is reduced from $2 per unit to $1.25 per unit.

Retailers may increase sales volume by offering discounts, packaging items together, or providing loyalty-pricing incentives to their best customers. Coupons and sales are also used to entice customers to purchase more.

Maximize Profit

The amount of profit before subtracting the cost of doing business is known as *gross profit*. Maximizing gross profit involves generating as much revenue as possible in relation to total cost of each item. To accomplish this, retailers charge the highest price per unit that customers will pay.

FYI

The phrase "what the market will allow" refers to the practice of pricing products as high as possible before sales fall due to the price.

Break-Even Point

In order to make a profit, prices must be high enough to cover costs. If products are priced too high, customers will not buy. If the price is too low, the retailer will lose money. A product starts generating a profit after the break-even point. The **break-even point** is when revenue from sales equals the costs. Any revenue earned after this point is profit. The formula for break-even is as follows.

$$\frac{\text{fixed costs}}{\text{selling price} - \text{variable costs}} = \text{break-even point}$$

For example, a retailer sells tennis racquets. The total fixed cost for the company to sell racquets is $4,000. As you recall, fixed costs include expenses such as rent and insurance. Each racquet that the retailer purchases from the vendor costs $20. This means that the variable cost is $20 per racquet. The selling price for the racquets is set at $100 each.

$$\frac{\$4,000 \text{ (fixed costs)}}{\$100 \text{ (selling price)} - \$20 \text{ (variable costs)}} = 50 \text{ units (break-even point)}$$

50 racquets must be sold in order for the retailer to break even. If more than 50 racquets are sold, the retailer will make a profit.

Return on Investment

Return on investment (ROI) is a common measure of profitability based on the amount earned from the investment made in the business. ROI is determined by dividing net profit after taxes by total assets. This shows how effectively the retailer has generated profits with the existing assets in the business. The formula for ROI is as follows.

$$\frac{\text{net profits}}{\text{total assets}} = \text{return on investment}$$

For example, a retailer had net profits for the quarter of $70,000. The assets of the business are $60,000. The retailer had an ROI of 116 percent.

$$\frac{\$70,000}{\$60,000} = 1.16 \text{ return on investment}$$

Move the decimal point two places to the right to convert the ROI number to a percent.

$$1.16 = 116 \text{ percent}$$

Base Price

The **base price** is the price at which a retailer expects to sell a product. This is the price before any discounts or extra charges are added. Base price is one element of pricing strategy. Individual retailers select their own pricing strategies. However, there are three common methods of setting the base price: demand-based pricing, competition-based pricing, and cost-based pricing.

Demand-Based Pricing

Demand-based pricing is a pricing strategy based on what customers are willing to pay. It reflects the customers' perceptions of value and is also known as *value-based pricing*. This strategy is used mostly for unique products and is generally short-term. When demand for the product decreases, the pricing will likely decrease as well.

Competition-Based Pricing

Competition-based pricing is a pricing strategy primarily based on what competitors charge. This strategy usually results in pricing that is near or below the prices of competing businesses. This is done to attract customers based on the retailer's low prices. Competitive pricing can be effective when prices are still high enough to maintain a profit. However, competitive pricing may result in reduced profits, or even losses.

Competitive pricing may create a price war. A *price war* is where two or more competitors battle to have the lowest price to retain market share.

When retailers go to extremes with competitive pricing or become involved in a price war, they may lose money. This may be an acceptable risk for a short period of time in order to attract new customers. However, when the circumstances that created the non-profitable pricing come to an end, retailers will raise prices to a profitable level.

Cost-Based Pricing

Cost-based pricing is a pricing strategy that uses the cost of a product to set the selling price. Cost-based pricing is the most common pricing method used in retail. This type of pricing takes into account the cost of the product, operating costs, and the profit goals of the business. These factors are used to establish the cost of each item. A markup is then added to the cost. *Markup* is a dollar amount or percentage added to the cost of the product to reach the desired profit level. The formula for cost-based pricing is as follows.

cost + markup = base price

Social Media

Social-Media Dashboards

One of the biggest challenges with social media is managing the time it takes to monitor multiple business social sites. For example, retailers need to keep profiles current, interact with followers, and send messages on a consistent basis. Social-media dashboards, such as HootSuite, TweetDeck, or Social Oomph, can help manage the time spent on social media more effectively. A social-media dashboard is an interactive tool, much like a car dashboard, that organizes and presents information in an easy-to-read format. These tools allow retailers to schedule alerts and notifications, create groups, browse site activity, and send automatic updates or messages. While everything cannot, and should not, be automated, a social-media dashboard can make the process of keeping social media updated easier and more efficient.

Dollar Amount

One method of calculating markup is to add a dollar amount to the price of each item to reach the desired profit. For example, a retailer orders one dozen (12) swimsuits at a cost of $12 each. In order to make a profit, the fixed expenses of the business must be taken into account along with the cost of each swimsuit. Taking this into consideration, the retailer decides that a $12 profit needs to be made on each unit. Therefore, the base price of the swimsuits is $24 each.

$$\$12 \text{ (cost)} + \$12 \text{ (markup)} = \$24 \text{ (price)}$$

Percentage

Another method of calculating markup is to add a percentage to reach the desired profit. Using a percentage provides a consistent level of profit. The formula for the percentage markup method is as follows.

$$\text{cost} + (\text{cost} \times \text{markup percentage}) = \text{price}$$

Using the swimsuits example, the retailer knows that each item sold must have a 90 percent markup in order to make a profit. Considering the cost, the base price of each swimsuit is $22.80.

$$\$12 + (\$12 \times 90\%) = \text{price}$$

$$\$12 \times 90\% = \$10.80 \text{ (markup)}$$

$$\$12 + \$10.80 = \$22.80 \text{ (price)}$$

Keystone Pricing

Keystone pricing is a method of determining the base price of a product in which the total cost of the product is doubled. Keystone pricing is the easiest method of setting the base price. The formula for keystone pricing is as follows.

$$\text{cost} \times 2 = \text{price}$$

Using keystone pricing for the swimsuits example results in a $24 base price.

$$\$12 \text{ (cost)} \times 2 = \$24 \text{ (price)}$$

Keystone pricing was once a very common method of pricing in retail. However, retailers typically prefer to determine and set their own profit margin to be competitive.

Price Adjustments

The final step in determining a product's price is to determine whether or not the base price should be adjusted. The adjusted base price is the list price. To set the list price, most retailers use either a type of psychological pricing or discount pricing to attract customers.

Psychological Pricing

Psychological pricing is a pricing technique that creates an image of a product to entice customers to buy. Some common psychological pricing strategies are odd pricing, even pricing, prestige pricing, price lining, promotional pricing, and bundling.

Exploring Retail Careers

Product Manager

Retail stores, such as department stores, clothing shops, and electronics superstores, offer a large variety of products and usually several different brands of each product. Product managers decide which products the store will carry. A product manager investigates new products, analyzes buying trends, and reviews sales records of current products to determine how profitable each product is likely to be. Based on this information, the product manager buys products for resale to the store's customers. Typical job titles for a product manager include *buyer, merchandiser, merchandise manager, purchasing manager,* and *procurement specialist*.

Some examples of tasks that product managers perform include:
- use spreadsheet software to organize, locate, and analyze sales figures on products in inventory
- meet with sales personnel to get information about customer wants and needs
- analyze sales records and trends to determine how much of each product to purchase
- negotiate prices and discounts in order to purchase selected products
- set markups and selling prices for products

Product managers must be able to analyze product performance based on financial figures. They also need good negotiation skills in order to get the best prices and terms for the products they buy. Most jobs in this field require an associate's degree or equivalent training in a vocational school, but on-the-job training may be substituted for these.

Odd Pricing

Odd pricing is a strategy in which a product's price ends with an odd number, usually just lower than an even dollar amount. Research shows that customers tend to ignore the most insignificant numerals in a price. For example, customers tend to look at the price $9.99 and pay most attention to the first nine, slightly less to the second nine, and even less to the last nine. As a result, although people know that $9.99 is only 1 cent less than $10, they look at the price as $9 rather than $10.

Even Pricing

Based on the same psychology as odd pricing, even pricing is a strategy in which a product's price ends with an even number. Some retailers, particularly those selling high-end products, do not want to portray an image of bargain through their pricing. They want their prices to project a higher price because we often equate higher prices with quality. For example, a luxury car dealer may set a car's price at $70,000 rather than $69,999 in an attempt to convey quality rather than a bargain.

Prestige Pricing

Prestige pricing is setting product prices high to convey quality and status. This strategy is used by retailers who want to project a high-end image. Typically, these businesses want to attract a more status-minded customer who is willing to pay higher prices. An example of this might be Rolex. The company charges high prices for quality watches that are a status symbol. Their customers are willing to pay higher prices for the combination of quality and status.

Price Lining

Price lining is setting various prices for the same type of product to indicate different levels of quality. For example, paintbrushes might be sold for $1, $3, and $5. The product tags on each may say "Good," "Better," and "Best." Price lining helps consumers make a decision based on both quality and price. Price lining is commonly used with medium-priced goods, such as computers and appliances.

Prestige pricing is used by retailers who want to project a high-end image.

Tupungato/Shutterstock.com

Promotional Pricing

Promotional pricing is reducing the price of a product for a short period of time. Promotional pricing gives customers a sense of getting a better value compared to the normal list price of a product. Pricing to promote a product is a popular retail practice. There are many examples of promotional pricing. One popular type of promotional pricing is *buy one, get one free (BOGO)*. There are many BOGO variations, such as *buy two, get one free* or *buy one, get one half-off*.

Bundling

Similar to promotional pricing, *bundling* combines two or more products for one price. For example, a necklace may cost $75 and the matching earrings $50. However, if the customer buys both, the retailer may offer the products in a bundle for $99. This increases sales for the retailer and offers value to the customer.

Bundling is a popular way for retailers to move stock and help merchandise turnover. Bundling may also be used to move stock that is dated or obsolete.

Discount Pricing

Retailers often discount the price of merchandise to encourage customers to purchase. **Discount pricing** is a reduction in the normal selling price. There are several different discount pricing strategies that retailers commonly use.

Grocers often use milk as a loss leader by pricing it low to entice customers to shop for all the rest of their groceries in the store.

Stephen Coburn/Shutterstock.com

Leader pricing is when only select merchandise is offered at special or reduced rates. Product that is priced just at or below a profit level is called a *loss leader*. Retailers use this pricing strategy hoping that customers will buy other merchandise at the regular price. For example, a grocery store may sell milk at a very low price to entice customers to do all their weekly grocery shopping at the store.

A *quantity discount* is given for purchasing a large number of items. The more a customer buys, the greater the discount earned. *Seasonal discounts* are offered to encourage customers to purchase items outside of the typical season of use. An example of an off-season purchase is buying a snow shovel in the summer.

A *markdown* is a reduction in the original price of a product. Retailers markdown products when they have too much inventory and need to reduce the amount of product on the shelf. They may also mark down product to encourage more sales. These markdowns may be permanent or temporary reductions.

Checkpoint 8.2

1. Name two pricing objectives used by most retailers.
2. What is the formula used to determine return on investment (ROI)?
3. What is the formula used to determine the base price of a product with a percentage markup?
4. Identify the common types of psychological pricing adjustments.
5. What is a loss leader? What is the purpose of using a loss leader?

Build Your Vocabulary

As you progress through this course, develop a personal glossary of retailing terms and add it to your portfolio. This will help you build your vocabulary and prepare you for a career. Write a definition for each of the following terms, and add it to your personal retailing glossary.

pricing objective

volume pricing

break-even point

base price

demand-based pricing

competition-based pricing

cost-based pricing

keystone pricing

psychological pricing

odd pricing

even pricing

prestige pricing

price lining

promotional pricing

discount pricing

Chapter Summary

Section 8.1 Retail Pricing

- Pricing products correctly plays a major role in the success of a business. Retailers consider multiple factors when setting a price. The price of a product establishes value for the customer.
- Retail pricing is influenced by both controllable and uncontrollable variables. Company goals, expenses, and product life cycle are examples of controllable factors. Uncontrollable factors that can influence price include competition, the economy, and supply and demand.

Section 8.2 Determining Prices

- Pricing objectives are usually set to maximize either sales or profits. A business can maximize sales by increasing its market share. Charging the highest price per unit that customers will pay can maximize profits.
- The base price is the price at which a retailer expects to sell the product before discounts or extra charges. Demand-based pricing, competition-based pricing, and cost-based pricing are the three common methods of determining a base price.
- Once the base price is set, the retailer can adjust the price using a type of psychological pricing or discount pricing.

Review Your Knowledge

1. How does unit pricing benefit customers?
2. Name the two examples of controllable factors that influence price.
3. Explain how a company's image can factor into setting prices.
4. Why is it important for a retailer to know its competition when setting prices?
5. Describe the law of supply and demand and its impact on prices.
6. What is market share?
7. What is the formula to determine the break-even point?
8. What is the formula for cost-based pricing?
9. A retailer knows that in order to make a profit on a certain product, the price must include a 25 percent markup. The cost of the product is $21. Show the calculation to find the price of this product.
10. List and explain three of the common psychological pricing techniques used by retailers.

Apply Your Knowledge

1. Competition is one factor businesses use in determining pricing policies. Some retail businesses match the prices of a competitor if the customer brings in an advertisement showing the price of exactly the same product. Select three retailers that sell computer equipment. For each, research the policy for meeting the competition. How does the policy to match the competitor prices among these businesses compare?
2. Supply and demand is one factor that affects the pricing policies of a business. Note the current price of gasoline at several local gas stations. Contrast the prices advertised by five gas stations. Do the prices vary among the businesses? Why or why not? What do you think the pricing policy is for gasoline?

3. Some of the factors that can affect prices are outside of the retailer's control. Uncontrollable variables include competition, economy, and supply and demand. These variables must be considered when setting prices. Imagine you are in charge of pricing at a neighborhood bookstore. Research how bookstores have been impacted by the uncontrollable variables mentioned. Write a paragraph describing how each uncontrollable variable would impact prices at the bookstore.

4. Return on investment (ROI) is a common measure of profitability for a business. Create a presentation that describes ROI and explains the process. Use the example of a retailer that sells mobile phone accessories. The business has a net profit of $50,000 and assets of $150,000. Explain how to calculate the ROI.

5. To make a profit, a product must be priced high enough to cover the costs associated with that product. A sporting goods store sells a variety of hiking boots. The fixed costs for selling the boots total $2,660. The variable price that the retailer pays to purchase the boots from the manufacturer is $59 per pair. Taking those costs into consideration, the retailer sells each pair of boots for $120. Pair with a classmate and explain to them how to calculate the break-even point. Explain the formula used and describe why the formula is used. Did your classmate understand break-even point?

6. Most retailers use psychological or discount pricing strategies to make the final adjustment to the base price for products. Find four different examples of these pricing strategies at local or online home improvement stores. Explain each pricing strategy and why it is a good strategy for that product.

7. Each retail establishment sets its own pricing objectives, or strategies, usually with the intention of maximizing either sales or profits. Select a pair of athletic shoes that you would buy. Use the Internet to find prices from various retailers for the shoes you selected. Make a chart that shows each retailer and price. How do the prices compare among retail establishments? Do you think these retailers are using the pricing objectives to maximize sales or maximize profits? Explain your opinion.

8. Using the pricing information gathered in the last activity, contrast the pricing objectives of the retailers. Why do you think the prices were different?

9. Cost-based pricing is a pricing method that uses the cost of a product plus a markup to set the selling price. A surf shop is setting prices for new boards that just arrived. The cost for the new boards is calculated to be $250 each. The retailer decided a 30 percent markup is necessary in order to be profitable. Calculate the markup using the cost-based formula using markup percent. What is the amount (in dollars) of the markup? What is the selling price of the boards? If the retailer wants to use the odd pricing strategy, what would the final selling price be for the boards?

10. Base price is one element of pricing strategy. Imagine two art supply stores, one uses cost-based pricing and the other uses demand-based pricing. Consider how each store sets its prices. Compare the pricing strategies of the two retail establishments. Which is most likely to have higher prices? Share your findings with the class.

Check Your Retail IQ

Now that you have finished the chapter, see what you learned about retail by taking the chapter posttest. If you do not have a smartphone, visit the G-W Learning companion website.

G-W Learning mobile site: www.m.g-wlearning.com
G-W Learning companion website: www.g-wlearning.com/marketing/

College and Career Readiness

Career Ready Practices There will be instances in which you will need to use critical-thinking skills to solve a problem. One way to approach a problem is to create a pros and cons chart. Imagine that you have to decide whether or not to hire a vendor to use for a promotion. Place all of the positive things about the vendor on the pro side and all the negative things on the con side. Circle the items on your list that you consider the most important. Did the pros and cons chart help you make a decision? Why or why not?

Reading Analyze the influence that folklore has on retail. Do an Internet search for folklore and select an article about folklore in the country of your choice. After you read this article, make a list of ways that folklore impacts how people shop.

Speaking Select three of your classmates to participate in a discussion panel. Acting as the team leader, assign each person to a specific task, such as timekeeper, recorder, etc. Discuss the topic of trade-offs and opportunity costs. Keep the panel on task and promote democratic discussion.

Teamwork

Working with your team, discuss the possible operating expenses of a bagel shop. Make a list of the fixed and variable expenses that could impact the price of the products and services offered. What did you learn from this exercise?

College and Career Portfolio

School Work

Your portfolio should contain items related to your schoolwork. These items might include report cards, transcripts, or honor roll reports. Diplomas or certificates that show courses or programs you completed should also be included.

At some point, you will likely apply for a job or volunteer position. At that time, list the classes you took that helped prepare you for the particular job or volunteer position. Describe the activities you completed or topics you studied in these classes that relate to the job or volunteer duties. This information will be helpful when you apply for the position by letter or talk with an interviewer.

1. Identify a job or volunteer position for which you could apply. Write a paragraph that lists the classes you took and activities completed that relate to the position. You can use this document as a model when you are actually ready to apply for a position.
2. Scan other documents related to your schoolwork, such as grade reports, transcripts, and diplomas. Place the model paragraph and other documents in your e-portfolio.
3. Place hard copies in the container for your print portfolio.

◇DECA. Coach

Tent Cards

When walking into an impromptu event, you are not given much to work with other than your brainpower. You are given instructions for your event, something to write with, and scratch paper. While that may not sound like a lot, if you use them wisely, you may have presentation tools that you had not thought about.

Most competitors think of the paper and pencil as a way to take notes and organize their thoughts. While you should use those supplies for this purpose, there is another way to use them—you can create your own personal presentation tools.

It is very easy to forget what the performance indicators are as you go through your presentation. When you begin your preparation, take a sheet of paper and fold it in half. On one-half of the page, list your performance indicators. Keep this page and carry it with you when you begin your presentation. DECA allows you to do this. When you sit or stand in front of your judges, use this piece of paper as a tent card presentation tool. Place it on the table in front of the judges, positioning it so that you can both see it. As you go through your presentation, use it as a reminder of each point that you need to address.

Visit www.deca.org to learn more information about DECA.

G-W Learning Mobile Site

Visit the G-W Learning mobile site to complete the chapter pretest and posttest, and to practice vocabulary using e-flash cards. If you do not have a smartphone, visit the G-W Learning companion website to access these features.

G-W Learning mobile site: www.m.g-wlearning.com
G-W Learning companion website: www.g-wlearning.com/marketing/

Unit 4
Promotion

Introduction

Communication is the process of sending and receiving written, verbal, and nonverbal messages. Retailers use various communication techniques in promotions that are intended to either inform or motivate customers to buy products or services.

Retail is all about sales. Effective sales associates prepare to sell before a customer ever enters the store. But, sales associates are only one part of a retail customer service strategy. Both brick-and-mortar retailers and e-tailers use elements of customer service to set themselves apart from the competition.

Green Retail

Recycle and Save

Many socially responsible retailers work with the community to encourage participation in recycling efforts. Several retailers have in-store recycling bins for customers to deposit used batteries, CFL lightbulbs, used ink cartridges, and plastic shopping bags.

Some retailers offer incentives for recycling items in the store. For example, when a Lowe's customer purchases a new appliance, Lowe's will haul away and recycle the customer's old appliance for free. Apple offers customers Apple Store gift cards for the value of old, reusable electronics. Best Buy offers a trade-in credit for unwanted video games and electronics. Both Apple and Best Buy will responsibly recycle electronics that do not have any trade-in value at no charge to the customer.

A great number of retailers have realized the importance of being environmentally conscious. Offering convenient recycling options benefits the retailer's existing customers and may help attract new customers.

Suranga Weeratunga/Shutterstock.com

Chapter 9
Retail Communication

Communication is the core of any business, but is especially important in retail. Successful retailers learn how to apply written, verbal, and nonverbal techniques to build relationships and close sales. Effective communication also includes good listening skills and the ability to read and understand documents.

Promotion is the process of communicating with potential customers to influence their buying behavior. Effective promotional activities inform, persuade, and remind customers of products that will meet their needs and wants. The promotional mix includes the elements of advertising, sales promotion, public relations, and personal selling. Each of these elements can be used alone or together to create an integrated marketing campaign.

Case Study

Nintendo

Nintendo launched its handheld, three-dimensional (3D) video game console, the Nintendo 3DS™, in August 2012. This gaming product was the first of its kind. Games could be played without wearing 3D glasses. Initially the Nintendo 3DS had a premium price, which created a high value for the product.

To promote the Nintendo 3DS, special launch events were scheduled throughout the United States. Many of the launch events began at midnight to add to the excitement. At the events, contests were held that challenged customers to play with the new game console. Most of the events also offered free giveaways, such as T-shirts, carrying cases, and beanie toys that promoted the Nintendo 3DS and its games.

Nintendo also spent millions of dollars on television advertising prior to the launch. Nintendo addressed each of the four *P*s of marketing (product, price, place, and promotion) in their successful marketing efforts for the Nintendo 3DS.

College and Career Readiness

Reading Prep

As you read this chapter, stop at the Checkpoints and take time to answer the questions. Were you able to answer these questions without referring to the chapter content?

Check Your Retail IQ

Before you begin the chapter, see what you already know about retail by taking the chapter pretest. If you do not have a smartphone, visit the G-W Learning companion website.

G-W Learning mobile site: www.m.g-wlearning.com
G-W Learning companion website: www.g-wlearning.com/marketing/

Sections

9.1 Effective Communication

9.2 Marketing Communications

Stuart Jenner/Shutterstock.com

Section 9.1 Effective Communication

Objectives

After completing this section, you will be able to:
- **Identify** the elements of the communication process.
- **Describe** the characteristics of written, verbal, and nonverbal communication.
- **Discuss** the importance of good listening skills.
- **Explain** why reading skills are necessary in the retail business.

Key Terms

communication
communication process
sender
encoding
channel
transmission
receiver
decoding
feedback
written communication
tone
verbal communication
pace
nonverbal communication
hearing
listening

Web Connect

Good communication skills are important in the workplace. How would you rate your communication skills? Search the Internet for resources used to evaluate communication skills. What did you learn?

Critical Thinking

Reflect on a recent communication that you had with a friend. Identify how the message was sent and received. What was the reason for the communication? Was your communication effective? Why or why not?

Communication Process

Communication is the process of sending and receiving messages that convey information, ideas, feelings, and beliefs. The communication process is a series of actions taken by both the sender and the receiver of a message. The communication process has six elements: sender, message, channel, receiver, translation, and feedback, as shown in Figure 9-1.

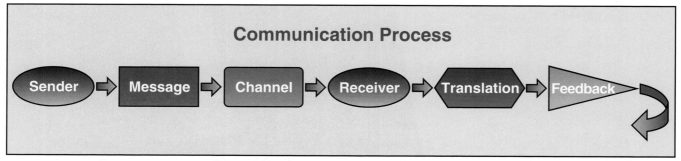

Goodheart-Willcox Publisher

Figure 9-1 Each of the six elements in the communication process is important.

Sender

The person who has a message to communicate is called the **sender**. The sender begins the communication process. Retail professionals send messages to people inside and outside of the organization. For example, when a sales associate talks to customers about products, he or she is the *sender* of those messages. As the starting point of the process, the success of any communication begins with the sender.

Message

The message is a critical element in the communication process. The sender of the message decides which form the message will take. The message can be in words, which will either be written or spoken. A message can also be in pictures or video. When the sender creates a message, he or she encodes it. **Encoding** is the process of turning the idea for a message into symbols that are communicated to others, such as words or images.

Channel

The sender chooses the best channel through which to send the message. The **channel** is how the message is transmitted. The channel may be a face-to-face conversation, a telephone call, an e-mail, or a text message. The act of sending a message is called **transmission**. The channel for a message is selected based on the type of promotion or communication that is being sent. For example, to communicate a message about a special sale, a text message may be sent to customers.

Text messages and e-mails are popular channels for sending messages.

Receiver

The person who physically receives the message from the sender is called the **receiver**. The receiver can be one person or many people. For example, the target audience for an e-mailed promotional coupon could be hundreds or even thousands of receivers.

Monkey Business Images/Shutterstock.com

Translation

Once a message is transmitted, the receiver decodes it. **Decoding** is the process of translating the message into terms that the receiver can understand. If the receiver does not understand the message, it has not been *received*.

Feedback

Feedback is the receiver's response to a message and is the last step in the communication process. It tells the sender if the receiver understood the message as intended. Feedback may be positive or negative. For example, a retailer sent an e-mail to customers about a new return policy. Customers objected and called customer service to complain. The phone calls voicing concern are the feedback.

Types of Communications

Three types of communication are written, verbal, and nonverbal. Words are used to build the message for written and verbal communications. Actions are used to communicate nonverbally. The success of communication is influenced by how well words and actions are used. Retailers use written, verbal, and nonverbal communication to meet specific needs.

Written Communication

In **written communication**, information is transmitted using symbols that are either printed or handwritten. Accurate written messages are important in retail.

Writing style refers to the way in which language is used to convey an idea. It reflects the many decisions that are made regarding word choice and construction of the message. **Tone** is an impression of the overall content of a message. Is it friendly or hostile? Demanding or courteous? Additionally, professional written communication must be free of all bias. *Bias-free writing* uses neutral words that convey neither a positive nor negative message. Gender, age, race, etc., cannot be inferred from bias-free writing.

Vocabulary is the selection of words used in written communication. The words chosen depend on the target audience, the purpose of the message, and the desired response from the receivers. Words carry most of the information in written communication and are very powerful. Think of the effect of the word *SALE* posted in the window of a store. The retailer is counting on that sign to entice customers to enter the store, look at merchandise, and possibly buy something.

Written communication is particularly important to e-tailers. E-tailers often depend on web pages as their primary way to communicate with customers. Much of the communication posted on websites is considered technical communication. *Technical communication* is professional material created by experts to help the reader understand a concept. *Technical documents* provide information, such as instructions or directions. User manuals, installation instructions, and application help files are examples of technical documents.

E-tail websites also provide specialized communication. *Specialized communication* is a task-specific message that provides information for the reader. An example is a message posted on an e-tailer's website informing customers of a product recall with instructions for returning the product for a refund. Another example is a public relations message that explains a community service project in which the store is participating. These written communications provide important information to customers.

Verbal Communication

Good verbal communication skills are also necessary in the retail business. **Verbal communication** is speaking. *Tone of speech* refers to the feeling conveyed to the receiver from the way words are spoken. A speaker's selection of words, or *vocabulary*, also affects the tone of speech.

Sales associates and customer service representatives often speak *informally* with customers in the store and on the phone. Retailers also have *formal* speaking opportunities, such as sales manager giving a formal sales presentation to a group. Before a formal presentation,

FYI

Anything that prevents clear, effective communication is known as a *barrier*.

When interacting with customers, tone of speech and choice of vocabulary can influence the customer's buying decision.

bikeriderlondon/Shutterstock.com

speakers often prepare by practicing in front of a mirror or a small group to build their confidence level. Whether informal or formal, effective speakers observe audience reaction and adjust their vocabulary and tone to meet the needs of the situation.

Another consideration in verbal communication is the pace of the presentation. Pace refers to how quickly information is delivered. The pace of verbal communication must be slow enough to allow the receiver to understand the information. It also needs to be fast enough to keep the receiver's interest. The speaker should be aware of audience reaction and adjust the pace accordingly.

Nonverbal Communication

Nonverbal communication refers to actions, instead of words, that send messages. When speaking, people send nonverbal messages through body language and behaviors. *Body language* is nonverbal communication through facial expressions, gestures, body movements, and body position. Raised eyebrows, smiles, sneers, and eye contact are considered facial expressions. *Eye contact* occurs when two people look directly into each other's eyes.

Exploring Retail Careers

Advertising and Promotions

One of the most basic needs of any company is to let the public know what it has to offer. Retailers rely on advertising and promotional events to inform customers about products and services. Advertising and promotions managers plan and coordinate advertising programs. They organize contests and other events to help make people aware of a company's products and services. Typical job titles for these positions include *advertising manager*, *promotions director*, *promotions manager*, *marketing and promotions manager*, and *advertising sales manager*. Some examples of tasks that *advertising and promotions managers* perform include:

- plan advertising and promotional campaigns to increase public awareness and increase sales of products or services
- review and approve layouts and advertising copy, including audio and video scripts
- coordinate or direct a campaign team to meet the company's goals
- prepare budgets for advertising or promotional campaigns

This position requires knowledge of media production and communication techniques. Managers must understand how to use written, oral, and visual media effectively to promote products and services. They should also have a basic knowledge of sales and marketing principles. This includes strategies and tactics for creating interest in products or services. Most positions for advertising and promotions managers require a bachelor degree. Many also require experience and knowledge both in the type of product or service the company sells and in advertising or promotions techniques.

Gestures that send messages include pointing, waving, a handshake, or a shoulder shrug. People also communicate through body movements, such as stepping closer to someone or turning his or her back to a person. Examples of body positions include straight or stiff posture, leaning back in a chair, and slouching.

Nonverbal communication can send subtle or loud messages. Retailers must be aware of what their nonverbal communications are expressing and make adjustments to meet the needs of their audience. If the words are positive, but the tone or actions are negative, the entire message may be lost.

Listening Skills

Retailers spend a great deal of time listening to vendors, sales associates, and customers. When *listening*, you make an effort to process what you *hear*. To process what is heard, you need to consider the speaker's purpose, relate what you already know to what you hear, and show attention.

Hearing is a physical process—sound waves reach the ears and send signals to the brain. Listening is an intellectual process that combines hearing with evaluation. In addition, listening often leads to follow-up. Sometimes people think they are *listening*, but they may be just *hearing*. When having a conversation with a customer, it is important for retailers and sales associates to listen rather than just hear what the customer is saying.

Employees of a service business, such as a car repair business, must pay close attention to what customers are saying.

michaeljung/Shutterstock.com

Active listening is fully participating in a communication interaction while processing what other people say. Active listeners often provide verbal and nonverbal feedback to the speaker. Nodding your head or saying "I understand" can let the speaker know that the message has been received. See Figure 9-2 for more tips on being an active listener.

Passive listening is casually listening to a speaker. Passive listeners let the speaker's words wash over them without processing the meaning or message. They can also miss important details of nonverbal communication. Passive listeners are more interested in hearing and less interested in listening.

Empathy is seeing things from the point of view of another person. Empathy helps people understand how someone else is feeling. The listener can understand even when he or she does not share the same feelings. Empathy is a key to effective listening. Being able to empathize with another person is important for those who work directly with customers. Customer service representatives and sales associates can benefit from having empathy when dealing with disappointed customers.

Reading Skills

Reading is something that many people may take for granted. However, it is a skill that should be perfected by those in the business world. Reading is one of the main ways to learn new information. Retailers read business e-mails and marketing materials to manage their business and keep up with industry trends.

Tips for Active Listening

- Think about the speaker's purpose.
- Evaluate what you hear by relating the information to what you already know.
- Make eye contact with the speaker to demonstrate attention.
- Take notes when necessary.
- Ask questions and make comments when appropriate.
- Adopt good listening habits, such as sitting in the front of the room.
- Fight distractions; never text or answer your cell phone when listening to a speaker.
- Focus your attention on the speaker.

Goodheart-Willcox Publisher

Figure 9-2 Being an active listener makes speakers feel valued.

Reading technical communication, such as product reports and trade and industry information, allows retailers to stay informed about what is going on in the economy.

Active reading is when the reader thinks about what he or she is reading. Active reading requires the reader to be involved and do something in response to the words. To do this, the reader should consider the purpose of the material that is being read. Why is the document being read? What is hoped to be learned? Becoming an active reader is an important skill for the workplace.

Reading product and industry-related materials helps retailers stay informed and be successful.

Minerva Studio/Shutterstock.com

Checkpoint 9.1

1. Name the six elements of the communication process.
2. What are the three types of communication?
3. What is writing style?
4. Compare and contrast active listening and passive listening.
5. Explain why reading skills are important in the retail business.

Build Your Vocabulary

As you progress through this course, develop a personal glossary of retailing terms and add it to your portfolio. This will help you build your vocabulary and prepare you for a career. Write a definition for each of the following terms, and add it to your personal retailing glossary.

communication
communication process
sender
encoding
channel
transmission
receiver
decoding

feedback
written communication
tone
verbal communication
pace
nonverbal communication
hearing
listening

Section 9.2 Marketing Communications

Objectives

After completing this section, you will be able to:
- **Explain** the goals of retail promotions.
- **Discuss** the elements of the promotional mix.
- **Describe** the concept of electronic promotion.
- **Explain** the use of integrated marketing communications (IMC).

Key Terms

product promotion
institutional promotion
persuasion
sales promotion
public relations (PR)
electronic promotion
quick response (QR) codes
viral marketing
blog
permission marketing
integrated marketing communications (IMC)

Web Connect

Use the Internet to research the best *viral marketing campaigns* within the past year. Make a list of the top five promotions. Do the top five promotions have anything in common? Do you remember seeing any of the campaigns? If so, why did you find them memorable?

Critical Thinking

Find an advertisement for a retail store in a magazine, newspaper, or material that was directly mailed to your home. What other types of promotions have you seen for this retailer (such as sales or electronic promotions, or public relations)? List all the types of promotions you find for the retailer. Why do you think the retailer selected this mix of promotions?

Promotion

Promotion involves all of the communication techniques used to inform or motivate customers to buy products or services. Promotion is one of the four *P*s of marketing. Any communication effort to promote a product or service is considered *marketing communication*. The coordination of communications to achieve a specific goal is a *marketing campaign*. While there are many types of marketing campaigns, they generally fall into two categories: product or institutional promotions.

A **product promotion** is when specific products or services are promoted. An example of a product promotion is shown in Figure 9-3. Most promotional campaigns are product promotions.

Goodheart-Willcox Publisher

Figure 9-3 A product promotion promotes a specific product or service.

An **institutional promotion** is when an organization or company is promoted rather than its products, as shown in Figure 9-4. These promotions are designed to increase awareness, build goodwill with customers, and create a favorable view of the retailer's reputation or brand, also called building *brand equity*. Hopefully, increased awareness will also lead to more sales.

Promotions inform, persuade, or remind people about the business or its products.

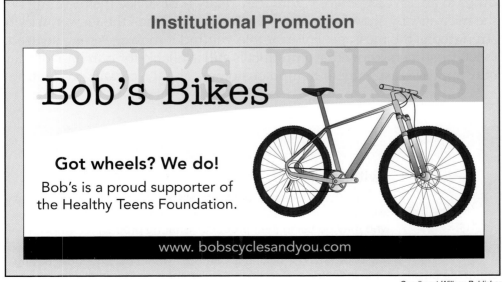

Goodheart-Willcox Publisher

Figure 9-4 An institutional promotion promotes the business.

Inform

Promotions that *inform* tell people something they want or need to know. Retailers typically spend more of their campaign dollars on direct mail than any other type of promotional material. Brochures, ads, e-mails, or catalogs make customers aware of the retailer's latest offerings. Promotions keep customers informed about:

- new features on existing products
- features and benefits of new products
- instructions on how to use and assemble products
- safety issues that may affect the use of a product
- charities and cultural organizations supported by the business
- events within the community sponsored by the business

Persuade

The end goal of most promotions is to *persuade* people to buy a product or service. **Persuasion** uses logic to change a belief or get people to take a certain action. Promotions provide information about product features and consumer benefits. The target market must consider the purchase worthwhile. If they do not, the message was not persuasive. Rebates, loyalty programs, and new product samples are examples of strategies used to persuade customers to take action.

Remind

Messages that *remind* appear in multiple places over a period of time. Research indicates that individuals must be exposed three or more times to an advertisement before they really hear or see the meaning of the message. By showing it often, the retailer reminds the viewer, which strengthens the message. For example, reminder messages may be used to let consumers know that a product is still available for purchase or they may appear seasonally to remind customers about a certain product.

Social Media

Twitter

Twitter is a useful tool for retailers to conduct conversations with customers. Retailers can "tweet" in real time with customers who may be using their products. Sharing product information or offering coupons or other industry "scoop" is a sure way to get followers. The business can hear what customers are saying about the business, the industry, or a topic that helps them gather intelligence about the competition. Twitter gives retailers a chance to network and expand their customer base.

Elements of the Promotional Mix

The *promotional mix* is a combination of the elements used in a promotional campaign. It can include advertising, sales promotion, public relations, and personal selling.

Advertising

Advertising is any nonpersonal communication that is not directed toward a particular individual. Advertisements, or *ads*, are generally available to anyone who might see or listen to them through broadcast media, in print, and online. The goal of advertisements may be to get a reaction from customers, generate sales, or motivate customers to action. For example, online advertising typically calls customers to action. Customers may be encouraged to click on the advertisements for sale information or visit the retailer's Facebook page for the latest news and offers.

An *advertising campaign* is a coordinated series of ads linked by a single idea or theme.

Print Media

Print media is one of the most effective forms of advertising. Advertising in print media may be found in newspapers, magazines, directories, direct mailings, outdoor signage, and transit promotion.

A *newspaper* is a daily or weekly publication printed on inexpensive paper. It can be in print or online and, normally, does not target any specific market. Although print newspaper sales have declined, newspapers are still a viable advertising medium. For a retailer, newspapers are a good place to run coupons to encourage consumers to come into the store. Some consumers are *coupon clippers*. They regularly cut newspaper and other printed coupons to save money on products.

Magazines are printed weekly, monthly, or quarterly and usually on high-quality paper. Magazines usually have a target audience and focus on a specific interest, such as golfing or travel. People tend to keep magazines for a longer period of time than newspapers.

Directories are books or online databases that list merchants by name and type of business. Contact information is often provided as well, such as address, phone number, and website. Consumers often turn to directories when they are trying to find a specific product or service.

Direct mail is any advertising message sent through the US Postal Service to current or potential customers. Direct mail includes catalogs, brochures, postcards, and letters sent to a targeted audience.

Outdoor signage is any type of advertisement that is placed outdoors and can be print or electronic. Outdoor signage includes billboards, bus benches, and arena placements, like sports stadiums.

Advertisements on digital billboards are very eye-catching and change every few minutes.

Suranga Weeratunga/Shutterstock.com

Digital billboards change images several times a minute. Outdoor advertising can be seen by many people, but may be very expensive.

Transit promotion is found on the outside or inside of buses, taxis, subways, and commuter trains. Transit ads are generally an inexpensive way to reach an often captive audience.

Broadcast Media

There are two forms of broadcast media: television and radio. Radio and television ads, or commercials, reach a large number of people daily.

Television advertising is the most expensive form of advertisement. This is partly because television broadcasts reach the largest possible audience. Similar to other forms of advertising, TV commercials are designed to appeal to specific target markets.

Radio advertising is similar to TV advertising, but the listener cannot see the ad. Radio ads can range in length and the audience is usually specific.

Sales Promotion

Sales promotion is a marketing method that encourages customers to take immediate action, usually to buy products or services. Sales promotion can be any type of marketing effort that is not considered advertising, public relations, or personal selling. Sales promotions may be used to promote a product or increase traffic into a store. Effective promotions are creative so that customers notice them and have a desire to enter or shop at that store.

Because sales promotions are intended to prompt consumer action, retailers and e-tailers can measure those actions. For example, if a retailer runs a contest, the increase in foot traffic, online hits, or sales during the contest period can be tracked. The cost of the promotion is compared to the increased profit to determine if the promotion was successful. If the promotion does not produce the desired results, the retailer can evaluate the process to identify flaws. See Figure 9-5 for possible cause-and-effect scenarios.

Coupons

Coupons are a type of discount found in newspapers, magazines, direct mail, online, and other places. They are like tickets that offer a discount when the customer comes into the store or goes online to redeem it. The purpose of a coupon is to get people to enter the store and make a purchase. Because coupons cannot be used after the expiration date, they create a sense of urgency.

Rebates

A *manufacturer's rebate* is a return of a portion of the purchase price of an item. Unlike coupons, rebates are received *after* a product is purchased. Rebates encourage potential customers to go to the store and make a purchase. Rebates also have an expiration date, which creates a sense of urgency.

To receive a rebate, the customer is required to complete a form and mail it to the manufacturer. Often, the process of submitting a rebate can be completed online. Once processed, the manufacturer sends a check for the rebate amount to the buyer. However, it may take months for the customer to receive a rebate.

Evaluating Promotions	
Promotion Effect	**Possible Cause**
No online or foot traffic is generated.	The ad piece, such as a coupon, may be poorly designed or is in some way unattractive. The promotional piece did not have the intended appeal.
Traffic is generated, but sales do not increase.	Something is unappealing to customers once they visit the store. Maybe the product is not as it appeared in the ad, the salespeople in the store are too pushy, or another flaw in the store must be discovered and corrected.
Sales are increased.	The promotion generated good traffic and increased sales. Additional profit should be compared to the expense involved in the promotion.

Goodheart-Willcox Publisher

Figure 9-5 The retailer can track the effects of a promotion and evaluate its success.

Promotional Items

Promotional items are given away to remind customers about a business and its products. These are also known as *marketing premiums*. The business name, address, phone number, and website are often printed on promotional items. These items can include key chains, calendars, pens and pencils, or more expensive items, like tote bags, calculators, or books.

Samples

Retailers may offer free product samples in the store to encourage customers to try new items. The goal is to persuade customers to buy the product that they sample.

Loyalty Programs

Loyalty programs are very popular with retailers. The most common loyalty program involves giving customers a free product or service after making a certain number of purchases. Other programs offer discounts on future purchases after the customer spends a specified dollar amount at the store.

Contests and Sweepstakes

Retailers often use contests and sweepstakes to get people into the store or to share their contact information. In *contests*, customers must do something to win, such as submit a photo of themselves using one of the retailer's products. *Sweepstakes* are games of chance where prizes are given to winners who are randomly selected from a number of entries. A sweepstakes can be as simple as placing a fishbowl near the cash register and customers place their business card in the fishbowl. Winners are drawn weekly and may receive a free product or a product discount.

Displays

Visual merchandising involves displaying merchandise in strategic locations where customers can clearly see the product. Stores use displays to create product awareness. Attractive visual merchandising can persuade potential customers to purchase. Many stores display merchandise at the checkout lanes to increase sales. These are called *point-of-purchase (POP) displays*.

Public Relations

Another element of the promotional mix is public relations. **Public relations (PR)** refers to the activities that promote goodwill between the company and the public. *Publicity* is unpaid media coverage for a newsworthy business, person, or product. This media coverage may be a news conference, press release, or local news story. Positive publicity is a way to form a good image of a business or product in the minds of consumers.

With personal selling, sales associates and customers interact with each other in person.

Proactive public relations is when the retailer presents itself in a positive manner to build an image. Companies issue PR communications to explain their contributions to the community, environment, and other socially responsible activities. *Reactive public relations* is used to counteract a negative public perception about the company.

Personal Selling

Personal selling is any direct contact between a sales associate and a customer. It is the direct, face-to-face delivery of information about a product or service. Sales associates are the people in a store who deliver this information directly to customers. Personal selling builds relationships. It also allows customers to ask questions or voice concerns.

Electronic Promotion

Electronic promotion is any promotion that uses the Internet, e-mail, or other digital technology. It may also be called *digital marketing*. Some campaigns combine electronic and traditional promotions for wider audience appeal. For example, a catalog sent to a customer through direct mail might include a quick response code, or QR code. The customer can scan the QR code and go directly to the business' website. **Quick response (QR) codes** are bar codes that, when scanned with a mobile device, connect the user to a website or other digital information.

Web Presence

A website is an online destination for retailers to connect with customers. In addition to selling products, retailers often use their websites to advertise and offer help to customers. For some, a website is the main way the company interacts with the public.

One way a customer gets to a retailer's website is by using a *search engine*. The customer enters a search term and the search engine sifts through all the websites related to that search term. The search engine provides a list of websites that best match the search term. For example, entering the search term "ringtones" into a search engine returns websites like iTunes, Billboard, and Myxer Inc. Examples of popular search engines include Google, Yahoo!, and Bing.

Online Advertising

Online advertising is placing ads on websites where typical visitors to that website are the retailer's target market. There is a cost for online advertising. One type of online advertising uses Internet *search engines*. Retailers purchase certain search terms, or *keywords*, used on different search engines. Small text ads show up on the side of the search results lists when those purchased keywords are used in a search. This practice is called *paid SEO* (search engine optimization). *Pay per click (PPC)* is a method of advertising that allows the business to pay for an ad only if someone actually clicks on it.

There are many online advertisement strategies available.

- *Display ads* are any type of online ads that are not interactive, but attempt to gain brand exposure.
- *Banner ads* are placed at the top of a website, typically in a box, and look similar to a print advertisement.
- *Transition ads* are advertisements that display while users are waiting for a website to load.
- *Behavioral ads* use cookies stored on a computer or mobile device to analyze the user's browsing habits. The ads selected for the user are similar to the searches previously performed and websites previously visited.
- *Floating ads* literally float across or around the web browser window and disappear after a few seconds.
- *Pop-up ads* appear on a page when it is first opened. *Pop-under ads* appear when the web page is closed.

Social Media

Social media is an Internet platform that connects people with similar interests. Social media sites create online communities. People share information, ideas, messages, pictures, and videos on social media sites. Social networking sites, such as Facebook and Twitter, provide opportunities to create a company page. For example, visitors can link directly from Facebook to a retailer or e-tailer and start shopping.

Viral marketing, or *buzz marketing*, is information about products that customers or viewers are compelled to pass along to others. This is also known as *word-of-mouth advertising*. Social media lets users share information about products and "buzz" about their experience with the products. Blogs also encourage customers to share comments and feedback. A **blog**, short for *web log*, is a website in a journal format created by a person or organization. There is no charge associated with this form of marketing.

Many customers view social media sites on mobile devices, such as smartphones and tablets. *Mobile ads* are advertisements sent to smartphones and other mobile devices. The use of mobile ads continues to grow.

E-mail Campaigns

E-mail can be an inexpensive and effective way to share information to both potential and existing customers. E-mail is used to introduce new products, provide product updates, and announce sales promotions. However, it is important that businesses are respectful and do not send e-mails to people who do not want them. Unsolicited e-mail is called *spam*. Spam may offend potential customers and may negatively influence their decision to visit the retailer. **Permission marketing** is the practice of receiving permission to send people company information through e-mail, text messaging, and other means. It is also called *opt-in marketing*. It is good business practice to get permission before sending e-mail.

Receiving spam may offend people and result in lost potential customers.

Qoqazian/Shutterstock.com

Before initiating an e-mail campaign, research e-mail etiquette and the 2004 *CAN-SPAM Act*. This act is enforced by the Federal Trade Commission (FTC). It allows individuals to report companies that send spam. E-mails that violate the CAN-SPAM Act rules are subject to penalties of up to $16,000.

Integrated Marketing Communications

A promotional strategy is the process of deciding the best way to use the promotional mix. Integrated marketing communications is one approach that businesses use. **Integrated marketing communications (IMC)** combines all the forms of marketing communication in a coordinated way. This means that advertising, sales promotion, public relations, and personal selling all work together to strengthen the retailer or its products. Using IMC makes a promotion much more effective.

Once the promotional strategy has been decided, the promotional plan can be put in place. The *promotional plan* is a detailed list of goals, activities, and other important information about how to promote a product or service. The steps to complete a promotional plan are outlined in Figure 9-6.

The plan becomes a road map to guide the business to reaching its promotional objectives. The objectives could be to promote a product or service, to promote the brand, or raise customer awareness. Promotion objectives vary depending on the company goals.

Developing a Promotional Plan

1. Identify the goals and objectives for the promotion: create goals that can be measured.
2. Identify the target market: use research, sales information, and other sources to decide which people are most likely to purchase.
3. Develop the message of the campaign: determine the theme and desired actions to be taken.
4. Select the promotional mix that meets the campaign goals and best reaches the target market.
5. Establish a budget for the campaign: make sure all the elements of the promotional mix are addressed.
6. Implement the campaign: create the action plan.
7. Use metrics to evaluate the campaign: determine what, if anything, could be improved for the next campaign.

Goodheart-Willcox Publisher

Figure 9-6 A promotional plan serves as a roadmap to meet the objectives of the business.

Most businesses use metrics to evaluate the effectiveness of the promotional plan. *Metrics* are a standard of measurement. Metrics help the retailer evaluate if the goals were met and the cost of the promotion was justified. For example, one metric may be to count how many customers used the retailer's coupons during a sales promotion. A goal is set at the beginning of the campaign for the optimum number. At the end of the campaign, the goal is measured. If the promotional plan generated the expected results, it may be considered successful. If the plan failed, the retailer may choose not to use that idea for the next promotion.

Promotional plans may be developed for just one product or service. However, some retailers create an overall promotional plan for the entire year and product line. Company objectives generally drive the format and timeframe of a promotional plan.

Checkpoint 9.2

1. What are the three goals of promotion?
2. What is sales promotion?
3. List four common types of electronic promotion.
4. Explain permission marketing.
5. What is the integrated marketing communications strategy?

Build Your Vocabulary

As you progress through this course, develop a personal glossary of retailing terms and add it to your portfolio. This will help you build your vocabulary and prepare you for a career. Write a definition for each of the following terms, and add it to your personal retailing glossary.

product promotion
institutional promotion
persuasion
sales promotion
public relations (PR)
electronic promotion

quick response (QR) codes
viral marketing
blog
permission marketing
integrated marketing communications
   (IMC)

Chapter Summary

Section 9.1 Effective Communication

- Communication is the process of sending and receiving of messages that give information and share ideas, feelings, and beliefs. The communication process includes six elements: sender, message, channel, receiver, translation, and feedback.
- Three types of communication are written, verbal, and nonverbal. In written and verbal communication, people use words to build the message. In contrast, body language is used to communicate nonverbally.
- Listening skills are important in the workplace. Listening is an intellectual process that combines hearing with evaluation.
- Reading is one of the main ways to learn new information. Active reading occurs when the reader thinks about what he or she is reading.

Section 9.2 Marketing Communications

- Promotion is all of the communication techniques used to inform or motivate customers to buy products or services. Promotions are used to inform, persuade, or remind people about the business or its products.
- The promotional mix is a combination of elements used in a campaign that can include advertising, sales promotion, public relations, and personal selling.
- A web presence, online advertising, social media, and e-mail campaigns are examples of electronic promotion.
- Integrated marketing communications (IMC) combines several elements of the promotional mix. IMC becomes part of the promotional plan and helps the business reach its goals.

Review Your Knowledge

1. What are bias-free words?
2. Define tone of speech.
3. Give five examples of body language.
4. In order to process what you hear, what three actions must you take?
5. What is empathy?
6. What is marketing communication?
7. What is the difference between a product promotion and an institutional promotion?
8. Name the four elements of the promotional mix.
9. Describe proactive public relations.
10. What is online advertising?

Apply Your Knowledge

1. Retail businesses deal with many customers who have varied personalities. Conduct research on retail customer types. How many types did you find? Write a description of each personality type and prepare your findings to present to the class. Before you present, practice in front of a mirror or with just a few people to build your confidence levels before speaking in front of a large group.
2. Technical communication is professional material created by experts that help the reader understand a concept. The purpose of these documents is to provide

information, such as instructions or directions. Conduct an Internet search for a technical document that gives directions on how to tie a bow tie. Using the information you read, demonstrate to the class how to tie a bow tie. Were you successful? Did the technical document you located give you the directions you needed for the task?

3. Promotional plans play an important role in driving sales for the retailer. Setting promotional objectives and reaching them can mean success or failure. Use the Internet to research retail promotional goals and metrics. What did you learn? Next, make a list of five promotional objectives that a typical retailer might create. These could be to increase sales, promote brand awareness, generate goodwill, or other objectives that might be important for the business. Next to each objective, describe a metric to measure how the goal will be evaluated.

4. Integrated marketing communications is a strategy that helps the retailer be creative in applying the elements of the promotional mix. Make a chart with two columns. In the first column, list each element of the promotional mix. In the second column, list examples of promotional activities that use each element. After you have finished the chart, create *Plan A* and *Plan B*. Mix and match pieces of the mix to create ideas for a promotional plan.

5. Search the Internet for an example of a successful public relations campaign. Prepare a two-minute summary of the campaign and its impact on the business it represented. Explain your findings in an oral presentation to your class. Remember that body language is nonverbal communication through facial expressions, gestures, body movements, and body position. It is important that you are aware of the message your audience is sending through body language. Be mindful and observe your audience during your presentation. Adjust your body language to meet the needs of your audience.

6. For a sales associate, it is important to observe the customer's reactions when presenting features and benefits about a product or service. Write several paragraphs that explain how a sales associate can observe his or her audience and adjust the pace of their presentation to meet the needs of the audience.

7. Prepare a demonstration showing how to fill the gas tank in a car. While demonstrating, observe the audience's facial expressions and other body language. What types of verbal responses did you use to respond to the audience's body language? Did you adjust the message in response to an individual's facial expressions or body language? Did you change any of the explanation because you sensed that someone was not following your ideas? Describe your verbal responses.

8. In the previous activity, you delivered a demonstration to your class and noted the verbal responses you used to respond to the audience's body language. Did you also find it necessary to adjust your nonverbal responses? Did you change the position of your stance? Did you adjust your facial expressions? Describe your nonverbal responses.

9. Do an Internet search for a recent product recall. Read the specialized written information related to the recall. Note the product, its flaws, how to return it, and any other critical information. Using the information you read, demonstrate your findings to the class. Use a handout, slide presentation, or any other visuals that will help your classmates comprehend the information.

10. Consider how your instructor presented a section of this chapter. Think about the vocabulary used to present the information. Write a paragraph describing how your instructor used vocabulary in his or her presentation. Did he or she adjust the vocabulary used during the presentation? Was the adjustment based on reactions from the class?

11. You have been tasked with creating an IMC campaign for a bottled water product. Using visual and print displays, present your plan to the class. Observe your audience and adjust the tone of your presentation to suit their reactions. Ask your classmates to comment on the effectiveness of your IMC campaign.

Check Your Retail IQ

Now that you have finished the chapter, see what you learned about retail by taking the chapter posttest. If you do not have a smartphone, visit the G-W Learning companion website.
G-W Learning mobile site: www.m.g-wlearning.com
G-W Learning companion website: www.g-wlearning.com/marketing/

College and Career Readiness

Career Ready Practices Successful employees model integrity. What role do you think ethics and integrity have in decision-making? Think of a time when your ideals and principles helped you make a decision. What process did you use to make the decision? In retrospect, do you think you made the correct decision? Did your decision have any consequences?

Writing Writing style is the way in which a writer uses language to convey an idea. Research the topic of marketing communications and its importance for businesses. Once you evaluate the relevance, quality, and depth of the information gathered, write a one-page thesis describing what you have learned. Organize your material so that it is logical to the reader.

Reading Read a magazine, newspaper, or online article about the importance of personal finance for teens. Take notes to identify the purpose of the article and the intended audience. Determine the central ideas of the article and review the conclusions made by the author. Demonstrate your understanding of the information by summarizing what you read, making sure to incorporate the who, what, when, and how of the piece.

Teamwork

Meet with your teammates and discuss the communication process. Describe a recent situation where each of you observed negative interaction between an employee and a customer at a retail store. List the verbal and nonverbal communication that was used by each person. Describe how the employee could have used verbal and nonverbal communication to avoid or correct the negative interaction.

College and Career Portfolio

Skills and Talents
Your portfolio should contain samples of your work that show your skills or talents. Now is the time to start collecting items. You can decide which documents to include later when you prepare your final portfolio.

Look at past school or work assignments you have completed. Select a book report, essay, poem, or other work that demonstrates your writing talents. Include a research paper, letter, electronic slide show, or other items that illustrate your business communication skills. Look for projects that show your skills related to critical thinking and problem solving. Have you completed a long or complicated project? Write a description of the project and tell how you managed various parts of the assignment to complete it on time. Include samples from the completed project. What career area interests you most? Select completed work from classes that will help prepare you for jobs or internships in that area.

1. Save the documents that show your skills and talents in your e-portfolio. Remember to place the documents in an appropriate subfolder.
2. Place hard copies in the container for your print portfolio.

◇DECA Coach

Create a Summary of Your Presentation

During a competitive events conference, realize that judges sit through many presentations. As hard as they may try to focus, and as much as you might not like, there are times when judges lose focus. They may miss some of the details of what you have said. While that may or may not be the case during your presentation, there are certain things that you can do to ensure that they grasp your content. One way to be sure that they know what you have said is to summarize your content at the end of the presentation.

If you are giving a prepared presentation, use the main headings from your scoring rubric to prepare your summary. Touch on each heading to remind your judge that you have addressed each issue. If you have delivered an impromptu presentation, use the performance indicators to summarize. Address them directly, reviewing each one by using the words verbatim, such as "and we have described the price function by…"

There are two advantages to summarizing your presentation. The first is that you are reminding the judges how you have addressed each performance objective. The second is to address the fact that you *have* addressed each performance objective. When you summarize, even if you overlooked an objective during your presentation, it gives you a second chance to convince the judges that you have addressed it. A summary helps the judges understand that you have not overlooked any of the scoring factors.

Visit www.deca.org to learn more information about DECA.

G-W Learning Mobile Site

Visit the G-W Learning mobile site to complete the chapter pretest and posttest, and to practice vocabulary using e-flash cards. If you do not have a smartphone, visit the G-W Learning companion website to access these features.

G-W Learning mobile site: www.m.g-wlearning.com

G-W Learning companion website: www.g-wlearning.com/marketing/

Chapter 10
Selling

Retail is all about sales. In order for a retailer to generate sales, sales associates are needed to provide the personal selling element of the promotional mix. Since sales associates are often the only contact a customer has with a retail business, ethics, personality, and dress are important.

Effective sales associates spend time learning about the products and building customer relationships before the sales process even begins. The sales process includes six steps that begin with approaching the customer and end with following up after closing the sale. Each step is important and focuses on the customer. However, no matter how well a sales associate executes the steps of the sales process, sales may still be lost. All sales opportunities are valuable learning experiences.

Case Study

Banana Republic

Banana Republic is a leading global specialty retailer with about 136,000 employees. The retailer is very selective about hiring sales consultants. Once hired, Banana Republic sales associates become some of the industry's best. They receive significant sales and product training through Banana Republic's service training. Most importantly, Banana Republic demands that each sales associate demonstrate a "customer first" mindset. The retailer expects each sales consultant to provide an optimal shopping experience for customers. From the moment customers walk into the store, they receive special treatment. All customers are greeted by a sales associate within seconds of entering the store. The sales associates are accessible at all times to ensure a positive shopping experience. Sales associates engage each customer by asking open-ended questions, establishing the customer's needs, and making relevant merchandise suggestions. Banana Republic's sales associates are familiar with the merchandise on the sales floor, as well as styles, fit, fabrics, price, and trends. The retailer invests in its sales associates by providing regular and ongoing training. Banana Republic understands that customer-focused, solution-oriented selling helps to build a loyal customer base.

College and Career Readiness

Reading Prep

Before reading this chapter, go to the Review Your Knowledge section at the end of the chapter and read the questions. This exercise will prepare you for the content presented in this chapter. Review questions at the end of the chapter serve as a self-assessment to help you evaluate your comprehension of the material.

Check Your Retail IQ

Before you begin the chapter, see what you already know about retail by taking the chapter pretest. If you do not have a smartphone, visit the G-W Learning companion website.

G-W Learning mobile site: www.m.g-wlearning.com
G-W Learning companion website: www.g-wlearning.com/marketing/

G-W Mobile

Sections

10.1   Personal Selling
10.2   Retail Sales Process

Kzenon/Shutterstock.com

Section 10.1 Personal Selling

Objectives

After completing this section, you will be able to:
- **Describe** the value of personal selling in retail.
- **Discuss** the expectations of a sales associate.
- **Explain** the role of a sales associate.

Key Terms

personal selling
punctuality
dependability
people skills
dress code
selling tasks
cash transaction

credit card transaction
debit card transaction
sales return
adjustment
nonselling task

Web Connect

Conduct an Internet search for retail sales position openings in your area. Select four positions that interest you. As you read each job description, list the requirements that each employer details in the job ad. What does each ad have in common?

Critical Thinking

When you are in the market for a personal electronic device, such as a new smartphone, how do you prefer to shop? Do you prefer to visit a store and solicit help from a salesperson, or do research on your own? List the advantages and disadvantages of each approach.

Personal Selling

Retail stores make great efforts to ensure that they have the right products, at the right price, at the right time. Retail is all about sales. However, to make sales happen, sales associates, also called *salespeople*, are needed to provide the personal selling function. Personal selling is an important element of the promotional mix.

Personal selling is direct contact between a sales associate and a customer for the purpose of persuading the customer to make a purchase. Face-to-face interaction allows the sales associate to help a customer find the right products, solve problems, and make buying decisions. Information can be provided that may not be found in an advertisement or a brochure. Customers can provide feedback so their individual needs can be met. Without salespeople, it would be difficult for a retailer to sell products or services.

Sales associates are often the only source of direct contact between a retailer and the customer.

Most personal selling occurs inside a retail establishment. However, some businesses visit the customer in his or her home to sell a product. An example is a home furnishings consultant who brings special order catalogs to a customer's home.

Sales Associate

A key element in most successful retail settings is effective sales associates. Without them, it would be difficult to serve the customer and generate sales.

Each type of retailer has different expectations of its sales associates. A retailer that offers simple and inexpensive items might depend on sales associates to answer questions and take orders. Retailers that have more complicated or expensive products may depend heavily on the sales team to interact with customers, rather than just answer questions. Each retailer determines what is expected of sales associates based on the type of business and its business plan.

Retailers expect the sales associates they hire to help the business generate sales. For that reason, retailers must hire the best people possible for the important role of sales associates. They depend on their sales associates to work to the best of their abilities and follow company rules. It is expected that salespeople are ethical, punctual, willing to learn the business, and helpful to customers. Good people skills and personal grooming habits are imperative in the retail business.

Ethical

Ethics are the rules of behavior that help people make decisions. Salespeople must be ethical and willing to do the right thing for both the customer and retailer. They are often the only person with whom a customer comes in contact. Customers may relate the sales associate with the image of the retailer. In a customer's eyes, an unethical employee may work for an unethical company.

Punctual

Punctuality means being on time. Frequent lateness indicates a negative attitude about the job. Missing work without an excuse and being consistently late is inconsiderate and is not tolerated by employers. Coworkers have to take on the work of employees who are late or absent. It is important for sales associates to show up ready for work every day and on time.

Punctuality is a sign of dependability. **Dependability** shows a person's ability to be reliable and trustworthy. Being dependable means that others can count on a person to do what needs to be done. A dependable person keeps his or her word, is honest, and carries a fair share of the workload.

Exploring Retail Careers

Copywriter

Have you ever wondered how the people who make radio, television, and other live advertisements think of what to say? Actually, they rarely have to think about it. A retailer's image is too important to allow these people to say whatever pops into their heads. The job of a copywriter is to write the advertisements a company uses to promote its goods or services. A good copywriter presents the company's products in the best possible way, encourages people to buy them, and uses a "hook" that helps ensure people will remember the company. Other typical job titles for a copywriter include *advertising copywriter*, *advertising writer*, *advertising associate*, and *web content writer*. The following are some of the tasks that copywriters perform.

- Consult with experts in the company to learn about the product or service to be advertised.
- Write advertising copy for use in written publications, broadcast media, or Internet media.
- Present drafts to clients or company executives.
- Edit copy based on feedback received from the company.
- Work with the company's art department or director to develop visuals.

Copywriters must have an excellent knowledge of the English language and must understand how to use language to persuade people to purchase products and services. They must have good communication skills to get the information they need about the product or service and to present the information in an appealing way. Copywriters should also have a sound understanding of the principles of sales and marketing. Most copywriting jobs require a bachelor degree.

Willing to Learn

Sales associates must constantly learn about new products and procedures. Ongoing training and education is a must in the retail business. Sales associates must attend new product training on a regular basis. They are also required to learn about business systems and procedures as they are updated. It is important that associates understand the products and business in order to respond to customer questions.

Helpful

Sales associates must want to help customers. Just being at work and on the sales floor is not enough. Bad habits and manners, such as talking with coworkers while ignoring customers, are not acceptable. Sales associates are required to help each customer by answering questions, presenting products, and providing good customer service.

Good People Skills

Sales associates must have good people skills. **People skills** include the ability to get along with others, resolve issues with others, and communicate effectively with people. Positive interaction with customers creates an environment of helpfulness and friendliness. Salespeople with poor people skills not only harm the retailer's reputation, but may also jeopardize sales.

Personal Grooming

Many businesses have dress codes that must be followed. A **dress code** is a set of rules or guidelines about the acceptable clothing in a certain place. In the workplace, dress codes may be enforced for safety reasons or to ensure a professional atmosphere. Some businesses expect sales associates to be dressed professionally. Other employers may prefer casual attire or uniforms. It is important to follow the dress code to project the correct image.

Retailers often enforce a dress code or require employees to wear a uniform to make sure everyone's appearance is appropriate.

bikeriderlondon/Shutterstock.com

Employers who require employees to wear a uniform usually provide the uniform clothing or will reimburse employees for purchasing the required uniform clothing.

A neat, clean appearance starts with good personal grooming. Clean, neatly combed hair, clean hands, and trimmed nails are expected. Employees who care about how they look also care about their jobs and want to do their best. The appearance of each sales associate is the first thing a customer sees when being approached. Grooming and dress typically reflect the retailer's image.

Role of Sales Associates

There are many tasks required of sales associates that may not be directly related to selling. Retail sales associates are involved in both selling and nonselling tasks.

Selling Tasks

Selling tasks are duties performed by sales associates when they are in direct contact with customers. One of the most important selling tasks is answering product questions in an effort to persuade the customer to make a purchase. However, all interaction with customers is considered a part of selling tasks. For example, ringing up a sale at the cash register and handling merchandise returns are selling tasks. Each of these interactions can influence purchases today or in the future.

Cash Sales

A cash transaction is a purchase for which a customer pays with cash. The sales associate must understand how to use the cash register to record the sale. Typically, the cost of each item is entered into the cash register or computer. If there are multiple items, the amount for each item is added together. The register automatically calculates sales tax on the sales total. The amount of the sales total plus tax is displayed on the register.

The following is the formula to calculate sales tax for a cash transaction.

$$\text{sales total} \times \text{sales tax rate} = \text{sales tax}$$

$$\text{sales total} + \text{sales tax} = \text{total sale amount}$$

For example, a grocery store customer bought a can of beans for $1.28, a package of rice for $3.95, and a half pound of tomatoes for $1.77. The sales total is $7. The grocery store is in a city with a 3 percent sales tax on food. The total amount of the sale with tax is $7.21.

$$\$7 \text{ (sales total)} \times 3\% \text{ (sales tax rate)} = \$0.21 \text{ (sales tax)}$$

$$\$7 \text{ (sales total)} + \$0.21 \text{ (sales tax)} = \$7.21 \text{ (total sale amount)}$$

To complete the cash sale, the sales associate enters the amount of cash given by the customer into the register. The amount of change is calculated, and the associate gives the customer the difference between the sale price and cash given.

The following procedure is one suggested method for counting change.

1. Place the cash from the customer on, rather than in, the cash drawer until the transaction is complete.
2. After the amount received is entered, remove the amount of change indicated by the register from the cash drawer.
3. Count the change aloud to the customer. Start with the largest denomination.
4. Give the customer the change.
5. Place the cash from the top of the cash drawer inside the drawer.

A check is also considered a cash transaction. Sales associates should know the store policy for accepting customer checks. Most stores require some form of identification from a person to pay by check. Photo identification is generally requested. Sales associates should be knowledgeable about any other check acceptance guidelines the retailer has in place.

Credit and Debit Card Sales

A **credit card transaction** is a purchase for which the customer pays with a credit card. Credit cards are issued by many major department stores and chain businesses. Credit cards are also issued by banks and can be used at most retail locations and sites. Visa and MasterCard are examples of bank-issued credit cards.

A **debit card transaction** is a purchase for which the customer uses a bank card to transfer money from a bank account to the retailer to pay for the merchandise. The funds must be in the customer's account to pay for the sale.

To record a credit or debit card sale, the initial steps are the same as a cash sale. The item amounts are entered and tax is automatically calculated. Instead of accepting cash, the credit or debit card is swiped. The amount of the purchase is recorded with the financial institution or business that issued the credit or debit card to the customer.

Properly recording sales transactions is one of a sales associate's selling tasks.

stockyimages/Shutterstock.com

High-Pressure Selling

Sales associates working in retail are usually expected to meet established sales quotas. Because of the pressure to meet these sales goals, sales associates may sometimes put pressure on customers to purchase a product or service. High-pressure selling techniques are an unethical practice. Pressuring a customer into a purchase that he or she does not want to make willingly is not only unethical, but could cost the company future business.

Sales Returns and Adjustments

A **sales return** is merchandise brought back to the retailer for a refund or credit. A retailer's return policy is often posted close to the cash register or is printed on the sales receipt. Many retailers require that customers return merchandise within a specific period of time, such as 30 or 45 days. Most stores are happy to make a refund or exchange within the retailer's policy.

To record a sales return, the customer is given full credit for the amount paid. The customer receives the amount for items sold plus sales tax. If the original purchase included items that are not being returned, the sales associate must calculate how much the customer will receive for the return.

The formula used to calculate a cash sale should also be used for returns. For example, a customer originally purchased a backpack for $30 and a binder for $8. The sales total for this purchase was $38. The sales tax applied was 6 percent of the sales total. If the customer decided to return just the binder, the refund amount would be $8.48.

$8 (sales total) × 6% (sales tax rate) = $0.48 (sales tax)

$8 (sales total) + $0.48 (sales tax) = $8.48 (total return amount)

If the original purchase was made using a credit or debit card, the card is swiped and the total return amount is transferred back to the customer's account. If the original purchase was a cash sale, the total return amount is given to the customer in cash.

An **adjustment** is a discount on the purchase price of an item given to a customer by the retailer. An adjustment is usually given when the merchandise purchased is damaged or defective. An adjustment can be a specific dollar amount or percentage off the original price of an item. To find the final purchase price of an item after an adjustment, use the following formula.

regular price − amount of adjustment = final purchase price

Nonselling Tasks

Nonselling tasks are duties performed by sales associates while not in direct contact with customers. One common nonselling duty is keeping the sales floor neat and in order. Sales associates are often responsible for returning stray items to their proper place and keeping fitting rooms tidy. These tasks can be time consuming. However, it is important to enhance the store's appearance when not working with a customer.

Another nonselling responsibility is restocking supplies, such as pens, register tape, and shopping bags at the checkout area. Making customers aware of happenings in the store is also helpful. Something as simple as placing an "out of stock" sign on the sales floor can make the difference between a happy customer and a frustrated one.

Shopping should be made as easy as possible when customers enter the store. This can be done by making sure products are stocked and organized by color, size, style, or other criteria. Sales associates should always note when merchandise is low or out so that stock can be replenished. They may physically replace the merchandise from stock or inform the manager that stock is running low.

Checkpoint 10.1

1. What is personal selling?
2. Give some examples of a retailer's expectations of its sales associates.
3. Why is it important for sales associates to have good people skills?
4. What is the formula used to calculate the total sale amount of a purchase?
5. What are some important nonselling tasks performed by sales associates?

Build Your Vocabulary

As you progress through this course, develop a personal glossary of retailing terms and add it to your portfolio. This will help you build your vocabulary and prepare you for a career. Write a definition for each of the following terms, and add it to your personal retailing glossary.

personal selling	cash transaction
punctuality	credit card transaction
dependability	debit card transaction
people skills	sales return
dress code	adjustment
selling tasks	nonselling task

Section 10.2 Retail Sales Process

Objectives

After completing this section, you will be able to:
- **Describe** the tasks involved in the pre-approach.
- **Explain** the steps of the sales process.
- **Discuss** how to learn from lost sales.

Key Terms

pre-approach
feature-benefit selling
customer relationship
   management
   (CRM) system
referral
sales process
approach
social greeting

service greeting
merchandise greeting
AIDA
feature
benefit
substitute selling
upsell
buying signal
suggestion selling

Web Connect

The Internet is a good resource for gathering sales information about a product. Research two cars that you would be interested in purchasing. After reading the details, consider how a sales associate might add to your shopping experience. Make a list of all of the questions you would ask a salesperson before making your purchase.

Critical Thinking

Consider your own shopping experiences in which you interacted with a salesperson and made a purchase. Describe what was said and done that persuaded you to make the purchase.

Pre-Approach

A sales associate does not just go on the sales floor and begin to sell. There is much preparation necessary before customers enter the store. The **pre-approach** includes all of the tasks sales associates complete before coming in contact with customers. This begins with many of the nonselling tasks that need to be conducted each day, such as straightening displays. These activities may take place during slow traffic periods or after the store is closed. Pre-approach also includes product training and managing customer relationships.

Product Training

Product training is necessary so that sales associates are knowledgeable about products they sell. Sales associates gain product knowledge in many ways. *Product knowledge* is being familiar with products so they can be presented effectively. Some retailers conduct formal training for their sales team. During this training, the features and benefits approach to selling is usually taught. **Feature-benefit selling** is the method of showing the major selling features of the product and how they can benefit the customer. This is also known as *solution selling*. Formal training may be conducted by the retailer or by a vendor of the product.

Informal sales training happens every day. Product knowledge may be shared by coworkers when talking during a lunch break or when business is slow. Customers may provide personal knowledge about a product during a conversation with a sales associate. Another way to learn informally is to read product tags, manuals, or other information that may accompany a product. Conducting a demonstration of a product is an excellent way to learn firsthand about selling features. Sales associates should always be learning about the products they sell.

Sales associates gain product knowledge during both formal and informal product training.

Monkey Business Images/Shutterstock.com

Customer Relationships

Retail sales usually take place in a store or online. Businesses do not simply send out marketing messages and wait for customers to shop. Many successful retailers actively try to identify potential customers and give each of them a personal reason to shop at the retailer's store.

Many businesses use a customer relationship management system. A **customer relationship management (CRM) system** is software that is used to track contact information and other data for current and potential customers. Customer data may include names, e-mail addresses, phone numbers, birthdays, past purchases, buying preferences, and even names of family members. With this information, personal messages can be sent to customers to urge them to visit and shop. Birthday cards can be sent to customers, as well as messages of appreciation for their loyalty. All of these activities make a customer feel appreciated and help to build a relationship with the retailer.

Social Media

Using #Hashtags on Twitter

The *hashtag* symbol (#) can help a retail business optimize tweets. Twitter converts any word or URL with a hashtag in front of it into a searchable term. For example, when promoting a new product offering called GreenTote, #GreenTote should be included in every tweet. This will create a searchable stream of relevant tweets about that product. Anyone searching Twitter for a topic related to that product can find all tweets containing the hashtagged word in a single location. This is a way to identify potential Twitter followers for that business. The retailer can connect with non-followers that have conducted the search to turn them into followers. In addition, long-standing hashtagged terms relating to the business can become part of that stream of tweets.

Some retail businesses may ask satisfied customers for **referrals**, or the names of other people who might buy the retailer's products. Once trust in a retailer has been established, many customers are happy to refer their friends and family to the store, and possibly to a particular salesperson. These referrals can be entered in the CRM system as potential customers.

Sales Process

Once a customer enters a store, the sales process begins. The **sales process** is a series of steps that sales associates take to help customers make satisfying buying decisions. There are generally six steps in the sales process.
1. Approach the customer.
2. Determine the customer's needs.
3. Present the product or service.
4. Handle objections.
5. Close the sale.
6. Follow up after the sale.

Approach the Customer

When a customer enters a store, the sales associate makes an approach. The **approach** is the first in-person contact a sales associate makes with a potential customer. The sales approach is also known as the *greeting*. The purpose of the greeting is to engage the customer in conversation. To be effective, the greeting should be friendly and the sales associate should make eye contact with the customer. The sales associate should communicate clearly and focus his or her attention on the person who has entered the store.

It is important that sales associates not be overly aggressive or pushy. If a customer resists the approach, the sales associate should be friendly and try again in a few minutes. The purpose of the greeting is merely to engage the customer in conversation.

There are three general types of greetings typically used in retail: social, service, and merchandise greetings.

Social Greeting

A social greeting acknowledges the customer's presence in the store. Simple greetings, such as "Hello" or "Welcome to our store," are examples of a social greeting. The sales associate should greet the customer with a genuine smile and sense of sincerity. Customers expect to be greeted. If they are not greeted, they may feel ignored. If the sales associate knows the customer, it is acceptable to call the person by name. The person should be recognized as a repeat customer and thanked for returning to the store.

Sometimes, a simple but pleasant "Hello," or other social greeting, is not enough to engage a customer. Additional conversation may be necessary, such as a comment on traffic or the weather. However, these comments should only be made when the weather or traffic is good. Research shows that comments about bad weather or heavy traffic can put customers in a less enthusiastic mood. An alternative is to engage customers by commenting on something personal. For example, the sales associate might compliment the customer on what they are wearing or ask how the day is going for them.

Service Greeting

A service greeting is one that immediately offers assistance to the customer. A common service greeting is, "May I help you?" This greeting may be useful if the customer knows that he or she needs assistance. In a store or department where products are technical or complex, this greeting may be especially helpful.

However, asking a simple question like "May I help you?" may get a response of "No, thanks." Many customers prefer to browse the store on their own, and approach a sales associate only if assistance is needed. If a service greeting is used, it is best to use an open-ended question or one that requires more than a one-word response. This type of greeting is more likely to engage the customer in conversation. For example, an open-ended service greeting might be, "What may I help you find today?"

Merchandise Greeting

A merchandise greeting is used when a sales associate approaches a customer with a comment about a product or in-store event, such as, "We just received a shipment of the latest smartphones with new features. They have a new motion-activated keyboard." This approach works best when the sales associate already has an idea of what the customer is looking for.

Determine Needs

Some customers may prefer a few minutes of small talk to warm up to the sales associate. However, it is important to determine the customer's needs and wants as early in the sales process as possible. A sales associate cannot be helpful until he or she knows what the customer needs or wants.

Customers go through a four-stage *buying process* before making a purchase. One buying process model is called AIDA, as shown in Figure 10-1. AIDA stands for attention, interest, desire, and action.

- *Attention.* Capture the customer's attention immediately.
- *Interest.* Get the customer's interest by showing something that appeals to his or her buying motives.
- *Desire.* Convince the customer that this product is what he or she needs or desires.
- *Action.* Persuade the customer to take action and purchase the product.

Customers have motives for buying. *Rational buying motives* are based on reason. *Emotional buying motives* are based on feelings. Sometimes both motives are combined when making a purchase. The sales associate may determine a customer's motives by observation, questioning, and listening.

Observation

Ideally, customers are greeted when they enter a store. However, this may not always be possible. Business may be brisk and too many customers may enter at once for a personal greeting to be delivered immediately. In some situations, customers may resist an initial greeting. These situations provide a new opportunity—observation.

Figure 10-1 AIDA is a model that describes the four stages of the buying process.

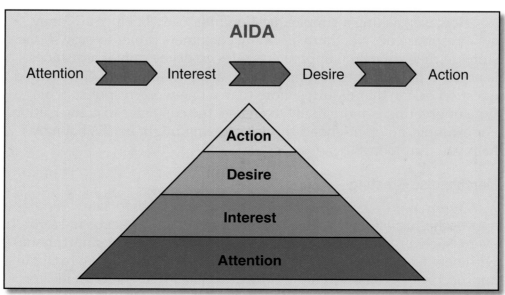

Observing the behavior of a customer can reveal many things. If a customer goes to a specific department or section of the store, this may indicate the type of product needed. If a customer picks up an item, the sales associate may have an idea of the specific product needed. If a person is moving quickly through the store, time may be important. When a customer looks at price tags, this may signal that price is a factor. The more observation that can be done, the better prepared a sales associate can be to assist the customer.

Questioning

Once the customer is greeted, or re-greeted, and is willing to engage in conversation, the sales associate can determine the customer's needs by asking questions. Open-ended questions are often best to encourage the customer to provide more information. Questions should address who, what, when, where, and why, as they relate to the customer's needs. Much can be learned from a questioning session.

Clarifying questions are very important in the process. Customers know their needs and sometimes oversimplify their answers. Statements like, "If I understand you correctly…" can help the sales associate better understand the customer's needs.

Once engaged in conversation, questions should be refined. Each question may lead to an additional question. The goal is to fully understand the customer's needs. If the needs are simple, only a few questions may be required. More complex or expensive purchases may require more questions.

Sales associates should not bombard customers with questions. This may make customers feel like they are being grilled. Personal questions such as, "What is your income?" or "What size do you wear?" are inappropriate. Allow the conversation to lead to that information, if needed.

Listening

In addition to questioning, listening is an important skill for a sales associate. *Listening* combines hearing words and evaluating them for their true meaning. Questions are pointless if the listener does not truly hear the response. Listening may provide answers to questions about the customer's needs that were not even asked.

Often, customers do not completely know or realize their needs. They may recognize a problem to be solved, but do not know what solutions exist. For example, someone shopping for a new desk lamp may comment, "Before mine broke, I always had to move it to the opposite side of the desk because it was so bright. I'm very sensitive to light." From this comment, the sales associate might recommend a desk lamp with a three-way switch for different levels of brightness. The customer may not have been aware that a three-way switch was an option to fulfill the need. Once this information is learned, the sales associate can solve the customer's problem, as well as replace the broken desk lamp.

Present the Product or Service

The presentation of a product or service is an important step in the sales process. This is the opportunity to create desire and show how a product will fulfill the customer's needs. Once customers have entered the store, successful selling requires that the steps in the sales process be followed. Personal selling is an example of an *informal presentation*.

Select the Product

Once customer needs are identified, products can be selected to present. Product knowledge gained from training can help sales associates select appropriate products. Ideally, only one product at a time should be shown in order to keep the customer's attention. Showing more than two or three products at a time may cause confusion. If a customer is not interested in a product, the sales associate should listen to the reasons and select a more suitable product that fits the need.

This may be a good opportunity to address some of the personal questions that were not addressed earlier. For example, if the sales associate is not sure how much the customer wants to spend, he or she should start by presenting a medium-priced product. The customer will indicate if more or fewer features are desired. Adequate questioning will continually refine the selection process.

It is important to get customers engaged in the presentation. Allowing them to touch, handle, and try the product will help in the decision-making process. The more they can experience what the product is like, the more likely they are to purchase it.

A sales demonstration is an effective way to engage customers.

dotshock/Shutterstock.com

Conducting a sales demonstration is an effective way to engage customers. A *sales demonstration* is when the sales associate shows the performance of a product. Product knowledge gained from training gives a sales associate the information he or she needs to conduct a sales demonstration.

For businesses that offer a service, a sales demonstration may be different. For example, if a retailer offers personal shopping as a service, sales associates would use their knowledge of the service and describe what the customer would receive, such as a personal consultation and all of the elements that are included.

Retail sales demonstrations are generally informal. However, there are times when a *formal presentation* is needed. For example, the training provided to sales associates on a new product is a formal presentation. There are occasions when a group of customers gather together to learn about a product or service. For these situations, a formal presentation may be the best approach to share product knowledge.

Formal presentations typically take place in front of a group of people. A slide show may be used for formal presentations. The slide show can include visuals such as charts, illustrations, or photos. Handouts that summarize the information presented may be distributed to the audience. The information in Figure 10-2 outlines steps for making a formal presentation.

Many of the same guidelines for personal selling are followed in a formal presentation. Remember that being prepared creates confidence.

Identify Features and Benefits

Customers understand features, but they buy benefits. A **feature** is a physical characteristic of a product. A **benefit** is how a product feature fulfills a need. The benefits of a product answer the question,

Guidelines for Creating a Formal Sales Presentation

1. Identify the product or purpose.
2. Analyze the audience and who will be in attendance.
3. Determine how much time is available.
4. Gather information.
5. Create a features and benefits list.
6. Prepare the content.
7. Create the slides.
8. Create the handouts.

Goodheart-Willcox Publisher

Figure 10-2 Use these guidelines to develop a formal sales presentation that will be delivered to a group.

"What will the product do for me?" An example of features and benefits is shown in Figure 10-3.

Effective sales processes include stating the feature, then explaining what the benefit is for the customer. For example, a *feature* of a television may be that it is high definition. The *benefit* to the customer is that high definition provides a clearer picture than standard definition. Features are intended to inform, while benefits are intended to persuade.

Substitute Sell

If a particular item is not available, it is acceptable to substitute sell. **Substitute selling** is when a different product is offered that still meets the customer's needs. There is often a variety of products that will meet a customer's needs. This selling technique does *not* mean that a sales associate should convince someone to buy a product that does not fulfill the need simply because it is available. Substitute selling requires the sales associate to help the customer understand that the alternate product will equally fulfill his or her need.

Upsell

To **upsell** a product is to suggest a product of higher quality or quantity, normally at a higher price. Upselling requires the sales associate to focus on additional features and benefits of the higher quality products. The customer must be convinced that the additional benefits provide a good value, which makes the purchase worth the extra cost. Simply pointing out that money can be saved per unit by buying more is an example of upselling. This is a common method of increasing sales.

Features and Benefits	
Product: Sunglasses	
Feature	**Benefit**
Ninety-nine percent ultraviolet blockage	Protects your eyes from sun damage
Polarized	Prevents glare
Titanium frames	Strong and lightweight
Spring hinges	Can be bent without breaking

Goodheart-Willcox Publisher

Figure 10-3 Features are physical characteristics of a product. Benefits describe how the product will fulfill a need.

Handle Objections

Once the product has been presented, customers may express *objections*, or reasons why they are not prepared to make a purchase. An objection may be a concern regarding a feature of the product, such as the price or quality. It may also mean that there are still unresolved questions, and more information is needed before the purchase is made. An objection is not necessarily a rejection of the product.

An objection cannot be addressed without fully understanding it. To address an objection, the sales associate should restate it. Often, such questions result in the customer providing more information. Once the reason for not buying is expressed, another opportunity is presented to directly manage concerns. This may be done by restating the features and benefits, the retailer's policies, or other factors that may influence the purchase.

Empathy and concern should be shown for a customer's objections. There are times when people do not express the real reason for not making a purchase. For example, a customer may not say that he or she cannot afford an item. Only through empathy and continued conversation can the true objection be uncovered. Having genuine concern for a customer's objections helps to build trust and confidence. This trust can build relationships and future sales, even if the immediate sale is not completed.

Close the Sale

The most important step of the sales process is closing the sale. It is important to ask the customer to make the purchase.

A key to closing the sale is knowing when to ask for the sale. During a product or service presentation, customers often exhibit **buying signals**, or clues that they are ready to buy. The customer may be direct and state that they are ready to buy. Or, they may be subtle, such as a nod of the head in agreement during the presentation. There may also be verbal clues during the conversation, such as, "That necklace would look great with my new dress." When customers start to plan how to use a product, they are picturing themselves owning it. This is a powerful buying signal.

There are several ways to close a sale, but it is essential to be *assumptive*, or to assume that the customer wants the product. Using questions such as, "Would you like to pay by cash or credit?" or "Are you available for delivery on Monday at six o'clock in the evening?" assume the customer wants to buy. Once a relationship has been developed, being assumptive makes it harder for the customer to say no.

Another important key in closing a sale is to know when to stop. Once a customer has agreed to make a purchase, the product presentation should stop. Unless there are additional questions, continuing to push the features and benefits of a product can cause frustration.

Once the sale is closed, the sales associate may offer related products that the customer had not considered. **Suggestion selling** is offering items that work with the product just purchased. For example, a sales associate who just sold a new tablet might offer screen protectors, a case, or insurance on the tablet. Most customers appreciate sales associates who suggest products that enhance their purchase.

Follow Up After the Sale

The last step of the sale is follow up. *Follow up* often means making sure the transaction is properly recorded as a cash or credit sale. If the customer is taking the product out of the store, it should be carefully wrapped in a bag or box. If the product is being delivered, all the details for the time and place of delivery should be verified and accurate. Sales associates should assure customers that they made the right purchase, and that the product will satisfy their need or want. Saying "Thank you" and "We look forward to future business" is a way to finalize the transaction.

For expensive purchases or specialty store sales, follow up often extends beyond the customer's in-store visit. Sales associates may make contact with customers to ensure that everything occurred as promised. This type of genuine concern gives the sales associate an opportunity to quickly correct anything that did not go right following the sale. Personal attention can reduce returns, and is an opportunity to continue building a relationship with the customer.

The most important step of the sales process is closing the sale.

Once items have been delivered and the customer is satisfied, many sales associates send thank you cards. This not only shows appreciation for the purchase, but it helps to continue building the relationship. This may lead to future sales or referrals.

Lost Sales

No one closes every sales attempt. Even sales professionals who perfectly execute the sales process do not close every sale. Lost sales may happen for a variety of reasons—not asking enough questions, presenting the wrong product, or a customer who is not ready to buy. Realizing this is an important part of a career in sales.

A key to becoming a sales professional is learning from each sales opportunity, whether the sale is closed or not. Reflecting on what went well and what did not is part of the process. Talking about presentations with other sales professionals, managers, or trainers is a good way to learn. Asking others how they might have handled the same situation helps develop sales strategies for use with future customers. Asking others to watch as you sell and give feedback is also helpful. Having a positive attitude and always trying to improve is an important part of being a successful sales associate.

Checkpoint 10.2

1. Explain the pre-approach to selling.
2. How do retailers use customer relationship management systems?
3. Identify the six steps in the sales process.
4. Explain three ways that sales associates determine a customer's needs.
5. What steps can a sales associate take to learn from a lost sale?

Build Your Vocabulary

As you progress through this course, develop a personal glossary of retailing terms and add it to your portfolio. This will help you build your vocabulary and prepare you for a career. Write a definition for each of the following terms, and add it to your personal retailing glossary.

pre-approach	merchandise greeting
feature-benefit selling	AIDA
customer relationship management (CRM) system	feature
	benefit
referral	substitute selling
sales process	upsell
approach	buying signal
social greeting	suggestion selling
service greeting	

Chapter Summary

Section 10.1 Personal Selling

- Retail is all about sales. To make the actual sales happen, sales associates are needed to provide the personal selling function.
- Retailers expect the sales associates they hire to help the business generate sales. A retailer depends on its sales associates to do their best and follow company rules.
- Retail sales associates are involved in both selling and nonselling tasks. Selling tasks include persuading customers to make purchases and recording sales transactions. Nonselling tasks include enhancing the store's appearance to make shopping as easy as possible for the customer.

Section 10.2 Retail Sales Process

- The pre-approach includes all of the tasks sales associates complete before coming in contact with customers. This includes learning about products in both formal and informal ways, and establishing and managing customer relationships.
- Once the customer enters the store, the sales process begins. There are generally six steps of the sales process. The steps in the sales process include the approach, determining needs, presenting the product, handling objections, closing the sale, and following up.
- Lost sales may happen for a variety of reasons. Sales associates can learn from each sales opportunity, whether the sale is closed or not.

Review Your Knowledge

1. Why is it important for retailers to hire the best possible sales associates?
2. Why is it important for sales associates to display ethical behavior with customers?
3. What is the formula used to calculate a cash sale, including sales tax?
4. Explain the process of recording a credit card sale.
5. Identify some of the nonselling tasks that sales associates may be required to perform.
6. Describe the importance of product training for sales associates.
7. Identify and describe the three types of greetings sales associates use in the sales process.
8. When questioning customers to determine their needs, what types of questions should a sales associate ask?
9. Explain the difference between the features and the benefits of a product.
10. What is suggestion selling? In which step of the sales process would a sales associate try suggestion selling?

Apply Your Knowledge

1. Demonstrating product knowledge can be illustrated through presentation of features and benefits of the product or service being offered. Your store has just added e-book readers to its merchandise selection. As the sales manager, you need to prepare a demonstration for the sales team to get them up to speed on the new product. Select an e-book reader with which you are familiar. Make a list of at least five features and benefits of the product that would be included in a sales demonstration.

2. The store manager has asked you to make a formal sales presentation on the new e-book reader to the members of a book club. Using the formal presentation guidelines in this chapter, create your presentation. Use your list of product features and benefits from the previous activity. You may create visuals or handouts as part of the presentation.

3. When delivering a formal sales presentation, being prepared creates confidence. Deliver the sales presentation for the e-book reader to your class. Ask your audience for feedback on your presentation. What did you do well? What could you do to improve?

4. A customer purchased five T-shirts from a retailer. Two of the T-shirts were $12.50 each, and the other three were priced at $10.75, $9.95, and $15.00. The sales tax rate is 7 percent. The customer paid for the T-shirts with a $100 bill. First, calculate the sales total of the purchase. Next, calculate the sales tax and total amount due. Ask a classmate to act as the customer. Explain the formulas you used to calculate the amount due. Next, count aloud the change that the customer should receive from this purchase. Ask your classmate to rate your efficiency.

5. Demonstrating the importance of a service to potential customers is similar to presenting information about product. The first step is to be confident and know the service that you are selling. The next step is to create the features and benefits chart for the service, similar to the features and benefits chart created to sell a product. The manager of a bike shop wants to promote the shop's bike maintenance service. Conduct research on the Internet to gather information about the features and benefits of such a service. Create a features and benefits chart. Present a sales demonstration to your class and allow time at the end for questions. Did your service knowledge provide you with enough information to answer the questions you received?

6. A sales return is merchandise brought back to the retailer for a refund or credit. A video game store has a return policy that gives customers a full refund if the game is returned within 30 days of the purchase date. A customer that purchased four games with cash would like to return just one of the games. The price of the game being returned is $40. The sales tax is 8 percent. Describe to a classmate how a sales associate should complete this return of a cash sale using a cash register. Show the formulas used to calculate the returned amount.

7. Conduct an Internet search on a customer relationship management (CRM) system that could be used in retail. Make a list of the important information that should be retained about customers. Prepare a presentation to persuade the manager of a small retail business to purchase the CRM system.

8. In this chapter, you learned about the three greetings that can be used to approach a customer. Imagine you work in an electronics store. Develop two different statements you would use to approach a customer for each greeting type: social greeting, service greeting, and merchandise greeting. Practice using each with another student in your class.

9. A customer is interested in purchasing a model train set for $125. However, one of the pieces is slightly damaged. The customer still would like to purchase the set. The store manager agrees to adjust the price on the damaged product by $12.50. Manually calculate the adjustment. Describe to a classmate how a sales associate should complete this adjustment using a cash register. Show the formula used to calculate the adjusted amount.

10. A retail sales manager is looking to hire a sales associate for an auto parts store. Make a list of personal requirements that you think are needed for this position. In addition, write two paragraphs describing the selling and nonselling tasks required of the position.

Check Your Retail IQ

Now that you have finished the chapter, see what you learned about retail by taking the chapter posttest. If you do not have a smartphone, visit the G-W Learning companion website.

G-W Learning mobile site: www.m.g-wlearning.com

G-W Learning companion website: www.g-wlearning.com/marketing/

College and Career Readiness

Career Ready Practices As a student, you will be planning for your future career. Describe a plan on how to align career paths to your personal goals.

Reading Active reading involves concentration. Select an article about the cost of a college education. Identify the explicit details, as well as the author's main idea for the article. Draw conclusions about the author's purpose for writing the article. Retell or summarize this information to your classmates.

Writing Rhetoric is the study of writing or speaking as a way of communicating information or persuading someone. List the three common categories of rhetorical devices. Provide an example from each category.

Teamwork

Working with your team, debate the importance of product knowledge as opposed to understanding the sales process. Which is more important to a sales associate's success? Make a list of the pros and cons of each aspect.

College and Career Portfolio

Activities

You have collected documents that show your skills and talents. However, some skills and talents are not effectively represented using only documents. Do you have a special talent in an area such as art, music, or design? Have you taken part in volunteer activities? Create a video to showcase your talents and activities. For example, if you are an artist, create a video that shows your completed works. If you are a musician, create a video with segments from your performances. If you have taken part in a volunteer or service activity, create a video that tells viewers about it. Suppose you volunteer with a group that helps repair the homes of elderly homeowners. The video could show scenes from the worksites and comments from the residents. (Be sure you have permission to include other people in your video.)

1. Place the video file in an appropriate subfolder for your e-portfolio.
2. Print a few screen shots from the video. Create a document that describes the video. State that the video will be made available upon request, or identify where it can be viewed online. Place the information in the container for your print portfolio.

◇DECA Coach

Create Introductions and Conclusions

Judges sit through a lot of back-to-back presentations and see a lot of presentations. Therefore, it is important that you do something to set yourself apart from your competitors. It is important that the judges remember who you are after you have finished the event and the next presenter steps up to the table. Keeping that in mind, the most memorable portions of your presentation are your introduction and your conclusion.

Most of your competition will walk to the judges' table, make an introduction, and then begin to explain his or her concept. A better way is to develop a creative introduction that includes some simple theatrics. After walking into the judge's booth and setting up your materials, try doing a 30 second skit, announcement, or other type of introduction. This will not only take your judges by surprise, but you will create a memorable moment for both you and them. For example, you might walk in and pretend that you are a news reporter opening the daily news. That news just so happens to be the problem you are about to solve with your presentation. After a brief intro, you can then introduce yourself to the judges. At the end of your presentation, you can pretend to be that reporter with another news report, identifying how the problem has been solved with your solution.

The key to creativity is to keep it brief, to address the problem in the introduction, and then to address the solution in your closing. Be creative and help the judges remember who you are.

Visit www.deca.org to learn more information about DECA.

G-W Learning Mobile Site

Visit the G-W Learning mobile site to complete the chapter pretest and posttest, and to practice vocabulary using e-flash cards. If you do not have a smartphone, visit the G-W Learning companion website to access these features.

G-W Learning mobile site: www.m.g-wlearning.com

G-W Learning companion website: www.g-wlearning.com/marketing/

Chapter 11
Customer Service Strategies

Retailers use customer service to set themselves apart from the competition. By having well-trained personnel and a wide array of customer services, a retailer can increase sales and ensure customer satisfaction.

Good customer service is important for both brick-and-mortar stores and e-tailers. In both environments, the service provided should encourage customers to return for future purchases. Retailers with a storefront have the benefit of face-to-face interaction with customers. However, e-tailers can also provide high-quality customer service. Call centers allow customer calls to be taken in real time and provide personal phone contact. In addition, online support can provide help at the customer's convenience. Immediate response to customer needs equals total customer satisfaction.

Case Study

Nordstrom

Founded in 1901, Nordstrom is one of few department store retailers to survive for more than 100 years. In a market where many retailers compete to provide the lowest prices to customers, Nordstrom does not. The secret to Nordstrom's success is its reputation for excellent customer service. The retailer believes that a word-of-mouth reputation exceeds anything that could be gained from traditional advertising.

While many companies claim to put customers first, Nordstrom actually does. The retailer takes customer service risks that other retailers do not, such as its liberal return policy. Nordstrom's return policy is that there is no return policy. There is no time limit, receipt, or other required paperwork to return Nordstrom merchandise.

Customer service stories abound for Nordstrom, such as a woman who returned shoes after twenty years with no questions or hassle. Think about how many times she told that story to others. This type of word-of-mouth advertising only cost the retailer the price of one pair of shoes. Nordstrom provides unforgettable customer service, which has created great loyalty among its customers.

College and Career Readiness

Reading Prep

Before reading this chapter, write the main heading for each section on a piece of paper. Leave space under each heading. As you read the chapter, write three main points you learned related to each heading.

Check Your Retail IQ

Before you begin the chapter, see what you already know about retail by taking the chapter pretest. If you do not have a smartphone, visit the G-W Learning companion website.

G-W Learning mobile site: www.m.g-wlearning.com
G-W Learning companion website: www.g-wlearning.com/marketing/

Sections

11.1 In-Store Customer Service

11.2 E-tail Customer Service

Section 11.1 In-Store Customer Service

Objectives

After completing this section, you will be able to:
- **Discuss** the roles of personnel and services as elements of in-store customer service.
- **Explain** why retailers extend credit to customers.

Key Terms

customer service
attitude
gift registry
personal shopper

corporate gift service
consumer credit
installment loan
customer loyalty

Web Connect

Using the Internet, search for *retail customer service jobs*. What are some of the qualifications that you see in your search results? List the five most common qualifications expected of customer service representatives. Explain why you think each is important.

Critical Thinking

Retailers must pay fees for accepting credit cards as a form of payment, yet most retailers accept major credit cards. What are some of the reasons you think retailers are willing to pay these additional costs? List your reasons.

Personal Customer Service

Customer service in an important strategy that retailers use to set themselves apart from the competition. **Customer service** is the ability to provide a product or service in the way it has been promised. Retailers who do this better than expected are said to provide *good customer service*. Retailers who fall short of customers' expectations are said to provide *poor customer service*.

Sales associates and other employees interact with customers each time they enter a retail store. Good customer service does not happen by chance, yet it is easy to create. With trained personnel and a good mix of service offerings, a retailer can meet the expectations of most customers. While some businesses fall short in this area, others go above and beyond the expectations of their customers. This distinction is one way that customers develop their image of the retailer.

Personnel

The first person to come in contact with a customer is often the sales associate. However, the sales associate may not be the only person who provides service. Customers may also interact with cashiers or clerks, managers, or customer service representatives. All of these retail employees are responsible for providing service to the customer.

The first step in providing good customer service is to ensure that the employees who come in contact with customers share the retailer's values. Management is responsible for putting in place employee standards that help create customer satisfaction.

Employees who provide customer service are held to the same standards established for sales associates:

- appropriate grooming and dress
- willingness to help customers
- ethical behavior
- good people skills

Common customer service values most retail employees share include product knowledge, company knowledge, attitude, communication skills, and tolerance.

Product Knowledge

Product knowledge is necessary for employees to be confident in their customer service skills. New employees generally receive training before they come in contact with customers. The training may include product demonstrations or other methods that show the features and benefits of the product. Ongoing training is typical for experienced employees. As a retailer adds new products, training is needed to learn new features and benefits. Sometimes a vendor will train a retailer's employees on new products.

Thorough product training allows both sales associates and customer service employees to be confident in their product knowledge.

Pressmaster/Shutterstock.com

Company Knowledge

Company policies and procedures are also covered in employee training. Most companies have a policy handbook that helps employees understand information that is important to both the retailer and the customer. This handbook is typically updated on a regular basis so all employees are aware of any procedures that change over time.

An example of important company policies and procedures is how the retailer addresses a product warranty. A *warranty* is a written document that states the quality of a product with a promise to correct specific problems that might occur. Warranties are generally provided by the product manufacturer. However, the sales associate or customer service representative must be able to explain to the customer how the warranty works. For example, a computer might be under warranty for one year. If the computer should need repair, the customer needs to know where to go for service. Most warranties require that a product be sent back to the manufacturer. It is important that retail employees understand the retailer's policy on warranties so they can accurately convey this information to customers and avoid any misunderstandings.

FYI

A manufacturer's product warranty often expires after a certain period of time, such as two years after purchase. Retailers often sell *extended warranties* that offer product repair or replacement services beyond the manufacturer's warranty.

Exploring Retail Careers

Customer Service Representative

No matter how hard a company works to provide quality products, customers may have questions or complaints. How these are handled can determine the success or failure of the company. Customer service representatives (CSR) serve as a direct point of contact for customers. They provide information, answer questions, and resolve complaints for customers. Some CSRs may even take orders and process returns. They may communicate with customers face to face, on the telephone, through fax, or over the Internet. Other typical job titles for a customer service representative include *customer service specialist*, *hub associate*, *account service representative*, and *call center representative*. The following are some examples of tasks that customer service representatives perform:

- provide product information for customers
- keep records of customer comments, complaints, and the actions taken to resolve issues
- solve customer problems by exchanging merchandise, offering a refund, or making adjustments
- refer unresolved issues to the appropriate departments for further research
- check to make sure customer problems were solved and the customers are satisfied

People skills are important for customer service professionals. They must be active listeners, giving their full attention to what the customer is saying. They also must speak well and persuasively. Critical thinking skills are also necessary to provide solutions for the customer. Most customer service positions require a high school diploma and up to a year of on-the-job training.

Some retailers offer a guarantee on products sold. A *guarantee* is a promise that a product has a certain quality or will perform in a specific way. A guarantee is similar to a warranty, but is generally not a written document. Some businesses guarantee services or products. If the service or product does not meet the guarantee, the retailer typically refunds the amount the customer paid. Retail employees must understand what the retailer will or will not provide under a guarantee statement.

Attitude

Attitude is the way a person looks at the world and responds to events. Employees and managers are expected to have a positive attitude on the job. In fact, managers set the tone for the attitude that employees demonstrate.

Customers want to interact with employees who make them feel positive. Employees who show enthusiasm help to provide a good atmosphere for the customer. It is a well-known fact that an employee's positive attitude can result in customer satisfaction. A positive attitude can also increase the chance of making a sale. However, this does not mean that the employee needs to be pushy and obnoxious.

A positive, optimistic attitude is reflected in a genuine smile.

Tyler Olson/Shutterstock.com

Positive employee attitude is reflected in a genuine smile. Believing in the product can make customers feel confident in the product and the company. An optimistic attitude shows the customer that the employee is there to help solve a problem or find a product.

Communication Skills

Communication skills are crucial in the workplace. Each customer contact creates a first impression of the employee and the business. First and foremost, employees must listen to the customer. It is important to use active listening skills so the customer's needs can be understood.

Once the customer's need has been identified, appropriate grammar and vocabulary should be used to communicate. An appropriate tone of speech should be used and empathy applied when necessary.

Retail Ethics

Truth in Advertising

Even though it may be tempting to focus on sales hype or other persuasive techniques to convey a message to customers, retailers must keep the information honest. Embellishing the message about a product or service and intentionally misrepresenting it is unethical and may be illegal. The facts should be communicated in a positive manner to create interest or demand for the product or service. Truth-in-advertising laws must be followed.

Tolerance

You may have heard the expression, "The customer is always right." This phrase does not actually mean the customer actually is *always* right. Rather, it means that an employee always *pretends* the customer is right, even if he or she believes the customer to be wrong.

When working in retail, employees will encounter customers who have a conflict or complaint. Knowing the best way to deal with a conflict is critical in providing good customer service. The concept behind "the customer is always right" is to keep the customer happy, even if he or she may be wrong. A happy customer may return to the store another day; an unhappy one probably will not.

Customer Services

Customer service is not limited to just interaction with an individual customer. Customer service has a broader meaning that includes specific *services* provided by a retailer. Some services are fairly standard and are expected by all customers. For example, customers expect that a store's return policy will make it easy to return an item.

Special services, outside the realm of the expected ones, can be expensive for a retailer to provide. The cost for these services may be passed on to the customer or must be absorbed by the retailer. Therefore, lower-priced stores do not offer as many services as higher-priced stores because they cannot, or do not want to, increase their selling prices. The following are some examples of special services retailers may offer their customers.

- *Alterations.* Many retailers offer the opportunity to have products altered or customized for the customer's individual needs.

- *Returns.* Customers expect to be able to return products that do not meet their expectations. Easy returns can make customers confident to purchase, knowing they can return items if necessary.

- *Delivery and installation.* Delivery for large or heavy items is important to customers. Assembly or installation services are also appreciated.

- *Extended store hours.* Retailers know that some customers want to shop at times outside of normal retail hours. Many businesses are open twenty-four hours a day, seven days a week.

- *Child care.* Some retailers offer child care services so that customers can shop without interruption. This benefits the retailer because it has the customer's full attention. The service benefits the customer because it allows free time to ask questions and make shopping decisions.

- *Gift registry.* A **gift registry** is an in-store *wish list* compiled by the customer. Potential gift-givers can see which items the person would like to receive. This service makes the gift-giver's job easier and greatly increases the chances that the gift-giver will make a purchase at the store.

In-store alterations is an example of a special service offered by some higher-priced retailers.

bikeriderlondon/Shutterstock.com

- *Personal shopper.* Some high-end retailers offer personal shoppers. A **personal shopper**, or *store consultant*, helps select products for individual customers based on the customer's preferences. The customer and the personal shopper meet to review the personal shopper's choices and make a purchase selection.

- *Corporate gift services.* Like a personal shopper, a **corporate gift service** connects a store consultant with a corporate representative to make gift selections. The store consultant helps the representative decide on gifts for clients, for retirements and promotions, and other corporate gift-giving occasions.

Market research can help the retailer decide which customer services are appropriate for the store. Retailers collect primary data to see what their existing customers want. They also use data to learn what the competition is doing. Employees' opinions can also be an important source of information.

Credit

Credit is often considered to be a customer service strategy. *Credit* is an agreement or contract to receive goods or services before actually paying for them. **Consumer credit** is credit given to individual consumers by a retail business.

One form of consumer credit issued by businesses is a proprietary credit card. A *proprietary credit card* is a credit card that may only be used at the stores that issued them. Examples are Macy's and Dillard's department store credit cards.

Some businesses extend credit by accepting debit or credit cards from their customers. It may be preferable to accept bank cards, such as MasterCard and Visa. An advantage of accepting these cards is that the responsibility for collecting the money owed for the purchase is transferred to the financial institution instead of the retailer. The bank pays the retailer for the customer's purchase and collects the money owed for the sale directly from the customer. This service is not free for the retailer or the customer. For the retailer, the bank adds a service charge to each purchase made using one of its debit or credit cards. For the customer, he or she must pay monthly interest on unpaid balances to the bank that issued the credit card.

If the retailer sells big-ticket items, like appliances or cars, consumer credit may be offered in the form of an installment loan. An **installment loan** is a loan paid in regular payments, or *installments*, usually with interest, until the loan is paid in full. Installment loans may be *secured loans*. Secured loans require *collateral*, or assets pledged to guarantee that the loan will be repaid. If the loan is not repaid, the asset can be taken by the creditor. The asset is then sold to cover the cost of the loan. Most retail loans are not secured, but do require that the customer qualify for credit.

Extending credit to customers is beneficial to retailers. The most obvious benefit is the generation of sales. Offering credit through proprietary credit cards, bank credit cards, and installment loans can create a steady income for the retail business. Research shows that people will often spend more money when using credit than if they are paying cash.

Another benefit of extending credit to customers is building customer loyalty. **Customer loyalty** is the continued and regular patronage of a business, even when there are other places to purchase the same or similar products. There are many reasons that customers are loyal to a business, but one of the reasons is convenience. Customers appreciate using a bank card for in-store and Internet purchases. Businesses that offer customers credit tend to generate more sales than if they only accepted cash.

A car loan is an example of an installment loan, with monthly payments.

wavebreakmedia/Shutterstock.com

Checkpoint 11.1

1. Explain the concept of customer service. Describe good customer service and poor customer service.
2. Describe the common customer service values that all employees should share.
3. Explain what the phrase "The customer is always right" really means in the retail business.
4. What is the difference between a proprietary credit card and a bank-issued debit or credit card?
5. How is extending credit to customers beneficial to retailers?

Build Your Vocabulary

As you progress through this course, develop a personal glossary of retailing terms and add it to your portfolio. This will help you build your vocabulary and prepare you for a career. Write a definition for each of the following terms, and add it to your personal retail glossary.

customer service	corporate gift service
attitude	consumer credit
gift registry	installment loan
personal shopper	customer loyalty

Section 11.2 E-tail Customer Service

Objectives

After completing this section, you will be able to:
- **Explain** the importance of e-tail customer support.
- **Describe** training considerations for off-site customer service personnel.
- **Summarize** the importance of ergonomics in the workplace.

Key Terms

call center
customer service
  flowchart
asynchronous service

automated e-mail
synchronous service
ergonomics

Web Connect

Visit two e-tailers online and research the ways each e-tailer provides customer service. Which one do you think is better? Compare and contrast the services offered to address customer inquiries.

Critical Thinking

Customer support for e-tail purchases may be different from customer support for in-store purchases. Make a list of the differences that you think exist between the two types of customer support. How are the processes similar? How are they different?

E-tail Customer Support

Customer service is key in attracting and retaining customers. Retailers make great efforts to provide the best customer service possible. If a retailer has a brick-and-mortar store, it is easy to offer face-to-face service to customers who come in to make a purchase, return an item, or visit for any other reason.

When a retailer sells products over the Internet, face-to-face customer contact is not possible. E-tailers must create a customer service strategy that supports their Internet customers who do not come in to a store. E-tail customer service is usually provided through a call center or online support.

Call Centers

Call centers are remote facilities that are typically operated by third-party customer support organizations. These centers represent the e-tail business so that the caller believes he or she is talking directly to the retailer. Call center representatives are trained to answer customer questions and concerns in a similar fashion as on-site customer service personnel. However, because call center representatives do not have the benefit of direct customer or employee communication, they depend heavily on customer service flowcharts. A **customer service flowchart** is a graphic map of possible questions and answers that directs the call center representative through the process of questioning the customer. An example of a flowchart is shown in Figure 11-1. Based on the customer's responses, the representative knows what questions to ask next. Eventually, the customer's problem is narrowed down and a solution can be provided.

Online Support

The Internet provides many opportunities to provide customer service for brick-and-mortar retailers, as well as e-tailers. As shown in Figure 11-2, online service can be categorized in two ways: asynchronous and synchronous.

Asynchronous Service

Asynchronous means "not in real time." **Asynchronous service** is when a customer asks a question and the response comes at a later time or date. For example, a customer sends an e-mail to a retailer asking a question. The e-mail is expected to get a timely reply, but the customer does not expect to get a response in real time or right away.

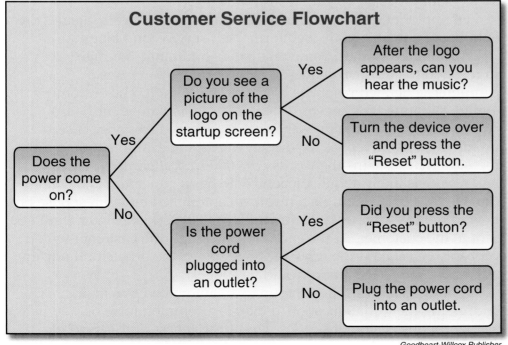

Figure 11-1 A typical customer service flowchart presents a series of questions to help find the solution to a customer's problem.

Goodheart-Willcox Publisher

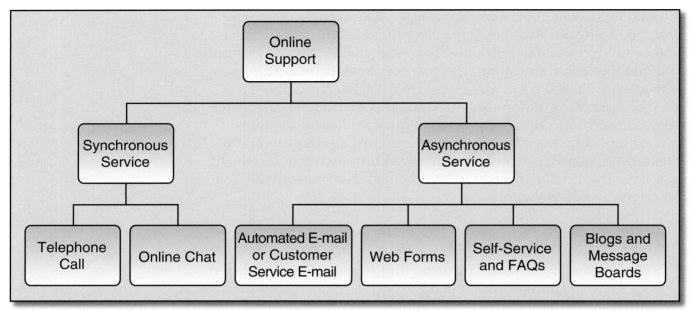

Goodheart-Willcox Publisher

Figure 11-2 Methods of online support can be either synchronous or asynchronous.

While most forms of online service still require human interaction, retailers do not have to staff an office during specified hours to provide this type of online service. Asynchronous service allows retailers to schedule off-hours for their employees. With this type of online service, retailers may even allow employees to work from home. Smaller companies with fewer service needs may even use existing employees to respond to service requests while business is slow. Online customer service representatives do not need telephone skills, but they must be good communicators.

Examples of asynchronous online customer service strategies are automated e-mail, e-mail, web forms, self-service, and blogs.

Automated E-mail. Some retailers use automated e-mail to respond to customer requests. An automated e-mail is a computer-generated response to a customer e-mail. The customer's e-mail is scanned for keywords. Once keywords are identified, a computer replies to the message with a prepared response based on the most likely replies for the keywords. For example, an e-mail message that contains the words *HP 1000 Deskjet printer*, *paper jam*, and *remove* is likely about someone who has a paper jam and cannot remove the obstruction. As a result, an automated e-mail response on how to remove a paper jam from an HP 1000 Deskjet printer would be sent to the customer. At the end of the message, the customer would probably be asked if the reply message solved the problem. If not, an alternative contact solution would be suggested.

E-mail. Whether following up to an automated e-mail or addressing the initial question, e-mail is a common form of asynchronous customer service. The effectiveness of this type of service depends on the customer's ability to clearly state the nature of the problem. Since customers are not always clear in what they are looking for, multiple e-mails may be required.

Web Forms. Many retailers provide web forms for customers to complete online, including contact information and a description of the issue. Similar to e-mail, service representatives may respond to the question at a later time.

Self-Service. By offering a robust website, self-help can be offered to customers without direct retailer contact. Online product manuals, frequently asked questions (FAQs), and other resources enable customers to try solving a problem on their own. Self-service resources can reduce customer frustration when a customer service representative is not available the moment the customer needs information. Another benefit is that customers can find this information online 24/7, making it very convenient.

Of course, an unhappy customer may want an immediate answer, and a deferred solution may make the customer angry. Companies using self-service resources should also consider other options to provide customers help when needed.

Blogs and Message Boards. Many retailers have message boards that encourage customers to post their concerns or issues for others to read. The hope is that another customer with a similar problem will respond to the issue. Customers helping customers can be a very efficient way to provide customer service.

Retailers commonly schedule a customer service representative to scan the message boards and provide additional responses to customer issues. This ensures that the customer receives an answer if a reply has not been posted. It also makes certain that the customer is given correct information.

Social Media

Blogs

Web logs, or *blogs* as they are known, are online journals. Blogs typically provide information or news about subjects that the owner of the site chooses to discuss. The entries are posted in a reverse chronological order so that the line of communication is easy to follow. Blogs are a great opportunity for a business to direct customer attention to the specific products and services that they carry. A blog is often used to share information with current or potential customers. There is no maximum word count, so blogs allow customers and retailers to communicate freely. Many people follow blogs to look for product information or learn more about a company. Blogs are indexed on search engines, which is great for retail business promotion. As an added benefit, the messages are permanently posted, so readers can go back at any time to review past information.

A live person on the telephone is often the most efficient way to assist a customer.

Diego Cervo/Shutterstock.com

Synchronous Service

Synchronous service is when a customer asks a question and receives a response in real time. For customers who want immediate assistance, real time service meets their needs. The most common real-time forms of customer service are telephone calls and online chat sessions.

Telephone Call. The simplest type of real-time customer service is a telephone call. It is also the most costly for retailers. Having a staff of representatives to answer calls takes manpower, equipment, and space.

Phone calls can be the most efficient way to help a customer. Many customers like the personal service of talking with someone when they need assistance. However, if the wait time is too long or the hours of service are limited, the customer may become frustrated.

Online Chat. Online chat enables the customer to communicate with a customer service representative in real time. Customer questions are answered using an instant message format. If the issue is a complaint, chat can hopefully resolve it and make the customer happy. If the customer asks a sales question, real-time chat can close a sale the same way an on-site sale would be closed.

E-tail Customer Service Personnel

Personnel for off-site customer service are as important as customer service employees on site. In some ways, e-tail customer service representatives require more rigid training than those in a brick-and-mortar store because they cannot interact with the customer face-to-face. On-site personnel have the opportunity to ask questions to clarify the situation. However, e-tail customers can easily get frustrated and leave the online conversation. It is much easier for an e-tail customer to give up than it is with face-to-face dialog.

Product Knowledge

Product knowledge is critical for customer service employees who do not have face-to-face contact with customers. Employees working in a store receive informal training from their peers, as well as customers. Being in the store allows them to touch and see the product. E-tail customer service employees may not be able to experience the product first hand. Product training must be thorough for these employees. E-tail customer service representatives may depend heavily on reference materials, such as product manuals and customer service flowcharts, to respond to questions.

Communication Skills

Customer service representatives who talk to customers on the phone must understand how to convey interest and concern. Not everyone has a natural telephone voice, so some employees may need special training.

Positive employee actions result in customer satisfaction. An example of a positive action is *listening*. Active listening is fully participating in and processing what the customer is saying. Since the customer's face cannot be seen over the phone, it is important to focus on what is being said. Full attention must be given to the purpose of the call. Above all, telephone representatives must learn to be calm regardless of how frustrated the customer may get.

Providing information in a way the customer can understand is an action that results in customer satisfaction. On each call, the customer service representative should *pace* the amount of information that is conveyed. It is important to listen to the customer and react accordingly. The pace must be slow enough for the customer to understand the information, yet fast enough to keep the call moving.

E-tail customer service representatives must use appropriate grammar and vocabulary when communicating with customers. When answering e-mail, the message should be proper and professional. Most e-mail questions have a prepared response that can be copied and pasted into an e-mail message. However, if the response must be drafted for an individual, professionalism is critical.

Workplace Ergonomics

Ergonomics is the science concerned with designing and arranging things people use so they can interact efficiently and safely. For employees in a call center, ergonomics can include designing workstations to fit the unique needs of the worker and the equipment used. Call center employees spend long periods of time working on computers. They may be at risk for eyestrain, back discomfort, and hand and wrist problems. Applying the principles of ergonomics results in a comfortable, efficient, and safer working environment.

There are many types of accessories available that may make a computer workstation more ergonomic, including wrist rests, specially designed chairs, and back supports. In addition, Figure 11-3 identifies a few things the employee can do to create a comfortable environment and help prevent injury or strain to the body.

Eyes

Position the computer monitor to minimize glare from overhead lights, windows, and other light sources. Reduce light intensity by turning off some lights or closing blinds and shades. Images on the computer screen should be seen clearly without glare.

Move the monitor so that it is 18 to 30 inches away from your eyes—this is about the distance of an arm's length. To help reduce eyestrain, employees should look away from the monitor every 15 to 20 minutes and focus on an object at least 20 feet away for one to two minutes.

Wrists and Arms

Forearms should be parallel to the floor. Employees should periodically stretch their arms, wrists, and shoulders. It is suggested that an ergonomic keyboard and mouse be used. This type of keyboard keeps the wrists in a normal body position. An ergonomic mouse fits the hand more comfortably.

Figure 11-3 Ergonomic workstations help prevent muscle pain, eyestrain, and headaches caused by improper placement of monitors, desks, and chairs.

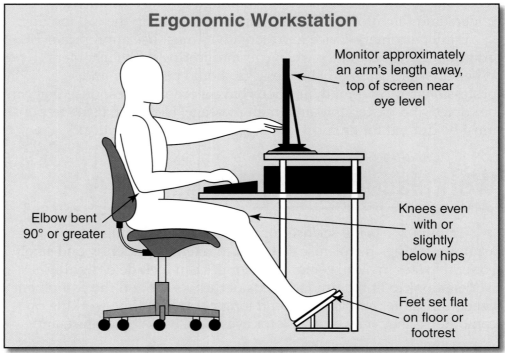

Ergonomic Workstation

Monitor approximately an arm's length away, top of screen near eye level

Elbow bent 90° or greater

Knees even with or slightly below hips

Feet set flat on floor or footrest

Goodheart-Willcox Publisher

Neck and Back

The computer monitor should be adjusted so that the employee's head is level, not leaning forward or back. The top of the screen should be near the line of sight. A chair that is comfortable and provides good back support is necessary for call center employees. The chair should be adjustable and provide armrests.

Good posture is important. Employees should try standing up, stretching, and walking every hour. This also reduces neck and back strain.

Legs

Thighs should be parallel to the ground. Feet should be flat on the floor or a footrest should be used. When taking a break, walk around to stretch the muscles and promote circulation.

Checkpoint 11.2

1. Describe the unique aspects of e-tail customer service.
2. Compare and contrast asynchronous services with synchronous services.
3. Explain the difference in how e-tail customer service representatives acquire product knowledge compared to on-site employees.
4. Why is it important to have ergonomic workstations for employees in a call center?
5. Which areas of the body are at risk for injury from sitting at a desk using a computer for long periods of time?

Build Your Vocabulary

As you progress through this course, develop a personal glossary of retailing terms and add it to your portfolio. This will help you build your vocabulary and prepare you for a career. Write a definition for each of the following terms, and add it to your personal retailing glossary.

call center	automated e-mail
customer service flowchart	synchronous service
asynchronous service	ergonomics

Chapter Summary

Section 11.1 In-Store Customer Service

- In-store customer service is in an important strategy that retailers use to set themselves apart from the competition. A retailer with well-trained personnel and a good mix of service offerings can meet the expectations of most customers.
- Offering credit is often considered a customer service strategy. Extending credit to customers generates sales and builds customer loyalty.

Section 11.2 E-tail Customer Service

- E-tail customer service is as important as customer service in a brick-and-mortar store. However, e-tailers must overcome the lack of face-to-face customer interaction. By providing call centers to take live calls in addition to online support resources, e-tail customers can have a positive experience when they need help.
- E-tail customer service representatives must have thorough product training to be helpful to customers. These employees may depend heavily on reference materials, such as product manuals and customer service flowcharts, to respond to customer questions.
- Call center employees spend long periods of time working on computers. Applying the principles of ergonomics results in a comfortable, efficient, and safer working environment.

Review Your Knowledge

1. What is the first step in providing good customer service?
2. Explain why lower-priced stores may offer fewer services than higher-priced stores.
3. How does a retailer benefit by accepting credit and debit cards issued by banks or other financial institutions?
4. What is the purpose of collateral in a secured loan?
5. Explain how extending credit builds customer loyalty.
6. How do customer service flowcharts assist call center employees?
7. What types of self-help resources can e-tailers offer their customers?
8. Why is active listening important in a live call taken in a call center?
9. Explain the importance of pacing the amount of information passed on to a customer during a customer service call.
10. How can an employee prevent injuries to the wrists and arms through proper ergonomics?

Apply Your Knowledge

1. Customer services are important to everyone who goes into a retail store or shops online. As a customer, which services provided by a retailer are most important to you? List three services and describe the reasons you chose each.
2. Every retail employee is responsible for providing customer service. Describe employee actions that result in customer satisfaction. Give examples from your own experiences as a customer or as an employee.

3. Employee attitudes can influence a customer's decision to return to a business or never enter the store again. Describe employee attitudes that result in customer satisfaction. Give examples from your own experiences as a customer or as an employee.

4. Personal shopping is a service often provided by higher-end businesses. Using the Internet, locate an e-tail store that provides a personal shopper service. Explain how the e-tailer provides this service and why it is beneficial for both the e-tailer and the customer.

5. Many large retailers offer proprietary credit cards. Research a retailer that offers a proprietary credit card, such as Target or Kohl's. What incentives does the retailer offer to customers who apply for a credit card? Why do you think incentives are offered?

6. E-tailers, like brick-and-mortar stores, must offer quality customer service. Create a chart with two columns. In column one, list types of e-tail customer services. In column two, list types of brick-and-mortar customer services. Highlight the services that are common between the two. What was unique about the e-tail customer services that differentiated them from the brick-and-mortar services?

7. Imagine that you are an e-tail customer who has received a defective product in an online order. You need to contact the company to resolve the issue. Choose the method of making contact that you prefer: asynchronous or synchronous. Explain your choice.

8. Customer service flowcharts are often used by customer service representatives who do not interact with customers face-to-face. Create your own customer service flowchart to address a problem that might be presented to a customer service representative of an electronics retailer. Choose a product and identify a question or problem that a customer might ask a retailer's customer service department. Create a graphic map of possible questions and answers.

9. Customer service representatives must be able to give accurate, timely, and polite answers to questions. Send a question about a product or service to one of your favorite e-tailers using online chat or e-mail. You might ask about a product's availability, where it is manufactured, or about shipping and delivery information. Evaluate the response you receive from customer service. Did you receive a timely response? Did the customer service representative have the product knowledge you required? Was appropriate grammar and vocabulary used in the response? Share your experience with the class.

10. It is important that management is aware of ergonomics in the workplace. Why is it important to implement ergonomics in the workplace? How do ergonomic workstations prevent potential employee injuries?

Check Your Retail IQ

Now that you have finished the chapter, see what you learned about retail by taking the chapter posttest. If you do not have a smartphone, visit the G-W Learning companion website.

G-W Learning mobile site: www.m.g-wlearning.com

G-W Learning companion website: www.g-wlearning.com/marketing/

College and Career Readiness

Career Ready Practices Most people use technology on a daily basis. Using technology in the workplace can help employees be more productive than working without it. In other instances, technology can be a distraction. Create a list of five types of technology and how people can use each to be more productive in the workplace.

Reading Read a magazine, newspaper, or online article about e-tailing. Analyze the article and distinguish the facts from the author's opinions on the subject. Write a report in which you draw conclusions about the importance of e-tail. Use visuals, such as graphs, to share specific evidence from the article with your class to support your understanding of the topic.

Research Using the Internet, research information on ergonomic solutions. What are some products available to businesses that need to create an ergonomic work environment? Write a short paper on your findings. Cite all of your sources.

Teamwork

Working with your team, debate the effectiveness of synchronous and asynchronous customer service. Share your personal customer service experiences. Which type of customer service does your team favor? If the entire group does not agree on which type is more effective, try to persuade each other with facts and experiences.

College and Career Portfolio

Diversity Skills

As part of a job interview, you may be asked about your travels or other experiences with people from other cultures. Companies are interested in this information for good reasons. Many companies serve customers from a variety of geographic locations and cultures. Some companies have offices or factories in more than one region or country. You may need to work closely with people from diverse cultures. Your job may involve travel to company locations or vendors in different countries. Employees that speak more than one language and have traveled, studied, or worked in other countries can be valuable assets. These employees can help the company understand the needs and wants of its diverse customers. They may also be better able to communicate and get along with coworkers.

1. Identify travel or other educational experiences that helped you learn about another culture, such as foreign languages studied.
2. Write a paragraph that describes the experience. Explain how the information you learned might help you better understand customers or coworkers from this culture.
3. Save the document file in your e-portfolio. Place a printed copy in the container for your print portfolio.

◇DECA Coach

Read the Guidelines

Each of DECA's prepared events come with a set of guidelines. It is critical that you read the guidelines thoroughly before you begin. The guidelines not only describe the event itself, but also provide each subtopic that you must address. You will learn the judging criteria, how long your presentation and written manual should be, and how to avoid penalty points.

It is a good idea to appoint one person on your team to be responsible for the guidelines. This person should not only read them thoroughly, but should also review them regularly. He or she can then check each part of the written manual as it is completed, examining it for possible violations of the rules.

Before prepared events go to competition, they will be checked by judges for violations to the guidelines. Simple mistakes, like single-spaced text, hand-written page numbers, and using inexact wording for headings and subheadings, can cost you penalty points. One page of the guideline is titled "DECA Competitive Event Checklist." This is a list of possible penalties that judges may assess to your written manual. Penalty points can make the difference between winning and losing. Make sure that at least one person on your team becomes an expert on the rules.

Visit www.deca.org to learn more information about DECA.

G-W Learning Mobile Site

Visit the G-W Learning mobile site to complete the chapter pretest and posttest, and to practice vocabulary using e-flash cards. If you do not have a smartphone, visit the G-W Learning companion website to access these features.

G-W Learning mobile site: www.m.g-wlearning.com

G-W Learning companion website: www.g-wlearning.com/marketing/

Unit 5
Visual Merchandising

Introduction

For retailers, a store's image is an opportunity to stand out from the competition and be memorable to customers. Store image is enhanced by visual merchandising. Visual merchandising for a brick-and-mortar store involves signage, product placement, displays, lighting, colors, store layout, and much more. Retailers know that visual merchandising impacts how a customer shops.

Principles of visual merchandising also apply to e-tail websites. Customers should be able to find what they are looking for and make a purchase with ease. The look, organization, and interactivity of an e-tail site are planned in the web-design process. Successful e-tailers build reputable and trusted websites that attract and keep customers.

Green Retail

Digital Coupons

Many retailers offer convenient digital coupons that are sent directly to customers through e-mail, text messages, or QR codes. Digital coupons eliminate the costs and resources involved in printing and physically distributing coupons. The customer simply presents the coupon or QR code on the screen of their smartphone or tablet device to receive the discount or special offer. Some retail customer loyalty cards can store digital coupons. When the customer's loyalty card is scanned, any digital coupons loaded onto the card are applied to the total purchase. Digital coupons are a convenient and green solution that benefits both customers and retailers.

260

Jeff Whyte/Shutterstock.com

In This Unit

Chapter 12
In-Store Merchandising

For retailers, the store image is a customer's first impression of both the retailer and the merchandise. Visual merchandising is used to project the store image and create interest in the merchandise. The storefront, store layout, store interior, and interior displays are all elements of visual merchandising that a retailer can control and customize.

When creating visual displays, the goal is to grab the customer's attention and encourage a purchase. Many display components are used to create a display. But, the most important component of any visual presentation is the merchandise. A visual merchandiser knows how to apply many design principles to develop an appealing and effective merchandise display.

Case Study

Disney Stores

Every toy store has aisle after aisle stocked with almost every toy a child would want. This used to describe Disney Stores, as well. However, Disney drastically changed its approach to visual merchandising in its retail stores. Rather than having shelves stacked with toys, Disney redecorated and reorganized. Now, the toys may not even be the first thing customers notice. The goal in revising the visual merchandising plan was to make the retail stores more like the Disney theme parks—a place where children want to visit and stay longer. Disney hoped this philosophy would also lead to more sales.

Once inside a Disney Store, there are many interactive experiences for children and adults. For example, some stores have mini theaters where customers can watch clips of Disney movies. Others may have karaoke contests or chats via satellite with Disney Channel stars. At the push of a button, 13-foot-high Lucite trees rise, crackle, project video fireworks, and even diffuse a scent through the store. Disney understands that visual presentation can lead to a better shopping experience for customers.

College and Career Readiness

Reading Prep

As you read this chapter, determine the point of view or purpose of the author. What aspects of the text help to establish this purpose or point of view?

Check Your Retail IQ

Before you begin the chapter, see what you already know about retail by taking the chapter pretest. If you do not have a smartphone, visit the G-W Learning companion website.

G-W Learning mobile site: www.m.g-wlearning.com
G-W Learning companion website: www.g-wlearning.com/marketing/

Sections

12.1   Store Image
12.2   Creating Displays

zhu difeng/Shutterstock.com

Section 12.1 Store Image

Objectives

After completing this section, you will be able to:
- **Describe** the importance of creating a store image.
- **Explain** the meaning of visual merchandising.
- **List** each of the four elements of visual merchandising.

Key Terms

store image
brand
visual merchandising
visual merchandiser
storefront

marquee
store layout
display
point-of-purchase
   display

Web Connect

Visit the website of one of your favorite brands. How does the website contribute to the image of the brand? Describe the visual elements, organization, and other characteristics of the website that support the brand's image.

Critical Thinking

What retailers come to mind when you hear the phrase *store image*? Do some stores have a stronger image than others? How do stores with a distinct store image leave a lasting impression on customers?

Creating the Store Image

You never get a second chance to make a first impression. For retailers, the store image is an opportunity to stand out from the competition and be remembered by the customer. **Store image** is the perception or impression created by the location, design, and décor of a retail business. Store image can best be described as the "personality" of a store.

Studies indicate that a retailer has only seconds to capture the attention of passing customers. A store's image attracts individuals who identify themselves in distinct ways, such as youthful and trendy or mature and sophisticated. The way a store looks and feels must convey this image to the target customers.

A **brand** is the name, term, or design that consumers relate to a business or product. While manufacturers build brands for their products, individual retailers and e-tailers create distinctive brands for their businesses. A business's brand sets it apart from its competition and is a key element of the store image. The elements of branding a retailer may use include the name, slogan, and symbols associated with the business.

Retailers try to develop a brand that best represents the products or services they offer. A retailer's name, the graphics and colors used in the store and on promotional materials, and any store slogans support the retailer's brand in a visible and memorable way.

Visual Merchandising

Store image is enhanced by visual merchandising. **Visual merchandising** is the process of creating floor plans and displays to attract customer attention and encourage purchases. Physical elements are used to project an image to the customer that creates interest. Customers are more likely to buy attractive and interesting merchandise. When done well, visual merchandising increases retail sales.

A **visual merchandiser** is the person in charge of carrying out the plan to develop the store image. In small retail operations, the tasks of visual merchandising are usually carried out by the owner or a store employee. Department stores generally have the largest visual merchandising budget and have a dedicated person or team for the job. Chain stores may have a central team that oversees all the stores to ensure a consistent store image.

Visual merchandising involves signage, product placement, displays, lighting, colors, store layout, and much more. Retailers know that visual merchandising impacts how customers shop. Merchandising can even determine which direction customers walk while in the store.

When you see a display in a store, you might not think much about what went into creating it. However, retailers spend a lot of time making sure that displays grab the attention of their customers. The design and layout of a store play major roles in the success of the store. Retailers must consider how the store looks from the outside, as well as how it looks once a customer enters.

Visual merchandising creatively displays products in a way that draws the attention of and is appealing to customers. Customers are motivated to buy what they see if they can picture themselves using the product. This is often referred to as the *silent salesperson*, as it may influence customers' decisions. Effective visual merchandising sells the merchandise without the help of a sales associate. It can turn a browser into a buyer, increasing the dollar amount of a sale.

Visual Merchandising Elements

There are four elements of visual merchandising:
- storefront
- store layout
- store interior
- interior displays

NRF Tip

Branding increases customer awareness of a business. Effective branding stimulates a reminder or memory about the retailer's product or service in the mind of the customer. The NRF website provides productive branding strategies specific to the retailer's location and target market.

Storefront

A customer's first impression of a retailer is influenced by the exterior of the business. The exterior of a retail business is commonly known as the storefront. The **storefront** is the exterior signs and logos, marquee, display windows, entrances, outdoor lighting, landscaping, and the building itself. All the elements of a storefront represent the brand of the business. The storefront elements help create the exterior image of the retailer.

- Exterior signs and logos help identify the business and also help brand it.

- A **marquee** is an overhanging structure located at the entrance to the store that contains a signboard. It usually displays information that can be changed, such as current sales promotions happening in the store.

- Display windows are an important element of visual merchandising. Windows are used to show merchandise and entice customers to enter the store.

- The entrance, or front door, may influence a customer's decision to enter the store. It should be inviting, easy to locate, and should leave no question whether the store is open for business.

- Outdoor lighting is important to create visual appeal. It is also necessary for the safety of customers and employees.

- Landscaping adds color and makes a business look more inviting. An inviting entrance helps customers feel that they are welcome.

The image of a retailer is supported by storefront elements, such as signage, display windows, displays, and landscaping.

Albert Pego/Shutterstock.com

Store Layout

Store layout is a floor plan that shows how the space in a store is used. Well-designed store layouts consider the customer's needs, as well as how to efficiently use the space. The layout also takes into consideration how many square feet of the store space will actually be used to generate sales for the business.

There are many store layouts a retailer may use, as shown in Figure 12-1. Floor plans are dictated by the type of business and what works best for customers. The following are some floor plan examples.

- A *straight floor plan* aligns the counters or racks in straight lines. This is a simple design that works for almost any retailer.

- A *diagonal floor plan* angles the counters or racks. This design adds interest to the overall look of the store.

- A *loop floor plan* organizes merchandise by function and forces customers through the store. IKEA is an example of a retailer that uses a loop floor plan. Customers start at the beginning of the loop and are guided throughout the store to the registers at the end of the loop.

Within a store layout, there are typically four areas of the business: selling area, sales support area, customer area, storage area.

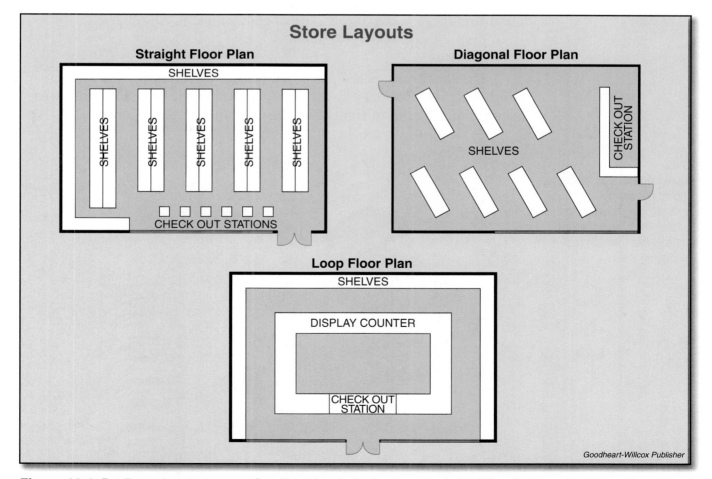

Figure 12-1 Retail store layouts are most often dictated by the business type and what is best for customers.

Selling Area

The *selling area* is the place where merchandise is presented to the customer. This area should maximize the sales per square foot, so the retailer can get the most return for the investment.

Wide aisles for traffic flow are important to people who are shopping. No one wants to feel crowded when in a favorite store.

The selling area should also be organized in a way that discourages shoplifting. Merchandise security is important to the success of a business. Employee and customer safety are also important factors to consider.

Customer Area

Customer areas are places in the store available for customers to use, such as fitting rooms, restrooms, and other comfort features that customers appreciate. These spaces have become popular in retail stores, as they cater to individuals looking for a positive shopping experience.

Sales Support Area

The *sales support area* is the place where employees take breaks, change clothes, and engage in other personal activities. It is important that this space is out of the view of customers.

Storage Area

The *storage area* is the place that houses merchandise, supplies, and other items necessary for the operation of the business. This area should also be out of sight from the customers.

Store fixtures used for displays should not distract attention from the merchandise. In this display, the sunglasses are more visible than the rack displaying them.

Kzenon/Shutterstock.com

Exploring Retail Careers

Visual Merchandiser

The way products are displayed in a store is the result of the work of a visual merchandise manager. A visual merchandise manager builds the image for the store. This person creates displays inside the store as well as for the window displays. Maintaining the look of the store interior and visual environment is part of the job tasks. Budget responsibilities are also part of the duties. Other titles for the position are *visual designer*, *visual merchandise manager*, and *merchandise displayer*. Some examples of tasks that visual merchandise managers perform include:

- develop ideas for designing window displays and signage
- build window displays and create signage to reflect seasons, trends, promotions, and changes in inventory
- arrange furniture, lighting, and other interior features to establish a feeling in the store that meets with the retailer's image
- communicate with sales and marketing to determine what products should be displayed and featured
- create and monitor budgets

Visual merchandise managers must be able to predict customer reactions to displays. They must also analyze customer reactions. A basic understanding of math is necessary to create and maintain budgets. A minimum of a high school diploma is required for the position. Some stores may require a bachelor degree in a related marketing or fashion merchandising field.

Store Interior

Store interior refers to everything on the inside of a store. After customers enter a retail business, they will notice the interior of the store. Attractive paint, fixtures, and lighting are important to the customer shopping experience.

Fixtures and equipment are chosen with the store's image in mind, as well as the merchandise that may be displayed. For example, a store with a high-tech design may use glass and metal.

Everyone has a favorite color. In retail, skillful use of color can motivate customers to buy. Color is essential in attracting attention and creating moods. For example, a restaurant may use a lot of red in its décor because research shows the color red can stimulate hunger.

Lighting is a vital part of store design and the visual presentation of merchandise. Lighting can transform appearances from average to dramatic. It defines a store's image by creating an overall atmosphere and feel for the store. Lighting can be used to entice customers into the store, lead them through selling areas, call attention to specific merchandise, and draw customers through the transaction process by conveying specific moods or enhancing merchandising themes. Effective use of light can dramatically enhance the performance of most retail environments.

Background music plays a role in defining a store's image. For example, many stores that target teenage customers play loud, upbeat music. Conversely, the Disney Store plays Disney songs. Both types of background music help *set the mood* for customers.

Smell also has an impact on the perceived image of a store. Many retailers intentionally use certain scents inside their stores to enhance the store image. For example, citrus scents are said to be energizing, while vanilla is relaxing.

Interior Displays

Displays help sell merchandise and reinforce the store's image. A **display** is a presentation of merchandise designed to attract customers so they will notice and examine the merchandise. Retailers use displays to draw the customer into a store, promote a slow-moving item, announce a sale, or launch a new season.

An *interior display* is located inside a store. There are various types of interior displays that retailers use. Some of the common displays are point-of-purchase display, open display, closed display, architectural display, and kiosks.

- A **point-of-purchase display** is a special display usually found near a cash register where goods are purchased. The displays sometimes hold impulse items, such as magazines.

- An *open display* is a display from which a customer can pick up an item. A clothing rack is an example of an open display.

- A *closed display* is usually a case that can be locked, if needed. Generally, items in a closed display have a high dollar value. The retailer does not want customers to pick up items in this type of display without assistance. A jewelry case is an example of a closed display.

- An *architectural display* is one that shows items in a way that customers can imagine how the items would look in their home. An example is a dining room set with a seasonal centerpiece on the table and place settings arranged, inviting someone to sit down.

- *Kiosks* are very small structures with one or more open sides to display and sell a limited number of goods. They are commonly found in shopping malls and airports.

A *window display* is a display that can be seen from the outside of a store. Both window and interior displays have many elements in common. Both are visual displays that show products and other promotions, such as a table displaying sale items or a wall showing featured products.

Window displays should attract customers' attention and draw them into the store.

littleny/Shutterstock.com

Checkpoint 12.1

1. Why is store image important?
2. Explain the concept of visual merchandising.
3. Name and describe the four elements of visual merchandising.
4. List four of the elements of a storefront.
5. What are the four common areas of a business within a store layout?

Build Your Vocabulary

As you progress through this course, develop a personal glossary of retailing terms and add it to your portfolio. This will help you build your vocabulary and prepare you for a career. Write a definition for each of the following terms, and add it to your retail glossary.

store image	marquee
brand	store layout
visual merchandising	display
visual merchandiser	point-of-purchase display
storefront	

Section 12.2 Creating Displays

Objectives

After completing this section, you will be able to:
- **Differentiate** between display types.
- **Explain** the function of various display components.
- **Identify** the use of design principles in a visual merchandising display.
- **Summarize** the role of centralized visual merchandising.

Key Terms

promotional display
institutional display
prop
balance
symmetrical balance
asymmetrical balance

rhythm
harmony
proportion
centralized visual merchandising

Web Connect

Window displays help sell merchandise for retailers. Use the Internet to research retail window displays. What makes a display attractive to customers?

Critical Thinking

Think about a display you recently saw in a retail store. What made you stop and look at the display? Did the display make you want to purchase the merchandise that was featured?

Display Types

When a display is created to help sell merchandise, it is called a **promotional display**. When a display is created to promote the store image, rather than a product, it is called an **institutional display**. Retailers may create institutional displays that promote charitable events or local organizations, like the American Society for the Prevention of Cruelty to Animals (ASPCA). These displays are not intended to sell merchandise, but to create goodwill with the shopping community. Retailers hope that their support of these events will create loyalty to their brand.

When creating visual displays, the goal is to grab the customer's attention and encourage a purchase. Retailers typically use one of three common display approaches for merchandise: traditional, thematic, and minimalist.

The *traditional approach* to creating a display involves using seasonal themes, holidays, or special events. This is a good way to let the customer know that the next season or holiday merchandise has arrived. Spring themes in February and back-to-school in July are common in grocery stores, as well as large department stores. Using the traditional approach, retailers hope to stimulate sales by inviting customers to shop the new merchandise.

Some merchants keep the same visual concept throughout the year. This is known as a *thematic approach*. This approach can be used to incorporate an element of the store image, such as a color, logo, or mascot, as a centerpiece of the retailer's operations. Retailers must be certain of their thematic concept, because it will likely last a long time. An example of a thematic retailer is Foot Locker, where employees wear sports officials' uniforms.

Some merchandisers design the interior so it ties into the product assortment. However, using the *minimalist approach*, few or no props are used to display merchandise. The merchandise itself must attract customers' attention. Upscale merchants use this approach with stark floors and walls and just a few racks of merchandise. This builds their brand with a certain look, and makes customers feel like they are buying unique products.

Other merchants, such as factory outlets, take a similar approach using minimal props and amenities. These merchants go to the opposite extreme, with concrete floors and a warehouse appearance. Their strategy is to save customers money by not investing in fancy surroundings.

Retail Ethics

Code of Ethics

Most retailers establish a set of ethics that employees must follow. The code of ethics outlines acceptable behavior when interacting with coworkers, suppliers, and customers. Some businesses even post their code of ethics on their websites. As a retail professional, it is important to know the code of ethics for your company so you can make correct decisions on behalf of the company.

Display Components

Display components help define the presentation. These elements can be expensive. The visual merchandiser must establish an inventory system to keep track of each item, either an electronic inventory system, a paper log inventory, or both. Also, it is important to regularly evaluate the display components used to make sure they are meeting the goals. Evaluating the effect of display components is similar to evaluating the results of a sales promotion. The retailer decides if the display was successful in reaching established goals and determines which display components were effective and which can be improved upon.

The most important component of any visual presentation is the merchandise. To be successful, there must be a balance between the merchandise and the elements used to create the display. Elements such as mannequins, props, lighting, color, signage, and graphics are used as enhancements in a display.

Mannequins

Mannequins are used to display clothing or to complement a display. They can be dramatic and artistic. Mannequins that are basic in style and form may cost a few hundred dollars, while more elaborate designs can cost more than a thousand dollars. Retailers select mannequins that are appropriate for their store and budget.

Mannequins are frequently used to display clothing both inside a store and in window displays.

hxdbzxy/Shutterstock.com

Props

Props are objects used in a display to support the theme or to physically support the merchandise. For example, a swimsuit display may include sand and seashells that are not for sale. Creative merchandisers may choose to make props using repurposed pieces or even everyday items. Items like old picture frames, furniture, ladders, musical instruments, and gardening tools can produce an excellent visual impact when used in a display.

Many large department stores, such as Macy's, Saks Fifth Avenue, Nordstrom, and Lord & Taylor, are known for their brilliant animated window displays during holiday seasons. It takes a staff of designers, sculptors, modelers, welders, and craftspeople many months to bring these windows to life. People wait in long lines just to view them. Window displays are a very important form of promotion.

Lighting

Lighting is an essential part of visual presentations. It adds dramatic effects that quickly enhance a routine visual display. Lighting can make products shine and bring colors to life. There are three types of display lighting used: primary lighting, secondary lighting, and atmosphere lighting.

Primary lighting is the overall level of brightness of the store. Outdoor lighting includes 150 watt bulbs used as basic window lighting, marquee lights that brighten the walkways, and lighting for general lobby areas. Inside the store, primary lighting is the lighting that fills the selling floor from overhead lighting fixtures. It provides the bare essentials of store brightness.

Secondary lighting provides store illumination and accent for display areas. Incandescent bulbs are most often used for secondary lighting. They come in a variety of sizes, from strings of tiny lights to full size globe- or reflector-type bulbs. Accent lighting creates visual interest and magically puts products in the customers' sight. It provides change from light to dark, highlights, and shadows to prevent boredom.

Atmosphere lighting is used to play light against shadow to create a distinctive effect on specific displays. Generally, atmosphere lighting uses color filters, spotlights, and backlighting to create dramatic effects. Spotlights are great for merchandise displays. The angle at which a spotlight is directed is very important. Any angle sharper than 45 degrees is likely to momentarily blind customers.

Color

Color can have a dramatic effect on visual presentation and store image. Visual merchandisers are aware of how color can create moods which generate interest and motivate customers to buy. The color wheel in Figure 12-2 is an example of one of the tools designers use to create a visual message or create a store's image. Using the color wheel can help the visual merchandiser choose pleasing and stimulating color arrangements.

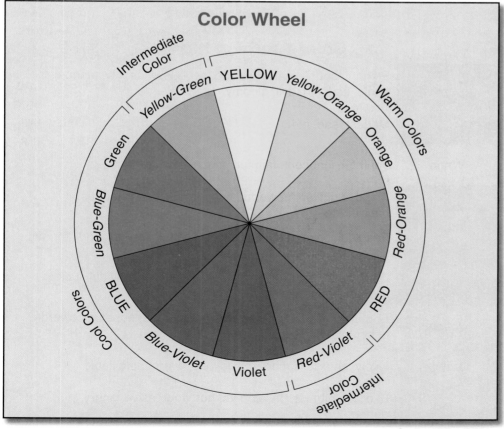

Figure 12-2 A visual merchandiser may use the color wheel to help choose attractive color arrangements.

Everyone is influenced by the colors that surround them. Color can be associated with emotions, special occasions, and genders. Figure 12-3 explains common connections between colors and emotions in US culture. The retailer's challenge is to create a successful color palette that influences its customers in a positive way. The right choice of colors in a display can convert browsers into customers. Therefore, it is vital to choose the right theme with the right colors for a display.

Signage and Graphics

Walk through a mall or past a retail store and you will see a variety of signs and photo enlargements that catch your eye. Signs are important for retail stores because they identify departments, announce special events, and are the first visual support of a store's brand. Signs may be temporary or permanent, used for special events or displays, or used to identify departments and direct traffic. They can take many different forms.

- Hanging signs are perfect to direct customers to the point of purchase.
- Illuminated signs catch the customers' attention.
- Letter display signs allow retailers to change a message and use various fonts and letter sizes.
- Many retailers use photographs to dramatize interior and window displays. Vendors often provide these photographs at little or no cost.

Figure 12-3 The right choice of colors can influence customers' buying decisions.

Colors and Emotions	
Black	Elegant, sophisticated, strong, serious, wise, mysterious, tragic, sad, old, evil, gloomy
Gray	Modest, sad, old
White	Youthful, innocent, faithful, pure, peaceful
Violet	Royal, dignified, powerful, rich, dramatic, mysterious, passionate
Blue	Peaceful, calm, restful, tranquil, truthful, serious, cool, formal, spacious, sad, depressed
Green	Cool, fresh, natural, friendly, pleasant, calm, restful, lucky, envious, immature
Yellow	Bright, sunny, cheerful, warm, prosperous, hopeful, cowardly, deceitful
Orange	Lively, energetic, cheerful, joyous, warm, hospitable
Red	Exciting, vibrant, passionate, hot, aggressive, angry, dangerous

Printed signs and photographs must be specifically designed to meet the retailer's need, and are created using graphic design software. The graphic is then printed on paper, vinyl, cloth, transfer paper, or another appropriate medium to be displayed in a retail store.

More expensive digital graphics, such as video feeds on flat-screens, enhance visual merchandising by targeting customers in certain areas of the store. For example, the video shown to customers waiting at the deli counter of a grocery store may display deli specials and recipes that prompt customers to make additional purchases.

Any of these display components can be used as a background for a display. A physical background can be created using mannequins, props, signs, or video screens. Lighting may be used as a background when it separates the merchandise on display from the surrounding environment. However, the display background should never be more noticeable or interesting than the merchandise on display.

Design Principles

A visual merchandiser must apply many design principles to develop an appealing and effective display that is recognized as *good* visual merchandising. Balance, emphasis, rhythm, harmony, and proportion are the design principles that must be followed to ensure the best results.

Balance

Balance is the way items are placed around an imaginary centerline. To achieve balance, an imaginary line is drawn down the center of the area to be featured. The area might be a window, a platform, or any other space that holds a display. Balance may be either symmetrical or asymmetrical.

Symmetrical balance, also known as *formal balance*, involves the placement of identical items on either side of the imaginary line. For example, if a mannequin is used on one side of the imaginary line, another mannequin is used on the other side.

This window display is an example of symmetrical balance. All of the items are equally placed on both sides of the imaginary centerline.

Northfoto/Shutterstock.com

Asymmetrical balance, also known as *informal balance*, involves the equal distribution of items, but the placement of pieces is not mirrored. The items used to balance each other may be different. For example, if a mannequin is used on one side, a ladder of similar height might be used on the other side.

Social Media

Facebook Pages

With more than 1 billion users, Facebook has become a *must* for most retail businesses. Retail businesses create pages to share their stories and connect with customers and potential customers. Like personal timelines, business pages can be customized by adding apps, posting stories, hosting events, and more. People who like a business page will get its updates in their news feeds.

The best way to use social media is to engage customers. It is important to understand that building a Facebook business page will not automatically drive current or potential customers to the business' website. A business must drive customers to like its Facebook page and interact with it on a regular basis. After customers like the business on Facebook, the retailer must continue to give them reasons to return and tell others about it. Facebook offers analytics to help businesses track how many people visit the page, visitors' demographics, and other important marketing information.

Emphasis

Emphasis means that the focal point of a display should be the merchandise. When the customer sees the display, attention should be drawn to the merchandise. The purpose of any visual presentation is to sell the merchandise, not the props. Color and lighting are used to create emphasis.

Rhythm, Harmony, and Proportion

Rhythm describes when all elements of a display help to move the eye smoothly from one item to another. An example of this is a display where arrows are used to point to products. **Harmony** is when all of the display elements blend to form a unified picture. **Proportion**, or *scale*, refers to the size and space relationship of all the items in a display. The items should fit the space they occupy.

Simplicity is important—less is more. Retailers must know when to stop adding items to a display. If it becomes too cluttered, the message may be lost. Like any other aspect of retailing, creating an attractive display takes skill and trial and error. As merchandise changes, so do the opportunities for visual displays.

Centralized Visual Merchandising

Many specialized chain stores, like Gap and Pottery Barn, use the concept of centralized visual merchandising. **Centralized visual merchandising** is the practice of developing merchandise displays at the company's home office. Typically, window and interior designs are created at the company headquarters by a centralized staff. The sample display is photographed and directions to build the display are written. The individual retail stores use the necessary props, signage, and other elements to construct the display.

Retailers that use centralized visual merchandising want customers to feel familiar with the store layout, no matter which of the chain's stores the customers enter. This practice establishes a uniform look for all store locations and maintains a consistent brand and store image. Using this approach saves money by eliminating the need for professional visual merchandisers at each store location.

Large retail department stores, like Macy's and Nordstrom, may elect to have in-house visual merchandisers or individual design teams within each store. These employees create the ideas and execute the plans for all the displays in their particular store. The designs are not necessarily the same in all of the stores, as the team in each store decides their own merchandising strategy. Having an in-house visual merchandiser allows the retailer to be creative and meet the unique needs of its customers.

Smaller retailers may hire a freelance designer for a specific promotion or particular season. Freelance designers are paid on a fee basis and are not on the retailer's staff. The retailer will maintain the display throughout the promotion or season. Using a freelancer designer gives the retailer flexibility to use the talents of an expert when needed. However, some small retailers decide to create displays on their own, without outside help.

FYI

Freelance is a term used to describe people who earn money by being hired to work on different jobs for short periods of time. They do not have a permanent job with one employer. Freelancers exist in various industries.

Checkpoint 12.2

1. How does a promotional display differ from an institutional display?
2. List the components that are commonly used as enhancements in displays.
3. Why is lighting important when creating a display?
4. Identify and describe the design principles that should be considered when developing a display.
5. Describe how chain stores carry out centralized visual merchandising.

Build Your Vocabulary

As you progress through this course, develop a personal glossary of retailing terms and add it to your portfolio. This will help you build your vocabulary and prepare you for a career. Write a definition for each of the following terms, and add it to your retail glossary.

promotional display	asymmetrical balance
institutional display	rhythm
prop	harmony
balance	proportion
symmetrical balance	centralized visual merchandising

Chapter Summary

Section 12.1 Store Image

- The store image is an opportunity for a retailer to stand out from the competition and be remembered by the customer. A store's image must appeal to the target customers.
- Visual merchandising is the process of creating floor plans and displays to attract customer attention and encourage purchases. Customers are more likely to buy attractive and interesting merchandise.
- The four elements of visual merchandising are the retailer's storefront, store layout, store interior, and interior displays.

Section 12.2 Creating Display

- A *promotional display* is created to help sell merchandise. An *institutional display* is created to promote the store image, rather than a product.
- Elements such as mannequins, props, lighting, color, signage, and graphics are used as enhancements in a display.
- Many design principles are applied to develop an appealing and effective display, including balance, emphasis, rhythm, harmony, and proportion.
- Centralized visual merchandising establishes a uniform look for all store locations and maintains a consistent brand and store image.

Review Your Knowledge

1. How does a store's image attract specific customers? What physical components are used to portray a retailer's image?
2. Explain the use and impact of visual merchandising.
3. List and describe the different types of floor plans.
4. What factors are important to consider in the selling area?
5. Define open and closed displays and give an example of each.
6. What is the *traditional approach* to creating visual displays?
7. Describe the use of props in displays.
8. Identify and describe the three types of lighting used in a display.
9. Why are signs important for retail stores?
10. Differentiate between symmetrical and asymmetrical balance.

Apply Your Knowledge

1. Recall the purpose of merchandising in retail. Explain how merchandising and visual merchandising are related activities. How does visual merchandising impact retail sales?
2. Visual merchandising involves many different physical elements, including the storefront, store layout, store interior, and displays. Visit a local retail business. What characteristics of the storefront would entice customers to go inside to shop? Are there any characteristics that would make customers stay away? Write a critique of the physical environment of the retail business.

3. Store layout has a significant impact on a retail business. Some layouts lead customers through the store. Other layouts aid in store security. Think of a retail business with which you are familiar. What is the type of layout does the store use? Why do you think the retailer chose that particular layout?

4. Some display techniques encourage customers to associate the display with a certain brand or store image. Visit a retail business in your community that has visual merchandising displays. Describe how the display is designed to represent a certain brand or store image.

5. Displays can be either promotional or institutional. Visit a retail business in your community and make notes on the different interior displays you see. Identify each display arrangement as promotional or institutional. Explain why.

6. Imagine that you are a visual merchandising manager working for one of your favorite retailers. You need to design a special-purpose, holiday sale display for the retailer's merchandise. The display must have a color scheme with products attractively arranged. Choose a product and draw a picture of your display. Write several paragraphs explaining how you chose your color scheme and which products to display.

7. Your holiday sale display must include at least one sign. Design a sign (or signs) to include in the display. Use the Internet to research sign printing and production procedures. Based on how you want to use signs in your display, explain how you would have the sign produced or printed.

8. The holiday sale display must be constructed. Construct a display background. Select and use display fixtures. Use the Internet to research visual merchandising display construction. How will you construct your display background and choose fixtures based on your display design?

9. The holiday sale is ending very soon. Evaluate the effectiveness of the display you designed for the holiday sale. List three metrics that could be used to evaluate your display. For example, if your display included holiday home décor items, sales of those products may have increased.

10. The time has come for you to disassemble your holiday sale display. The store manager was so impressed with your visual merchandising work that the display will be used for next year's holiday sale. Explain how you will take apart and store the display for use next year. Inventory each piece used in the display and write instructions for rebuilding the display.

Check Your Retail IQ

Now that you have finished the chapter, see what you learned about retail by taking the chapter posttest. If you do not have a smartphone, visit the G-W Learning companion website.

G-W Learning mobile site: www.m.g-wlearning.com

G-W Learning companion website: www.g-wlearning.com/marketing/

College and Career Readiness

Career Ready Practices You may have been taught to treat others how you would like to be treated. This is often called the *golden rule*. Working well with others who have a background different from yours may require that you also learn to treat others as *they* wish to be treated. Conduct research on the Internet about cultural differences related to personal space, time, gestures, body language, and views of authority figures. List four differences and how you would approach each.

Listening Informative listening is the process of listening to gain specific information from the speaker. Interview a person who works in the human resources department of a company. Ask that person to explain employee attendance policies for his or her company. Make notes as the policies are described. Evaluate the speaker's point of view and reasoning. Select and organize key information that the speaker shared. Did you listen closely enough to write accurate facts?

Reading Imagery is descriptive language that indicates how something looks, feels, smells, sounds, or tastes. Using this text, find an example of how the author used imagery to describe a concept. List the page number and paragraph where you found the example. Why did you think this was a good example? How does learning about imagery improve your vocabulary?

Teamwork

Working with your team, describe a retail display for a popular product. Identify the color scheme, describe the display background, and categorize the display fixtures. Evaluate the use of the design principles for visual merchandising in the retail display your team selected.

College and Career Portfolio

Technical Skills

Your portfolio should not only showcase your academic accomplishments, but the technical skills you have. Are you exceptionally good working with computers? Do you have a talent for playing a musical instrument? Technical skills are very important. Interviewers will want to know what talents and skills you have.

1. Write a paper that describes the technical skills you have acquired. Describe the skill, your level of competence, and any other information that will showcase your skill level.
2. Save the document file in your e-portfolio folder. Create a subfolder named Skills. Save each a document for each skill with the file names Skills01, Skills02, etc.
3. Place a printed copy in your container for your print portfolio.

◇DECA Coach

▲ Written Manual

Because they tend to be a lot of work, many competitors avoid prepared events, especially those that include lengthy written manuals. Many can be as long as 30 pages. While that sounds like a lot, do not let it intimidate you. Take a look at exactly how much writing is really required.

First, assume that at least five or six pages of your manual will be graphs, charts, tables, photographs, and other images. It may be more. That reduces your manual to 24 pages. Still sound like a lot? Consider that most manuals allow for three-person teams. If you have 24 pages split evenly amongst three people, then you have reduced the amount of writing down to eight pages each. Now consider how much time you have to write it. If you plan during the month of September, that gives you at least October, November, and December to write. That means that you have 13 weeks to write eight pages. That is just a little over half a page per week.

Now compare that to what you do for your English class. Suddenly, it does not sound like too much. The key to writing an effective manual is to break it down into manageable pieces. Stick to a timeline that you set early in the year. By competing at a prepared event with a written manual rather than an impromptu event, the odds of earning your way to the International Career Development Conference (ICDC) go through the roof!

Visit www.deca.org to learn more information about DECA.

G-W Learning Mobile Site

Visit the G-W Learning mobile site to complete the chapter pretest and posttest, and to practice vocabulary using e-flash cards. If you do not have a smartphone, visit the G-W Learning companion website to access these features.

G-W Learning mobile site: www.m.g-wlearning.com
G-W Learning companion website: www.g-wlearning.com/marketing/

Chapter 13
Online Merchandising

Good e-tail sites make it easy for customers to find what they are looking for, whether they want something specific or are just browsing. A main consideration for e-tailers is to determine how their online site is organized. When customers visit the site, it should be easy for them to find products, make a purchase, and leave the store.

When customers visit an online store, the e-tailer can influence and direct customers' shopping experiences. This practice can be compared to the visual merchandising strategies of a brick-and-mortar store. E-tailers do not have fixtures, signs, walls, or floor space. Instead, they use website design elements to influence buying decisions.

Case Study

Nikon USA

Nikon USA makes some of the most technologically advanced digital imaging equipment in the world. Sometimes, having the best products is not enough. The company believed that a website face-lift would improve both online and in-store sales. A web design company overhauled the site. Some changes were more obvious to customers than others. For example, modifications that helped the site show up higher in search engine rankings were probably not apparent to customers. The file size of Nikon USA web pages was reduced so the pages displayed more quickly. Customers may have noticed pages that originally took ten seconds to load could be viewed in less than one second. Just these two changes increased site traffic by 214 percent.

The addition of a learning center was a very visible change to the site. Nikon products can be complex. So, a section of the website is dedicated to helping customers understand and use the equipment. The Learn & Explore section includes how-to articles, key terms, equipment recommendations, photography expert tips, and videos. After the learning center launched, sales increased in all product lines, but particularly for the most complex and expensive products. Nikon USA created a more effective and useful e-tail store that led to increased sales.

College and Career Readiness

Reading Prep

The summary at the end of the chapter highlights the most important concepts addressed in this chapter. Read the summary first. Then, make sure you understand those concepts as you read the chapter.

Check Your Retail IQ

Before you begin the chapter, see what you already know about retail by taking the chapter pretest. If you do not have a smartphone, visit the G-W Learning companion website.

G-W Learning mobile site: www.m.g-wlearning.com

G-W Learning companion website: www.g-wlearning.com/marketing/

Sections

Denys Prykhodov/Shutterstock.com

285

Section 13.1 E-tail Merchandising

Objectives

After completing this section, you will be able to:
- **Identify** common visual elements e-tailers use as merchandising tools.
- **Explain** how e-tailers use digital displays.
- **Describe** the benefits of a *sticky* website.
- **Explain** how suggestion selling is accomplished on an e-tail website.

Key Terms

digital display
above the fold
stickiness

Web Connect

Visit the e-tail site of three companies that sell very different products. For example, you might select an automobile manufacturer, a clothing retailer, and a pet-sitting service. Browse the sites and make note of how each business is visually represented on its site. How is the type of business identified in the site's design?

Critical Thinking

Recall a time when you became frustrated with an e-tail site. Explain why the site was difficult to use. What could the e-tailer have done differently in its site design to avoid the difficulty you experienced?

Online Merchandising

All merchandising techniques are efforts to increase sales. Basic marketing activities must be applied to e-tailing, just as with brick-and-mortar retail stores, in order to increase sales. The merchandising techniques previously discussed for retail stores are also used for e-tail. How the techniques are carried out changes because the store is online rather than in a physical location. All merchandising strategies focus on the four *P*s: product, price, place, promotion.

- The *product* or service for the e-tail business is selected. If e-tailers also have brick-and-mortar stores, they need to decide which products will be offered online. Some products may be unique to the online store or to specific locations. Online product and service offering criteria is typically based on the cost of products, profit margins, and similar criteria. The e-tailer's marketing plan will define the selection.

- The *prices* are set using methods described in Chapter 8, *Pricing Strategies*. The cost of doing business online is different from brick-and-mortar retailing, so different metrics may be used to determine pricing.

- *Place* is the Internet.

- The *promotion* techniques used, discussed in Chapter 9, *Retail Communication*, are chosen based on budgets and forecasted sales and are outlined in the marketing plan. Promotion methods for e-tail are similar to those used for brick-and-mortar retail, but fewer printed pieces may be used.

Merchandising efforts also incorporate the seven functions of marketing, as described in Figure 13-1. Notice that the application of the functions of marketing for both retail stores and e-tail stores is very similar.

Seven Functions of Marketing		
Marketing Function	**Retail Operations**	**E-tail Operations**
Channel Management The route product takes from the supplier to the customer	Producer → Brick-and-mortar store → Customer	Producer → Online store or Customer (through online store order)
Marketing Information Management Gathering and analyzing information about customers	Market research uses internal records, secondary data, primary data.	Market research uses internal records, secondary data, primary data.
Market Planning Creating a plan to achieve established business goals	The marketing plan is based on budgets and forecasted sales, and includes criteria to reach sales goals.	The marketing plan is based on budgets and forecasted sales, and includes criteria to reach sales goals.
Pricing Establishing product prices that will generate a profit, including researching and analyzing competitors' prices.	Product prices are determined based on market research and competition.	Product prices are determined based on market research and competition. Potential lower costs of doing business online are also considered.
Product/Service Management Determining which products or services a business should offer to meet customer needs	Products or services offered are determined by customers' needs and wants.	Products or services offered are determined by customers' needs and wants.
Promotions Communication techniques used to inform customers and influence purchasing.	Included is promoting the business, products, or events through advertising, in-store displays, and public relations.	Included is promoting the business, products, or events through advertising, online digital displays, and public relations.
Selling Personal contact with individual customers to encourage purchasing.	Sales representatives and customer service personnel interact primarily in person with customers.	Automated services, sales representatives, and customer service personnel interact with customers online or over the telephone.

Goodheart-Willcox Publisher

Figure 13-1 Applying the seven functions of marketing to both retail and e-tail operations.

Because an e-tail store has no walls or physical elements, these techniques are applied through web design. Recall that brick-and-mortar merchandising uses floor layout, displays, color, lighting, smells, sounds, and interactive elements designed to catch the attention of customers and persuade them to purchase. Though the merchandising techniques are applied differently, web designers can control an e-tail store's layout, image, colors, mood, music, and other elements to catch visitors' attention.

E-tailers make online merchandising decisions during the web design process. The design of an e-tail store should suit the target market in every way. If it does not, their customers may choose to shop in more appealing online stores. Merchandising choices, particularly on a site's home page, create a visitor's first impression of the e-tail store.

As with a physical store, one important element of online merchandising is the *look and feel* of an e-tail site. While brick-and-mortar stores consider elements such as wall color, signage, and product displays, e-tailers must use other merchandising tools. The look and feel of an e-tail store helps customers understand they are in the right type of store, making them more confident to purchase. The most apparent visual design elements of merchandising on an e-tail site are colors, fonts, balanced elements, and graphics.

Color

Web designers consider the use of color when creating an e-tail site. Many stores use specific colors in their brand and logo. Customers identify the stores with their characteristic colors. For example, Target uses red and white, Best Buy uses yellow and blue, and Toys "R" Us uses the many bright colors contained in their logo.

Social Media

Using Apps on Facebook

According to Facebook, there are over 550,000 active apps that businesses can use on the Facebook platform. And, more are offered daily. Many of the apps were created to improve business practices or more efficiently integrate Facebook into a company's operations. For example, there are apps for surveys, blogging, testimonials, contests, and sweepstakes, to name just a few. YouTube, Twitter, and Flickr have apps that automatically embed information posted on the sites into the business' Facebook page. Many business apps are free. Fee-based apps often offer a basic service at no charge. Also, custom apps can be created specifically for a business' needs. Many large brands use custom apps because they enhance the user experience. When users are happy, they will interact more with the retailer's page, which can mean more business.

Some e-tailers choose colors that reflect the look and feel of their *products*. For example, Scotts lawn and gardening products are focused on healthy lawns and plants. As a result, the company uses many shades of green throughout its website.

Font Choice

Font choice also plays an important role in online merchandising. Most e-tail stores use plain fonts to describe their products and policies. However, other fonts may be used throughout the site to emphasize their brand or product. For example, a party supply e-tailer might choose to use **Playbill** as the font for western-themed promotions and sales. Consider the following two headlines:

Click here for your Wild West costume.

Click here for your Wild West costume.

The first headline supports the e-tailer's *Wild West* merchandising efforts and may make customers more eager to shop.

Balance

Recall that *balance* is a design principle in which elements in a display appear to be evenly distributed. Balance is also used on a web page. Web designers try to create balance using the right combination of text, graphics, and web page elements. Balanced elements make web pages readable and appealing to visitors.

Graphics

Using the right amount of graphics is an important merchandising tool. For example, visitors expect a children's products e-tail store to be filled with bright colors, fun fonts, and a lot of graphics. This combination helps create a fun atmosphere for site visitors.

On the other hand, an online bookstore typically has limited graphics. Customers who visit bookstore sites do so for information about books. Book covers are shown graphically. But, the information describing the book, reader reviews, author bio, and other product detail needs to be read, not viewed.

Recall that branding involves the name, phrase, or design that consumers relate to a business or product. The graphics used on a site send a visual message that helps build and reinforce the brand image of a company or product. If the graphics are inconsistent with the brand, visitors receive mixed messages and the brand is diluted. For example, Toys "R" Us uses a cartoon giraffe and other cartoon figures throughout its e-tail stores. Imagine if the Toys "R" Us e-tail site was filled with images of business people dressed in suits. These images would confuse visitors and they would question if they were even in the right store.

Digital Displays

E-tail stores do not have physical displays, but they do have online displays that are seen by visitors. **Digital displays** are images and text strategically placed on a web page to draw visitors' attention to specific promotional products, sales, or other special events. These online displays are intended to direct visitors' attention to something that they might not have seen otherwise and encourage them to make a purchase. For example, a customer visiting a department store's e-tail site may be shopping for a blouse. A display on the home page announces a sale on women's shoes. The e-tailer hopes that customers will consider visiting the sale, even though they might not have been shopping for shoes.

E-tailers may also use digital displays for other activities that keep visitors at the site, such as customer contest displays or customer opinion and voting displays. E-tailers hope that visitors will be interested enough to click on the display and interact with features on the site.

Just as with in-store promotional displays, e-tailers carefully consider where digital displays are placed on a web page. Digital displays need to be obvious and *jump out* at site visitors. For example, when placed properly on a web page, the digital display in Figure 13-2 is intended to draw the attention of customers. The e-tailer hopes customers will click on the display to get free shipping or shop for clearance bargains.

Online displays are often placed **above the fold**, so they can be seen on a web page without scrolling down the page. By placing the display above the fold, the e-tailer hopes that visitors will immediately see the display when they visit the web page.

Figure 13-2 A typical e-tail digital display promotes special sales, offers, products, and events.

Up to **75% off** all merchandise!

Summer Clearance This Week Only—

FREE SHIPPING!

Click here for coupon code.

Cheryl Casey/Shutterstock.com; Goodheart-Willcox Publisher

Interactivity

Interactivity is a key difference between the Internet and other types of media, such as radio and television. Interactive content can help to keep a customer at an e-tail site for longer periods of time. This content can also help to build brand image and ultimately sell more products. E-tail stores have an enormous advantage over brick-and-mortar stores in providing entertainment and interactive features to customers. These may include games, polls, news, blogs, and other interactive features. Interactivity on e-tail sites improve their **stickiness**, or how long a visitor stays on a site. Having a sticky website has several advantages to e-tailers.

- Helps build the brand image by keeping logos and other brand messages in front of customers for longer periods of time.

- Encourages customers to revisit the site.

- Allows e-tailers to charge more for advertising on their site.

Anything that engages visitors will likely keep them in the online store longer. The longer customers stay in the store, the more likely they are to find something they would like to buy. Many e-tail sites offer nonshopping-related features, such as games. These features allow the e-tailer to build brand equity while a visitor plays a game. The type of interactivity included on a website is limited only by the web designer's imagination. For example, an e-tailer might create a catalog flip book that requires visitors to flip, or turn, each page. This may sound minor, but it keeps visitors engaged as they flip through each catalog page.

When interactivity is used creatively, it can also help present products in a more favorable light. For example, when viewing a product image online, interactive features may allow customers to click on the image to move it, see it in action, examine it up close, rotate it, view it in different colors, or even click through a slideshow. This type of interactivity keeps customers engaged with the product, and provides a maximum amount of visual information.

Suggestion Selling

In brick-and-mortar stores, sales associates may not be with each customer every moment they are in the store. E-tailers have a unique opportunity to virtually track customers during every step of their shopping experience. E-tail sites can be programmed to make recommendations to customers based on where in the site they are, what they have clicked on, which items are in their shopping cart, and which products others have purchased.

Based on a customer's product selection, e-tailers can automatically suggest more expensive products or less expensive clearance products.

NRF Tip

As a result of e-tailing, competitors are often no longer down the street from the retailer's location. Competitors can be in other states or even other countries. NRF has conducted research on global businesses and global market trends that can help business owners better understand trends outside of their own neighborhood.

E-tail customers may not be as annoyed by product suggestions online as they might be when a "pushy salesperson" tries to sell them additional products in person. The online product suggestions may simply appear on screen at some point during the customer's shopping trip.

E-tailers may also suggest their best selling products, assuming that the most popular merchandise has widespread appeal. An e-tail site may also be programmed to make connections between related purchases. For example, e-tailers may note that 30 percent of customers who purchased a particular necklace also bought the matching ring. Knowing this, the matching ring may appear as a product suggestion when a customer places the necklace in the shopping cart.

Checkpoint 13.1

1. List the most apparent visual design elements of merchandising on an e-tail site.
2. How does balance benefit the design of an e-tail site?
3. What is the purpose of a digital display on an e-tail site?
4. Describe how e-tailers benefit from creating a *sticky* e-tail site.
5. Explain how e-tailers use suggestion selling.

Build Your Vocabulary

As you progress through this course, develop a personal glossary of retailing terms and add it to your portfolio. This will help you build your vocabulary and prepare you for a career. Write a definition for each of the following terms, and add it to your personal retail glossary.

digital display
above the fold
stickiness

Section 13.2 Structuring an Online Store

Objectives

After completing this section, you will be able to:
- **Identify** the five structural elements common to retail websites.
- **Discuss** the importance of consistency in site design.

Key Terms

home page
splash page
navigation bar
navigation label

pop-up menu
shopping cart
wish list

Web Connect

Select a specific product, such as an article of clothing, that you would buy from an e-tailer. Comparison shop for the item online. Visit at least three e-tail websites that carry the product. Which website made it easiest for you to find the product? Analyze which aspects made the website customer friendly.

Critical Thinking

Think of an item that you might purchase online. What would you want to know about the company before making a purchase from its e-tail site? List the criteria you would use before making a purchase online.

E-tail Site Organization

When e-tailing began in the 1990s, business owners did not understand why some e-tail stores worked and others did not. They simply created a website to sell something and hoped customers would visit the site and buy their products. Over time, a model was developed based on which e-tail sites were successful. While there is no one formula for success, there are certain qualities common to all successful e-tail sites that are based on solid research.

Perhaps the most important rule of e-tail site design is to organize the online experience to make shopping easy. Customers want to be able to find products, buy them, and move on. Customers do not think about how this works on a website, but e-tailers should put a tremendous amount of thought behind these functions.

For e-tailers, the organization and structure of a website is equivalent to the floor layout of a brick-and-mortar store. Many e-tail store sites have thousands of web pages. A website that does not easily guide customers through the store runs the risk of losing them. Customers will leave a website if they cannot find what they are looking for or become frustrated with site functionality.

Imagine a brick-and-mortar store with the aisles and products laid out as shown in Figure 13-3. Customers would find this store very difficult to navigate. This unclear, confusing layout is inconvenient and makes it hard to find things. Customers who are looking for multiple items must backtrack within the store, which means they may easily become lost. There is a good chance customers would give up and go to another store.

E-tailers must pay close attention to how their stores are organized. A poor site layout can cause customers to go to another store, just like the poor layout of a brick-and-mortar store. There are several common elements to the structure of successful e-tail sites:

- home page
- navigation bar
- content pages
- product pages
- effective checkout system

Home Page

Every brick-and-mortar store has a front door. So does every e-tail store. The front door of an e-tail store is its home page. A **home page**, or *index page*, is usually the first page a person sees when visiting an online store. It is a gateway to the rest of the pages and content on the site. It may also be called a *landing page* because the home page is where most people land after clicking on a link to the site. Layout of the home page is critical. Its appearance should reflect the image of the store. The home page should also look inviting so the visitor will want to see more.

Some sites include a **splash page**, which is a page that appears before the website home page. E-tailers often use splash pages for language selection, to promote a special offer, or to grab the visitor's attention for another purpose. However, research shows that a splash page may distract visitors. Splash pages often use cutting-edge

Figure 13-3 Customers may easily get lost in a retail store with a poor layout.

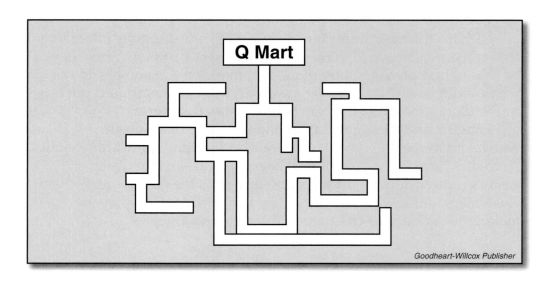

Goodheart-Willcox Publisher

technology that some visitors may not be able to view. Also, splash pages tend to push an e-tail site further down the list on search engine rankings.

Good e-tail websites have a home page that represents the image of the business. The home page should include company contact information and a consistent navigational system. Contact information may appear as text or a link on the page, or as a *Contact Us* button.

The home page should include an e-mail sign-up box, which allows visitors to provide their e-mail address. Entering an e-mail address allows the company to make regular contact with the visitor through newsletters or regular e-mails with sales and promotions. Customers may also be willing to provide an e-mail address if something is offered in return, such as a coupon or discount code.

An e-tail home page should provide links to the store's social media accounts, such as Facebook, Twitter, and Google Plus. Social media site providers have graphic buttons that may be used on a website and can link directly to the e-tailer's social media page.

Navigation Bar

Well-designed e-tail sites have a useful and clear navigation system. The **navigation bar**, or *nav bar*, is the primary tool customers use to locate products and services on an e-tail site. Because of this, the design and location of a website's nav bar are critical to online sales.

Exploring Retail Careers

E-tail Director

Businesses with an online presence employ a director to oversee the e-commerce site. An e-tail director manages the online activities of a retailer. The e-tail director is responsible for the online presence, brand, and image of the business. This person oversees the webmasters and other personnel who contribute to the website. The e-tail director also interacts with management and marketing to make sure company goals are being met. Other typical job titles for an e-tail director are *e-commerce director*, *online manager*, and *e-commerce manager*. The following are some typical tasks that e-tail directors perform:
- organize activities to maximize online sales
- create search engine optimization (SEO) strategies
- oversee website maintenance
- negotiate with suppliers
- ensure products are shipped efficiently
- process customer payments electronically
- perform online customer service tasks

An e-tail director position requires a bachelor degree. It is preferable that the degree be in marketing or management. The position also requires experience in information technology or website marketing and management.

Location

The nav bar is usually a horizontal list of links at the top of each page. It may also be a vertical list of links in a left-hand column of the page. Product categories are usually prominently displayed either near the top or along the left side of a page. Research shows that online visitors tend to look for a nav bar in these two locations.

Labels

The navigation labels are titles placed on the nav bar buttons. These labels should be clear, concise, and easy to understand. E-tailers should avoid labels that visitors may have difficulty understanding.

For example, typical navigation labels for a video game e-tailer are shown in Figure 13-4. Most video game customers know what to expect when they click on those navigation buttons. However, suppose this video game e-tailer is holding a contest called *Around the World* and has added a nav bar button with that label. If visitors are not aware of the contest, the *Around the World* navigation label has no meaning to them. As a result, the visitors probably will not click on the button. If the e-tailer gives the nav bar button a more descriptive label, such as *Contests*, the meaning is clear. Visitors interested in contests may click on the button to learn more.

Complex Nav Bars

A well-planned and organized navigation system can be built with simple text, images, buttons, and links. However, sites containing many pages may require a more complex navigational system for customer convenience.

Pop-up menus are nav bars that display a submenu when a site visitor places the cursor over or clicks on a navigational button or link. Pop-ups allow e-tailers to build more complex nav bars that take up less screen space, as shown in Figure 13-5. These menus are also easy to navigate without clicking through multiple pages.

E-tailers need to provide information about company policies, refunds, customer service, store locations, contact information, careers, and other nonproduct information on their website. A second navigation bar is often placed at the bottom of a web page to address these topics, as shown in Figure 13-6. Usability research shows that users look to the bottom of a page for specific nonproduct information.

Goodheart-Willcox Publisher

Figure 13-4 The navigation bar for a video game e-tailer may have navigation labels for all the different gaming platforms available.

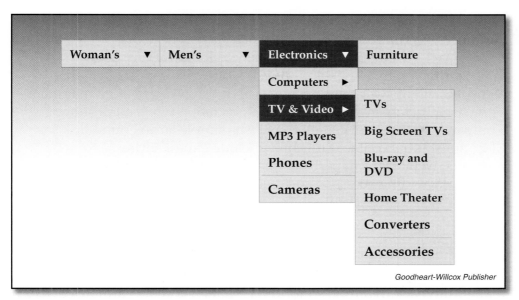

Figure 13-5 Pop-up menus are easy to navigate and take up less screen space.

Content Pages

Content pages are web pages that support the goals of the website. The content on an e-tailer's site can play a role in how customers find products to buy. For example, the content pages for a women's clothing e-tailer may sort products into categories, such as:

- New Arrivals
- Tops
- Bottoms
- Dresses
- Workwear
- Outerwear

Using categories helps visitors find the products they need and want.

Content pages may also provide information that is not directly related to products. For example, an e-tail site may have size charts, privacy and security policies, shipping rates, live customer service, and much more.

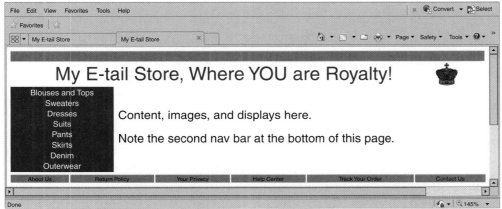

Figure 13-6 Navigation labels for nonproduct topics are often available on a nav bar at the bottom of a web page.

Goodheart-Willcox Publisher

This type of content may be as important as product information in helping customers feel comfortable enough to make a purchase.

Contact information should be easy to find on every page. When shopping in a brick-and-mortar store, customers expect that someone will answer their questions about a product before making a purchase. Customers have the same expectation when e-tail shopping. Company contact information may be as simple as an e-mail link. More substantial contact links may include e-mail addresses, phone numbers, web forms, department listings, and other communication options. Providing access to customer service on content pages, whether responses are delayed or live, is effective in encouraging sales.

Product Pages

Providing product detail for online customers is critical. Recall that a drawback to online shopping is that customers cannot see, feel, or try products before making a purchase. So, the more product detail provided on product pages, the more likely a customer is to complete the purchase. An ideal product page has most, or all, of the following information: product name, price, image, description, options, available stock, customer reviews, and a Buy button.

Product Name

While this may seem obvious, the customer needs to know what they are looking at. A descriptive product name is helpful to customers. For example, "Cotton V-neck tee" is better than "T-shirt." Ideally, each product should have a different name so customers can compare items.

Price

Customers are not likely to make a purchase without knowing the selling price. Some e-tail sites do not list the product price on the product page, but say "See shopping cart for price" instead. This approach does not move the customer any further into the purchasing process. If the price displayed in the shopping cart is too high or low, the customer will lose trust in the site.

Product Image

Customers want to see the products they are going to buy. Images of the actual product should be provided. Product images should include various angles, such as the front and back or inside and outside of the product. Customers also appreciate the ability to zoom on the product image in order to see details.

Product Description

Detailed product descriptions are crucial for sales. The e-tailer should address every potential question about the product in the description. For example, product dimensions may be important in buying a piece of art. The customer needs to be sure the art will fit in the available wall space. If dimensions are not provided, the customer most likely will not buy the art. If the product description is long, it can be placed on a pop-up page.

Product Options

Customers need to understand the options available for products, when applicable. For example, some products are offered in different sizes, colors, or materials. While some e-tail sites do not display these selections until checkout, having options may influence a buyer's decision.

Available Stock

Indicating whether product is in stock may be a factor in customer's decision to purchase. Some e-tail sites do not show this information until the checkout process. However, having product availability information on the product page can aid the customer in making a decision and avoid frustration.

Customer Reviews

Once considered a novelty, customer reviews have become a critical element in the online shopping experience. Customers want to know other people's experiences with products and services. A high percentage of negative reviews can hurt the sales of a product.

Buy Button

Customers must be able to easily make their purchase. The on-screen purchase button may say, "Add to cart," "Buy," "Add to basket," or another similar phrase. No matter what the button says, how to buy an item must be clear to the customer.

Many website visitors rely on product and customer reviews when making buying decisions.

Raywoo/Shutterstock.com

Checkout System

A good checkout system is essential to convert customers into buyers. **Shopping carts** are software applications that help online customers select and place items in the cart, pay, and get a receipt for their purchase. The key to an effective checkout system is the ability to see what is being purchased at any point in the checkout process. Customers must be able to see the items in the cart, how much each item costs, and shipping charges for the order. If the customer cannot see this information while on the e-tail site, they will likely lose trust in it.

Web designers have many choices in checkout system software. The price of each software product reflects the features available to the e-tailer. Basic shopping cart software has fewer options, but is still functional. Pricier software may contain additional features to make shopping easier and purchasing more likely.

A checkout system shows not only the quantity, cost, and shipping charges, but also allows customers to edit their purchases before payment. They may choose to change the quantity, size, or color of a product, or may remove an item from the cart entirely. E-tailers often build checkout systems that allow items to be saved as a wish list. A **wish list** saves selected items in a shopping cart for a future purchase when the customer returns to the site. Customers appreciate special features, such as a wish list, and they are more likely to return for a future purchase.

Brick-and-mortar businesses know that the longer you keep people waiting in line, the more likely they are to lose patience and leave your store. While online customers do not have to wait in line, it is important that the e-tail store is designed to make purchasing simple and to the point. Overly complex checkout systems can make visitors abandon their purchase and look elsewhere.

A website's checkout system should be easy to understand and navigate.

JMiks/Shutterstock.com

Site Consistency

Consistency is extremely important to an e-tail site's organization. Web designers should consider consistency in both the overall visual design and the placement of features. When walking through a brick-and-mortar store, customers expect to see similar elements throughout the store. While each page of an e-tail store will not look exactly the same, using some uniform elements provides page-to-page consistency.

Site Elements

Consistent elements build brand image and let visitors know they are on a page within the same e-tail site. For example, in a grocery store, customers expect to see company logos, labeled directional signs on aisles, and signage at checkout areas and near exits. A good e-tail store consistently uses identifying elements in the same way.

There are several elements that should always appear in the same place on an e-tail site to help navigation and reduce distractions. For example, the navigation bar should be in the same place on every page. Other items that should be similar from page to page include the logo or tagline, font, and other brand identifiers.

Breaking the Rules

The home page is one page of an e-tail website that does not need to be consistent with the other pages. There are many acceptable ways to design a home page, but it should always introduce the visitor to the brand image and navigation categories. For example, a tennis e-tail site may have a nav bar on every page. However, the e-tailer chose to make the home page more enticing and to lead visitors to product pages without a nav bar. This e-tailer's home page introduces visitors only to the main product categories, as shown in Figure 13-7.

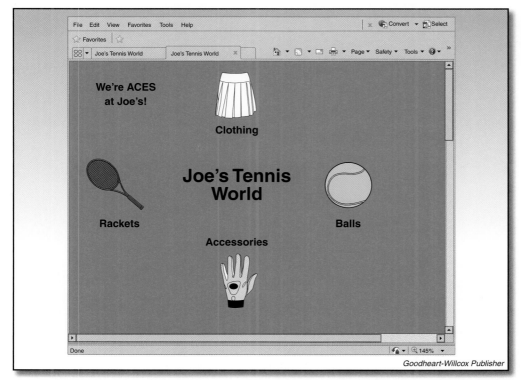

Figure 13-7 This e-tailer's home page does not have a nav bar and displays only the main product categories.

Goodheart-Willcox Publisher

Checkpoint 13.2

1. List the five fundamental design elements that successful e-tail sites have in common.
2. How is a splash page used on an e-tail site?
3. What is the typical location of the nav bar on a web page?
4. What is an online shopping cart?
5. Identify some site elements that should be consistently located on every page of an e-tail site.

Build Your Vocabulary

As you progress through this course, develop a personal glossary of retailing terms and add it to your portfolio. This will help you build your vocabulary and prepare you for a career. Write a definition for each of the following terms, and add it to your personal retail glossary.

home page   pop-up menu
splash page   shopping cart
navigation bar   wish list
navigation label

Section 13.3 User-Friendly E-tailing

Objectives

After completing this section, you will be able to:
- **Identify** the qualities of a user-friendly website.
- **Explain** how hyperlinks are used as a navigation tool.
- **Describe** readability strategies for text and graphics used on a website.
- **Explain** ways to optimize the functionality of a website.

Key Terms

site usability
orphaned page
hyperlink
readability
thumbnail image

serif fonts
sans serif fonts
functionality
plug-ins

Web Connect

Which elements of a website do you use to navigate the Internet? Pay attention to how you "get around" online. Do you prefer using navigation bars, hyperlinks, or the back button? What elements of a website make it easy for you to use?

Critical Thinking

A printed book must be easy to read in order for the reader to understand the material. What considerations for readability should be applied to a website? Are criteria for website readability similar to or different from a printed product?

Site Usability

Site usability describes how effective a website is for visitors. It explains how easily customers can accomplish basic tasks on the site, such as accessing product pages and making purchases. E-tail web designers base a site's design on proven tactics. There have been many studies on how web design affects visitors' time spent at a website. Longer periods of time spent on an e-tail site often lead to increased sales. A user-friendly e-tail site should be easy to navigate, readable, and highly functional to increase the time customers spend at the site.

Ease of Navigation

Research has found that customers grow frustrated or lose interest if merchandise takes too long to find on an e-tail site. Nearly 40 percent of online customers will leave an e-tail site because they cannot find exactly what they want quickly or easily enough.

This means that the e-tailer will lose sales if products and other information are hard to find. The easier it is to find things, the quicker customers can make their purchases.

One general rule of creating a website is to avoid creating orphaned pages. An **orphaned page** is a web page that does not have an obvious way for a visitor to move around the site. The only way a visitor can leave an orphaned page is to click on the browser's back button. Making visitors backtrack wastes their time and leaves an unfavorable impression of a site.

In addition to nav bars, hyperlinks are another way to navigate through a website. **Hyperlinks**, or *links*, are the elements on a web page that visitors can click to connect to another location. They take the viewer to another place on the same page, within the same website, or to another website entirely. Hyperlinks provide a basic form of Internet interactivity by allowing the user to interact with a web page rather than just read it.

Hyperlinks are essential to building a successful e-tail site and can be attached to both text and graphics. By clicking on links, visitors can connect to pages that provide product or company information or view special sale pages. Customers can select products, read more product detail, and make online purchases by clicking on hyperlinks.

Readability

Readability describes how clear and easy something is to read. Highly readable websites are more user friendly, and visitors spend more time at them. Web designers use a number of text and graphic-design strategies to improve readability. These strategies direct visitors' attention to exactly what the e-tailer wants them to see.

Clear and accessible product categories help customers to easily and quickly find what they want.

Annette Shaff/Shutterstock.com

Text Strategies

Generally, online visitors do not thoroughly read the text on a web page unless they are looking for specific, detailed information. Users tend to quickly scan the text on a page until something catches their eye. Because online visitors tend to scan rather than read, it is important to understand where visitors look first on a web page. Using this information, the most important text is placed in the most viewed locations.

Eye tracking studies indicate that visitors tend to look at the top and left portions of a page first. Then, they move their eyes backward and forward, forming an *F* shape. E-tailers can place keywords in these areas to capture the visitor's attention.

Use Headings to Break up Long Pages

If content cannot be spread over multiple pages, such as a news article, it may be necessary to put a large amount of text on one page. When this happens, use headings and subheadings to break up the text. Headings and subheadings help readers stay visually organized as they read through the text. In addition, if visitors are forced to scroll down three or more screens on a single page, the page should include links that bring them *back to the top* of the page.

Use Bulleted Lists

Use bullets when it is important for a list to stand out on a page. Bullets help viewers stay visually organized. Bullets also direct the reader to focus on the list itself, in addition to placing it in context with the rest of the page.

Use Hyperlinks in Text

Text posted on the Internet can be hyperlinked to other information. Hyperlinks allow visitors to click on the linked text and connect directly to a page or site without revisiting the nav bar or site search tool. This functionality makes navigation easier and more efficient for the customer.

Keep Content Concise

Information on a web page should be provided in the fewest number of words necessary. Visitors often skip over long sections of text and look for *quicker* information. Finding the right balance between detailed information and the length of text is critical. However, there are times when details are necessary. For example, the details provided about return policies are necessary to inform customers and protect the e-tailer.

Graphic Design Strategies

Photos, charts, graphs, and illustrations are worth a thousand words. Effectively using visuals can enhance readability when they replace or reinforce blocks of text. In fact, an eye-tracking study conducted by Nielsen revealed that Internet users pay "close attention to photos and other images that contain relevant information."

Give Text Blocks Enough Spacing

Web pages generally include text, graphics, and other visual information. So, it is important to give text blocks adequate room to be read. Elements of design, including text blocks, should not be crowded together. Blocks of text with no breaks are very frustrating for the reader.

Use Images Strategically

The type and number of images on a web page may vary from site to site depending on the target audience. For example, a children's site may be well-served with bright colored cartoons and animated images. However, it is important not to overuse visuals. The most important images should immediately attract visitors' attention, and should not be lost on a page full of visuals.

Notice that each block of text in this web page design has plenty of empty space around it, which improves the readability of the page.

little Whale/Shutterstock.com

Avoid Large Image Files

Research shows that the average web customer will only wait for eight seconds while a page is loading. If the page takes longer to load, typical visitors will leave the page. Web designers can do several things to improve the speed at which a page loads.

If it is necessary to use a large image file, make the visitor aware with a warning. For example, a link to a large picture might have a caption beside it stating how large it is, such as *300KB*. This lets the customer know that the feature may be slow to download. It is best to avoid inserting large-size images and documents into a page. A better option is to provide a link to the image or document, which gives customers the option to click on the link if they are interested.

Use Thumbnail Images

A **thumbnail image**, or *thumbnail*, is a small product image that has a very small file size. If customers like what they see, they click on the thumbnail to open the larger size image for closer viewing. The page that opens also usually contains detailed product information.

A common practice on e-tail sites is to limit how many images are listed on each page. Often, only 10 or 20 thumbnails will download on a page. At the bottom or top of the page it may display the number of pages available, such as "page 1 of 5." This lets the customer know that there are more pages to view. Limiting the number of thumbnails on a page helps to speed up each page. Some sites give customers the option to choose how many product thumbnails they want to view on each page, including a "View all" option.

Avoid Advertising-Like Images

While advertising is everywhere on the web, research shows that customers have learned to tune out web ads. As a result, e-tailers do not want their own important images to be confused with ads placed on the site. To avoid this confusion, e-tailers should not use images that look like online advertisements on their site.

Limit Animation

Animation is a beneficial feature when used wisely, especially for e-tail sites geared toward young people. However, animation may slow down a site and can look amateurish when overused. It is important that animations support the e-tailer's brand.

Use Readable Fonts

Serif fonts have short lines near the top and bottom of the long parts of some printed letters. Times New Roman and Courier are common serif fonts. *Sans* means without. Therefore, **sans serif fonts** are those without the serifs. Arial and Helvetica are common sans serif fonts.

There was once a rule of thumb stating that pages should be 50KB or less in total size. However, increased computing speed and bandwidth has made the use of larger pages possible and practical.

Look at these *fs* side by side: **f** f. Notice the *foot* at the bottom of the second *f*, which is a serif font. Research shows that sans serif fonts that are at least 10 point in size are better for online viewing. However, research indicates that serif fonts are easier to read in printed materials, such as books and magazines.

Limit Emphasis

Using colored, bold, and italic text should be carefully considered. If overused, the emphasis of these treatments will lose impact. Underlined text should rarely be used on web pages because it is easy to mistake the text for a link. Also avoid using uppercase text in sentences. UPPERCASE TEXT IS ACTUALLY HARDER TO READ because your brain receives fewer visual cues. Uppercase text can be effective in short headlines, but that is one of the few places it is effective.

Optimize Functionality

Functionality is the quality of having a practical use. To determine what makes any site functional, identify the purpose of the site. The ultimate purpose of an e-tail site is to generate sales. Therefore, web designers do what they can to make the buying process more practical for customers. Shopping carts are the most obvious way to increase sales functionality on an e-tail site. However, there are several other considerations.

Scroll Down, Not Across

The space on a web page is valuable. Sites should be designed so that visitors can see it all. Many pages require customers to scroll down, but visitors should not need to scroll horizontally across a web page. Customers need to see the entire width to get a feel for the page.

Limit Cutting-Edge Technology

Cutting-edge technology includes features that utilize the latest computer and display technologies. However, these features are not always supported by every browser. Some of this technology can produce unique web pages that attract customers. In order for new technology to work, customers must have the most current **plug-ins**, or browser software applications that read and interpret the technology. Customers without the needed plug-ins cannot view the content, which makes the page appear to be broken.

For example, some iPads and iPhones cannot read Flash, yet Flash is an important feature on many sites. If a site has a nav bar that uses Flash, iPad and iPhone users will not be able to navigate the site.

Rather than remove Flash components from the site, a second nav bar that does not use Flash may be available on the site. If Flash is used elsewhere on the page, the e-tailer may redirect the user to an alternate site for mobile devices that does not use Flash.

Most sites that use plug-ins recognize whether or not a visitor's browser has the plug-in installed. If not already installed, the visitor is prompted or redirected to install the plug-in. However, many users choose not to view the page rather than installing the plug-in on their computer. Web designers need to balance the ability to create unique, feature-packed pages with how many visitors will actually be able to access and use the page.

Open a New Browser Window

Keeping visitors at an e-tail site is crucial to sales. When using hyperlinks that connect visitors to another website, the linked site should open in a new browser window. When the outside web page is closed, visitors are returned to the original e-tail site. This encourages customers to continue browsing the e-tailer's site, which increases the likelihood they will make a purchase.

Checkpoint 13.3

1. What are the qualities that make a website user friendly?
2. How do hyperlinks make navigating a website easier?
3. List three text strategies to improve the readability of a website.
4. Describe two graphic design strategies that are related to text on a website.
5. Explain the disadvantages of using cutting-edge technology on a website.

Build Your Vocabulary

As you progress through this course, develop a personal glossary of retailing terms and add it to your portfolio. This will help you build your vocabulary and prepare you for a career. Write a definition for each of the following terms, and add it to your personal retail glossary.

site usability

orphaned page

hyperlink

readability

thumbnail image

serif fonts

sans serif fonts

functionality

plug-ins

Chapter Summary

Section 13.1 E-tail Merchandising

- Merchandising techniques are efforts used to increase sales. An e-tail store has no walls or physical elements, so these techniques are applied through web design. The most apparent visual elements of merchandising on an e-tail site are colors, fonts, balanced elements, and graphics.
- E-tail stores use digital displays of images and text to draw attention to specific promotional products, sales, or other special events. E-tailers hope that visitors will be interested enough to click on the display and interact with features on the site.
- Interactive content can help to keep a customer at an e-tail site and build brand image which ultimately sells more products. Interactivity keeps customers engaged while providing visual information.
- Suggestion selling is used to recommend that customers buy additional items. Sites can be programmed to make recommendations based on where in the site the customer is, what has been clicked on, which items are in the shopping cart, and which products others have purchased.

Section 13.2 Structuring an Online Store

- Successful e-tail sites have several common fundamental design elements: a home page, navigation bars, content pages, product pages, and effective checkout systems.
- Consistency is extremely important to an e-tail site's organization, both in the overall visual design and the placement of features. Each page of an e-tail store does not look exactly the same, but uniform elements provide page-to-page consistency.

Section 13.3 User-Friendly E-tailing

- Site usability describes how easily customers can accomplish basic tasks, such as accessing product pages and making purchases, on a website. A user-friendly e-tail site should be easy to navigate, readable, and highly functional.
- Research shows that customers grow frustrated or lose interest if merchandise takes too long to find on an e-tail site, which means sales are lost. The easier it is to find things, the quicker customers can make their purchases.
- Highly readable websites are user friendly, which encourages visitors to spend more time on the site. E-tailers should place keywords and graphics in places on a web page that are most likely to capture a visitor's attention.
- A site that is functional can make the buying process more practical for customers. Shopping cart functionality, screens that do not require horizontal scrolling, and limiting technology are ways to increase the functionality of an e-tail site.

Review Your Knowledge

1. Explain how merchandising techniques are applied to e-tail stores.
2. How do e-tailers use digital displays on their e-tail sites?

3. What is the purpose of including interactive content on an e-tail site? Give some examples of common interactive features.
4. Explain how the phrase "above the fold" applies to websites.
5. Explain the importance of organization to website design.
6. Why is a website's home page often called a *landing page*?
7. Identify some of the non-product information that e-tailers need to provide on their websites.
8. What is an *orphaned page*? How does it affect a visitor's experience at the site?
9. How do bulleted lists contribute to the readability of a website?
10. What are some of the functionality considerations when designing an e-tail site?

Apply Your Knowledge

1. Browse the website of an upscale watch retailer, like Rolex. Then, browse the website of a less expensive retailer with a younger target market, like Slap™ Watch. What visual elements are most noticeable to you on each site? While both e-tail sites sell watches, each attempts to reach very different target markets. Identify the visual design elements of each site that create the unique look and feel that appeals to the e-tailer's target market.
2. Create a list of five very different products, such as a beverage, item of clothing, piece of sports equipment, personal electronic device, and gardening item. For each item, guess which colors, fonts, and images would be used in the visual merchandising design on the product's web page. Search the Internet for the products and compare your guesses to the visual merchandising elements e-tailers actually use.
3. Recall that the four *P*s of marketing are product, price, place, and promotion. Analyze how these basic elements of marketing apply to e-tailing. Search some e-tail sites to find current examples.
4. The seven functions of marketing apply to both retail and e-tail businesses. Interpret how each marketing function applies to an e-tail business that sells running shoes.
5. E-tailers develop a list of criteria before products are selected to sell on a website. List the criteria an e-tailer that sells books might use to decide which children's books will be sold on the site. Next, list the criteria that would be used to decide if the e-tailer should offer gift-wrapping service for books purchased on the site.
6. Successful e-tail websites are organized in a way that is familiar and comfortable to customers. Go to the website of an e-tailer with which you are familiar. Locate the home page, a navigation bar, content pages, product pages, and checkout system. Analyze how these five structural elements, as well as the site design components, contribute to the successful structure and organization of the website.
7. The use of graphics, digital images, and animation on an e-tail site must be purposeful, otherwise the website appears unprofessional. Go to the website of an e-tailer with which you are familiar. Analyze the use of graphics, digital images, and animation on the website.
8. Hyperlinks used within text create increased interactivity on an e-tail site. Go to the website of an e-tailer with which you are familiar. Analyze the use of hyperlinks in a selected block of text. How do the hyperlinks relate to the text or content?

9. Make a list of the five common elements of website structure: home page, navigation bar, content pages, product pages, and checkout system. Go to the Amazon.com website. Analyze how Amazon.com addresses each structural element on the e-tail site.

10. Review ten e-tail websites for the use of text on the home page. Record your observations, indicating the use of serif fonts and sans serif fonts for the main information presented, appropriate spacing of text blocks, and the use of upper-case text. Create a chart from the data you collected. Analyze the readability of each home page based on your data.

Check Your Retail IQ

Now that you have finished the chapter, see what you learned about retail by taking the chapter posttest. If you do not have a smartphone, visit the G-W Learning companion website.
G-W Learning mobile site: www.m.g-wlearning.com
G-W Learning companion website: www.g-wlearning.com/marketing/

College and Career Readiness

Career Ready Practices Most people in the United States act as responsible and contributing citizens. How can a person demonstrate social and ethical responsibility in times when disaster relief is needed in the community? Participate in a group discussion about how citizens can go beyond the minimum expectations of helping others in the community.

Writing You have decided to volunteer for a nonprofit organization. Compose an informative letter or e-mail that you might send to an organization. Convey information clearly and accurately by effectively organizing the content.

Reading Figurative language is used to describe something by comparing it with something else. Locate an advertisement for a product. Scan the information for figurative language about the product. Compare this with a description using literal language. Draw conclusions as to which product appeals to you more. Did the use of literal or figurative language influence your opinion of the products? Did the advertisement help you understand the product?

Teamwork

Working with your team, select an e-tail business that you think needs a new website. Or, propose a site revision to your school's Career and Technical Student Organization website. First, analyze the selected website. Create a list of structural elements that need to be addressed. Identify what components work and what needs improvement. Make a list of tasks that must be considered to improve the website's structure. Outline each step that would be necessary if your team is awarded the opportunity to update and revise the website.

College and Career Portfolio

Soft Skills

Employers and colleges review various qualities of candidates. For example, the ability to communicate effectively, get along with customers or coworkers, and solve problems are important skills for many jobs. These types of skills are often called *soft skills*. Make an effort to learn about and develop the soft skills needed for your chosen career area.

1. Search the Internet for articles about soft skills and their value in helping employees succeed.
2. Make a list of the soft skills important for a job or career that currently you possess. Select three of these soft skills. For each soft skill, write a paragraph that describes your abilities. Give examples to illustrate your skills.
3. Save the document describing your soft skills abilities in your e-portfolio. Also place a printed copy in your physical portfolio.

◇DECA Coach

Create a Time Line

If you choose to compete in a prepared event, the first step is to determine in which event you will compete. The second step is to create a time line. Generally, you have three to four months to develop your manual, so start early. Determine when your project is due. Break your manual down into "little chunks" and decide how long you need to complete each part.

Use the written guidelines provided by DECA to help organize your time line. Take each section in the guidelines and determine about how much time you will need to complete each section. Then, go to work and stick to it. When developing your time line, understand that things do not always go as planned. You should allow yourself extra time. For example, if you have four months to complete your manual, create a time line that will allow you to finish in three. This gives you time to come up with new ideas, make changes, and to schedule time with your instructor and advisory panel.

While planning your manual, stick to the written portion. When that is complete, begin developing your presentation. Ask your advisor to help develop your time line. As you develop it, write down your deadlines. Be sure your advisor has a copy. Check off each section as it is completed. Use your time line as a visual guideline to walk you through the process.

Visit www.deca.org to learn more information about DECA.

G-W Learning Mobile Site

Visit the G-W Learning mobile site to complete the chapter pretest and posttest, and to practice vocabulary using e-flash cards. If you do not have a smartphone, visit the G-W Learning companion website to access these features.

G-W Learning mobile site: www.m.g-wlearning.com

G-W Learning companion website: www.g-wlearning.com/marketing/

Chapter 14
Creating an E-tail Website

Brick-and-mortar retailers make sure customers can walk through the front door, select merchandise, make their purchase, and leave the store. For e-tailers, the type of planning and work that goes into creating a pleasant customer experience is much different. To accomplish a seamless online shopping experience, e-tailers must plan their sites to be user-friendly and easy to navigate. This involves understanding what is important to the customers in the target market.

The actual building of an e-tail website can be complicated. The look, content, and functions of an e-tail website are constructed using a coded computer language. It is important for e-tailers to understand how a web page is constructed and the tools and resources necessary, even if they are not building their own websites.

Case Study

Salon Savings

Salon Savings, a leading e-tailer of discount hair and skin care products, noticed it was receiving a lot of telephone calls from online customers. These customers could not find the products they were looking for and could not complete their online purchases. To address these concerns, Salon Savings set three goals for their e-tail site:
- make products easier to find
- improve online customer service
- increase online sales

To make products easier to find, the search functionality was changed to allow customers to find products in multiple categories, such as by product type and by brand. To improve online customer service, Salon Savings streamlined their shopping cart system and payment process. Also, features were added to improve the customer's experience, such as order status information and past order history. To increase sales, a "Recommended for You" section was added that suggests other relevant items during checkout.

Because Salon Savings identified their website goals, the company understood what actions needed to be taken to improve the e-tail site. As a result of the site improvements, the number of customer telephone calls is greatly reduced, and Salon Savings has more than doubled its business.

College and Career Readiness

Reading Prep

Examine the list of key terms. What clues do they convey about the chapter topics you will study?

Check Your Retail IQ

Before you begin the chapter, see what you already know about retail by taking the chapter pretest. If you do not have a smartphone, visit the G-W Learning companion website.

G-W Learning mobile site: www.m.g-wlearning.com

G-W Learning companion website: www.g-wlearning.com/marketing/

Sections

DeiMosz/Shutterstock.com

Section 14.1 Building a Website

Objectives

After completing this section, you will be able to:
- **Identify** the preplanning decisions for an e-tail website.
- **Describe** the five phases of website creation.

Key Terms

outsourcing
contractor
web authoring software
web host
storyboard
site map
template

web browser
uniform resource
   locator (URL)
domain registrar (DR)
file transfer protocol
   (FTP)
webmaster

Web Connect

Conduct an Internet search for "web design firm" and select one or two that appeal to you. Examine the client list for each. What are some of the reasons you suspect these companies hired a web design firm rather than build their own site?

Critical Thinking

One of the obvious purposes for building an e-tail website is to generate sales. However, a retailer may have other reasons for creating a commerce site. What are some other reasons you think a retailer might have to build a website? Make a list of your opinions.

Preplanning Considerations

The first consideration in creating an e-tail store is whether to hire someone to build the website or have a current employee develop the site. Hiring a professional web designer or web author to build a website can be expensive. Some retailers, especially small ones, may choose to build their own sites using available software programs and online tools to save money. Ultimately, e-tailers should examine the pros and cons of site-building options and determine the most effective and efficient way to create the site.

Outsourcing the Website

Outsourcing means to contract with an expert to perform specific work. Outside experts hired to complete a task are also called **contractors**. The entire job of creating a website may be outsourced, or a professional web designer may be hired to develop only a portion of the site. For example, many small e-tailers may build their own websites, but use a contactor to help them connect their online sales with an inventory database. Large e-tailers often hire their own full-time employees to design, build, and maintain their site, rather than outsource the tasks to contractors.

Building an e-tail website requires the appropriate technical knowledge and tools to be done well. For example, a site may have an online form for feedback, a game, or the ability to take credit card payments online. These types of features require programming skills that an e-tailer may not have or have access to.

E-tailers should research and examine web design companies to see which best suits their needs. It is important to evaluate both the costs and the services provided by each web design company.

Building the Site In-House

When e-tailers opt to build their own sites, they must choose a software product that offers the features and functions needed to build the site they envision. **Web authoring software** is the computer software used to build a website. It may also be called *web design software*. Adobe Dreamweaver® is an example of commonly used web design software. While this software is expensive, the cost is much less than hiring a professional web design company or contractor.

Web design software is also available through some web-hosting services. A **web host** is a company that provides a place for an e-tailer to post its website onto the Internet. Many web hosts provide several tools needed to build and maintain a website. For example, Google provides *Google Sites*, which helps simplify the task of building a website. *Google Sites* provides web authoring software and offers many professional-looking site templates. Web authoring software may be available to install on a computer or be used only online.

Exploring Retail Careers

Web Designer

A web designer plans, designs, creates, and updates the e-tail website. They are responsible for the look and feel of the site. Designers work with usability experts, graphic designers, and online merchandisers to build a website that is user-friendly for online shoppers. If the e-tail store also has companion brick-and-mortar stores, they must ensure that the image of e-tail store is consistent with the brick-and-mortar stores. Other job titles for this position are *web developer* and *web author*. Some examples of tasks that web designers perform include:

- plan, design, and develop a website
- select software to handle specific jobs, such as tracking inventory or storing data
- test software and hardware to ensure performance and capacity
- coordinate efforts with the marketing team
- analyze data and write reports
- update and maintain the website

Web designers should be creative and have the ability to identify and solve complex problems. The education required may range from a high school diploma to an advanced college degree.

Software programs are also available to help the e-tailer to produce professional-looking graphics, blogs, shopping carts, and many other website components.

Building and maintaining a website is time consuming. If the e-tailer uses an employee within the company to plan and build the website, his or her other job functions are put on hold. E-tailers should analyze the cost of using a web design company or contractor against an employee's abilities and time constraints.

Five Phases of Website Creation

Once an e-tailer decides who will build the website, the creative process can begin. Successful online stores take significant time to develop. As shown in Figure 14-1, there are five general steps in building an e-tail site: plan, design, develop, publish, and maintain.

Plan

During the planning phase, information is gathered to define the website's goals, profile the intended audience, determine technical requirements, and begin outlining the site structure and organization. This may be the most important phase in building an e-tail site. If the site is not properly planned, the web designer may be required to go back and make changes over and over again. The web designer must meet with the store's ownership to determine what they hope

Figure 14-1 These are the five general steps in building an e-tail site.

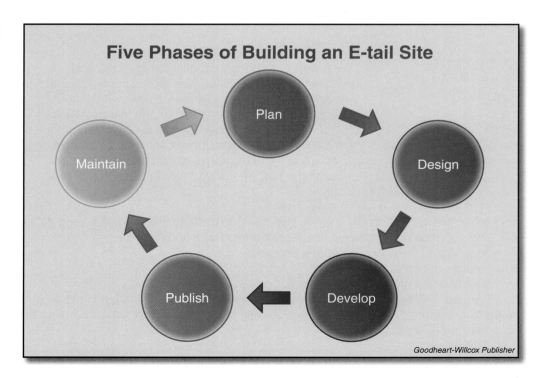

Five Phases of Building an E-tail Site

Maintain • Plan • Design • Publish • Develop

Goodheart-Willcox Publisher

to accomplish by having an e-tail store. By asking questions, the web designer can determine the goals, or *objectives*, of the e-tail site. The goals of a business may not always be as simple as *generate sales.*

Retailers decide exactly what they want their website to accomplish by establishing *website goals*. A common business objective is to generate sales. However, placing products on a site is not enough to generate sales. There needs to be reasons for customers to return to the site. An e-tail site should entice customers to visit the site, as well as achieve the goal of making sales.

For example, Skateboard Sam's is an online skateboard and accessories retailer. The owners know that their target market is people who like to skateboard. They set the following goals for their e-tail site:

- Enhance Skateboard Sam's image in the skateboard community so that 5,000 new people *like* the store on Facebook.

- Accumulate 10,000 new e-mail addresses for the Customer Relations Management (CRM) system within a year.

- Provide a communication forum that attracts 5,000 new skateboard enthusiasts within a year.

- Encourage repeat visits to the site so that 50,000 visitors return to the website at least once this year.

- Generate $250,000 in online annual sales.

Skateboard Sam's believes that each of these goals is important. With the goals in mind, the retailer can decide the type of content needed on their site to help accomplish each one. The owners of Skateboard Sam's examined each goal and developed specific actions and content, as shown in Figure 14-2. Note that some content can serve more than one goal. For example, a skateboard game may help to generate a mailing list, as well as encourage repeat visits.

Retailers may also use mathematical models in planning their site. *Mathematical models* are processes used to simulate real-world situations by using mathematical equations to predict future behavior or situations. These complex math equations require a computer to calculate a large range of possible outcomes. For example, mathematical models can be used to predict population demographic changes, customer behavior patterns, and employment trends. Many variables are entered into a statistical software program and the computer calculates all of the possible outcomes, as well as the probability of each outcome occurring.

There are several different types of mathematical models that can be used, depending on the application. The following are some common models that apply to retail:

- *Decision Theory.* This model helps management make decisions based on the amount of data available. There may be so much data that it is impossible to see patterns without modeling. Or, there may not be enough data and modeling is needed to predict additional data.

Skateboard Sam's Website Goals

Goal 1: Enhance Skateboard Sam's image in the skateboard community so that 5,000 new people *like* the store on Facebook.
- Provide information about awards Skateboard Sam's has received.
- Identify affiliations with charities and skateboard organizations.
- Showcase celebrities using Skateboard Sam's equipment.

Goal 2: Generate a contact mailing list to include 10,000 new e-mail addresses within a year.
- Provide an online skateboard game that requires user registration.
- Offer a weekly e-mail skateboard newsletter to those who sign up with their e-mail address.
- Provide a contest or giveaway that requires registration.

Goal 3: Provide a communication forum that attracts 5,000 new skateboard enthusiasts within a year.
- Provide a chat room, blog, or other community forum on the e-tail site.
- Provide links to Skateboard Sam's Facebook and Twitter sites.

Goal 4: Encourage repeat visits to the site so that 50,000 visitors return to the website at least once this year.
- Provide a section of the site for skateboarders to submit their favorite skateboard action photos; update the section weekly.
- Provide up-to-the-minute news about the skateboard community.
- Post skateboarding competition schedules and results.

Goal 5: Generate $250,000 online annual sales.
- Provide a wide array of products and price points.
- Provide free skateboard lessons to anyone who purchases a skateboard from Skateboard Sam's.
- Offer detailed product information and close-up pictures.
- Have a checkout system that is fast and easy to use.
- Add pages for clearance and sale items.
- Provide a coupon for *liking* Skateboard Sam's on Facebook.

Goodheart-Willcox Publisher

Figure 14-2 Website goals established during the planning phase for Skateboard Sam's.

- *Game Theory.* This model takes into consideration competition, conflict, and the "rules" that are in place. If a manager makes one decision, this model predicts the probable outcomes resulting from that decision.
- *Queuing Theory.* This model takes into account supply and demand, and attempts to predict the amount of resources required to meet a particular level of demand.
- *Linear Programming.* This model attempts to find how resources should be allocated to achieve the most profit for the least cost.

Design

The information gathered during the planning phase influences the design of the content, navigation, and special features of the site. In the design phase, web designers create sample pages that include the major screen elements, such as the page layout, colors, fonts, themes, and navigation. Design is a critical step. If not done properly, the functionality and user experience with the entire site is affected.

The first step in designing a website is to create a storyboard. A **storyboard** is a series of drawings that helps the web designer see what the site should look like. It shows the look and feel of each segment of the site. The storyboard also illustrates the navigation system and structure of the site. An accurate site layout should be on paper before it is built. This step can save a lot of time and redesign work.

In addition to a storyboard, web designers build a site map. A **site map** is an overview of the pages within the website, often in the form of an outline. Together, the storyboard and site map provide a visual representation of the e-tail store. A site map also allows both the web designer and site visitors to better identify the location of each page on the site. Generally, a site map has links to each of the different pages, so users can jump directly to the page they want.

The web designer must review all of the site goals to and include website content to meet each goal. It is much easier to build a navigation bar that visitors can easily follow when the content is identified.

A final step in the design phase is to visit websites of the e-tailer's competition. It is important to know what the competition is doing, and this may spark ideas for the site. For example, a fishing tackle store is preparing to build an e-tail site. In visiting other sites, the owners noticed that a competitor has tide charts on their site. Why? The purpose is to get customers to continually visit the site to check the tides, which is important information for those who fish. Once at the e-tail site, the competing tackle store hopes visitors will also make a purchase. Tide charts may be a feature that the fishing tackle store e-tailer should consider putting on its site.

The structure, components, and navigation of an e-tail site must be determined in the design phase.

alphaspirit/Shutterstock.com

Develop

Once the e-tail site is planned and designed, development can begin. The most changes are made during the development phase. Changes should be viewed as opportunities for improvement, making the site more user-friendly and efficient.

Most web designers work from a template. A **template** is a page that contains all of the elements that will be common to every page on the site. Using a template, web designers can add content to each individual page without rebuilding the common elements. Common elements include the colors, fonts, logos, navigation bars, and footers that will be carried over from page to page.

A **web browser** is the software program used to view websites. There are many different web browsers, such as Microsoft Internet Explorer®, Mozilla Firefox®, and Safari. Different web browsers may display websites and web pages differently. The look and feel, as well as the layout of a website, may appear different to customers based on their browser. Web designers need to know how sites look on different browsers and operating systems, such as Mac versus Windows platforms, to provide the intended experience to all customers.

Uniform Resource Locator (URL)

A **uniform resource locator (URL)** is the unique Internet name and address of a document, web page, or website. It is like the unique street address of buildings and properties where mail is delivered. Because each URL must be unique, it can only be purchased and used by one owner.

Determining and buying a URL is part of the development process. In order to buy a URL, the e-tailer must visit a **domain registrar (DR)**, which is a company that verifies, sells, and registers URLs. There are many domain registrars on the Internet. To determine if a URL is available, the DR compares the names entered by visitors to existing registered URL names. If the desired URL is not available, the DR usually makes recommendations for similar URL addresses

Visitors enter or link to a website using the site's unique address.

Claudio Divizia/Shutterstock.com

that are available. The buyer can accept one of the alternatives or try searching for another URL. When an acceptable URL is found, the e-tailer purchases it online through the DR. The DR immediately registers the URL so that others may not purchase it.

Internet Identity

Every website URL should appropriately represent the related organization. For example, Kohls.com is the site of Kohl's department store. While many businesses are fortunate to buy their own name, others may not be so fortunate. It is important that the URL provide online customers with a sense of the e-tailer's identity. For example, if a small jewelry store owner named John Kohl wanted to build a website, he could not use Kohls.com because it is already taken. To represent his business' identity on the Internet, he may choose JKohls.net, JKohlsjewelry.com, or another combination that provides the appropriate Internet identity.

Publish

When an e-tail site is built and developed, it is ready to be posted online, or *published*, through the web host. The most common way to upload web pages to the Internet is to use **file transfer protocol (FTP)** software. FTP software provides tools to transfer files from a computer to the Internet, so others can view them online. Most web authoring software has built-in FTP software for easy uploading.

In order to publish a website, the web designer must know the settings that allow the FTP program to communicate with the site. Once the settings are in place, pages can be uploaded with the click of a button. Each time a change is made to a web page, no matter how minor, the entire page must be uploaded again so the changes are reflected on the website.

Once a page is posted on the Internet, the site should be tested. Tests for mistakes or errors on the web pages should be completed before the pages are posted "live" on the Internet. Once the site has passed the tests, the web designer should view the site live on the Internet to ensure it looks and performs as intended. The site should also be viewed using several different web browsers, as each may display the pages differently.

Maintain

Keeping an e-tail site current is critical to sales. Products and information need to be updated on a regular basis so customers can see what is available. Some large e-tail sites are updated several times a day. Sales, pricing, promotions, and other announcements must always be current. Imagine if an e-tailer ends an advertised sale, but forgets to remove the sale information from the website. Customers would be unhappy if they were not able to purchase items at the sale price.

Retail Ethics

Competition

Retailers are always looking for a chance to evaluate the competition. However, caution should be taken on how those products are obtained. Ethical practice is to buy the product or ask the competitor if it is okay to take a sample. Taking product from a competitor without its approval, such as at a trade show, is unethical.

Maintenance can be very time consuming. Each time an image, text, or other site element needs to be added or removed, the content is altered through the web design software and the revised pages are uploaded. With potentially thousands of web pages on a site, including product pages, maintenance is an ongoing process. A **webmaster** is the person responsible for maintaining and updating a site once it has been published. Sometimes, webmasters also take full responsibility for the site, including designing and building it.

Checkpoint 14.1

1. Explain the preplanning considerations of building an e-tail site.
2. What is a *web host*?
3. What are the five phases of website creation?
4. How do website visitors use the site map?
5. What is the function of a domain registrar (DR)?

Build Your Vocabulary

As you progress through this course, develop a personal glossary of retailing terms and add it to your portfolio. This will help you build your vocabulary and prepare you for a career. Write a definition for each of the following terms, and add it to your personal retail glossary.

outsourcing	template
contractor	web browser
web authoring software	uniform resource locator (URL)
web host	domain registrar (DR)
storyboard	file transfer protocol (FTP)
site map	webmaster

Section 14.2 Web Design Tools and Resources

Objectives

After completing this section, you will be able to:
- **Discuss** the factors that contribute to a good e-tail website.
- **Identify** additional website products and services a web designer may include on a site.
- **Explain** the importance of search engine optimization to e-tail websites.

Key Terms

web widget
image cruncher
JavaScript
search engine
keyword
indexing

search engine
   optimization (SEO)
organic SEO
metadata
meta tags

Web Connect

Select an e-tailer and visit its online store. Study the look and feel of the site. Now, open the same web page on a mobile device. Do the sites appear to be identical or different in some way? Describe what you discovered.

Critical Thinking

When shopping online, there are many different ways to find what you are looking for on a website. Compare the advantages and disadvantages of using a search tool, the navigation bar, and simply clicking on hyperlinks to find your desired product.

Good E-tail Websites

Aside from the product selection, what makes people shop at some e-tail stores over others? There are many sites that sell the same brands and products. According to research by The Nielsen Company, two factors that drive online shopping are brand recognition and the trustworthiness of a retailer. E-tailers have limited control over who else sells similar merchandise, but they can control building the trustworthiness of their site.

Successful e-tailers build reputable and trusted websites that attract and keep customers. When building an e-tail site, its accessibility, simplicity, site-search tools, ease of purchase, customer service options, and return guarantees should be considered.

Accessibility

Visitors to an e-tail website will likely be using a variety of web browsers. Different browsers, especially the browsers on mobile devices, may display websites differently. Web designers must ensure that visitors can view the site the way it was intended to be seen.

Online customers want to find what they are looking for quickly. Effective web design considers the *three-click rule*. Visitors may get frustrated if they do not find what they are looking for within three clicks. This frustration might lead them directly to a competitor's site.

According to mobiThinking™, more than 700 million people access the Internet through a mobile device. In some countries, such as China, more people access websites through mobile devices than through computers. Mobile devices are expected to become the dominant method of accessing the Internet in the near future. Therefore, it is important for e-tailers to have websites that are compatible with mobile devices, like smartphones and tablets.

Mobile devices are not capable of viewing websites in quite the same way as computers. To accommodate this, web designers may develop a separate e-tail website for mobile users that is more compatible with mobile-device browsers. The site should recognize mobile devices and redirect visitors to the mobile site. Mobile e-tail sites should be simple, small in size for fast downloading, and retain the brand equity by using the same colors, logos, and other visual elements used by the main site.

Simplicity

Flashy *bells and whistles* on a website may be distracting to customers who just want to buy products. While flashy features may work well on some sites, they should be limited to only what is necessary to build the brand. For example, a rock star's website that sells music, T-shirts, and other items for fans might be expected to have music and videos. However, a retailer of adult apparel would not need music and videos on its e-tail site. E-tailers should eliminate unnecessary features on their sites that might distract visitors.

Site-Search Tools

Site-search tools, such as a *Search* box on the home page, help users easily find products on an e-tail site. In fact, 57 percent of users are likely to use a site-search tool. E-tail site visitors who use a site-search tool are more likely to make a purchase than visitors who do not use a site-search tool.

Site-search tools also help visitors find items that do not necessarily fit neatly into a navigation bar category. For example, if a customer wants to find a pair of red shoes, *red shoes* would be keyed in the *Search* box. The search returns all of the products on the site with the words *red* and *shoe* in the product descriptions, details, or coded data. The key to an effective site-search tool is to make sure products on the site are described properly.

A search box helps visitors quickly find items on an e-tail site.

alexskopje/Shutterstock.com

Ease of Purchase

Once customers find a product they want to buy, completing the purchase transaction should be easy so they do not abandon the site. An uncomplicated checkout system contributes to a positive customer experience.

It should be clear that the e-tail site is secure, so that customers feel safe providing personal information. E-tailers should also clearly state their privacy policies, letting customers know if and how their personal information will be used.

Recall that good checkout systems are essential to an e-tail store, and the shopping cart is a primary element in that system. While there are free choices available, shopping carts often have fees associated with them. For example, PayPal™ offers an easy-to-use shopping cart that is used throughout the world. Google and Yahoo! also offer shopping cart systems for businesses that host their e-tail site with them. Whether free or not, e-tailers cannot make online sales without a shopping cart system.

A common way customers pay for online purchases is a debit or credit card. However, some people are uncomfortable with this form of payment because they fear identity theft through hacking. Other payment options, such as electronic checks, should be available for online customers. Giving customers the ability to order and pay by phone is also a good option.

Customer Service Options

Customer and e-tail site visitors should have multiple options to contact the retailer, including e-mail, phone, postal service mail, and online chat. Prompt attention helps customers feel valued and builds trust in the e-tailer. According to *Internet Retailer Magazine*, retailers hoping to boost online sales should focus on what is important to customers. The magazine conducted a survey that showed online customers want the following capabilities:

- track deliveries online (79 percent)
- online access to customer service reps (45 percent)
- access video demonstrations for using, assembling, or installing products (49 percent)

Return Guarantees

E-tailers can increase customers' comfort to make purchases by providing guarantees, whenever possible. Recall that some customers are not comfortable buying products online because they cannot touch and feel the items. Providing guarantees on returned products may ease hesitation about online purchasing. If a product arrives that does not work or meet their expectations, customers must be able to easily return it. All details of guarantees should be available

When shopping online, many e-tail sites offer customer support through live chat with a customer service rep.

Syda Productions/Shutterstock.com

before a purchase is made. Customers should know if the product is guaranteed, how return shipping works, who pays the postage, and any other information relevant to returns and exchanges.

Additional Web Authoring Tools

Based on the website's goals and objectives, there are many other website products and services a web designer may include. *Enhanced web pages* include more than informational content and basic functions. An enhanced web page may include features that keep visitors engaged, provide up-to-the-minute news, or can collect customer information, opinions, and preferences. Most enhanced features and elements for web pages can be built using tools and software that may be found online.

Web Widgets

Web widgets are programs that run when a visitor opens the web page. For example, a weather widget may be included on a web page to show the current weather conditions. Many widgets can be found on the Internet that require little or no programming. The web designer can simply copy and paste the widget items into the web page code.

Widgets can add value and greatly increase visitor interaction with a site, which gives visitors a reason to return. To be useful, the e-tailer must find widgets that fit the company's image and that suit the target market.

Forms and Databases

Forms enable an e-tailer to collect information, receive feedback, and take orders. The simplest forms send data to a designated e-mail address. More complex forms can place data into a spreadsheet or database and even help keep track of inventory. Forms also provide a method of communication between the customer and the e-tailer. Once a visitor completes and submits a form, the information is captured for future use. If the completed form is an order, it goes to a fulfillment address where the order can be filled and sent to the customer. If a visitor completes a feedback form, the information is recorded in the customer relation management (CRM) system for market research and customer contact.

Forms should be efficient in design and function so the information entered can be directly fed to a database. Forms and databases with advanced features can be complex. But, simple and moderately complex forms can be built to effectively meet the goal of the business.

Message Boards, Blogs, Listservs, and Chat Rooms

Message boards, blogs, listservs, and chat rooms allow visitors to communicate with each other. These online sources are also used as a source of marketing research data for the retail business. Market research is important for retailers to understand the needs and wants of customers. Using these features, an e-tailer can build a sense of community among its visitors. Additionally, the e-tailer can monitor and evaluate comments, conversations, and opinions about both its store and products. The customer communities give e-tailers insight into what they are doing right and wrong from their customers' perspectives. These site features can be constructed using online tools or the appropriate plug-ins for web authoring software.

Polls and Surveys

Like blogs and chat rooms, polls and surveys add interactivity to an e-tail site. These features also help e-tailers keep up with customer needs and preferences. A good poll is short and interesting enough to entice users to participate. Relevant polls may attract daily visitors to the site. Changing the poll questions regularly is critical. If the questions do not change, visitors have no reason to return.

E-tailers can use polls and surveys to collect market research information and opinions from site visitors. However, most people

Online polls and surveys are used to engage site visitors and collect market research information.

Brian A Jackson/Shutterstock.com

do not want to be bothered with surveys. So, e-tailers often offer something to visitors in return for taking the survey. They may provide a coupon, a chance to win a prize, or something else the visitor values.

Tracking

Site tracking features can provide e-tailers with market research information about their customers. These features can help e-tailers understand who is visiting their site, how their site was found, which search engine keywords are most effective, what country the visitors are currently in, and much more. This information can be used to improve the site and make it more effective. For example, Google Analytics offers tools to analyze mobile device traffic on a site, measure user activities on web pages, understand how web searching led visitors to the site, and many other data-gathering and tracking tools.

Games

Having games on an e-tail site can be a great way to get visitors to return. The games should be appropriate for the site visitors and be related to the industry of the e-tailer. For example, a teen's clothing site might have a game that allows visitors to "try on" separate pieces of clothing to see how they look together, while a newspaper site may have a crossword puzzle.

Not all customers will play games when visiting a site. However, for visitors who enjoy them, games are a good way to get them to return to the site. Even if they return only to play the game and not to shop, the games help to build brand equity. Remember, every time someone visits the site, they see the logo, slogan, and other elements that keep the brand in front of them.

Image Crunchers

Image crunchers reduce the file size of an image so it opens faster. File sizes are generally measured in kilobytes (KB) or megabytes (MB). Image crunchers compress an image file to a smaller file size for faster downloading and can reduce image height and width. Reducing the file size of images reduces the size of the entire web page, which helps the site download much faster. Crunchers allow web pages to have more images without slowing the download process. Most professional web designers crunch images when building a site. This can be done with graphics software programs, such as Adobe® Photoshop®. However, there are many easy-to-use, free image cruncher tools on the Internet.

JavaScript

JavaScript is little pieces of code that can be inserted into web pages to perform many different functions. JavaScript can provide a site with practical functions, such as forms, password protection, games, and navigation bars. It also allows the creation of "fancy" website features. For example, using JavaScript a web designer can create an astronaut floating around the page, add a custom tail to the user's mouse pointer, add a countdown clock, or have scrolling text at the bottom of a page. There are thousands of ready-to-use JavaScript examples available. However, only JavaScript that adds value to the site should be used.

Collections

Some web design sites feature all of the site creation tools previously discussed, and many more, in one location. These *collections* create a one-stop-shopping site that provides most or all of the tools needed to build and enhance an e-tail site. For example, some sites feature web hosting and web authoring tools, as well as an array of widgets and scripts. Finding a collection can make adding features to a site easy for a webmaster.

Search Engines and E-tailing

A **search engine** is a computer program that online visitors use to look for information on the Internet. A person enters **keywords**, or search terms, describing the content he or she wants. The ability to be found through a search engine is critical to the success of a website.

Some essential website elements are invisible to or hidden from online visitors. These hidden elements allow the web designer to build a site that is easily found on search engines, such as Google, Yahoo!, and Bing. Search engines are programmed to retrieve a list of websites that match the keywords entered. Search engines operate by **indexing** each web page, or associating web pages or sites with particular keywords and phrases. Once indexed, search engines rank each page to match a particular set of keywords. When someone uses a search engine, the indexed keywords are paired up with the keywords entered to find and display the most likely matches on the search results pages.

Search Engine Optimization (SEO)

Search engine optimization (SEO) is the process of getting a website ranked higher on the results pages when an Internet search is conducted. This process includes adding special coding and typical search terms in the website text. The goal of SEO is to attract more profitable traffic from search engines to the website.

E-tailers want to be found as a result of Internet searches. They also want to be near the top of the results list. Customers tend to start clicking on sites from the top of the indexed list and work their way down. Good SEO can mean the difference between a customer visiting one store over another store. There are two ways that e-tailers can attempt to have their websites ranked higher in search indexes: organic SEO and paid SEO.

Organic SEO

Organic SEO is the process of *creating* a website so that it will be ranked high in search engine indexes. The best SEO strategy is to make SEO an integral design consideration from the early stages of planning and designing a website.

Metadata is a key element that impacts how a website is viewed by a search engine. Metadata are hidden data within a site that provide information about the content of particular items. For example, an image may include metadata describing how large the picture is, the color depth, image resolution, file name, and when the image was created. A text document's metadata may contain information about the document's length, who the author is, when the document was written, and a short summary of the document.

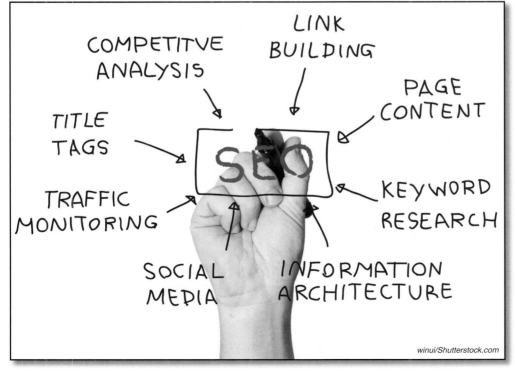

The goal of search engine optimization is to be near the top of an Internet search results list.

Meta Tags

Web pages often include metadata in the form of meta tags. **Meta tags** are specific types of metadata associated with a web page. For example, title, description, and keyword meta tags are commonly used to describe the content of a web page. Most search engines use these data when adding pages to the search index.

The title includes the words seen by a website visitor at the top of the web browser. It is also the default name given when a visitor bookmarks the web page.

Keywords are the words and phrases customers might use if they are looking for a specific product on a website. Those keywords are added to the metadata in order of importance or relevance, and are separated by commas. Businesses usually develop a standard list of keywords applied to all their web pages, which may include products, brand names, and even commonly misspelled words. Web designers may also add page-specific keywords to the standard list, as applicable.

If the same keywords are repeated too often in a meta tag, some search engines will not index the document. Search engines typically process only the first 1000 characters of the keywords list. Search engines also read, or *crawl*, the text on every web page to find the most commonly repeated words. The search engine matches these repeated words with the metadata. Keywords must match the web page text, or the page may be ranked lower in the search engine results.

Keywords should be listed by importance in the meta tags. The closer the tag or word is to the beginning of the code, the higher its ranking. For example, if the main product is a Coach purse, keywords in the meta tags might read *Coach, purse, handbags, accessories.* Keywords in this order would rank higher than if listed as *accessories, handbags, purse, Coach.* Web pages are assigned higher rankings by search engines based on the order of the page's keywords. This is true for all wording in metadata.

This description is the text that is found when a web search is performed. For example, when a search is performed on Google, a ranked list of websites is returned with hyperlinks and brief descriptions of each site. The description displayed in the search engine results list is pulled from the meta tag text. To avoid being shortened by search engines, descriptions should be brief with no more than 200 characters.

Alt Tags

Alternative text tags, or *alt tags*, are hidden code used to name or describe images on a web page. Alt tags make images searchable because they contain the text shown when an image cannot be displayed in a browser. For example, an image of a Black & Decker® drill should be given an alt tag in the code that says *Black & Decker drill*. The model number may also be included. Visitors do not see this text, but search engines do. Alt tags can be seen using some web browsers by hovering the mouse pointer over an image. To maximize SEO results, the web designer should assign an alt tag to every image.

Paid SEO

As discussed in Chapter 9, *Retail Communication*, retailers purchase certain search terms, or keywords, used on different search engines. This practice is called *paid SEO*. Websites are coded to include the purchased keywords, and the search engine links to the business' site. Paid SEO increases the chances of higher rankings in a search engine's results.

Checkpoint 14.2

1. What are the six things to consider when building a reputable and trustworthy e-tail site?
2. Identify payment options e-tailers should consider for their shopping cart systems.
3. Why are message boards, blogs, listservs, and chat rooms important to an e-tail website?
4. How are collections used in the creation of a website?
5. Explain the importance of search engine optimization (SEO) to e-tail websites.

Build Your Vocabulary

As you progress through this course, develop a personal glossary of retailing terms and add it to your portfolio. This will help you build your vocabulary and prepare you for a career. Write a definition for each of the following terms, and add it to your personal retail glossary.

web widget	indexing
image cruncher	search engine optimization (SEO)
JavaScript	organic SEO
search engine	metadata
keyword	meta tags

Section 14.3 Elements of a Web Page

Objectives

After completing this section, you will be able to:
- **Summarize** how code is used to build a website.
- **Discuss** how visual elements impact the look, feel, and navigability of a web page.

Key Terms

code	Flash®
HTML	WYSIWYG
Java	cascading style
Java applets	sheets (CSS)
dynamic HTML	style
(DHTML)	frames
extensible markup	tables
language (XML)	bandwidth

Web Connect

Visit the website of your favorite e-tailer. On your browser's tool bar, select the **View Source** or **Page Source** button. Describe what you see.

Critical Thinking

Some online businesses want their websites to be very *flashy* and use the latest technology to accomplish this look. Make a list of businesses that might want flashy websites. Why do you think a flashy look appeals to these businesses?

How to Build a Website

Once a website is planned and designed, it must be built. While a web page may appear to be simply text and graphics, there is much more involved. Unlike a document built with a word processing program, websites are built with a computer language using code. Code is a set of instructions for a computer directing it to perform certain activities. It is also called *source code*.

Code is invisible to the person viewing a web page. Web browsers read the code and translate it into what is seen as a web page. For example, Figure 14-3 shows an example of a typical sentence that might appear on an e-tail website. Below it is the code needed to create that sentence and make it appear the way the web designer wanted. This same type of code is used to build text, images, and all other elements of a web page.

> **A sentence as simple as this on a web page...**
>
> **ON SALE NOW!** *Get free shipping* **with every order over $75!**
>
> **...is created using this "invisible" code to be visible in a web browser.**
>
> <p><font face="Arial, Helvetica, sans-serif"><strong><font color="#0000FF" size="+1">ON SALE NOW!</font></strong><font size="+1"> Get <em><strong>free shipping</strong></em> on purchases over $75!</font></font></p>

Figure 14-3 An example of code used to create web pages.

Goodheart-Willcox Publisher

Web Page Languages

In order to build an e-tail site, web designers need to understand how to write the code that creates web pages. Writing code can be time consuming, and there are many languages available.

HTML

The fundamental language for a web page is called HTML. HTML stands for hypertext markup language. This type of code tells a web browser how to read the web page. Figure 14-3 is an example of HTML coding. HTML code helps the web designer to design and layout a page, determine the types of fonts, insert background colors or images, and much more. It is essentially the framework for the entire page.

HTML pages have two main sections, which are the *head* and the *body*. The head is a section that is never seen by website visitors. It stays in the background, but contains critical elements of a web page. For example, the brief web page description displayed in a search engine results list is written in code in the head of the HTML page. The second part of HTML page is the body. The body contains the rest of the web page elements.

Java

Java (not to be confused with JavaScript) is a language that enables web designers to build entire web pages or to build separate small programs to be inserted into web pages. These small programs, called Java applets, act as additional features inserted into an HTML web page. Java applets can be used to create a variety of functions on a web page, such as charts, online photo albums, slideshows, and much more. Web page visitors must have Java installed and enabled, or turned on, in their web browsers before they can view the content.

DHTML

Dynamic HTML, or *DHTML*, combines HTML, JavaScript, and cascading style sheets (CSS) to create vibrant visual effects on a web page. HTML can layout and display elements of a web page but has limited dynamic features. DHTML can provide visual effects that are not possible using HTML. For example, many nav bars are created using DHTML. If you have ever clicked on a nav bar button that displays a submenu, there is a good chance that nav bar was built with DHTML.

XML

Extensible markup language (XML) is a language that can be viewed by most web browsers. XML allows web designers to build advanced web page features that HTML does not. For example, XML is commonly used to create online databases. An XML application can read a database and display the result on a web page, while updating the results as the data change. XML is often used within HTML pages.

Flash®

Adobe® **Flash**® is a program based on ActionScript code that can create dynamic animated and video elements on a web page. Flash may be used as a stand-alone web page or may be inserted into a web document. For example, buttons that become animated, spin, or light up when clicked may be created using Flash. It can also be used to create full-feature videos on the web. Flash supports streaming video on sites like YouTube.

Nonlanguage Features

Aside from writing code, there are other considerations that impact the construction of a website. The type of web design software used, as well as the way it portrays a website, are important considerations.

WYSIWYG Software

While all websites are built using code, web designers most often do not write and key in every line of code. The most common method of building a site is to use WYSIWYG software. **WYSIWYG** (pronounced WIZ-ee-wig) stands for "what you see is what you get." Much like a word processor, WYSIWYG software allows web designers to see exactly what the web page looks like while building it. This software is easy to use because it automatically converts content and design elements into code.

It is important to note, however, that web authoring software is not perfect and may not always do exactly what the web designer wants it to do. As a result, web designers need a basic understanding of the code to effectively use web authoring software. For example, to build special features that are not part of the web authoring software, web designers may need to modify the code by hand.

Cascading Style Sheets (CSS)

HTML coding has evolved, and other HTML-based languages now make building web pages easier. One improvement to HTML is cascading style sheets. Cascading style sheets (CSS) is a type of style language used to more easily format the layout and design a web page.

CSS defines new styles, or visual elements in HTML, displayed on completed web pages. It allows the web designer to choose and apply different styles to items that are repeated on a web page, such as fonts and other graphic elements. For example, a style could be created for the bold, blue fonts shown in Figure 14-3. Once the style is created, CSS allows the web designer to simply select a style to create the same bold blue fonts, instead of writing HTML code for each instance. Most web design templates are created with CSS.

Frames

Another way to layout a web page is to use frames. Frames allow the web designer to display more than one web page within a single browser window, as shown in Figure 14-4. For example, a web page could have a nav bar in one frame on the left side of the page, and the main content in a larger frame filling the center of the page.

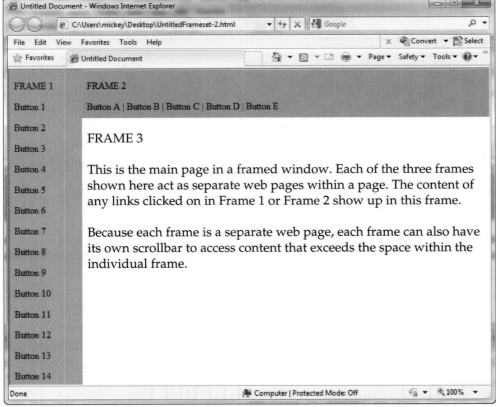

Figure 14-4 The red, gray, and white portions of this page were built using frames.

Using frames does have drawbacks. When a search engine analyzes a framed site, it reads the site and thinks it is a blank page. So, the search engine gives the web page a low ranking in the search results. Understand that using frames to create a website can greatly reduce the chance that it will be highly ranked in search engine results.

Visual Elements in Web Pages

There are plenty of elements in a web page that visitors can see. Selecting these elements impacts the look, feel, and navigability of the site. Some are viewable by visitors, such as graphics, while others lie in the background and control how other elements are viewed. Visual elements of web pages include graphics, tables, fonts, hyperlinks, and multimedia.

Graphics

As web browsing speed continues to get faster, the use of graphics is increasingly important. Text allows web visitors to read information, but graphics allow the e-tailer to send a powerful message. Graphics are used to make a web page more visually appealing, help to build a brand, send a message, and create a visual theme throughout a site.

The two most common types of image files used on websites are GIFs and JPEGs. Both file types are compressed, or reduced in size, to download quickly into a web browser. *Graphic interchange format (GIF)* is commonly used for images that are simple in nature, such as cartoons, logos, and other graphics that do not contain much shading. GIFs also allow the background of an image to be transparent, so they can blend in with the background of a web page.

Joint photographic experts group (JPEG) (pronounced JAY-peg) files allow for wide variations in color. For example, most photographs on web pages are JPEGs.

Tables

Tables are used to display data in rows and columns, keeping the elements neatly aligned for easy reading. Tables may be used in web pages for the purpose of page layout.

Most web page languages do not give web designers the flexibility of placing elements exactly where they want them to be. As a result, many web pages have invisible tables within the pages that provide more control over how the web page appears to visitors. Figure 14-5 shows an example of how tables might be used in a web site. Tables keep page elements, such as text and graphics,

Goodheart-Willcox Publisher

Figure 14-5 In this example, tables are used to layout elements in a website's header.

fixed so that they appear the same on all browsers. When tables are used to control appearance, they are built without borders and lines. In doing this, the edges of tables, rows, and columns cannot be seen on screen.

Fonts

Font selection may appear to be a basic choice, but web designers put a lot of thought into font selection. The type of font used helps set the tone for a web page, and can even send a brand message. For example, the font in *this* part of the sentence sends a different branding message than the *Jokerman font used in this part of the sentence*.

One challenge faced by web designers is the visitor's ability to read a font. Most web browsers can only read approximately eight specific fonts. If a web page includes a font that is not readable by a browser, it is automatically converted to one of eight readable fonts. According to Macromedia, the eight readable fonts are:

- Arial
- Helvetica
- Times New Roman
- Times
- Courier
- Georgia
- Verdana
- Geneva

When fonts are converted, the appearance of the web page changes. To avoid this, web designers often create a limited amount of text using either graphics or Flash. The browser will view text as images or Flash files and will not convert the font style. However, overusing this solution can create web pages that are very large in size.

Social Media

Creating Shopping Events on Facebook

There are apps that allow a retailer to create shopping events for fans directly through the business' Facebook page. Most apps of this type are fee-based. Pop-up shop apps can be used to sell a product to Facebook fans of the page for a short time. A business can offer a new product or a discount on an existing product for people that like a Facebook page to create an inside shopping event. Knowledge of this type of activity is often shared between Facebook users and can quickly increase likes for a Facebook page. Retailers then need to give people a reason to return with other shopping events or engaging content.

Hyperlinks

Hyperlinks connect visitors to another location within the site or on a completely different website. Visually, hyperlinks must stand out from the rest of the text on the page. Typically, hyperlinked text is underlined and in bright blue, but any color can be used, as long as it is clear that the text is a hyperlink. Hyperlinks can be attached to text and graphics, as well as other dynamic features.

Multimedia

One of the things that makes the Internet different from other mediums is that it is interactive. When properly used, sound, animation, video, games, and other multimedia components on a website can provide a rich experience for visitors.

Audio

Audio, or sound, can be effective on an e-tail website when used properly. Audio can be as simple as a *click* sound when a button is pushed. Background music or sound may play while visitors navigate the site. While sound can help enhance the brand, it should be used with caution. Audio can use a lot of bandwidth, or the amount of data that can be transmitted in a certain amount of time. Using audio that consumes a great amount of bandwidth can make downloads slow or choppy. The result may be an impatient customer who leaves the site. If large audio files are used on a web page, give visitors the option to turn the sound off.

Video

Video on an e-tail site can provide demonstrations of a product or process, provide tips, or entertain visitors. However, like audio, viewing video should be optional. Some visitors love videos, while others are impatient and prefer to read instructions or other information. Most video should not play automatically when a visitor reaches a page. The e-tailer should give visitors the option to watch videos. Most video players also allow viewers to pause or stop the video, if they so desire.

Checkpoint 14.3

1. How is code used to create a website?
2. How is DHTML different from HTML?
3. Explain how frames are used on a web page.
4. How do tables add to the visual look and feel of a web page?
5. Identify the eight fonts that are readable by most browsers.

Build Your Vocabulary

As you progress through this course, develop a personal glossary of retailing terms and add it to your portfolio. This will help you build your vocabulary and prepare you for a career. Write a definition for each of the following terms, and add it to your personal retail glossary.

code	WYSIWYG
HTML	cascading style sheets (CSS)
Java	style
Java applets	frames
dynamic HTML (DHTML)	tables
extensible markup language (XML)	bandwidth
Flash®	

Chapter Summary

Section 14.1 Building a Website

- When deciding to build a website, retailers must decide whether to outsource the site building tasks or build the website in-house. They should examine the pros and cons of their site-building options and determine the most effective and efficient way to create the site.
- There are five general steps in building an e-tail site: plan, design, develop, publish, and maintain.

Section 14.2 Web Design Tools and Resources

- E-tailers can build the trustworthiness of their site by considering its accessibility, simplicity, site-search tools, ease of purchase, customer service options, and return guarantees.
- Many website features and elements can be built using tools and software found online to meet the website's goals and objectives. These include image crunchers, web widgets, JavaScript, message boards, blogs, listservs, chat rooms, forms, databases, polls, surveys, and games.
- Search engine optimization (SEO) is the process of getting a website ranked higher on the results pages when an Internet search is conducted. The goal of SEO is to attract more profitable traffic from search engines to the website.

Section 14.3 Elements of a Web Page

- Code is a set of instructions for a computer directing it to perform certain activities. In order to build an e-tail site, web designers need to understand how to write the code that creates web pages.
- Selecting visual elements impacts the look, feel, and navigability of a site. Graphics are used to make a web page more visually appealing, help to build a brand, send a message, and create a visual theme throughout a site. Tables are commonly used in web pages to keep the elements neatly aligned for easy reading. The type of font used helps to set the tone for a web page, and can even send a brand message.

Review Your Knowledge

1. Describe the considerations involved when building a website in-house.
2. Explain the importance of defining the goals and objectives of a website during the planning phase.
3. Explain how to obtain an Internet name. How does this relate to a business' Internet identity?
4. Explain ways to make purchasing easy for online customers.
5. How do image crunchers improve the performance of a web page?
6. What is the difference between organic SEO and paid SEO?
7. What is HTML?
8. How can web designers use graphics and Flash to manage unreadable fonts on a web page?
9. Explain how tables are used in website design.
10. What is bandwidth?

Apply Your Knowledge

1. Select your favorite search engine. Visit the business solutions information on the search engine site and investigate the information provided on SEO. Write a summary of your findings.
2. Technology has made marketing research quicker and more accurate. Marketing information can be obtained from search engines, customer relations management (CRM) system databases, blogs, and listservs. Create a table that has two columns. In the first column, list each of these sources of information. In the second column, write examples of the type of marketing information that can be found using each of these activities. What did you find in common that all of these sources provide as marketing research information?
3. Using the information about the web site you are constructing, select a simple form that you could post on the site such as a product survey, user poll, or other activity of your choice. Keep the form simple and easy to use. Write the questions in a manner that allows data to be collected, such as contact information or user information. This data collection should be constructed so it can be used for market research. Also, use frames as you develop the pages.
4. E-tailers have preferences as to payment collection options that are used on their websites. Visit your favorite e-tail site. What options does the retailer offer customers? How are these options described? Are there icons, text only, or both?
5. Do an Internet search for *Java applets*. There are many applets that are free of charge. Write down several of the ones that you found. What is their purpose?
6. There are many multimedia components that make an e-tail site both useful and interesting for visitors. Make a list of several of the components you think are most important. Explain your reasoning for each component listed.
7. Research data modeling. How do retailers consider data modeling when designing a website?
8. Review a few of the e-tail websites that you visit often. Find examples of features added to create enhanced web pages. List several of the examples you find and explain how each adds value to the website.
9. Research the history of coding languages. Create a time line that notes each milestone development and new code languages to the present date.
10. Choose one e-tail site that you visit often. Review the pages on the site and make a list of all the keywords you think the web designer should include for search engine optimization.

Check Your Retail IQ

Now that you have finished the chapter, see what you learned about retail by taking the chapter posttest. If you do not have a smartphone, visit the G-W Learning companion website.

G-W Learning mobile site: www.m.g-wlearning.com

G-W Learning companion website: www.g-wlearning.com/marketing/

College and Career Readiness

Career Ready Practices Conduct an Internet search for *desirable workplace skills*. Pick five skills from your search results. Beside each of the five you selected, indicate an academic skill that directly relates to the workplace skill.

Reading Read a magazine, newspaper, or online article to find the current US unemployment rate. Identify the audience and the purpose of the message. How did you apply your prior knowledge of the subject to understanding the article?

Listening Practice active-listening skills while listening to your teacher present a lesson. Focus on the message and monitor it for understanding. How did you use prior experiences to help you understand what was being said? Evaluate your teacher's point of view and use of material in the presentation.

Teamwork

Working with your team, continue the **Teamwork** website revision project started in Chapter 13. Review the website analysis and the list of tasks necessary to update and revise the website. Make a list of the goals and objectives for the revised website. Choose the appropriate website products and services, and begin building web pages. Include a simple form to post on the site, such as a product survey, user poll, or other activity that can be used to collect visitor information for market research. Create complex web pages that include frames, JavaScript applications, hyperlinks, and tables. Review keywords in the meta tags on the existing website. Revise and reorganize the keywords to optimize the page's search engine ranking.

College and Career Portfolio

Hard Skills

Employers review candidates for various positions and colleges are always looking for qualified applicants. When listing your qualifications, you may discuss software programs you know or machines you can operate. These abilities are often called *hard skills.* You should make an effort to learn about and develop the hard skills you will need for your chosen career.

1. Do research on the Internet to find articles about hard skills and their value in helping employees succeed.
2. Make a list of the hard skills that you possess that you think would be important for a job or career area. Select three of these hard skills. Write a paragraph about each one that describes your abilities in this area. Give examples that illustrate your skills.
3. Save the document file in your e-portfolio. Place a printed copy in the container for your print portfolio.

◇DECA Coach

Teambuilding

When you work as part of a team on one of DECA's competitive events, understand that you may be working with the same team members for a long time. You may work together from the beginning of the school year all the way through the International Career Development Conference (ICDC), which is held in late April. Therefore, you need to be sure to pick teammates with whom you are comfortable. Look at the strengths and weaknesses of each member, but also consider compatibility.

One of the best ways to build team camaraderie is to do something together outside of school. Ask your advisor to establish some "friendly competition" between your team and other teams in your DECA chapter. It may be things that you do during class, but do not hesitate to take it outside of class. For example, you might set up a bowling competition between your team and other teams in your chapter. You might play tennis or video games against another team. Friendly competition will strengthen your team.

Visit www.deca.org to learn more information about DECA.

G-W Learning Mobile Site

Visit the G-W Learning mobile site to complete the chapter pretest and posttest, and to practice vocabulary using e-flash cards. If you do not have a smartphone, visit the G-W Learning companion website to access these features.

G-W Learning mobile site: www.m.g-wlearning.com

G-W Learning companion website: www.g-wlearning.com/marketing/

Unit 6
Managing the Business

Introduction

Managers are in charge of everyday operations of a business to ensure that it functions efficiently and meets established goals. Managers must also lead, support, and guide their teams to success. Effective team members work well with others, share responsibilities, and cooperate in reaching the team's goal. Successful teams are developed through five stages: forming, storming, norming, performing, and adjourning.

Like other businesses, retailers are obligated to operate in an ethical manner. Many businesses have a code of ethics that employees are expected to follow. In addition, there are local, state, and federal laws under which retailers must abide.

In the operation of a business, both retailers and e-tailers assume controllable and uncontrollable risks. Risk management involves anticipating risks and taking the necessary steps to prevent or minimize them to help ensure the success of the business.

Green Retail

Sustainability Training

Green retailers lead by example and educate their employees on sustainable business practices. Through sustainability training, employees learn the importance of "going green" at work and the best practices to reduce waste, lower energy consumption, and even apply sustainability principles to the supply chain. Employees also learn about the carbon footprint of businesses and individuals, and positive actions they can take to protect the environment. Actions as simple as turning off lights when not in use, recycling paper, and reusing boxes contribute to the sustainability of a business.

In This Unit

Ruta Production/Shutterstock.com

349

Chapter 15
Retail Management

Taking control and making decisions about a business requires the type of person who can lead. Executing the functions of management—planning, organizing, staffing, leading, and controlling—can be challenging. Some personalities are better suited to perform these functions than others. Management styles are generally classified as laissez-fair, democratic, autocratic, or consulting.

Managers are typically responsible for the direct supervision of personnel. Recruiting, hiring, training, supervising, and terminating employees fall within management tasks. Managers are also in charge of everyday operations of a business to ensure that it functions efficiently and meets established goals.

Case Study

Gap Inc.

Gap Inc. is a global fashion retailer, with brands that include Gap, Old Navy, Banana Republic, Piperlime, and Athleta. Gap Inc. created their Retail Management Program to train and develop management candidates who are dedicated to the challenging and rewarding business of fashion retailing. Through the program, management candidates acquire a thorough understanding of the company's product lines, operations, and the pillars of successful retailing.

During this nine-month program, candidates are assigned cross-brand rotations in inventory management, merchandising, and production. They gain hands-on experience running both brick-and-mortar and online businesses and are immersed in the Gap Inc. culture. While participating in business functions, candidates also attend professional training classes and general education sessions to build their management skills and abilities.

By providing the Retail Management Program, Gap Inc. trains effective managers who will successfully manage a Gap Inc. store or operation. This contributes to the company's overall profitability and image.

College and Career Readiness

Reading Prep

As you read the content of this chapter, try to determine which topics are fact and which are the author's opinion. Research some of the topics and verify which are facts and which are opinions. Identify the sources you used to verify facts.

Check Your Retail IQ

Before you begin the chapter, see what you already know about retail by taking the chapter pretest. If you do not have a smartphone, visit the G-W Learning companion website.

G-W Learning mobile site: www.m.g-wlearning.com

G-W Learning companion website: www.g-wlearning.com/marketing/

Sections

15.1 Management Functions

15.2 Managing the Store

mangostock/Shutterstock.com

Section 15.1 Management Functions

Objectives

After completing this section, you will be able to:
- **Identify** the functions of management.
- **Explain** the four styles of management.
- **Describe** the tasks involved in managing personnel.

Key Terms

manager
management
functions of
   management
planning
organizing
staffing

controlling
leading
store manager
human resources
   management
recruiting
supervise

Web Connect

Conduct an Internet search for *functions of management*. Write your own definition of each function. Next, make a list of skills that successful managers need to develop in order to carry out the functions of management.

Critical Thinking

Think about your personal style of dealing with other people. Imagine yourself as a store manager. What type of manager do you think you would be? List and describe the skills you possess that would make you an effective manager.

Functions of Management

A **manager** is the person responsible for carrying out the goals of the business. It is important for retail managers to match the right people with the right tasks in order to achieve the store's goals.

Management is the process of controlling and making decisions about a business. Management includes all of the activities required to plan, coordinate, and monitor the business. These activities are known as the functions of management. The **functions of management** include planning, organizing, staffing, controlling, and leading. Figure 15-1 illustrates the functions of management.

Planning

Planning is the process of deciding the actions that will guide the business in reaching its goals. In the planning process, managers consider both short-term and long-term goals. A goal is considered to be *short term* when it can be achieved within a year. For example, a monthly sales goal is short-term. A *long-term* goal takes more than a year to achieve. A business' goal of opening a second store within the next five years is an example of a long-term goal.

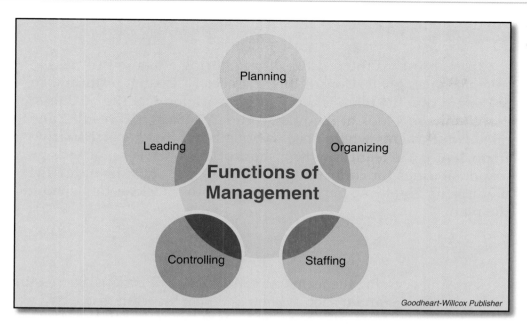

Figure 15-1 The functions of management.

Goodheart-Willcox Publisher

Successful managers generally put their plans in writing and share them with the team. Sharing this information with the team demonstrates good communication practices.

Organizing

Organizing is coordinating the efforts of a team to reach its goals. Organizing ensures that the business has everything it needs to function successfully. Managers use the plans they developed to figure out the best way to reach the team's goals. Managers may create a time line to achieve a goal, assign roles to employees, and establish methods for carrying out tasks.

Staffing

Staffing is the process of hiring people and matching them to the best position for their talents. Staffing is not an easy task. Managers must find employees who are trustworthy and team players. After being hired, a manager may train the employee. In some retail organizations, a coworker may provide training. In others, the human resources (HR) department may take responsibility for training new employees.

Managers must find employees whose talents match the responsibilities of the position.

Andrey_Popov/Shutterstock.com

Controlling

Controlling is the process of monitoring a team's progress in meeting its goals. Controlling involves assessing performance to ensure that the team is on the right path to meet the business plan. Managers look at the plan, compare it to actual results, and make adjustments where necessary. This process is particularly important if the team is falling short of its goals. A manager's responsibilities for controlling a business may include budgeting, monitoring employee performance, and other tasks established in the plan.

Leading

Leading is giving the team clear and concise directions. Successful managers understand the job at hand and help the team reach its goals. Leaders are ethical, recognize team member accomplishments, and lead by example.

Exploring Retail Careers

Webmaster

Most businesses have a website through which they do at least some of their marketing and selling. Logically, a website that looks interesting and is easy to use will be more successful than one that is poorly designed.

A webmaster manages web design and development, and maintains the website after it becomes active. Functionality and design are included in the responsibilities of this position. Webmasters also work with web designers and management, and ensure that the website reflects the image of the business. Other typical job titles for webmasters include *information technology (IT) manager*, *website manager*, and *corporate webmaster*. Some examples of tasks that webmasters perform include:

- work with web development teams to create an easy-to-use interface and solve usability issues
- install updates and upgrades as needed
- troubleshoot website and server problems, keeping downtime to a minimum
- implement and monitor firewalls and other security measures
- update content and links as requested or needed by the company

Webmasters must be proficient in application server software. They must also be proficient in graphics and web page creation software. An understanding of graphic design and web design is essential. If the website is used for sales, the webmaster must also be familiar with the company's products or services. They must be able to set up customer orders and payment processes. Most jobs in this field require an associate degree in web design or a related field, or training in a vocational school. Related job experience is also helpful.

Styles of Management

Each store manager has a different style of managing. *Management style* is the way a person leads a team. There are four common styles of management:

- *Laissez-fair management style* encourages team members to make their own decisions.
- *Democratic management style* encourages team members to participate and share ideas.
- *Autocratic management style* is when the leader makes all the decisions without input from the team.
- *Consulting management style* is a combination of democratic and autocratic in which the manager makes the decisions, but involves team members.

Retail business owners may prefer their store managers to use one style of management over another. Certain types of stores may require specific styles of management in order for the store to be successful. For example, a small department with only two or three employees may function efficiently with a leader who is democratic. On the other hand, a large department with many employees may function better with a manager who is uses the consulting style.

EDHAR/Shutterstock.com

Some managers invite employees to participate in the decision-making process and share ideas.

Managing Personnel

Understanding the functions of management leads to effectively managing the store's personnel. The **store manager** is the person in charge of the overall well-being of a retail store. Store managers are responsible for the people who work in the business. Managing the team is one of the most important job duties a store manager has.

Human resources management is facilitating and managing the employees of an organization. Human resources management is one of the functional areas of retail. Many retailers have a human resources department that takes responsibility for this function. However, managers often participate in the process. Personnel management includes recruiting, hiring, training, supervising, and terminating employees.

Recruiting

Recruiting is the process of finding suitable people and getting them to join a company. There are many ways to recruit potential employees. Exhibiting at trade shows is one common method of recruiting candidates. Employment agencies, social media, and online job boards are other good ways of finding qualified people.

Hiring

Once a pool of potential candidates is identified, the manager begins the process of hiring. Applications and résumés are reviewed and candidates are selected. Interviews are scheduled with the candidates.

Recruiting potential employees is a function of managing personnel.

Andresr/Shutterstock.com

The interview process helps the manager get to know the candidates. It also helps the candidates understand the position and the company. After much review, the manager makes a hiring decision.

Training

Employees rarely show up for their first day of work knowing exactly what to do. Employee training generally begins with introductions to other employees and management. New employees also learn the history and mission of the company, its policies and procedures, payroll and benefits, and related business skills, such as sales or product knowledge. Training takes time and is expensive for a retailer. While training may be more intense for new hires, good retailers consider training an ongoing process for both new and seasoned employees.

Supervising

To **supervise** is to make sure employees perform their jobs. Managers must deal with day-to-day behavior and incidents to make sure the business runs smoothly. Employee complaints and grievances must be addressed. There may be complaints about the work environment, employee equity, and other issues. Unresolved complaints can lead to low morale.

Managers also assess employee performance. Most retailers evaluate employees on a regular basis, typically once per year. The purpose of an evaluation is to make sure that employees are performing as expected. Many companies use good employee evaluations as a basis for pay raises.

Terminating

Occasionally, managers must release employees for performance or behavior issues. It is important that the manager make termination decisions objectively and act in the best interest of the business.

Social Media

Targeting Posts on Facebook

Facebook has tools for retail businesses that allow only the most relevant people to see certain posts. There are two ways to target a post: limit the audience who can see it or add newsfeed targeting filters. These tools make page posts more efficient and are useful for special offers and for information that only some people need. Even if people share a retailer's post with their friends, only those who are in the audience selected for the post will be able to see it.

Terminating an employee without just cause and proper documentation can leave the company open to lawsuits. The manager must make sure to follow company procedures before releasing an employee.

Checkpoint 15.1

1. List the functions of management.
2. Explain the difference between a short-term and a long-term goal.
3. What is *management style*?
4. What tasks are involved in personnel management?
5. What is the purpose of an employee evaluation?

Build Your Vocabulary

As you progress through this course, develop a personal glossary of retailing terms and add it to your portfolio. This will help you build your vocabulary and prepare you for a career. Write a definition for each of the following terms, and add it to your personal retailing glossary.

manager
management
functions of management
planning
organizing
staffing

controlling
leading
store manager
human resources management
recruiting
supervise

Section 15.2 Managing the Store

Objectives

After completing this section, you will be able to:
- **Describe** the operations activities required for a retail business.
- **Identify** ways to measure store performance.

Key Terms

chain of command
organizational chart
income statement

Web Connect

Research *retail store operations* on the Internet. List five of the retail store operations you find in your research. Rank each item in order of importance. Write several paragraphs to explain your ranking.

Critical Thinking

The attitude of a manager sets the tone for the rest of the staff. How do you think a manager influences attitudes in a business? How does attitude contribute to an environment that creates customer satisfaction?

Operations

Operations are the day-to-day activities necessary to keep a business up and running. Operations is also a functional area of retail. Store operations can be challenging for managers. Both retailers and e-tailers face many of the same challenges. While operational tasks can become routine, there are many details that need to be addressed. From opening the store first thing in the morning until closing the store at the end of the day, the store manager is responsible for all operations of the business.

In a retail business, operations activities can include the following:
- scheduling
- building maintenance
- managing merchandise
- interacting with customers
- interacting with superiors

A primary goal of the operations function is efficiency. Efficient operations lower expenses, increase profits, and help to keep product prices down. Managers oversee operations as an important part of their responsibilities.

Scheduling

A work schedule must be planned for the employees, telling them what days and times they are expected at work. The manager must balance the store's needs for staff with the employees' needs for hours and flexibility. Because retail stores are often open for long hours, the manager should make an effort to be fair in scheduling employees. Most large retailers use software developed for employee scheduling.

Building Maintenance

The retail building is a visual element that portrays the retailer's image. It is important that the store be safe and attractive, both inside the building and on the grounds outside. A clean, attractive store sends a positive message, while a sloppy or dirty store sends a negative one. Managers should have a system in place for regular store cleaning and maintaining a neat and clean appearance of the building's exterior.

Keeping the business' exterior neat and clean is part of a manager's regular building maintenance tasks.

senkaya/Shutterstock.com

Managers must also attend to safety issues in and around the building. Potholes in the parking lot, moisture or loose wires on the ground, and other hazards in or around the store must be dealt with immediately. These hazards are often not foreseeable, but management needs to make decisions as they occur. Many retailers hire a cleaning and maintenance crew to handle these tasks.

Managing Merchandise

The manager is responsible for merchandise from the moment it arrives at the store. The merchandise must be received and displayed appropriately. Although the manager may not always be the person performing each task, he or she is responsible for making sure the tasks are done correctly.

Once inventory is delivered from a vendor, it is recorded in the store's inventory. Managers should establish procedures for making sure that inventory is received and recorded correctly. It is important to match the merchandise received with the delivery invoice. Merchandise should be counted and inspected for damage. A good system for receiving merchandise helps ensure that inventory is correct.

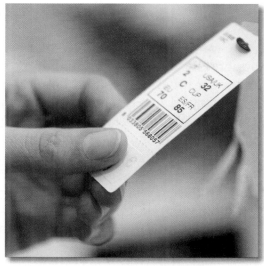

A merchandise ticket identifies the product and lists the price.

bikeriderlondon/Shutterstock.com

Once received, retail merchandise must be ticketed and priced before it can be placed onto the retail floor. The ticket states the price and identifies the product. As each item is sold, inventory can be adjusted and tracked using the ticket information. Improper ticketing can result in under- or over-charging customers for an item. It can also result in a skewed inventory.

Ticketed merchandise must be placed on the sales floor to be sold. Where to place merchandise is a strategic decision that may impact sales. The manager influences decisions about merchandise placement and display.

Interacting with Customers

Ultimately, managers are responsible for keeping customers happy. Customer relations duties are usually handled indirectly through sales associates, customer service reps, and other front-line employees. However, the manager is ultimately responsible for customer relations for the business.

Managers should dictate the behaviors expected from the staff. These behaviors can help ensure that new customers become repeat customers:

- Be friendly and call customers by name, when appropriate
- Offer the best service possible
- Maintain a clean, attractive shopping atmosphere

Managing customer relations is not always as simple as wearing a smile and being polite. Sometimes, customers have issues that are not easily resolved. The first step to resolution is to listen to the customer's issue. Issues cannot be resolved until they are fully understood. Once the issue is identified, the manager needs to offer solutions. Even if the manager believes a customer's issue is unjustified, he or she needs to weigh the cost of solving the problem against the cost of potentially losing a customer.

Interacting with Superiors

Store managers also have supervisors. The store manager's supervisor may be a regional manager or the store owner. The store manager must understand how to work with his or her supervisor.

Every business has a chain of command. The **chain of command** is an organization's structure of decision-making responsibilities, from the highest to the lowest level of authority. Most businesses create an organizational chart to show the chain of command. An **organizational chart** is a diagram of employee positions that shows how all the positions interact within the chain of command. An example of a retail organizational chart is shown in Figure 15-2.

It is important that the store manager listen to and understand the direction given by his or her supervisor. Those directions must then be conveyed to the store employees to make sure that the goals of the business are met.

Store Performance

The manager is responsible for the overall performance of a store. Store performance can be measured in many ways. One way is by calculating the operating expenses. Operating expenses are the expenses that keep a business functioning. This includes the cost of goods and services used in the daily operation of a business,

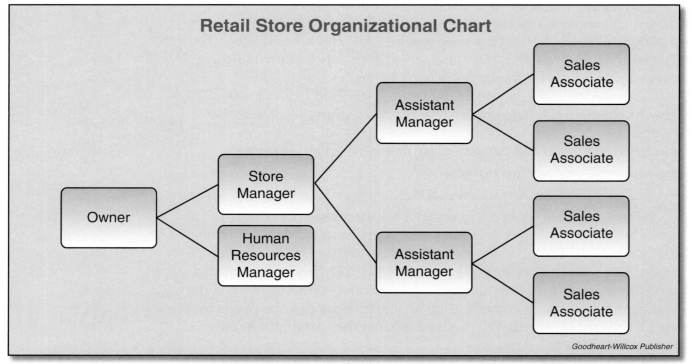

Goodheart-Willcox Publisher

Figure 15-2 An organizational chart illustrates the chain of command for a retail store.

like paper, computers, and janitorial services. Managers are often evaluated on how well they control the day-to-day expenses of a business. This can be done by comparing the prices of various suppliers and choosing one that offers the best value.

Store performance is also measured by the sales generated. The following are some of the sales data that may be used to evaluate performance:

- **Volume.** Sales may be monitored by the number and dollar amounts of sales transactions each day, week, quarter, or year.

- **Product.** Some businesses track the sales of individual products. This helps management evaluate which products are effective in generating sales.

- **Sales associate.** Number of products, product assortment, and sales volume for each sales associate may be evaluated as a criteria for store performance.

- **Territory.** Retailers who have multiple store locations may evaluate the sales of each store in relation to the performance of other stores in the same territory. Territory, or team, sales may also be calculated to reflect performance in various geographic locations.

- **Other metrics.** The number of website hits, customer website traffic, and specific channel sales are examples of other metrics used to measure performance.

Revenue is the money that a business makes from the products and services it sells. *Expenses* are the costs incurred to operate a business. Businesses create **income statements** that show the revenue and expenses during a specific period of time. The goal is to generate a profit. *Profit* is the difference between revenue and expenses. Profits may be recorded by each department or for the overall store.

Metrics are standards of measurement. In retail, metrics are used to measure a business' performance. Examples of metrics include sales figures and website traffic data.

The manager is responsible for the overall performance of a store.

Retail Ethics

Integrity

Integrity is defined as the honesty of a person's actions. Integrity and ethics go hand-in-hand in both personal and professional lives. Retail professionals help establish the reputation of a business in the community. A retail professional who displays integrity helps create a positive culture for the business, customers, and the community.

E-tailers and retailers may use similar, but different, performance metrics. E-tailers track website hits and traffic, customer purchases, customer activity on the e-tail site, customers' locations, and many other data using website analytic software, such as Google Analytics. An e-tailer can create tracking and sales reports to evaluate the performance of its e-tail site. E-tail management may then choose to make adjustments to improve the site's effectiveness.

Generally, upper management creates sales goals that the store must meet. It is the responsibility of the store manager to execute the plans and meet the sales goals.

Sales per Square Foot

Calculating the amount of sales generated per square foot may be used to evaluate performance. Some businesses use this metric as an indicator of success. The formula for sales per square foot is as follows:

$$\frac{\text{net sales}}{\text{square feet of selling space}} = \text{sales per square foot}$$

Average Sales per Transaction

The average amount sales per transaction may be used to show how much each sale contributes to the success of the business. The formula to calculate average sales per transaction is as follows:

$$\frac{\text{net sales}}{\text{number of transactions}} = \text{average sales per transaction}$$

Average Sale per Employee

Some stores may calculate the average sales amount per employee. The formula is as follows:

$$\frac{\text{net sales}}{\text{number of employees}} = \text{average sale per employee}$$

This information can help a store manager evaluate if an employee meets the store's or department's standards. However, other factors may affect this number, including days worked, time of day worked, territory or team assigned, sales promotions, and other job functions the employee needed to perform. For example, a sales associate working during the week might not sell as much as a sales associate who works only on the weekends or during other peak sales periods. Time away from the sales floor for tasks like store cleaning and merchandise stocking also affect the average sale per employee figure.

The average sales per transaction and average sales per employee figures may be further analyzed by channel. A *channel* is a specific source of sales. For example, a company may break down the average sales per transaction data into retail location sales, outlet location sales, and online sales. The sales data per channel may be a useful metric in a company's marketing decisions.

Checkpoint 15.2

1. List some of the daily operations activities for a retail business.
2. How does an organizational chart depict the chain of command?
3. What are the two general methods of measuring store performance?
4. How is profit calculated?
5. Identify factors that can affect the average sale per employee figure.

Build Your Vocabulary

As you progress through this course, develop a personal glossary of retailing terms and add it to your portfolio. This will help you build your vocabulary and prepare you for a career. Write a definition for each of the following terms, and add it to your personal retailing glossary.

chain of command
organizational chart
income statement

Chapter Summary

Section 15.1 Management Functions

- Management is the process of controlling and making decisions about a business. The functions of management include planning, organizing, staffing, controlling, and leading.
- The four styles of management are laissez-fair, democratic, autocratic, and consulting. The style of management used depends on the individual manager and the size of the staff.
- Understanding the functions of management leads to effectively managing personnel. Personnel management includes recruiting, hiring, training, supervising, and terminating employees.

Section 15.2 Managing the Store

- Operations are the day-to-day activities necessary to keep a business up and running. The operations function of retail includes scheduling, building maintenance, managing merchandise, interacting with customers, and interacting with superiors.
- Store performance can be measured by calculating the operating expenses or by calculating the sales generated. Commonly used sales data to evaluate store performance include volume of sales transactions, sales of individual products, sales per square foot, average sales per transaction, and average sales per employee.

Review Your Knowledge

1. Describe what *organizing* means as a function of management.
2. Who is responsible for training new employees?
3. Name and describe the four different management styles.
4. How can a retailer recruit potential employees?
5. Explain how a manager should handle terminating an employee.
6. Explain a manager's responsibilities related to building maintenance.
7. Describe the importance of proper merchandise ticketing.
8. Explain the store manager's role in handling customer complaints.
9. How can an e-tailer evaluate the performance of its e-tail site?
10. State the formula for calculating the average sales per transaction.

Apply Your Knowledge

1. Planning is an important function of management. How is time management related to planning? How can a manager use time management to create plans for his or her team?
2. As an employer hiring part-time sales associates, what are your expectations for new employees? Write several paragraphs describing how you expect new employees to behave while on the job.
3. There are times when employees need to be terminated for performance or behavioral issues. Create a list of inappropriate work habits that you think could lead to termination. Identify appropriate work habits that can lead to an employee's success on the job.

4. There are four types of management styles: laissez-fair, democratic, autocratic, and consulting. Which style do you think describes the type of manager you would be? Make a list of your behaviors that correspond to the management style.

5. Contact a retail store in your area and talk with the store manager. Ask if you can visit and conduct an interview about the importance of managing store performance. Make a list of questions before your visit. Summarize your visit and interview for the class.

6. This chapter states that a primary goal of the operations function is efficiency. Explain what this statement means to you. Give examples of the typical goods and services a retail business uses for its daily operations. Conduct Internet research on how a business can reduce operational expenses. Are there any strategies that result in greater operating expense efficiencies than others?

7. Sometimes, a customer's problem must be handled by a manager. There are certain management actions that can produce customer satisfaction, rather than dissatisfaction. Make a list of behaviors that qualify as positive manager interaction with an unhappy customer. Rank the behaviors in order of importance. Explain your choice of behaviors and ranking.

8. Retailers evaluate store performance using multiple metrics. One metric is to measure the volume of sales based on sales per square foot. Assume a retail store is 1,300 square feet. In one month, the store generated $214,200 in net sales. State the formula used to calculate sales per square foot. Next, calculate the sales per square foot for the month. Show your calculation.

9. Other metrics retailers use to evaluate their business are average sales per transaction, sales per time period, and sales per channel. Assume that a retail store generated $214,200 in net sales in one month. During that month, the store reported 12,600 transactions. State the formula used to calculate average sales per transaction. Next, calculate the average sales per transaction for the month. Show your calculation. The sales are further broken down by channel. In-store sales represented 51 percent of the store's total sales. Online sales account for the remaining amount. What is the total for each channel?

10. Average sales per employee and per product are metrics retailers use to evaluate the performance of their business. Each employee is typically part of a territory or team. Assume that a retail store generated net sales of $214,200 in one month. In the same month, the store employed eight sales associates who comprised one team. State the formula used to calculate average sales per employee. Next, calculate the average sales amount per employee for this team. Show your calculation. There are three product lines that generated these sales. Product A was responsible for 20 percent of total sales, Product B for 50 percent of total sales, and Product C for 30 percent of sales. What is the dollar amount for each product line?

Check Your Retail IQ

Now that you have finished the chapter, see what you learned about retail by taking the chapter posttest. If you do not have a smartphone, visit the G-W Learning companion website.

G-W Learning mobile site: www.m.g-wlearning.com

G-W Learning companion website: www.g-wlearning.com/marketing/

College and Career Readiness

Career Readiness Practices Communication is an important part of the job for any business professional. Cite ways that you can use technology to enhance and improve your communication skills.

Research Secondary research is data and information already assembled and recorded by someone else. Find secondary research on workplace safety. Validate and document your resources. Demonstrate your understanding by summarizing what you learn.

Listening Perform an Internet search to find information on the average age of students in college. Discuss your findings and reasoning with the class or a small group of your classmates. Respond to any questions you are asked. As you listen to your classmates' opinions on this topic, take notes, and ask questions about positions or terms you do not understand. If you hear any unfamiliar vocabulary or expressions used by your classmates, draw on prior knowledge to analyze the meaning.

Teamwork

Working with your team, make a list of ten managers whom you personally know. These could be your teachers or people for whom you have worked. Next to each name, indicate which type of management style you think each person uses— laissez-fair, democratic, autocratic, or consulting. What did you learn from this exercise?

College and Career Portfolio

Clubs and Organizations

Employers and colleges review candidates for various positions. They are interested in people who impress them as being professional or serious about a position. Being involved in academic clubs or professional organizations will help you make a good impression. You can also learn a lot that will help you with your studies or your career. While in school, you may belong to groups, such as National Honor Society and Future Business Leaders of America. When you are employed, you may belong to professional organizations related to your career area, such as American Nurses Association. Update your résumé and online information to reflect your membership in clubs and organizations. Make sure information about you on the Internet does not detract from your professional image. Review information you have posted on social network sites, blogs, wikis, and other sites. Remove any information that does not produce a favorable impression of you.

1. Identify clubs or organizations you can join that will help you learn and build a professional image. List the name and give a brief description of each.
2. Save the file in your e-portfolio. Place a copy in the container for your printed portfolio.

◇DECA Coach

Get in Character

Whether you are involved in an impromptu presentation or a prepared presentation, one common mistake that competitors make is that they forget to get into character. Each situation calls for you to play a certain role. Be sure to pretend that you are who you are supposed to be. The same holds true for your judge. For example, you may be a public relations representative for your company. You are asked to develop and present a public relations plan to your vice president that is directed at solving the issue at hand. Whatever the role calls for, be sure to be in character. Judges understand and expect this. When you do not play the right role, you reduce your chances of scoring well during your presentation.

Getting into and staying in character is another thing to focus on during your practice. Some of the best DECA chapters even invite a drama instructor or a member of the local Toastmasters chapter (a professional public speaking organization) to participate on their advisory panel. These professionals can help you understand your character and may also provide tips and hints. During your conversation, feel free to make character-related comments, like "I enjoyed the luncheon we had last week." Stay in character until after you have left the judge's table.

Visit www.deca.org to learn more information about DECA.

G-W Learning Mobile Site

Visit the G-W Learning mobile site to complete the chapter pretest and posttest, and to practice vocabulary using e-flash cards. If you do not have a smartphone, visit the G-W Learning companion website to access these features.

G-W Learning mobile site: www.m.g-wlearning.com

G-W Learning companion website: www.g-wlearning.com/marketing/

Chapter 16
Working as a Team

Employers look for employees that can be effective team members. Effective team members work well with others, share responsibilities, and cooperate in reaching the team's goal. There are five stages of group development that apply to any successful team: *forming*, *storming*, *norming*, *performing*, and *adjourning*.

Successful teams are supported and guided by effective leaders. There is no list of set skills for great leaders. But, effective leaders exhibit many similar traits and skills. These include being trustworthy, ethical, and decisive. Effective leaders also have excellent communication, motivational, and time-management skills.

Case Study

Kroger

Kroger is one of the nation's largest traditional grocers, with more than 2400 stores. The company performs many business functions well, including marketing, merchandising, and pricing. But, one of the main elements Kroger attributes to their continued success is *teamwork*. In fact, company executives and associates often refer to the grocery chain as "Team Kroger."

Kroger approaches teamwork from three perspectives: executive, associate, and total teamwork. Kroger's leadership team communicates continuously through several venues. For example, leadership team members have profiles on an internal company page that is similar to a "Kroger only Facebook." Through this platform, management can share ideas daily. They also talk regularly via conference calls. One of the most common themes in their communications is how to find, hire, and inspire quality associates. Associates also have profiles and may communicate with each other and with the executive team.

Associates from various areas of the business are often teamed up together to work on collaborative projects. Senior associates may also join these teams to build powerful teams that share fresh ideas, history, and a sense of solid teamwork. "Team Kroger" has more than 13,000 associates who have over 30 years of service with the company. Kroger understands that building winning teams at all levels of employment leads to retail success.

College and Career Readiness

Reading Prep

Skim the chapter by reading the first sentence of each paragraph. Use this information to create an outline for the chapter before you read it.

Check Your Retail IQ

Before you begin the chapter, see what you already know about retail by taking the chapter pretest. If you do not have a smartphone, visit the G-W Learning companion website.

G-W Learning mobile site: www.m.g-wlearning.com

G-W Learning companion website: www.g-wlearning.com/marketing/

Sections

16.1 Teams

16.2 Leading a Team

michaeljung/Shutterstock.com

Section 16.1 Teams

Objectives

After completing this section, you will be able to:
- **Identify** the qualities of effective team members.
- **Describe** the five stages of team development.

Key Terms

team
teamwork
collaboration
interpersonal skills
respect
forming

storming
norming
consensus
performing
adjourning

Web Connect

Conduct an Internet search for *team building*. In your own words, explain the goal of team building. Choose three team building activities that interest you. What team skills would be developed by each of the activities you chose?

Critical Thinking

Conflict in the workplace may be caused by many factors. Working with others can sometimes be a challenge. Give an example of a situation that may cause team members to disagree with each other. Then, list ways that the conflict can be solved.

Teamwork

A **team** is two or more people working together to reach a goal. **Teamwork** is the action of people who come together for the purpose of a common goal. A group of people working together to reach a goal is usually more productive than an individual working alone. Team members can share experiences, ideas, and talents to help accomplish a variety of tasks.

Being a team member of a company group is similar to playing on a sports team. Success is measured in terms of the team, not each player. Teamwork involves putting the team goals ahead of personal goals. A successful team reaches its goals.

The ability to be an effective member of a team ranks as one of the top skills employers look for in an employee. Effective team members are people who can work with others, share responsibilities, and come together to create a positive environment. Effective team members also know how to collaborate with others and focus on the goals of the group.

Just like on a sports team, workplace success is measured in terms of the team, not individual players.

Collaboration

Collaboration is working with others to achieve a common goal. When people work together as members of a team, they share ideas and responsibilities. However, collaboration may require team members to give up something important to them so the group can reach an agreement. This is called *compromising*, and it can often lead to conflict. It is important for team members to learn how to compromise so the team can reach its goals.

Conflict is a situation in which disagreements lead to hostile behavior, such as shouting. However, conflict does not always have to have a negative outcome. Disagreements may actually lead to discussions that create positive outcomes.

Conflict resolution is an important skill that team members should acquire. The first step in conflict resolution is to listen to each team member's ideas and not pass judgment. All ideas should be considered and discussed. Weigh the pros and cons of each idea. If the conflict cannot be resolved, a manager or human resources representative should be called to help resolve the issue.

Interpersonal Skills

Interpersonal skills are a group of skills that enable a person to interact with others in a positive way. Some common interpersonal skills include effective verbal and nonverbal communication, listening, problem solving, and being assertive. Retail managers expect team members to have good interpersonal skills. These skills are necessary to complete job duties and ensure a positive working environment.

Respect

Respect is the feeling that someone or something is good, valuable, and important. All people want to be respected, especially in the workplace. Team members are expected to be respectful and considerate of the feelings of coworkers.

The retail workplace is usually diverse. *Workplace diversity* means that people from many cultures, backgrounds, genders, and races come together in a place of employment. *Culture* incorporates the shared beliefs, customs, and social behavior of a particular group or nation. Individuals bring their personal life experiences and culture to the workplace. As team members, it is necessary to embrace these ideas to make the group a strong unit.

Team Development

Educational psychologist Bruce Tuckman created one of the most popular theories of team development. According to Tuckman, there are five stages of group development that lead to successful teams.

Figure 16-1 Teams progress through the stages of development at different rates.

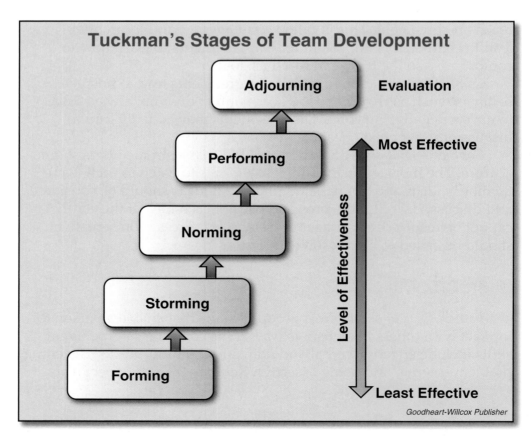

His model was first developed in 1965 with four stages, and he later added a fifth stage. The original four stages were *forming, storming, norming,* and *performing.* The fifth stage added is *adjourning.* These stages are shown in Figure 16-1.

Forming

Forming is stage one. **Forming** occurs when a group of people come together and meet the members of the team. There is no conflict and no ideas are exchanged. During this stage, team members get to know each other. This is very easy and pleasant for all team members. For example, forming occurs when the employees of a new retail store meet each other for the first time. They would likely be excited about the new venture and eager to get started. The forming stage also happens when a retailer hires new employees to join an established team.

Leaders can use team building activities to help bring team members together. Team building activities are meant to teach team members how to interact, communicate, and work together effectively. These may be indoor or outdoor activities in which team members solve a problem, create a plan, complete a task, or simply socialize. Team building activities can help a team reach its peak performance on the job.

Storming

Storming is stage two. The name provides a clue to what a team experiences in this stage. **Storming** is when team members become less patient with team processes, as well as with one another, and start to experience conflict. Members begin to express their ideas in trying to work toward team goals, which leads to either agreement or disagreement.

In the new retail store example, the storming stage might occur when employees battle for the best jobs, the best schedule, or a leadership position.

Norming

Norming is stage three. Norming is when teams finally come together on their ideas and reach a consensus. A consensus is when all members of a team support an idea. This stage occurs when the team has determined what the rules are and all members work to respect them. In this stage, the team focuses more on the goal and less on conflict. They begin to move with a clear and decisive understanding of the goal or common cause.

Norming is the time when a team may define the criteria for goals to accomplish. Criteria for measuring success may be defined in many ways. Setting a date for a task to be completed is one criterion. Hitting a sales target may be another. In the new retail store example, issues that arose in the storming stage have been resolved and team members work together.

Performing

Performing is stage four. Performing is the stage when a team is functioning at its best. This is the stage that all teams would like to reach, but sometimes do not. Trust, confidence, and passion for reaching the team's goal are necessary in the performing stage. Each member is equally involved and working. In the performing stage, teams measure results and evaluate if the goal was met. In the new retail store, this stage is carried out in the day-to-day operations. Employees help each other in the store, encourage each other, and do whatever is necessary to improve sales and customer relations.

Adjourning

Adjourning is stage five. Adjourning is when the team's work is finished and their efforts to meet a goal come to an end. This is a time when members of the team recognize a job well done. This stage might occur at the end of the year, as the team reflects on sales or other measurable goals. It may also occur when an employee leaves and the team changes. While most retailers do not have an *end date*, they do achieve goals and set new ones.

In some cases, it is difficult for teams to adjourn. Team members may develop loyalty toward a project or other team members. It is important to reflect on the accomplishments and prepare for the next journey.

Checkpoint 16.1

1. Describe the qualities of an effective team member.
2. What does it mean to compromise?
3. Explain the concept of workplace diversity.
4. What are the five stages of team development?
5. Describe the activities of the norming stage of team development.

Build Your Vocabulary

As you progress through this course, develop a personal glossary of retailing terms and add it to your portfolio. This will help you build your vocabulary and prepare you for a career. Write a definition for each of the following terms, and add it to your personal retail glossary.

team	storming
teamwork	norming
collaboration	consensus
interpersonal skills	performing
respect	adjourning
forming	

Section 16.2 Leading a Team

Objectives

After completing this section, you will be able to:
- **Identify** traits common to most effective leaders.
- **Describe** the skills necessary to be a good leader.
- **List** ways a leader can acknowledge team results.
- **Identify** professional development opportunities for leaders.

Key Terms

leadership
traits
trustworthy
flexible
ethics
decisive

skill
delegate
time management
professional
    development

Web Connect

Select one of the presidents of the United States who you admire. Conduct an Internet search to learn more about that president. List three positive leadership traits this person demonstrated. Write several paragraphs describing why this person was an effective leader.

Critical Thinking

Define the term *leadership* in your own words. What do you think it means? Make a list of people you consider to be good leaders. Next to each name, explain the leadership characteristics you think each person possesses.

Leadership

Leadership is the ability of a person to guide others to a goal. A person who guides others to a goal is called a *leader*. Leaders cast a vision for the team and inspire team members to work toward that vision. The true measure of a leader is whether he or she can help the team accomplish its goal.

Employee-centered leaders make an effort to treat their employees with fairness, respect, and consistency. Employees who are treated with respect are more likely to stay with the company. Employees who stay with a retail business for long periods of time are valuable to the business and develop a strong sense of loyalty to the company.

There is no formula for a great leader. However, there are many *traits* and *skills* that good leaders demonstrate. Some of these traits and skills may come naturally, while others may be learned and developed.

Traits

Traits are behavioral and emotional characteristics that make each individual unique. They are elements of one's personality that are consistent over time. A list of common traits is shown in Figure 16-2. Effective leaders are usually trustworthy, flexible, ethical, decisive, and calm.

Trustworthy

A person who is **trustworthy** is worthy of people's confidence. Leaders make decisions daily. Their decisions must always be in the best interest of the business. Good leaders are trusted to be team players and always look out for the organization.

Flexible

Leaders need know when to be flexible. Being **flexible** means being able to adapt to circumstances as they change. A leader who is flexible is willing to make a change when it is in the best interest of both the company and the team members. Exercising flexibility at the right times can help the company improve and grow.

Ethical

Ethics are rules of behavior based on ideas about what is right and wrong. Leaders must be *ethical* by consistently doing the right thing.

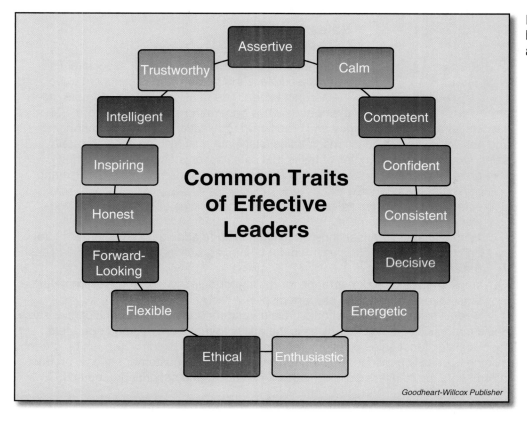

Figure 16-2 Effective leaders often possess some or all of these characteristics.

Goodheart-Willcox Publisher

Team members often follow the example of their leader's behavior. For example, if a leader has a positive attitude, that attitude tends to influence others. Ethics are no different. When a leader acts in an ethical way, he or she sets the standard for others to follow.

Consistent

Being *consistent* is a positive trait for a leader. Each team member is entitled to consistent treatment from a manager. Once a decision is made, leaders need to ensure that *all* team members abide by the decision. Leaders should use caution when making exceptions, as exceptions may be seen by team members as being inconsistent.

Decisive

Being decisive means having the ability to make decisions quickly and effectively. Decisive leaders are able to use the information provided, weigh possible decisions based on the information, and make a decision. Team members depend on leaders to make difficult decisions that impact both themselves and the company. A leader who cannot be decisive may quickly lose the confidence of team members.

Exploring Retail Careers

Sales Associate

The first person that a potential customer sees when entering a store is often a sales associate. The sales associate is the person who is expected to be the product expert. The goal is to help customers meet their needs while generating sales for the store. Sales associates also handle money and credit card transactions, process exchanges, and answer customer questions. A sales associate may also be called a *retail salesperson*. Some examples of tasks that sales associates perform include:

- greet customers, answer questions, and explain or demonstrate the use and benefit of merchandise
- communicate current sales, promotions, and policies about payments and exchanges to customers
- handle financial transactions, which can include adding up a customer's total purchase and accepting payment for a sale, as well as opening or closing cash registers
- stock shelves or racks, arrange for mailing or delivery of purchases, mark price tags, take inventory, and prepare displays

A retail sales associate should have an understanding of the principles of sales. Basic math skills are necessary, as is the ability to make change and operate a cash register. Most sales positions require a high school diploma, though on-the-job training is usually provided. Training topics often include customer service, product information, the retailer's policies, sales techniques, and security procedures.

Calm

Good leaders have to make difficult decisions on a regular basis. Some decisions may not make all team members happy. Such decisions can create a stressful environment. In these situations, leaders need to remain calm. A *calm* leader is able to make rational decisions without being influenced by emotions or stress. This is particularly important when making public decisions. If customers or team members see a leader getting upset or stressed, they will likely feel that there is something to worry about. This creates a negative situation that leaders should avoid.

Skills

A **skill** is the ability to do something well. Skills may be learned, developed, and improved. There is not an exact skill set common to all good leaders. A list of common skills is shown in Figure 16-3. Certain skills that are common to effective leaders include communication skills, conflict management skills, delegation skills, motivational skills, time-management skills, and problem-solving skills.

Communication Skills

One of the most important skills a leader must possess is communication skills. Leaders must be effective communicators

Figure 16-3 These skill sets help people become leaders both at school and work.

Goodheart-Willcox Publisher

Retail Ethics

Biased Language

As you begin your career, you may encounter others who categorize people using biased words and comments. Using age, gender, race, disability, or ethnicity as a way to describe others is unethical and sometimes illegal. Use bias-free language in all of your communication, whether verbal or printed, to show respect for everyone with whom you come in contact.

to ensure that all team members understand the goals and how to reach them. They must be able to give directions and make sure the directions are understood. Leaders must be able to send clear messages to customers, team members, and management.

Careful listening and purposeful responses are also hallmarks of good communication. Leaders must understand what someone wants and ask questions when necessary. As in every part of life, communicating in a positive manner gets better results than negativity or a poor attitude.

Conflict Management Skills

Conflict management is a beneficial interpersonal skill for leaders to develop. No matter how perfect an organization, all teams experience some level of conflict. The conflict may be within the team or with others outside of the team. A leader must be able to manage conflict and prevent it from escalating.

Negotiating conflict requires multiple steps. First, everyone involved must be respectful of each other during negotiations, in spite of the disagreement. Second, everyone must clearly understand the issue. Questions may need to be asked to clarify the issue before it can be resolved. Once the issue is clearly defined, multiple solutions should be explored. All parties involved should then collaborate to decide on the best possible solution.

Delegation Skills

An individual person cannot do everything required to operate a retail business. For that reason, good leaders must know how to delegate. To **delegate** means to assign other people tasks to complete. A leader should know the strengths and weaknesses of individual team members. Duties may be delegated based on a team member's ability and desire to complete a task. Delegation is how leaders can ensure all necessary tasks are completed.

Motivational Skills

The best leaders help employees perform at peak levels. And, the best team members are often those who truly *want* to perform well. There is no single best way to motivate others. Some people may be motivated by rewards, providing a fun work environment, being sensitive to special needs, or being firm at the right time. Good leaders can find ways to motivate almost everyone by using different methods with different people.

It is also critical that leaders be *self-motivated*. They must be able to do their job without constant supervision. Leaders must understand the company's goals, know how to reach them, and be willing to do whatever it takes to achieve them.

Time-Management Skills

Time management is the ability to organize time and assignments to increase personal efficiency. Leaders are expected to *multitask*. They must be able to look at the tasks to be completed, estimate the amount of time required to complete each task, and decide the best order in which to complete them. The end goal is to accomplish tasks efficiently, while meeting company goals. The difference between average and excellent leaders is often not how hard they work, but how well they prioritize assignments.

To be effective, leaders must have good time-management skills and be able to multitask.

Hasloo Group Production Studio/Shutterstock.com

Problem-Solving Skills

Problem-solving skills allow a person to identify a problem and take steps to solve it. Effective leaders are able to solve problems, always keeping the best interest of the business in mind.

Leaders may act as liaisons between other teams in the company. They may be seen as the "go to" person who employees, customers, and management seek out for answers. Employees may have questions about procedures or products. Customers may have questions about pricing or store policies. Management may need an explanation of something that happened during daily operations. A leader must be able to address any problem that arises.

Recognizing Team Results

Teams are measured by their results. The criteria for measuring results can take many forms:

- meeting an established monetary sales goal
- meeting an established number of units solds
- selling a set number of a specific type of product from a selected vendor
- perfect attendance during a specified time period

Effective leaders also recognize individual accomplishments. Teams work hard to meet goals and to be recognized by their managers. Individual team members, as well as entire teams, should be acknowledged when performance is stellar. There are many ways that hard work can be acknowledged.

- A public mention of thanks singles out a person or team in front of the company and builds pride.
- Creating an award that is given on a regular basis, such as an employee or team of the month, creates motivation to excel.
- Cash bonuses are effective motivators to succeed.
- Knowing that a promotion is a potential reward for excellent performance is a driving force.

Effective leaders encourage each individual to be part of the business' success, and acknowledge those who do a good job.

Professional Development

Professional development is training that builds on the skills and knowledge that contribute to personal growth and career development. Effective leaders continually seek opportunities to improve their management skills.

There are a variety of options for professional development. Many options involve a fee to participate. However, businesses are often willing to pay to provide professional development training for their employees.

Recognition encourages each individual to be part of the business' success.

michaeljung/Shutterstock.com

Professional organizations, such as Dale Carnegie Training®, sponsor seminars held in major cities. Some community colleges offer night and weekend classes in leadership. These classes are generally taught by local business executives. The classes typically do not follow a regular college schedule, but are created around the schedules of working people. Some retailers bring trainers on site to work with their leadership team.

Checkpoint 16.2

1. Give three examples of common *traits* that leaders typically possess.
2. Why is it important for a leader to remain calm?
3. What does it mean to be *self-motivated*?
4. Explain how a leader can recognize individual and team accomplishments.
5. What is *professional development*?

Build Your Vocabulary

As you progress through this course, develop a personal glossary of retailing terms and add it to your portfolio. This will help you build your vocabulary and prepare you for a career. Write a definition for each of the following terms, and add it to your personal retail glossary.

leadership	decisive
traits	skill
trustworthy	delegate
flexible	time management
ethics	professional development

Chapter Summary

Section 16.1 Teams

- Teamwork helps people accomplish goals more quickly than working alone. Being an effective team member calls for collaboration, interpersonal skills, and respect.
- The five stages of team development are forming, storming, norming, performing, and adjourning.

Section 16.2 Leading a Team

- Leadership is an important part of teamwork. Common traits of effective leaders include being trustworthy, flexible, ethical, decisive, and calm.
- Certain skills are common to effective leaders, including communication, conflict management, delegation, motivational, time-management, and problem-solving skills.
- When a team meets its goals, it is important for the leader to recognize the team's accomplishments.
- Professional development builds on a person's skills and knowledge. This leads to personal growth and career development.

Review Your Knowledge

1. Explain the purposes of teams in the workplace.
2. List and describe three skills that help individual team members be effective.
3. Discuss the concept of collaboration and challenges it may present.
4. During which stage of team development do team members often experience conflict?
5. Compare and contrast the performing stage and the adjourning stage of team development.
6. Discuss the importance of leadership in the workplace.
7. Why is it important for a leader to be consistent?
8. What skills are common to effective leaders?
9. Describe why time-management skills are important for a leader to possess.
10. Give an example of how a retail team's results may be measured.

Apply Your Knowledge

1. The goals of individual team members and leaders are similar. But, their roles are different. Compare and contrast the expectations and responsibilities of team members and leaders. Create a chart with two columns. Label column one "Team Member" and column two "Leader." Under each heading, list the specific responsibilities each person assumes. Share your findings with the class.
2. Successful teams learn how to function as one unit. Compare and contrast the influence of cultural diversity. How does diversity impact a team's performance?

Create a flowchart showing the stages that teams experience when coming together as a dedicated group.

3. Conflict resolution is an important skill that all team members must learn. Both individual team members and leaders need to understand the steps to resolve conflict. Create a flowchart detailing the steps that individual team members should follow to resolve conflict. Next, create a flowchart detailing the steps a leader should follow to resolve team conflict. How do the models compare?

4. Evaluate your own leadership qualities. List the traits you currently possess that would make you a good leader. Identify the traits you need to develop. What did you learn from this?

5. Employers have expectations of the employees they hire. What do you think an employer looks for in an employee? If you are currently employed, include characteristics that your manager expects of you. How would you rate yourself as an employee on a scale from 1 to 10?

6. Research various time management techniques and tips. Describe some of the techniques you find and how they can be used in the workplace. How can these skills help an employee develop and maintain schedules and meet deadlines? What can you do to improve your time-management skills?

7. There are many ways a team measures results. Think about a team effort in which you participated. How did the team measure its results or successes? List the criteria that the team used. Are there other criteria that could have been used to measure the results?

8. Develop a list of ways that team performance can be recognized. Relate your own experiences with team recognition. Research different ways that business teams and professional individuals can be given recognition for successful efforts. Next, develop a list of ways that team performance can be rewarded.

9. Leadership and career development are ongoing activities that most people find valuable to their personal success. What leadership and career development opportunities are available in your school? What activities would you like to pursue in order to develop your leadership qualities? What activities would you like to pursue in order to develop your career goals?

10. Interpersonal skills are an important asset. Make a list of interpersonal skills you currently possess. Which interpersonal skills do you need to develop to become a more productive team member? How can you develop these skills?

Check Your Retail IQ

Now that you have finished the chapter, see what you learned about retail by taking the chapter posttest. If you do not have a smartphone, visit the G-W Learning companion website.

G-W Learning mobile site: www.m.g-wlearning.com

G-W Learning companion website: www.g-wlearning.com/marketing

College and Career Readiness

Career Readiness Practices Everyone has a stake in protecting the environment. Taking steps as an individual to be more environmentally conscious is a behavior of responsible citizens. From a business standpoint, being environmentally conscious may also help a company be more profitable. What things can you do in the workplace to save energy or other resources?

Listening Passive listening is casually listening to someone speak. Passive listening is appropriate when you do not have to interact with the speaker. Listen to a classmate as he or she is having a conversation with you. Focus attention on the message. Ask for clarification for anything that you do not understand. Provide verbal and nonverbal feedback while the person is talking.

Reading Visit your local library and locate an informational book about retailing that was written at least ten years ago. How is it different from this text you are currently using? How has the culture of retail changed over the years? Share your findings with the class.

Teamwork

Working with your team mates, discuss the role of a team member and the role of a leader. Create a chart that lists *team member* in column one and *leader* in column two. Write the expectations for each in the appropriate columns. Compare and contrast the expectations. How are they the same? How are they different?

College and Career Portfolio

References

An important part of any portfolio is a list of references. A reference is a person who knows your skills, talents, or personal traits and is willing to recommend you. References can be someone for whom you worked or with whom you provided community service. Someone you know from your personal life, such as a youth group leader, can also be a reference. However, you should not list relatives as references. When applying for a position, consider which references can best recommend you for the position for which you are applying. Always get permission from the person before using his or her name as a reference.

1. Ask several people with whom you have worked or volunteered if they are willing to serve as a reference for you. If so, ask for their contact information.
2. Create a list with the names and contact information for your references. Save the document file in an appropriate subfolder for your e-portfolio.
3. Place a printed copy in the container for your print portfolio.

◇DECA Coach

Presentation Materials

Prepared presentation guidelines permit the use of presentation materials, such as presentation boards, PowerPoint presentations, props, etc. Presentation materials can make all the difference in telling your story to your judges.

Take advantage of this opportunity. Create flyers, business cards, and other professional-looking materials to give to your judges. If there is a product involved, be sure to bring a sample to pass to the judges. "Salesmanship 101" says that people believe what they can see and feel. When rules permit, pass the product to the judges and do not take it back until the end of your presentation. Let them handle it as you present to them.

However, the guidelines are very specific regarding presentation tools. They state exact sizes for flip charts, display boards, posters, laptop computers, and handheld devices. The guidelines even spell out the use of sound in your presentation. Any violation of these guidelines can result in disqualification. Your presentation materials will be evaluated before you present. For example, a display board that is one inch too long will result in disqualification.

Finally, be sure to practice setting up your presentation materials. While this may sound silly, you do not want to waste your presentation time setting up. Practice it many times to become as efficient as possible. If you cannot set up quickly, consider changing your presentation strategy.

Visit www.deca.org to learn more information about DECA.

G-W Learning Mobile Site

Visit the G-W Learning mobile site to complete the chapter pretest and posttest, and to practice vocabulary using e-flash cards. If you do not have a smartphone, visit the G-W Learning companion website to access these features.

G-W Learning mobile site: www.m.g-wlearning.com
G-W Learning companion website: www.g-wlearning.com/marketing/

Chapter 17
Ethics and the Law

Retailers are obligated to act in an ethical manner. Even though they are in business to make money, they should not lose sight of the importance of ethical and legal behavior.

Responsible pricing practices and sourcing products are two areas where retailers should pay special attention. Collecting customer data and using it properly is important, and the practices of the Federal Trade Commission (FTC) should be followed. Honest advertising that does not include puffery, false claims, bait and switch, or spam is a must. To make these practices a reality, businesses must set an example and require employees to comply with established workplace ethics.

In addition, retailers must abide by local, state, and federal laws. There are laws that protect the consumer, the employee, the retailer, and the environment. Proper respect must be given to all ethical and legal issues.

Case Study

Commemorative Brands, Inc.

Commemorative Brands, Inc. is the parent company of ArtCarved® and Balfour®. These names are well-known for high school and college class rings, as well as other commemorative jewelry. Ethical business and sourcing practices are important to this company.

The jewelry business is competitive and maximizing profits is important. Some jewelers choose to buy gold and diamonds mined in war zone areas. In these areas, the extraction processes often harm or violate the human rights of workers. The money generated from the sale of these materials is used to finance war. Lower costs of diamonds and gold mean higher profits for jewelers. However, Commemorative Brands, Inc. chooses to buy its gold and diamonds from reputable suppliers, even though the costs may be higher. It believes that ethical business practices are as important as making profits.

The company strongly believes in corporate social responsibility, and hopes its actions demonstrate a commitment to human rights and the environment. Commemorative Brands, Inc. understands that good ethics may just be what their customers are looking for when making purchasing decisions.

Reading Prep

Before reading this chapter, preview the figures referenced in the text. Translate the technical information in the illustrations into words. Assess the extent to which the illustrations support the content.

College and Career Readiness

Check Your Retail IQ

Before you begin the chapter, see what you already know about retail by taking the chapter pretest. If you do not have a smartphone, visit the G-W Learning companion website.

G-W Learning mobile site: www.m.g-wlearning.com

G-W Learning companion website: www.g-wlearning.com/marketing/

Sections

17.1 Retail Ethics

17.2 Legal Issues

Section 17.1 Retail Ethics

Objectives

After completing this section, you will be able to:
- **Explain** the importance of ethics in retail.
- **Analyze** pricing practices used in retail.
- **Describe** the role of sourcing in retail.
- **Explain** privacy protection of customer data.
- **Discuss** inappropriate advertising practices.
- **Identify** examples of inappropriate workplace behavior.

Key Terms

price fixing
price gouging
price discrimination
predatory pricing
deceptive pricing
price ceiling
price floor
sourcing
false advertising

puffery
bait and switch
spam
piracy
freeware
shareware
netiquette
cyberbullying

Web Connect

Unethical business practices are in the news every day. Research the phrase *unethical retailers*. Choose one story and write several paragraphs explaining why the retailer was questioned about ethics in its business practices.

Critical Thinking

Why do you think it is important that a retail business treat its customers ethically? Give examples of ethical and unethical conduct that a retailer might display. What are the consequences of unethical business conduct?

Ethics

Business ethics are the rules for professional conduct and integrity in all areas of business.

Retailers, like other businesses, are obligated to operate in an ethical manner. Being *ethical* means making a decision that most people consider to be the right thing to do. The difficult part about ethics is that people have different perspectives on what is right and wrong. Our personal values and experiences make up our ethics. These values guide us in the decisions we make every day. It is important to understand and respect different ethical opinions. This may involve discussions with others to fully understand different ethical opinions. It is important to find agreeable solutions to difficult ethical issues and determine how the solution will be carried out in the business.

Many businesses have a code of ethics that employees are expected to follow. A *code of ethics* is a written statement about the general values, often social or moral, that guide the business.

Those who work in retail make ethical decisions each day. For example, management decides how to approach public issues that may cause customer concern, like product recalls. Marketers decide how to word promotions to convey honest information. Salespeople give customers accurate product details that may influence buying decisions. All of these situations require ethical behavior.

One way employees can ethically approach a decision is to use a *decision-making model,* or a basic checklist, that can be customized for an individual retail business. An example of a decision-making model is shown in Figure 17-1.

Ethical decision making is a complicated issue. By using a decision-making model, retailers and their employees can objectively determine ethical conduct. Positive ethical conduct helps create strong relationships with employees, customers, and vendors.

Pricing Practices

Retailers are in business to make money. However, the goal of making a profit should not get in the way of legal and ethical operations. Pricing practices are of particular concern to retailers.

Price Fixing

Price fixing is when two or more retailers get together and agree upon a set price for similar products. For example, two retailers might agree to sell a particular brand of paint for an identical price. This practice may force the consumer to pay a higher price for the paint than they would have in an open market. Price fixing is illegal under the *Sherman Antitrust Act.*

Ethical Decision-Making Model

- **Define the issue.** What is the problem or situation?
- **Is it legal?** Retailers must comply with federal, state, and local laws.
- **Is it ethical?** How do I feel personally about the situation?
- **Is the information proprietary?** Proprietary information must be kept confidential and never be shared with people outside the retail business.
- **Is there a conflict of interest?** A conflict of interest is when an employee has competing interests or loyalties.
- **Are the facts accurate?** Is the information documented to be true?
- **What are the consequences of the action?** Will someone be harmed by the decision?

Goodheart-Willcox Publisher

Figure 17-1 A decision-making model is a checklist that can help a retailer or employee find ethical solutions.

Antitrust laws protect against unfair business practices that limit competition. The Sherman Antitrust Act, often called the *Sherman Act*, is one such law. It was passed in 1890.

Price Gouging

Price gouging is the practice of raising prices in times of emergency or great need. Some states consider this a form of price fixing. For example, following a snowstorm, a local hardware store tripled the price of snow shovels. Customers needed to clean their driveways and were forced to pay the high price because it was the only hardware store in the community.

Price Discrimination

Price discrimination is selling the same product at different prices to different customers based on customers' personal characteristics. The *Robinson-Patman Act of 1936* prohibits price discrimination against individuals.

Pure price discrimination is when a retailer sells its products for the highest price a person is willing to pay. With *imperfect price discrimination*, retailers target groups. For example, a movie theater may charge different prices for the same movie based on the time of day the movie is shown. This practice is not illegal.

Predatory Pricing

Predatory pricing is setting prices low to drive other companies out of business. If low pricing drives the competition out of business, a retailer can then set prices at any level it wishes. Predatory pricing is illegal and violates antitrust laws. It is illegal under the *Sherman Act*.

Deceptive Pricing

Deceptive pricing is pricing an item to intentionally deceive the customer. For example, a retailer advertises that a product is 70 percent off. In reality, that same product was sold at the same or a similar price before the sale. The retailer intentionally misled the customer to believe the product is on sale. This practice is unethical.

Retailers may compare a sale price to a *suggested retail price*. If the suggested retail price is actually the price regularly used, then the sale price is honest. If the suggested retail price is never used, then the retailer is misleading the customer.

Price Ceilings

Price ceilings are maximum prices for certain products or services that are set by the government. These ceilings are generally set on essential products. This is done to protect consumers from conditions that might make purchasing essential products or services difficult. For example, some cities have rent control. Property owners have a maximum amount they can charge for rent. This helps most people afford a place to live.

Price Floors

The opposite of a price ceiling is a price floor. A **price floor** is a minimum price for certain products or services that is set by the government. Price ceilings are set to protect *consumers*. Price floors are set to protect selected *industries*. For example, many agricultural products, such as milk, often have price floors. This helps dairies afford to stay in business.

Sourcing Practices

Sourcing is the process of finding and analyzing potential suppliers of products to be purchased for resale. Retailers must buy products at the lowest possible price and at the highest quality. However, retailers should not participate in any purchase that is not ethically and legally sound.

Recall that some products are less costly if purchased from another country. Buying products from other countries may be seen as an attempt to take sales away from manufacturers in the United States, which, in turn, creates unemployment.

Some countries outside of the United States can create lower-priced products for several reasons. One reason is that wages in those countries are much lower than in the United States. Consumers may consider it unethical to buy products from countries that pay their employees low salaries. Another reason is that some countries have few or no regulations that oversee the production of products. For example, during the height of the toy's popularity, Thomas the Tank Engine train sets were recalled from American retail shelves. The train sets were made in China and painted with lead paint, which is known to cause brain damage in children. The use of lead paint is regulated in the United States, but not in China.

Expensive products, such as designer handbags, watches, and jeans, are sometimes copied and sold at lower prices and often much lower quality. While this is not illegal, the products cannot be sold under the original brand names. When a product is copied and sold

Rent control in some major US cities is an example of a government-established price ceiling.

PathDoc/Shutterstock.com

as an original it is called a *counterfeit product*. This practice *is* against the law. For example, a Rolex watch may cost thousands of dollars and is desired by many. Yet, it is possible to buy a counterfeit Rolex watch that costs significantly less than the genuine product. Retailers who knowingly sell fake products are involved in both unethical and illegal practices.

Without regulations, the cost of making a product can be decreased. But, this may also lead to products that are much lower in quality.

Data Collection

By nature of the business, e-tailers have the opportunity to collect data from people who visit their websites. Online customers must give personal information in order to receive the correct product. Customer information, such as contact information, gender, and even product sizes, may be recorded when a customer places an online order. Individuals are entitled to privacy and to have a say as to how their information is used. E-tailers are ethically and legally obligated to use data in an appropriate manner.

The Federal Trade Commission (FTC) developed *Fair Information Practice Principles* that dictate the proper ways customer data may be used. There are five principles of this privacy protection.

- *Notice.* Consumers must be given information about how the e-tailer will use data gathered before the customer provides the data.

Selling imposter jewelry as an original, branded design is illegal.

dotshock/Shutterstock.com

- *Choice.* Individuals have the right to either allow or refuse the e-tailer use of their data for secondary purposes.
- *Access.* Individuals have the right to access and review for accuracy any data collected about them.
- *Security.* E-tailers must have policies in place to prevent the misuse of data collected.
- *Enforcement.* E-tailers should put safeguards in place to ensure compliance to the regulations.

It is necessary that both company data and customer data be protected against hackers who attempt to steal proprietary information.

Advertising

Another ethical challenge faced by retailers is the possibility of misleading customers through inaccuracies in advertising or other promotions. Customers use different media to make shopping decisions. Advertising helps them decide what they want to buy and where to shop. However, when advertising messages are not truthful, the retailer may directly mislead the customer.

False advertising is overstating the features and benefits of products or services, or making false claims about them. False advertising is both unethical and illegal.

The FTC prevents practices that are unfair to consumers. The FTC's Bureau of Consumer Protection works to prevent fraud, deception, and unfair business practices in the marketplace.

Examples of common unethical advertising practices include puffery, false price claims, bait and switch, and spam.

Puffery

Some advertising claims can be measured and others cannot. Claims that cannot be measured are considered **puffery**. This is not always against the law. For example, an advertisement may state, "Made from the finest silk on Earth" or "America's favorite store." These exaggerated claims are probably not measurable and may be false, but are not illegal.

False Claims

There are many ways retailers can make false claims in advertising. These claims may be simple, such as stating "prices start at $99" or "we have the lowest price." If the wording misleads customers, the statements are said to be *false claims*. Retailers may even claim to be going out of business just to make customers believe that everything is being sold at bargain prices. This practice is no longer legal. Any claims that lead customers to believe something that is untrue is unethical and may have legal consequences.

Bait and Switch

Bait and switch is the practice of advertising a product, usually at a very low price, so customers will come into the store. When customers arrive, the featured product is sold out and another product is substituted. Generally, the substitute product is more profitable for the retailer and may not be as desirable for the customer. Bait and switch practices are not illegal, but can be considered false advertising.

Spam

Spam is similar to junk mail that arrives in your home mailbox.

Spam is any electronic message sent in bulk to people who did not give a company permission to e-mail them. Retailers who spam potential customers hope that some of the people will read their message, but know that most will not. By sending spam, the company runs the risk of alienating potential customers.

Retailers who communicate with customers using mass e-mails must follow specific laws that describe what they may and may not include in the e-mails.

Workplace Ethics

Ethics is a guiding set of moral values that helps people make decisions. Employers typically have a handbook and code of conduct that outlines how employees should behave while at work. Companies may define specific issues as inappropriate, as well as unethical or illegal. For example, employers have rules for using company equipment, downloading software, and communication on the Internet.

Company Equipment

Company equipment is meant for business-related functions, not personal use. Business equipment includes everything from desktop computers and phones to the photocopy machine. All employees must be aware of appropriate use of office equipment. Many codes of conduct also have guidelines for visiting websites and rules for downloading to company computers. These rules protect the retailer's computer system and private information.

Hardware, such as computers and copiers, are provided to employees to improve efficiency. Company-owned mobile devices, such as smartphones and tablets, are also company property. They

Company-owned equipment should not be used for personal reasons without company approval.

michaeljung/Shutterstock.com

should not be used for personal reasons without company approval. Additionally, employees should follow company policies for appropriate communication and workplace behavior.

Scanners are a common piece of equipment in many business and home offices. A scanner is used to create a digital version of printed material. Whether scanning text, artwork, or a photograph, all rights of that material remain with the owners.

Software Downloads

It is unethical and illegal for an employee to download software that has not been purchased and registered by the employer. When buying software, a license is purchased. A *license* is the legal permission to use a software program. All software has terms of use that explain how and when the software may be used.

Some software may only be lawfully used if it is purchased. These programs are known as *for-purchase software*. Demonstration, or *demo,* software may be used without buying it. However, demos are limited in either functionality or time. If the retailer decides to keep using the software, it must be purchased. Piracy is the illegal copying or downloading of software, files, or other protected material. This includes scanning or downloading images or music.

Software known as freeware is fully functional and can be used forever without purchasing it. To be considered freeware, the software cannot be a demo or restricted version of software meant for purchase. Shareware is software that can be installed and used at no cost, but usually has a notice screen, time-delayed startup, or fewer features. Purchasing the software removes these restrictions. Figure 17-2 identifies the differences between software types.

Characteristics of Software Types

Characteristics	Software Type		
	For-Purchase	**Freeware**	**Shareware**
Cost	• Must be purchased to use • Demo may be available	Never have to pay for it	• Free to try • Pay to upgrade to full functionality
Features	Full functionality	Full functionality	Limited functionality without upgrade

Goodheart-Willcox Publisher

Figure 17-2 Different restrictions and fees apply to the various types of software products.

There are differences between a demo of for-purchase software and shareware. Typically, shareware can be used forever with certain restrictions. Use of shareware is on the honor system. Retailers who continue to use the software are expected to purchase it. Demos of for-purchase software, however, may stop working after a certain amount of time or have limited functionality.

Public-domain software, like freeware, is free. However, freeware is copyrighted, while public-domain software either has no copyright or the copyright has expired. Some photographs, music, videos, and textual information are also in the public domain.

Netiquette

For employees, *workplace etiquette* is a set of guidelines for appropriate behavior on the job. **Netiquette** refers to social and professional guidelines for online communications. Netiquette covers e-mails, social networking, blogs, texting, and chatting. For example, it is unprofessional to use texting language in a business environment. Also, employees should proofread and spell-check e-mails before sending them. Whether sending an e-mail to a customer in response to a question, texting a coworker, blogging about a company product, or engaging in any other communication, it is important to follow the same common courtesy used in face-to-face discussions.

Internet access provided by the company should be used only for business purposes. Checking personal e-mail or shopping online is not acceptable. When using the Internet, the employee is a representative of the company. Proper netiquette should be followed. **Cyberbullying** is harassing or threatening an individual through the Internet. Cyberbullying includes using social media or e-mails to harass or scare people. Cyberbullying is unethical and can be grounds for prosecution.

Checkpoint 17.1

1. Explain the importance of ethics in the workplace.
2. Name several pricing strategies that are illegal.
3. Explain the concept of sourcing.
4. What are the five principles of privacy protection regarding data collection under the Fair Information Practice Principles?
5. What is workplace *netiquette*?

Build Your Vocabulary

As you progress through this course, develop a personal glossary of retailing terms and add it to your portfolio. This will help you build your vocabulary and prepare you for a career. Write a definition for each of the following terms, and add it to your personal retailing glossary.

price fixing	puffery
price gouging	bait and switch
price discrimination	spam
predatory pricing	piracy
deceptive pricing	freeware
price ceiling	shareware
price floor	netiquette
sourcing	cyberbullying
false advertising	

Section 17.2 Legal Issues

Objectives

After completing this section, you will be able to:
- **Explain** the impact of business laws for retailers.
- **Summarize** the protection granted under the Consumer Bill of Rights.
- **Describe** the areas of employee protection laws.
- **Identify** ways retailers can get legal protection for information.
- **Discuss** the importance of environmental laws.

Key Terms

Consumer Product Safety Commission (CPSC)
recall
labor union
Occupational Safety and Health Administration (OSHA)
compensation
benefits
Equal Employment Opportunity Commission (EEOC)
proprietary information
confidentiality agreement
intellectual property
infringement
copyright
plagiarism
patent
trademark

Web Connect

There are specific workplace laws that retailers must honor. Research laws that relate to labor relations. Identify one law that is particularly important or interesting to you. Write several paragraphs describing your opinion of the value of that law.

Critical Thinking

Discrimination in the workplace is illegal. Give an example of discrimination that you have witnessed either at school or at work. How did the person in charge address the situation? Make a list of the steps that the person in charge pursued.

Business Laws

While successful retailers understand that they have an ethical responsibility to follow certain socially responsible guidelines, they are also bound by laws. All businesses must follow local, state, and federal laws set by legislators. Retailers and e-tailers must formulate business plans and activities to ensure that they and their employees follow the law.

Many ethical issues also cross legal borders. At times, it is difficult to distinguish between what is unethical and what is illegal. In many cases, poor retail practices fall under both classifications.

Laws that impact retailers and their stakeholders are put in place for protection. These laws are enacted for the protection of consumers, employees, the retailer itself, or the environment.

Consumer Protection Laws

Prior to 1962 there was a common phrase used in business: *caveat emptor*, or "buyer beware." In other words, the customer took the risk for the purchases they made. If something did not go as planned, the retailer had little responsibility to make things right.

In a message to Congress in 1962, President John F. Kennedy outlined four basic consumer rights. In 1985, the United Nations' Assembly added four more rights. These eight rights are now called the *Consumer Bill of Rights*. The original four basic consumer rights are:

- the right to safety
- the right to be informed
- the right to choose
- the right to be heard

Exploring Retail Careers

Publicist

Presenting a positive image to the public is important to the success of a business. Publicists plan and implement programs to create and maintain a good public image for the company. A publicist's job is to develop systematic communication that helps to inform the public about a retailer's accomplishments and special events. The job also includes managing any negative information about the retailer. Publicists generally work in an office. However, they may spend time attending meetings and community activities. They often must work long hours and may work in a high-stress environment. Typical job titles for these positions include *community affairs manager*, *public relations director*, *communications specialist*, and *press secretary*. Examples of tasks that publicists perform include:

- promote the retailer's image, activities, or brands
- prepare press releases, write newsletters, maintain blogs, give presentations, and answer questions from the media or the public
- work with community groups or charities
- oversee company communications
- respond to requests for information from the media
- create and implement fundraising campaigns

Publicists must have excellent oral and written communication skills. Basic computer skills are required. A bachelor degree is necessary. The degree may be in communications, business and marketing, or English. Previous public relations experience is usually required.

The four additional rights that were added in 1985 are:

- the right to satisfaction of basic needs
- the right to redress
- the right to education
- the right to a healthful environment

It was this bill of rights that changed the mindset of our nation regarding consumer protection. This bill of rights protected consumers and held retailers more accountable to the customer. Examples of consumer protection laws are shown in Figure 17-3.

Consumer Protection Laws	
Sherman Antitrust Act (1890)	Makes a monopoly illegal and protects against price fixing
Federal Trade Commission Act (1914, amended several times)	Series of regulations that requires all advertising to be truthful and not misleading
Robinson-Patman Act (1936)	Prevents unfair price discrimination for business and consumers
Truth in Lending Act (1968)	Requires disclosure of all terms of a loan in a clear way
Fair Credit Reporting Act (1970)	Provides consumers the right to examine their own credit report and correct inaccuracies
Consumer Product Safety Act (1972, amended 1990)	Protects the public from unreasonable risks of injury or death from unsafe products
Fair Credit Billing Act (1974)	Protects consumers against unfair charges and provides a way to challenge incorrect bills
Equal Credit Opportunity Act (1975)	Prohibits credit grantors from discriminating against consumers on the basis of sex, marital status, race, national origin, religion, age, or the receipt of public assistance
Electronic Fund Transfer Act (1978, amended 2009)	Sets guidelines for electronic transfers and payments, including ATM transactions and online payments
Trademark Counterfeiting Act (1984)	Makes it illegal to knowingly traffic a counterfeit product, or to misuse a trademark such as labeling
Nutrition Labeling and Education Act (1986)	Requires food labels to provide a complete disclosure of nutritional value
Identity Theft and Assumption Deterrence Act (1998)	Makes it illegal for someone to use another person's personal information for the sake of receiving credit
Truth in Domain Names Act (2003)	Protects consumers from being attracted to a deceptive or deceitful domain name (URL)
Wireless Telephone SPAM Protection Act (2003)	Prohibits companies from sending unsolicited advertisements to text messaging systems
CAN-SPAM Act (2004)	Sets regulations on what companies can and cannot do when sending group e-mail solicitations
US Safe Web Act (2006)	Protects consumers from fraud and deception, particularly to fight spam and spyware

Goodheart-Willcox Publisher

Figure 17-3 These are only a few examples of consumer protection laws in the United States.

Laws regulating the packaging and labeling of products aim to ensure that consumers have all the information they need to make purchasing decisions and are not deceived. The *Fair Packaging and Labeling Act* was passed in 1966 to support this aim. The most apparent function of packaging is to contain and identify a product. This legislation requires product packaging and labeling to meet more specific criteria to protect consumers. For example, the label must accurately list the contents of the package, identify the name and location of the manufacturer or distributor, and be easily legible.

Retailers and e-tailers may not sell products or services that are harmful to the public. The **Consumer Product Safety Commission (CPSC)** is a federal organization charged with protecting consumers from purchasing products that pose a risk of injury or death. The CPSC works to prevent unsafe products from reaching retail shelves. If products are found to be unsafe once they have been sold, the CPSC may demand a recall of the product. A **recall** is when a retailer or manufacturer requests that customers return a product for a refund or replacement.

Employee Protection Laws

The US Department of Labor has created more than 180 federal laws to protect employees in the workplace. These laws ensure that employees are treated safely and fairly. There are four general categories of workplace laws: labor relations, compensation and benefits, safety and health, and equal employment opportunity. Figure 17-4 explores several employee protection laws.

Social Media

Using Videos in Social Media

Videos posted on YouTube or other sites actively share information and engage customers or potential customers. YouTube has many features that encourage retailers and viewers to dialog about videos. For example, links and comments can pop up at certain points in a video. Viewers can post questions and comments and subscribe to a retailer's video channel. Viewers can also share a YouTube video on Facebook or Twitter. Plus, on YouTube, businesses can buy pay-per-click advertising to promote their videos. This option is a great way to get a target audience to view a certain video.

Videos can also position the company as a go-to expert for a specific product or service. When something important happens, such as new advance in the industry, create a video offering the latest information or advice. People will be searching for content on that topic, so any videos on that topic can take advantage of the interest. The video content can also be repurposed into blog posts, e-books, or webinars. This allows content to last longer and reach different audiences in a variety of ways.

Employee Protection Laws

National Labor Relations Act (1935)	Gives employees the right to form a union and negotiate with management as a collective group
Social Security Act (1935)	Established a system of lifetime retirement benefits based on age and/or disability
Fair Labor Standards Act (1938)	Established laws for overtime pay, set a minimum wage, and set strict rules for child employment
Equal Pay Act (1963)	Demands equal pay for equal work regardless of gender
Civil Rights Act, Title VII (1964, amended 1972 and 1991)	Prohibits discrimination based on a person's race, color, religion, sex, national origin, age, disability, or genetic information
Occupational Safety and Health Act (1970)	Sets safety standards for nearly all businesses
Consolidated Omnibus Budget Reconciliation Act (COBRA, 1985)	Provides workers and their families who lose their group health benefits the right to continue to purchase those benefits through the employer
Immigration Reform and Control Act (1986)	Makes it unlawful for employers to hire illegal immigrants
Worker Adjustment and Retraining Notification Act (1988)	Requires employers to provide notice 60 days in advance of plant closing or mass layoffs for businesses with more than 100 employees
Americans with Disabilities Act (1990, amended 2008)	Prohibits employers from treating qualified employees with disabilities differently with respect to hiring, advancement, and compensation
Workmans' Compensation (varies by state)	Protects workers when they are injured on the job and addresses wage replacement, medical treatment, etc.
Family Medical Leave Act (1993)	Grants medical leave under certain circumstances without the fear of losing one's job; prohibits employers from not hiring or promoting pregnant women; and allows family leave related to pregnancy
Health Insurance Portability and Accountability Act (1996)	Regulates the availability of group health insurance and states that employers must offer insurance to all members of the group

Goodheart-Willcox Publisher

Figure 17-4 US employee protection laws protect employees in the workplace.

Labor Relations

Labor relations laws give employees the right to form a labor union and negotiate with employers as a group. A **labor union** is a group of wage earners or salaried employees that join together to negotiate with management regarding workplace laws. Such negotiations, or *collective bargaining,* represent all employees eligible to be union members.

Safety and Health

In 1970, the US Department of Labor created the Occupational Safety and Health Administration to assure a safe workplace. The Occupational Safety and Health Administration (OSHA) is a federal agency that enforces safety and health regulations in the workplace. Most employees in the United States are protected under OSHA laws. Retailers that do not abide by these laws and do not meet OSHA standards may receive significant fines and penalties.

Compensation and Benefits

Compensation is an employee's wage or salary. Benefits are other types of noncash payments, such as insurance and paid time off. There are a variety of laws that regulate minimum standards on how retailers must compensate their employees.

Equal Employment Opportunity

The US Equal Employment Opportunity Commission is a federal agency that was formed in 1972 to prevent discrimination in the workplace. *Discrimination* is unfairly treating a person or group of people differently from others. The Equal Employment Opportunity Commission (EEOC) enforces federal laws that state it is illegal to discriminate against people in the workplace based on race, color, religion, sex, national origin, age, disability, or genetic information. Equal treatment, or *equality*, means that all people should be treated the same in the workplace. All people should be given the right to be considered for employment based on their abilities.

EEOC laws apply to all types of work situations including hiring, firing, promotions, harassment, training, wages, and benefits. Harassment is a form of discrimination. *Harassment* is unwelcome conduct that is based on race, color, religion, sex (including pregnancy), national origin, age (40 or older), disability, or genetic information. Employers should take steps to educate employees to prevent harassment from occurring.

Retailer Protection

There are a variety of laws that protect the consumer and the employer. There are also laws by local, state, and federal agencies that protect the business. One area of particular concern for retailers is protection of information. Examples of retailer-protection laws are shown in Figure 17-5.

Retail Ethics

Bribes

A *bribe* is an exchange of something of value for special consideration when doing business. Bribes are unethical, as well as illegal in the United States. In some foreign countries, however, bribes are considered legal. Regardless of where a company is located, US retailers should not accept a bribe from an individual, government, or business entity.

Retailer and Business Protection Laws

Copyright Act (1976)	Provides protection for authors of intellectual works
Lanham Act (1946, most recently amended 1996)	Provides trademark protection for words, symbols, phrases, packages, or other distinct features of a brand or product.
Digital Millennium Copyright Act (1998)	Series of laws to protect digital intellectual property. Most notably it identifies authors of online intellectual property as the rightful owner, including photographs, documents, video, recorded sounds and music, trademarks, and other elements for use in Internet publications. It also addresses the consequences of illegal, social, and unethical uses of information technologies, such as piracy; illegal downloading; licensing infringement; and inappropriate uses of software, hardware, and mobile devices in the United States. However, it does not bind other countries.
American Inventor's Protection Act (1999)	Protects owners of an invention to the exclusive rights to produce and sell their invention

Goodheart-Willcox Publisher

Figure 17-5 Many US laws protect the products, ideas, and information of businesses.

Confidential Information

Proprietary information, also known as *trade secrets*, is confidential information that a company needs to keep private. Proprietary information can include many things, such as product formulas, customer lists, and manufacturing processes. All employees must understand the importance of keeping company information confidential. The code of conduct should explain that company information may only be shared with permission from human resources. Employees who share proprietary information with outsiders are unethical and, possibly, breaking the law.

Before hiring an employee, a company may require the person to sign a confidentiality agreement. A **confidentiality agreement** typically states that the employee will not share any company information with those outside the company. Confidentiality agreements can also prevent former employees from working for a competitor for a specified length of time.

Intellectual property is something that comes from a person's mind, such as an idea, invention, or process. Generally any work created by company employees on the job is owned by that company. In business, these ideas are considered *proprietary information* and must be protected from theft. Any use of intellectual property without permission is called **infringement**. Ownership of all intellectual property is implied. However, there are three ways to register intellectual property to discourage infringement, as shown in Figure 17-6. The owner may choose to copyright, patent, or trademark the intellectual property.

FYI

US laws are not honored by all countries. For example, China does *not* have laws against copying movies and music.

Intellectual Property Protection	
Form of Protection	**Intellectual Property**
Copyright	Protects books, magazine articles, music, paintings, or other work of authorship for the life of the creator plus 70 years
Patent	Gives inventor the sole right to produce and sell an invention for a specific time
Trademark	Protects phrases, names, symbols, or any unique method of identifying a company or its product

Goodheart-Willcox Publisher

Figure 17-6 Registering intellectual property with the US Copyright Office or US Patent and Trademark Office discourages infringement.

Copyright

A **copyright** is the exclusive right to copy, license, sell, or distribute material. It acknowledges ownership of a work and specifies that only the owner has the right to sell the work, use it, or give permission for someone else to sell or use it.

A copyright lists the author or creator and the year the work was published. Copyrights are valid for the life of the author plus 70 years. Copyright laws in the United States are in place to protect the creators of original work. Another person cannot claim ownership of the work or use it without permission. The laws cover all original work, whether it is in print, on the Internet, or in any other form of media. All the material on a website is copyrighted unless the terms of use specifically state that an individual is free to copy and use any material provided. **Plagiarism** is claiming another person's material as your own, which is both unethical and illegal.

The © symbol and the "copyright by" statement indicate copyrighted material. However, lack of the symbol or statement does *not* affect a copyright. All original material is automatically copyrighted. A copyright can be registered with the US Copyright Office, which is part of the Library of Congress. However, original material is still legally protected whether or not the copyright is registered.

Fair use is a doctrine related to copyright law that allows limited use of copyrighted

Scanning or copying another person's work is plagiarism.

lightpoet/Shutterstock.com

material without permission from the creator of the original work. An example of fair use is when copyrighted material is used for teaching. However, this should not be taken advantage of. Copyright laws should always be followed.

Patent

A patent gives a person or company the right to be the sole producer of a product for a defined period of time. Patents protect an invention that is functional or mechanical. The invention must be considered useful, novel, and operational. This means that an idea may not be patented. A process can be patented under certain conditions. The process must transform a substance or item into a different state or thing, or be related to a particular machine.

The inventor must file a patent application with the US Patent and Trademark Office. Once granted, a patent protects the inventor's intellectual property for between 14 and 20 years from the filing date.

Trademark

A trademark protects taglines, slogans, names, symbols, and any unique method to identify a product or company. A *service mark* is similar to a trademark, but it identifies a service rather than a product. Trademarks and service marks do not protect a work or product. They only protect the way in which the product or service is described. The term *trademark* is often used to refer to both trademarks and service marks. The US Patent and Trademark Office handles trademark applications and enforces trademark laws. Once approved, trademarks never expire.

Graphic marks or *symbols*, shown in Figure 17-7, can be used without being formally registered. However, trademarks should be registered with the US Patent and Trademark Office. This prevents another company from claiming ownership of a trademark or using it without permission.

Environmental Law

Even retailers that are not green are required to comply with environmental laws. Environmental laws and regulations ensure that companies act in a responsible manner and make decisions that do not harm the environment. Examples of environmental laws are shown in Figure 17-8. The *Environmental Protection Agency (EPA)* has very specific laws that apply to different industries. For example, it regulates the output of pollutants by manufacturing facilities into the air and water.

Correct Use of Trademark Symbols	
TM	Trademark, not registered
SM	Service mark, not registered
®	Registered trademark

Goodheart-Willcox Publisher

Figure 17-7 The symbols used to indicate that material is registering intellectual property can be used without being formally registered.

Environmental Laws	
Clean Air Act (1970)	Established maximum air pollutant levels businesses can emit
Clean Water Act (1972)	Established maximum water pollutant levels businesses can emit
Noise Control Act (1972)	Protects the public from excessive noise coming from business
Energy Policy Act (2005)	Provides tax incentives for those companies that use energy-efficient methods
Energy Independence and Security Act (2007)	Requires companies to increase the energy efficiency of buildings

Goodheart-Willcox Publisher

Figure 17-8 Environmental laws and regulations apply differently to business within different industries.

Checkpoint 17.2

1. Describe business laws and their importance for retailers.
2. What did the Consumer Bill of Rights accomplish?
3. What are the four general categories of workplace laws?
4. What is the purpose of a confidentiality agreement?
5. What do copyright and trademark compliance infer?

Build Your Vocabulary

As you progress through this course, develop a personal glossary of retailing terms and add it to your portfolio. This will help you build your vocabulary and prepare you for a career. Write a definition for each of the following terms, and add it to your personal retailing glossary.

Consumer Product Safety Commission (CPSC)
recall
labor union
Occupational Safety and Health Administration (OSHA)
compensation
benefits
Equal Employment Opportunity Commission (EEOC)

proprietary information
confidentiality agreement
intellectual property
infringement
copyright
plagiarism
patent
trademark

Chapter Summary

Section 17.1 Retail Ethics

- Retailers are obligated to act in an ethical manner. To guide employees, many businesses create a code of ethics that outlines appropriate business behavior.
- Retailers are in business to make money. However, they should not lose sight that ethical and legal behavior is necessary. Pricing practices is one area that is of special concern to retailers.
- Retailers must buy products at the lowest possible price and at the highest quality. However, retailers should not participate in any purchase that is not ethically or legally sound.
- Businesses are obligated to use data collected from customers in a legal and ethical manner. Retailers must respect the rights of the customer and follow *Fair Information Practice Principles* developed by the Federal Trade Commission (FTC).
- Advertising helps customers decide what they want to buy and where to shop. No customer should be mislead due to puffery, false claims, bait and switch, or spam.
- Employers should outline the expected business ethics for employees and hold them accountable for their actions.

Section 17.2 Legal Issues

- All businesses must follow local, state, and federal laws set by legislators. Retailers and e-tailers must formulate business plans and activities to ensure that they and their employees follow the law.
- Consumer-protection laws protect the consumer when they make a purchase and hold retailers more accountable to the customer. The Consumer Product Safety Commission (CPSC) protects consumers from purchasing products that pose a risk of injury or death.
- Employee protection laws ensure that employees are treated safely and fairly. The US Department of Labor has created more than 180 federal laws to protect employees in the workplace.
- Certain laws by local, state, and federal agencies protect businesses. One area of particular concern for retailers is protection of information.
- Environmental laws and regulations ensure that companies act in a responsible manner and make decisions that do not harm the environment.

Review Your Knowledge

1. How can a decision-making model be helpful when ethics are at stake?
2. Differentiate between *pure price discrimination* and *imperfect price discrimination*.
3. Compare and contrast *price ceiling* and *price floor*.
4. Give examples of appropriate and ethical workplace behavior.
5. Explain why downloading software may present ethical issues.
6. Why are employee protection laws necessary?
7. Explain discrimination, harassment, and equality. How do these elements relate to each other?
8. Give examples of concerns retailers have regarding private information.
9. Explain the criteria necessary to receive a patent for an invention.
10. Name the federal agency that enforces environmental laws and regulations.

Apply Your Knowledge

1. Workplace ethics, or office ethics, are important to the employer and employee. Imagine yourself as a manager for a retail store. One of your employees reports another employee for using company equipment for personal use. Using the ethical decision-making model in Figure 17-1, analyze the situation.

2. Corporate ethics may require that an employee sign a confidentiality agreement. Imagine yourself working in the human resources department of a retail business. It has come to your attention that an employee who signed a confidentiality agreement has violated that agreement. Using the ethical decision-making model in Figure 17-1, analyze the situation.

3. You are a marketing manager working for a retail establishment. You have been asked to send an e-mail campaign to a list of customers that someone retrieved from the Internet. You know that this is considered spam and are not comfortable sending this campaign. Using the ethical decision-making model in Figure 17-1, analyze the situation.

4. Businesses have an obligation to be ethical in all communication, including advertising and promotional messages. You have probably seen an advertisement from an unethical retailer that intentionally misleads the customer. Find an advertisement, either in print or online, that you think is misleading. Using the ethical decision-making model in Figure 17-1, analyze the situation. State the unethical claim and why you think it is unethical. How common of a practice do you think this is?

5. Employee behavior is important in the workplace. You hear disturbing information about a coworker. Another coworker wants to discuss the issues. You are uncomfortable about spreading gossip about another person. It is unethical to share personal information about someone with whom you work. Using the ethical decision-making model in Figure 17-1, analyze the situation.

6. Most people have a perception as to what ethics are and what they are not. Define your perception of ethics in the workplace. Explain why people should understand and respect ethical opinions of others that may conflict with their personal ethics. What is the importance of public discussion in finding answers to difficult ethical issues?

7. Ethical businesses try to do the right thing when natural disasters hit their community. Rather than raise prices, these retailers try to minimize prices to help those in need. Businesses may even sell supplies and other needed items at break-even or lower prices. Choose a natural disaster that happened within the last year. Find an example of a retailer who helped the affected community. Write a paragraph describing the retailer's actions and how it assisted the community.

8. There are laws that protect businesses and consumers by implying ethical behavior. Research and identify the relevant laws that regulate advertising, copyrights, and trademarks. Write a paragraph about each topic including the name of the law and what it protects.

9. Research the application process for copyrights. List the steps that are necessary to obtain a copyright. Next, research the application process for a trademark. List the steps that are necessary to obtain a copyright. How are these processes similar? How are they different?

10. The *Fair Packaging and Labeling Act* is one of many laws passed regulating product packaging and labeling. Research US packaging and labeling laws. Choose one that applies to a product you commonly purchase. Explain the law and how it has been applied to the product you regularly purchase.

Check Your Retail IQ

Now that you have finished the chapter, see what you learned about retail by taking the chapter posttest. If you do not have a smartphone, visit the G-W Learning companion website.
G-W Learning mobile site: www.m.g-wlearning.com
G-W Learning companion website: www.g-wlearning.com/marketing/

College and Career Readiness

Career Ready Practices What do you think the old adage, "Necessity is the mother of invention" means? Find examples of how the need for something has led to the development of something new.

Listening Ask a classmate to give you directions on how to drive to the nearest mall. Take notes as the directions are given. Evaluate and summarize your notes. If necessary, ask the speaker to slow down or repeat a point. Use prior knowledge of the city to follow the directions that are given.

Reading Now that you have completed reading multiple chapters in this text about retailing and e-tailing, analyze the themes and structures that the author used. Create a concept map that illustrates how the themes of this text are related.

Teamwork

Legal issues were covered in this chapter. Working with your teammates, identify five legal issues that may be of concern in a retail business. These issues could impact the consumer, employer, or retail. After you have identified the issues, list ways each of the issues could be resolved.

College and Career Portfolio

Networking

The purpose of your portfolio is to help you get a job, a volunteer position, or be accepted to a college. You should build a network of people who can help you in these efforts. You have probably already begun to build one, even if you have not thought of it in these terms. People in your network include your instructors, employers, coworkers, or counselors who know about your skills and interests. Those who participate with you in volunteer efforts, clubs, or other organizations can also be part of your network. These people may help you learn about open positions and may be able to give you information that will help you get a position.

1. Identify people who are part of your career network as described above.
2. Create a database to contain information about the people. Include each person's name, contact information, and relationship to you. For example, the person might be a coworker, employer, or fellow club member.
3. Save the file in your e-portfolio. Place a printout in the container for your print portfolio.

◇DECA Coach

Visually Lead the Speaker

You have the ability to direct the focus of the judge anywhere you like. He or she will follow your lead. If you doubt this, next time you are talking to a friend, suddenly look out the window, hold your stare, and make a surprised face. The odds are that he or she will also turn around and look out the window. You can and should do the same thing with your judges.

Your eyes are very important. While speaking, make good eye contact with all the judges. However, if you wish to redirect their attention to a prop, a chart, or other visual, be sure to lead them. Simply direct your eyes to where you want them to look. Often, pointing is effective. If you are looking at something and pointing at it, others will look at it, too. If you continue looking them in the eye, they may not redirect their attention. When you are done, simply return to eye contact.

Team members are also important in redirecting attention, even when they are not speaking. Idle team members should always be looking at the speaker and nowhere else. An occasional nod of agreement from your teammates is helpful. If your team members are not watching the speaker, it shows a lack of interest to the judges. When the speaker leads the judges to something visual, nonspeaking members should also follow this lead. It reinforces to the judges the direction they should be following. As you practice your presentation, be sure to focus on leading the judges.

Visit www.deca.org to learn more information about DECA.

G-W Learning Mobile Site

Visit the G-W Learning mobile site to complete the chapter pretest and posttest, and to practice vocabulary using e-flash cards. If you do not have a smartphone, visit the G-W Learning companion website to access these features.

G-W Learning mobile site: www.m.g-wlearning.com

G-W Learning companion website: www.g-wlearning.com/marketing/

Chapter 18
Risk

Risk is part of the cost of doing business. Retailers and e-tailers manage both controllable and uncontrollable risks every day. They usually face four basic types of risk: natural, human, economic and political, and market.

Successful businesses practice risk management. Risk management involves identifying, assessing, and reducing risks. One way to manage risk is to avoid or reduce the risk through proper planning. Businesses also transfer certain risks by purchasing insurance to help protect against financial loss. However, not all risks can be insured, so a business must be prepared for those potential losses.

Case Study

Lowe's

In 2012, Hurricane Sandy struck the east coast of the United States and damaged or destroyed several hundred thousand homes and businesses in its path. Those who lived in the most afflicted communities experienced devastating losses. As retailers worked hard to replenish inventory and reopen their own stores, many reached out to assist those in need. Lowe's was one of the retailers that decided to champion the cause.

Lowe's partnered with national nonprofit organizations to generate relief and rebuilding funds. In addition to monetary donations to the American Red Cross, Habitat for Humanity®, and other relief organizations, Lowe's hosted relief and recovery events in New York and New Jersey stores and became a repository for American Red Cross donations. Groups of volunteer employees, known as Lowe's Heroes, distributed more than 100,000 pounds of food and cleaning supplies into affected communities. Thanksgiving came soon after Hurricane Sandy, so the Lowe's Heroes delivered more than 22,000 family-style Thanksgiving dinners to hurricane-impacted families.

While Lowe's was not required to make such efforts, it recognized that the company was part of a community in need. By participating in the rebuilding efforts and supporting local communities, the company hopes that customers will remember that Lowe's is a friend to their community.

College and Career Readiness

Reading Prep

As you read this chapter, take notes on the important points you want to remember. Record key terms and ideas. Is this helpful in understanding the material?

Check Your Retail IQ

Before you begin the chapter, see what you already know about retail by taking the chapter pretest. If you do not have a smartphone, visit the G-W Learning companion website.

G-W Learning mobile site: www.m.g-wlearning.com

G-W Learning companion website: www.g-wlearning.com/marketing/

Sections

Dusit/Shutterstock.com

Section 18.1 Identifying Risk

Objectives

After completing this section, you will be able to:
- **Explain** business risk.
- **Describe** four types of risks that a retailer might encounter.

Key Terms

business risk
controllable risk
uncontrollable risk
natural risk
human risk
shoplifter
burglary

robbery
fraud
embezzlement
economic risk
market risk
product
   obsolescence

Web Connect

Research the term *speculative risk*. Write a paragraph describing your findings. How do you think speculative risk applies to retail and e-tail businesses?

Critical Thinking

All businesses face risks. Create a list of risks that a brick-and-mortar retailer might face. Next, create a list of risks that an e-tailer might face. What risks do both types of businesses have in common?

Business Risk

Business risk is the possibility of loss or injury that might occur while operating a business. Business risks are similar for both retailers and e-tailers.

A risk can be controllable or uncontrollable. A **controllable risk** is one that cannot be avoided, but can be minimized by purchasing insurance or implementing a risk plan. Incidents, such as fire, will be covered if a retailer buys insurance. An **uncontrollable risk** is a situation that cannot be predicted or covered by purchasing insurance. For example, if the competition comes out with a new product, a retailer could lose business. This is an event that cannot be controlled. There is no type of insurance that will cover such a loss.

Types of Risk

As shown in Figure 18-1, there are four basic types of risk: natural, human, economic and political, and market.

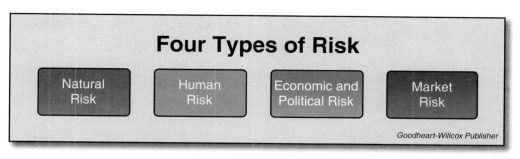

Figure 18-1 There are four basic types of risk, all of which can affect a retail or an e-tail business.

Natural Risk

A **natural risk** is a situation caused by nature. Humans have little control over natural events and often have no time to prepare for them. Examples of natural events include earthquakes, fires, floods, storms, and other natural phenomena. Natural risks may cause injury, loss of life, or loss of property.

Human Risk

A **human risk** is a situation caused by human actions. For a retail business, there is always a chance of theft, fraud, or accidental injury. These situations can be caused by employees, customers, or vendors.

Theft

The National Retail Federation estimates that retailers lost more than $37 billion through various types of theft in 2011. Some types of theft are shoplifting, burglary, robbery, and employee theft.

Of the losses due to theft, $12.1 billion were directly related to shoplifting. A **shoplifter** is a person posing as a customer who takes goods from a store without paying for them. A shoplifter may distract employees, change price tags on items to get a lower price, or intentionally confuse sales associates.

A **burglary** occurs when a person breaks into a business to steal merchandise, money, valuable equipment, or take confidential information. There are many different ways for burglars to enter a building. Picking locks, hiding in the business after closing, using stolen or duplicated keys, or breaking windows or doors are common methods. A **robbery** is a theft involving another person, often using force or the threat of violence.

Employee theft is when an employee steals from the business. There are a number of unethical ways in which employees steal from a business. Stealing directly from the register, giving friends discounts or free items, and taking merchandise from the store are examples.

Shrinkage is a term that identifies inventory losses due to shoplifting, employee theft, paperwork errors, and vendor fraud.

Employee theft is a human risk that retail businesses must be aware of.

Lisa F. Young/Shutterstock.com

Fraud

Fraud is cheating or deceiving a business out of money or property. Fraud can be committed by employees, vendors, and customers.

Employees can embezzle from the business. Embezzlement is a type of fraud that occurs when somebody entrusted with confidential company information, financial records, money, or other valuables takes it for personal gain.

Vendors may commit fraud by delivering less than what was ordered, but charging for the full order.

Customers may try to commit fraud by paying with checks from bank accounts that have insufficient funds. Others may try to use a stolen credit card or counterfeit money. Some customers may commit identity theft by using another individual's personal information.

Accidental Injury

Retail establishments are responsible for any accidents that happen on their property. Accidental injuries may happen to both employees and customers if the retailer is careless about taking care of the property.

Economic and Political Risk

An economic risk is a situation that occurs when the economy suffers due to negative business conditions either in the United States or someplace in the world. Negative business conditions may include high unemployment and low wages, high product prices and inflation, or increased competition for a product.

Risks caused as a result of a change in economic conditions are called *dynamic risks*. They are generally not predictable and do not occur in regular intervals.

Political changes can create political risk for global business. Retailers who buy or sell merchandise outside the country can be directly affected by political conditions. For example, if political changes affect trade agreements between the United States and other countries, global business may come to an end. This may directly impact retailers who depend on other countries for product and sales.

Market Risk

Market risk is the potential that the target market for products or services is much less than originally thought. A new product may not be as popular as expected. Also, customers may decide that a product is no longer desirable. A product may have a short shelf life and become obsolete quickly. This is known as product obsolescence. **Product obsolescence** occurs when customers no longer want to buy a product, leaving a retailer with merchandise it cannot sell.

> FYI
>
> *Planned obsolescence* is evaluating and updating current products, or adding new products to replace older ones.

Checkpoint 18.1

1. Explain the concept of business risk.
2. List the four basic types of risk.
3. Name and describe three common examples of human risk.
4. What is employee theft? Give examples of this behavior.
5. Discuss market risk and how it impacts the retailer.

Build Your Vocabulary

As you progress through this course, develop a personal glossary of retailing terms and add it to your portfolio. This will help you build your vocabulary and prepare you for a career. Write a definition for each of the following terms, and add it to your personal retailing glossary.

business risk

controllable risk

uncontrollable risk

natural risk

human risk

shoplifter

burglary

robbery

fraud

embezzlement

economic risk

market risk

product obsolescence

Section 18.2 Managing Risk

Risk Management

Risk management is the process of identifying, assessing, and reducing different kinds of risks. This process involves anticipating risks and taking the necessary steps to prevent or minimize the negative results that may occur.

There are several risk management techniques that may be considered. Risks may be avoided or reduced, transferred, or assumed by the retailer or e-tailer.

Avoid or Reduce the Risk

Avoiding risk is one of the best risk management techniques. While businesses take preventive measures to avoid risk, it is not always possible. It is necessary to have a plan to reduce the risk when it happens.

Human Risk

Human risks can generally be avoided or reduced. One risk that many businesses confront is improper use of its computer network by employees. The first line of defense for this type of risk is proper training and guidelines for employees. Every person in the company should understand the proper procedures for using company equipment. Education is the best way to avoid or reduce the risk.

Careless downloading of files can shut down an entire network. Some downloaded files and software programs contain computer viruses or other harmful software. *Software viruses* are computer programs that cause harm to computer systems. A virus may destroy company and customer data on the computer or collect confidential information from the company's network and transmit it to another location. Viruses can also be contained in e-mail attachments or be transmitted by visiting websites. Viruses can be file infections, boot-sector infections, worms, and Trojan horses. Most are **malware**, which is a computer program designed to damage or disrupt a computer or network. To help reduce this risk, a firewall should be installed. A **firewall** is software that prevents unwelcomed Internet access to data stored on a computer.

Passwords are another way of protecting company data. Each individual who has access to the company's network and computers should have passwords. The retailer can restrict the amount of information viewed by an employee by assigning rights to certain files.

To protect company data, each employee should be required to enter a password to access the company's network.

Syda Productions/Shutterstock.com

Phishing, pronounced *fishing*, is the use of fraudulent e-mails and copies of valid websites to trick people into providing private, confidential, and personal data. The most common form of phishing is done by sending a fake e-mail to a group of people. The e-mail message looks like it is from a legitimate source, such as a person's bank. The e-mail asks for certain information, such as an account number and password, or it provides a link to a website. The linked website may look real, but it collects private information that is used to commit fraud. Retailers can protect their customers and vendors from phishing e-mails by keeping their information secure. They can also warn customers and vendors if sensitive information has been stolen or if they are aware of phishing e-mails being sent from a fraudulent source.

Theft

Retailers can protect themselves against theft by being proactive with a preventative plan. It is difficult to totally eliminate theft, but it can be decreased.

The layout of a retail store is a critical element in reducing both customer and employee theft. Maximizing sight lines is one key factor in preventing theft. Employees should be able to see as much of the store as possible. They should be able to see their customers and each other. Mirrors can be used in areas that are hard to see. Expensive merchandise should be in locked cases or have security tags attached. Outside lighting, alarms, and security systems are also effective theft deterrents.

Security cameras can be used for surveillance inside a store and outside the building.

Surveillance is the act of closely observing activity within a store to detect and prevent crimes. It can be conducted using employees, security guards, or video cameras. Having an adequate number of salespeople on the floor to observe activity discourages shoplifting. Security cameras can record activity inside a store and outside the building. Installing the cameras in visible areas is effective in preventing both shoplifting and employee theft.

The retailer should establish cash handling policies. To prevent internal theft, employees should never ring up their own purchase or product return transactions. Also, employees should regularly remove cash from the registers and place it in a safe or secure drop box.

FYI

The *Better Business Bureau (BBB)*, established in 1912, is a nonprofit organization dedicated to consumer education and establishing a trustworthy standard of business practices.

Fraud

Fraud is an unwelcome challenge that confronts both retailers and e-tailers. Employee fraud is a situation that businesses need to avoid at all costs. A good deterrent to employee fraud is to hire honest people. Thorough background checks run on potential employees should be part of the hiring process.

Vendor fraud may be avoidable by investigating a vendor before conducting business. Before using a vendor, check its status with the Better Business Bureau (BBB). To make sure vendors deliver what they promise, deliveries should be verified while the delivery person is present. Deliveries should not be accepted if they cannot be checked in on arrival.

Customer fraud may take various forms. Identity theft poses a difficult challenge for retailers and e-tailers. A customer who steals another person's identity may be hard to detect especially online. If a person in the store writes a check, his or her identity should be verified. All information printed on the check should match the customer's driver's license or state ID. The best defense is to contact the customer's bank to verify there are sufficient funds in the account to cover the purchase.

E-tailers generally process orders using customer credit cards for payment. The sales transactions are not in person, so there is no easy way to verify the identity of the person using a credit card. An identity thief who has all of someone's personal information is nearly impossible to detect. One way retailers and e-tailers can try to avoid the risk is to confirm the information given by the customer with the credit card company.

Accidental Injury

Workplace safety in the United States has continuously improved since the beginning of the 20th century. Injury, death,

Social Media

Pinterest

Pinterest is a type of social networking called *visual networking* because it is primarily based on sharing images. It has over 20 million active users who avidly *pin* (the Pinterest word for posting) images or products from websites they find interesting or want to share with others. Users are encouraged to *re-pin* and *comment* on others' pins. Users are directed to company websites through hyperlinks embedded in the images. Creating a business profile and vision boards allows other users to follow pins established by the retailer. A Pinterest account can also be linked to the business' Twitter and Facebook accounts, which is highly recommended.

and illness related to working conditions have gradually declined. This is due to changes in the type of work done today and in the safety precautions that have been put in place.

Falling hazards, lifting hazards, and material-storage hazards account for most of the workplace accidents that occur in retail. A **falling hazard** is a source of potential injuries from slipping or falling. Falls are the most common workplace accident in a retail business. Falls can result in broken bones, head injuries, and muscle strains.

Lifting hazards are sources of potential injury from improperly lifting or carrying items. Most back injuries are caused by improper lifting. To avoid injuries from lifting, employees should take certain precautions:

- make several trips carrying fewer items
- use dollies or handcarts whenever possible
- lift with the legs, not the back
- never carry an item that blocks vision

Material-storage hazards are sources of potential injury caused by the improper storage of merchandise or equipment. A cluttered workplace is an unsafe workplace. For example, items that are stacked too high can fall on employees and customers.

Maintaining a safe workplace is the responsibility of both the employer and employee. The employer makes sure the facility and working conditions are safe so that accidents are unlikely to occur, and provides safety training when applicable. The employee uses common sense and care while at work.

Natural Risks

All businesses should have a plan for natural risks. With a disaster plan in place, lives and property can be saved. Fire drills and tornado drills should be practiced with employees on a regular basis. Signs should be posted that clearly identify storm shelters in case of an emergency.

Employees should be diligent in clearly identifying and cleaning up slipping hazards in the workplace.

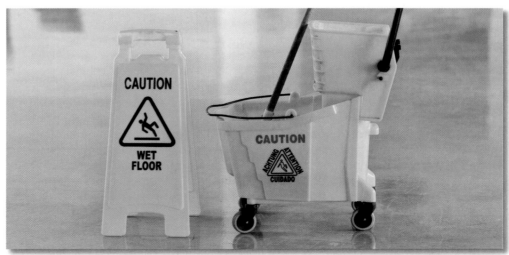

Businesses should meet with the local fire department for other important tips on preparing for natural risks. Insurance companies may also be a resource for safety and preparation suggestions.

Market Risks

All retailers take a market risk. Retailers cannot control which products consumers will prefer and they cannot control their competition. However, some of these risks can be avoided or reduced by conducting market research. While not an exact science, adequate research can help a business create comprehensive, well-informed plans.

Transfer the Risk

Damages and losses do occur. While damages may be unavoidable, the financial losses associated with damages from human, physical, and natural risk factors may be transferred by purchasing insurance. **Insurance** is a financial product that offers protection against a specific type of loss. In return for this protection, the insured pays a premium. A **premium** is the amount paid for insurance, which is often a monthly fee.

Exploring Retail Careers

Retail Loss Prevention Specialist

Theft can devastate even a strong retail business. A retail loss prevention specialist protects the building as well as employees and merchandise. This person is responsible for deterring illegal activity on the premises, especially theft and shoplifting. If a loss prevention specialist is able to identify a person engaging in illegal activity, it is his or her job to detain the violator. This position works with local law enforcement, as necessary. Other typical job titles for retail security officer are *loss prevention specialist*, *in-store detective*, and *director of security*. Some examples of tasks that retail security officers perform include:

- monitor closed-circuit TV camera systems in an effort to detect crime
- conduct physical security checks of the building and parking lots
- enforce laws in and around a building
- write observation and incident reports
- assist authorities with investigation of incidents, including interviewing witnesses of incidents, possibly for court testimony

A retail loss prevention specialist must be able to make quick decisions and determine the best way to handle situations. They also must have good observation skills and remain alert. Most security professionals have a high school diploma. Higher level security positions may require at least some college work in criminal justice. Most states also require security professionals to be licensed.

NRF Tip

NRF offers member participation in a Loss Prevention Advisory Council. This group meets frequently to discuss the problem of theft for retailers and to generate ideas on managing those losses.

There are several types of insurance that can be purchased to guard against financial losses. These types of insurance protect either the retailer or the employees. Some types of insurance that retailers may consider are shown in Figure 18-2.

Assume the Risk

All risks cannot be insured. An **uninsurable risk** is one that an insurance company will not cover. For example, insurance companies will not cover economic or market risks. The retailer must assume these risks and take responsibility for losses.

Insurance Coverage Available to Retailers	
Commercial Insurance	**How it protects the retailer:**
Business interruption	Protects against expenses and loss of income resulting from fire, theft, or other insured peril.
Fidelity bonds	Covers against losses due to employee actions that are not covered under normal theft policies, such as embezzlement or employee theft.
Fire and theft	Covers losses due to fire and the resulting smoke and water, as well as theft.
General liability	Provides protection for retailers and individuals against normal exposure for negligence resulting in bodily injury or property damage.
Product liability	Pays for damage or injury that results from the use of the retailer's goods or services.
Professional liability (also known as errors and omissions insurance)	Protects retailers against damages from not acting in their capacity as an expert in the field.
Surety bonds	Three-party contract in which the third party guarantees performance of one of the other parties.
Employee Insurance	**How it protects employees:**
Group health insurance	Offered to all employees in the organization and provides coverage for medical expenses.
Group life insurance	Offered to all employees in the organization and provides a predefined payment upon the death of an employee.
Workers' compensation	Provides compensation and rehabilitation benefits when an employee is injured as part of their job duties. Workers' compensation is mandatory in most cases.

Goodheart-Willcox Publisher

Figure 18-2 Various insurance products offer protection for employers and employees.

Some businesses may choose to *self-insure*. This can be accomplished by creating a savings account dedicated to covering risks. The retailer may deposit monthly installments, similar to paying a monthly insurance premium. The money accumulates in the savings account and can be used to pay for a loss that is not covered by insurance.

Checkpoint 18.2

1. Define risk management and explain what it involves.
2. How can retailers avoid or reduce the risk of computer viruses?
3. What can a retailer do to be prepared for natural risks?
4. Explain the concept of transferring risk.
5. Explain what it means to assume risk.

Build Your Vocabulary

As you progress through this course, develop a personal glossary of retailing terms and add it to your portfolio. This will help you build your vocabulary and prepare you for a career. Write a definition for each of the following terms, and add it to your personal retailing glossary.

risk management
malware
firewall
phishing
surveillance
falling hazard

lifting hazard
material-storage hazard
insurance
premium
uninsurable risk

Chapter Summary

Section 18.1 Identifying Risk

- Business risk is the possibility of loss or injury that might occur while operating a business. Risks may be considered controllable or uncontrollable.
- The four basic types of risk are natural, human, economic and political, and market.

Section 18.2 Managing Risk

- Risk management is identifying, assessing, and reducing risks. This process involves anticipating risks and taking the necessary steps to prevent or minimize them.
- While businesses take preventative measures to avoid risk, it is not always possible. It is necessary to have a plan to reduce the risk when it happens.
- The financial losses associated with damages from human, physical, and natural risk factors may be transferred by purchasing insurance. There are several types of insurance that protect either the retailer or the employees.
- All risks cannot be insured. The retailer must assume uninsurable risks and take responsibility for losses.

Review Your Knowledge

1. Describe the difference between controllable and uncontrollable risks.
2. List three examples of natural risk.
3. What is the difference between burglary and robbery?
4. Compare and contrast economic risk with political risk.
5. Explain the term *dynamic risks*.
6. How can human risks be avoided or transferred?
7. Can market risks be controlled? Why or why not?
8. Discuss the human risk of improper use of the business computer network. Why is this important?
9. Customer fraud takes on various forms. Give an example of customer fraud.
10. Explain how a retailer can self-insure.

Apply Your Knowledge

1. Locate an article in a newspaper, magazine, or online about a retailer that recently dealt with business risk. Write several paragraphs about the incident that includes answers to the following questions: What kind of risk did the retailer face? Was it controllable or uncontrollable? Did the business assume the risk?
2. List and describe controllable and uncontrollable risks for a retail business. List and describe controllable and uncontrollable risks for an e-tail business. How could these risks impact the prices of goods and services?
3. Think about the security concerns for retailers and e-tailers. Create a chart with two columns. Label column one "E-tailer" and column two "Retailer." Identify the security concerns that each might face. Examine the concerns that impact both. How similar or different are they?

4. In your own words, define *threats* for retailers. Create a chart with two columns. Label column one "E-tailer" and column two "Retailer." Identify threats that each might face. Examine the concerns that impact both. How similar or different are they?

5. Research the different types of surveillance tactics retailers might use. What types of surveillance tactics would an e-tailer use? Explain how these tactics help control risk.

6. Describe the security risks that an e-tailer might face. How are these security risks unique to e-tailers?

7. Brainstorm security procedures that retailers can put in place to guard against risk. How can these procedures be implemented? What security procedures are unique to e-tailers?

8. Using the Internet, research different security providers. What products and services do they offer? Summarize the information you find.

9. What types of safety training could a retailer or e-tailer provide for its employees? Outline training suggestions specific to sales associates, customer service representatives, and those working in the warehouse. How can safety training control risk?

10. Using the Internet, research professional liability insurance. What does a professional liability insurance policy need to cover for a retailer? for an e-tailer? How can purchasing this kind of insurance control risk? Present your findings to the class.

Check Your Retail IQ

Now that you have finished the chapter, see what you learned about retail by taking the chapter posttest. If you do not have a smartphone, visit the G-W Learning companion website.

G-W Learning mobile site: www.m.g-wlearning.com

G-W Learning companion website: www.g-wlearning.com/marketing/

College and Career Readiness

Career Ready Practices The ability to read and interpret information is an important workplace skill. As a consumer, it is important that you understand your consumer rights. Research the Consumer Bill of Rights. Read and interpret the information you locate. How do these rights influence consumer behavior? Write a report summarizing your findings in an organized manner.

Reading Research the laws in your state regarding truth-in-advertising laws. Read closely to determine what the text says. Identify two words and one concept that are unfamiliar to you. Define them using context clues or Internet research.

Research Combine primary research and secondary research on workplace safety to write a paper. Use an appropriate design for your report. Draw pictures or diagrams to illustrate the information included in your report.

Teamwork

Working in teams, research the most common natural risks for your geographic area. Find out how often these risks usually occur, what they cost retailers, and what recommendations are made by government and insurance companies to deal with these risks. Present your findings to the class.

College and Career Portfolio

Portfolio Organization

You have collected various items for your portfolio in earlier activities. Now you will organize the materials in your print portfolio. Your instructor may have examples of portfolios that you can review for ideas. You can also search the Internet for articles about how to organize a print portfolio. You should provide a table of contents for the items. This will allow the person reviewing the portfolio to find items easily. Keep the sections of the portfolio that are for your use only separate from the other documents, such as your contacts database. You should continue to add and remove documents as you complete assignments or gain new skills. Update the table of contents when you make changes to the portfolio.

1. Review the documents you have collected. Select the ones you want to include in your career portfolio. Make copies of certificates, diplomas, and other important documents. Keep the originals in a safe place.
2. Create the table of contents. You also may want to create a title page for each section.
3. Place the items in a binder, folder, or other container.
4. Conduct the same exercise for organizing your electronic documents in your e-portfolio.

◇DECA Coach

Handling Questions and Answers

Presentations allow for a question and answer period at the end of the presentation. No matter how good your presentation was, your performance during the question and answer period is critical to your success. Part of your performance is based on the content of your responses. However, it is not the only thing on which you will be evaluated.

One important rule during the questioning period is that teammates should never argue or show disagreement during the question and answer period. Even if you do not agree with what your teammate just said, discuss it after you have left the judge's table. One way to help correct a mistake made by a teammate is to wait until your teammate has finished his or her response. Then, you can add, "Another way we could consider addressing that is by…"

Another rule for the question and answer period is to understand that the judge is supposed to question you. Regardless of tone, do not get defensive. You may also recall parts of your presentation just in case they missed something. You can clarify or expand on your content, but do not be argumentative. All teammates should attempt to answer a portion of the questions.

One good habit is to acknowledge that the judge just asked a good question. If the judge has offered you advice, be sure to thank them for their professional advice. Making them feel good about themselves will do nothing but help your cause.

Visit www.deca.org to learn more information about DECA.

G-W Learning Mobile Site

Visit the G-W Learning mobile site to complete the chapter pretest and posttest, and to practice vocabulary using e-flash cards. If you do not have a smartphone, visit the G-W Learning companion website to access these features.

G-W Learning mobile site: www.m.g-wlearning.com

G-W Learning companion website: www.g-wlearning.com/marketing/

Unit 7

Retail Careers

Introduction

Most of us will start working at a job, and then pursue a career. Creating a career plan can help define your career goals and what is required to reach those goals, such as education requirements and professional experience. There are many career research resources available to evaluate which careers will make the most of your talents, skills, and interests.

When looking for your first retail job, your résumé must persuade the employer that your skills and experience fit the position. It is also the first impression potential employers will have of you. An interview is your opportunity to sell yourself in person. The employment process can take a substantial amount of time, but may result in a great start to a successful career.

Green Retail

Electronic Job Hunting

Digital technology has made finding and applying for jobs more eco-friendly than ever before. Before the widespread availability of the Internet, job seekers read through the want ads in piles of newspapers and either mailed their résumé or traveled to multiple business locations to complete job applications. Using the Internet, job seekers can locate and apply for open job positions on *job search lists* and *online job boards*. These websites allow multiple employers to post and update job openings. Job seekers can electronically upload and e-mail their résumé in response to a job posting. Some websites allow job seekers to fill out and submit their application online. Searching and applying for jobs electronically saves employers and job seekers time and money, in addition to conserving fuel and paper resources.

In This Unit

Chapter 19
Preparing for a Career

A job is the work a person does regularly in order to earn money. A career is a series of related jobs in the same profession. Most of us will start with a job and then pursue a career. Studying the career clusters will help you learn about the career opportunities that are available. Your career preparation will begin with a career plan that includes short- and long-term goals.

Many resources are available to help guide you in deciding a career pathway. Most careers require some type of formal education. Along with education, work experience is a great way to advance your knowledge about a profession. Career and technical student organizations are another source of potential learning opportunities. Professional organizations provide valuable industry and career information for those exploring a career in retail. Professional development is important for continued career success.

Case Study

Google

As you begin looking for a job to begin your career, it is important to understand what potential employers look for in candidates. The hiring process can be lengthy and intense. Each company has its own protocol, so make sure you understand what is expected when you apply.

Google offers extensive information on its website about how the company operates, the company culture, and its evaluation and hiring process. The website also offers candidates support from Google recruiters, as well as résumé and interview preparation tools. The company wants to ensure that candidates are "good for Google" in the long term. In addition to the traditional review of a candidate's education and experience, independent groups of Googlers meet with candidates to evaluate their leadership skills, role-related knowledge, how they think, and the intangible quality of Googleyness. The company believes that involving its great Google employees in the hiring process results in hiring more great people.

College and Career Readiness

Reading Prep

As you read this chapter, take notes on the important points you want to remember. Record the information in the form of an outline to help you understand the material covered.

Check Your Retail IQ

Before you begin the chapter, see what you already know about retail by taking the chapter pretest. If you do not have a smartphone, visit the G-W Learning companion website.

G-W Learning mobile site: www.m.g-wlearning.com
G-W Learning companion website: www.g-wlearning.com/marketing/

Sections

19.1   Creating a Career Plan
19.2   Retail Careers

Stephen Coburn/Shutterstock.com

Section 19.1 Creating a Career Plan

Objectives

After completing this section, you will be able to:
- **Differentiate** between a job and a career.
- **Identify** the five levels of careers on the career ladder.
- **Explain** the importance of career planning.

Key Terms

job
career
career clusters
career pathways
career plan

goal
short-term goal
long-term goal
goal setting
SMART goal

Web Connect

There are many interesting retail jobs that you may choose to pursue. Use the Internet to research a retail job that appeals to you. Note the educational requirements and specific job tasks for the position. After completing your research, determine if it would be a good future career for you. Why or why not?

Critical Thinking

Goal setting is an important activity for anything you do in life. Write three short-term goals and three long-term goals for yourself. These can be personal or professional. What did you learn from writing these goals on paper?

Job or Career?

A **job** is the work a person does regularly in order to earn money. A **career** is a series of related jobs in the same profession. A *job* may be a part-time position you work after school. A *career* is a position for which you prepare by attending school or completing specialized training. Over time, a job can turn into a career.

Planning a career in retail can be very exciting. There are many opportunities for those who are interested in the retail field. As brick-and-mortar stores evolve and e-tail continues to grow, there will soon be new careers and job titles that do not exist today.

Studying the career clusters is a good way to begin learning about careers. The **career clusters**, shown in Figure 19-1, are 16 groups of occupational and career specialties that share common knowledge and skills. Within each of the 16 career clusters are multiple career pathways. **Career pathways** are subgroups that reflect occupations requiring similar knowledge and skills. These pathways include careers ranging from entry-level to those that require advanced college degrees and many years of experience. All of the careers within any of the pathways share a foundation of common knowledge and skills.

The 16 Career Clusters

Careers involving the production, processing, marketing, distribution, financing, and development of agricultural commodities and resources.

Careers involving management, marketing, and operations of foodservice, lodging, and recreational businesses.

Careers involving the design, planning managing, building, and maintaining of buildings and structures.

Careers involving family and human needs.

Careers involving the design, production, exhibition, performance, writing, and publishing of visual and performing arts.

Careers involving the design, development, support, and management of software, hardware, and other technology-related materials.

Careers involving the planning, organizing, directing, and evaluation of functions essential to business operations.

Careers involving the planning, management, and providing of legal services, public safety, protective services, and homeland security.

Careers involving the planning, management, and providing of training services.

Careers involving the planning, management, and processing of materials to create completed products.

Careers involving the planning and providing of banking, insurance, and other financial-business services.

Careers involving the planning, management, and performance of marketing and sales activities.

Careers involving governance, national security, foreign service, revenue and taxation, regulation, and management and administration.

Careers involving the planning, management, and providing of scientific research and technical services.

Careers involving planning, managing, and providing health services, health information, and research and development.

Careers involving the planning, management, and movement of people, materials, and goods.

States' Career Clusters Initiative 2008

Figure 19-1   Each of the 16 career clusters contains several career pathways.

Retail is part of the marketing career cluster and is a component of each pathway. The pathways in the marketing cluster are:

- marketing management
- professional sales
- merchandising
- marketing communications
- marketing research

There are many foundation skills necessary for success in any career. The following are some of the skills needed for a retail career.

- Basic skills—reading, writing, listening, speaking, and math
- Thinking skills—decision making, creative thinking, problem solving, visualization, and reasoning
- Personal qualities—self-management, integrity, honesty, sociability, and responsibility
- Technology skills—social media knowledge, software skills, and systems skills
- Business skills—planning, organizing, negotiating, leadership, and communication

It is important to build and maintain these skills throughout your career. These foundational skills will help you get your first job, and will help you advance in your career.

Five Levels of Careers

Figure 19-2 Most careers have different position levels based on years of experience, education, and technical skills.

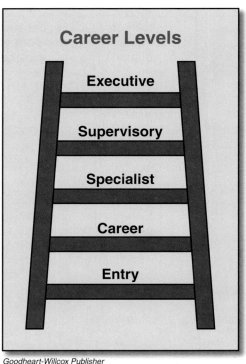

Goodheart-Willcox Publisher

In each career area, there are multiple opportunities for employment. The positions are generally grouped by skill level or education, as shown in the career ladder in Figure 19-2.

An *entry-level* position is usually a person's first or beginning job. It requires very little training. An example of an entry-level position in retailing is a sales associate.

A *career-level* position requires an employee to have the skills and knowledge for continued employment and advancement in the field. An example of a career-level position in retailing is a store manager.

A *specialist-level* position requires specialized knowledge and skills in a specific field of study. However, someone in this position usually does not supervise other employees. An example of a specialist-level position in retailing is a merchandise buyer.

A *supervisory-level* position requires specialized knowledge and skills and has management responsibility over other employees. An example of a supervisory-level position in retailing is a marketing manager.

An *executive-level* position is the highest level, and is responsible for the planning, organization, and management of a company. An example of an executive-level position in retailing is a vice president.

Career Planning

You may have already created a career plan as an activity in another class. A **career plan** is a list of steps to reach a career goal. A **goal** is something a person wants to achieve in a specified time period. A goal is also known as an *objective*. Figure 19-3 illustrates a career plan.

Career Plan: Retail Sales Manager		
Extracurricular and Volunteer Activities	**Work Experience**	**Education and Training**
During Junior High School • Help nonprofit groups and local youth groups with fund-raising efforts. • Choose behavioral and business themes for fairs and competitive events.	• Choose a part-time job or volunteer position that allows you to interact with a wide variety of people.	• Participate in business-related student organizations. • For optional or extra credit work, select topics and do projects pertaining to communication and sales techniques.
During High School • Participate in your school's business CTSO. • Attend informational sessions on effective public speaking.	• Work as a sales or customer service associate in a retail environment.	• Take classes in the business and marketing areas, as well as human behavior, accounting, and statistics.
During College • Help student, nonprofit, or local groups identify the best strategies to maximize their fund-raising efforts.	• Work on the management staff of a retail business.	• Follow the B.S. degree path for marketing and communication or business.
After College • Become a member of a sales professionals association. • Attend local business professionals and chamber of commerce events.	• Work as a sales manager in a retail environment.	• Participate in appropriate professional development opportunities. • Consider obtaining an advanced degree.

Figure 19-3 This table illustrates a potential career plan for a retail sales manager.

Part of career planning is to research the different steps necessary to reach your goal. Some career goals may require a college degree or industry certification. When creating your career plan, consider the qualifications, education, and years of experience that each step requires.

There are two types of goals: short-term and long-term. A short-term goal is one that can be achieved in less than one year. An example of short-term goal may be getting an after-school job for the fall semester. A long-term goal is one that will take a longer period of time to achieve—usually more than one year. An example of a long-term goal is to attend college to earn a four-year degree.

Goal setting is the process of deciding what a person wants to achieve. Your goals must be based on what you want for your life. Well-defined career goals follow the SMART goal model. SMART goals are specific, measurable, attainable, realistic, and timely, as illustrated in Figure 19-4.

Specific

A career goal should be specific and straightforward. For example, "I want to have a career" is not a very specific goal. Instead, you might say, "I want to have a career in retail." When the goal is specific, it is easier to track your progress.

Measurable

It is important to be able to measure progress so you know when you have reached your goal. For example, "I want to earn a bachelor

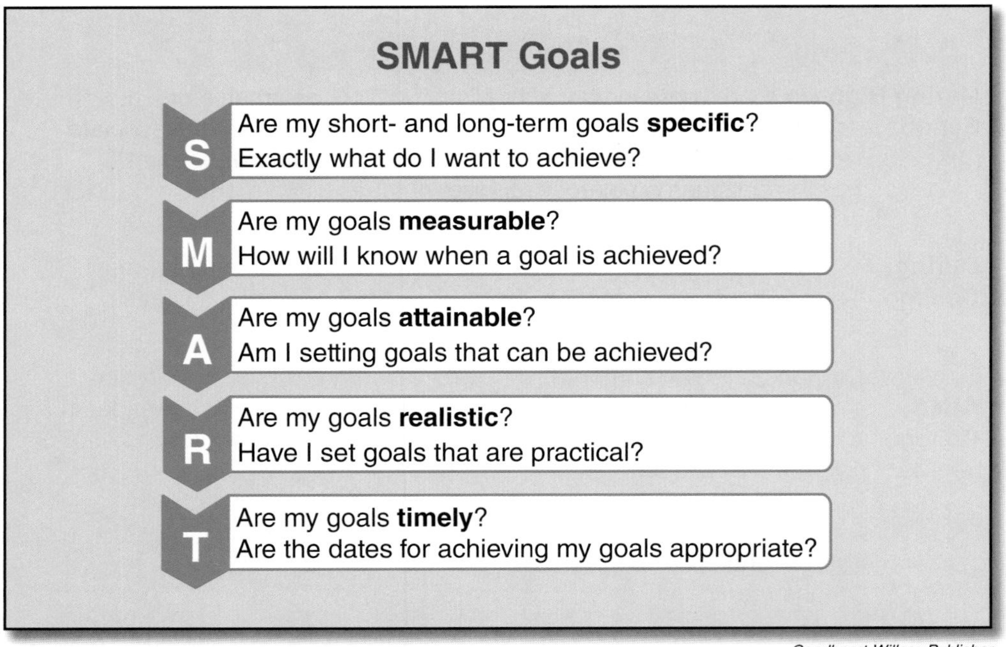

Figure 19-4 Well-defined career goals follow the SMART goal model.

SMART Goals

S Are my short- and long-term goals **specific**? Exactly what do I want to achieve?

M Are my goals **measurable**? How will I know when a goal is achieved?

A Are my goals **attainable**? Am I setting goals that can be achieved?

R Are my goals **realistic**? Have I set goals that are practical?

T Are my goals **timely**? Are the dates for achieving my goals appropriate?

degree in merchandising" is a goal that can be measured. When you earn the degree, you will know your goal has been reached.

Attainable

Goals need to be attainable. For example, "I want to be a vice president for a retail store when I graduate from college" is not reasonable for that point in a person's career. Gaining retail experience is necessary before obtaining a management position. This goal becomes more attainable when coupled with a plan to obtain the necessary aptitudes, skills, and experience.

Realistic

Goals must be realistic. Obtaining a position as vice president for a store may be practical with proper planning. Finding an entry-level position as a sales associate and working your way up to vice president over a period of years makes this a realistic goal.

Exploring Retail Careers

Telemarketer

Telemarketing, or soliciting orders for products or services, is a sales tool used by some companies as an alternative to more expensive marketing techniques. Charities also use telemarketing techniques to request donations. The two main types of telemarketers are those who place phone calls to potential customers, and those who answer phone calls from customers responding to advertisements. Other typical job titles for telemarketers include *telephone sales representative (TSR)*, *telesales specialist*, and *telemarketing sales representative*. The following are common tasks that telemarketers perform:

- research names and telephone numbers of potential customers from directories, magazine reply cards, and lists purchased from other organizations
- call businesses or individuals to solicit sales or to request donations for charitable causes
- read from prepared scripts to describe the products or services they are selling
- input customer information, including payment information, into computerized ordering systems
- answer telephone calls from potential customers who are responding to advertisements that state "call this number"

Telemarketers need a good understanding of sales and marketing methods and strategies. They should have good speaking skills, including proper diction and clear pronunciation, as well as a pleasant speaking voice. Because telemarketers sometimes encounter unpleasant responses, they should have an even temperament and be able to remain calm and pleasant at all times. Many telemarketing jobs require a high school diploma.

Timely

A goal should have a starting point and an ending point. Setting a timeframe to achieve a goal is the step most often overlooked. An end date can help you stay on track. For example, you may want to be a vice president by the time you are 35 years old. Aiming to get the experience and education to achieve this position by a specific age will help you remain motivated to reach your goal on time.

Checkpoint 19.1

1. Differentiate between a *job* and a *career*.
2. Under which career cluster is retail included?
3. List and describe the five levels of careers.
4. Explain the relationship between a career plan and a career goal.
5. What is the SMART goal model?

Build Your Vocabulary

As you progress through this course, develop a personal glossary of retailing terms and add it to your portfolio. This will help you build your vocabulary and prepare you for a career. Write a definition for each of the following terms, and add it to your personal retailing glossary.

job	goal
career	short-term goal
career clusters	long-term goal
career pathways	goal setting
career plan	SMART goal

Section 19.2 Retail Careers

Objectives

After completing this section, you will be able to:
- **Identify** available career research resources.
- **Summarize** how to prepare for a career.
- **Explain** how professional organizations can prepare you for a career.

Key Terms

career aptitude test
formal education
career and technical
   student organization
   (CTSO)

certification program

Web Connect

Before you begin your career exploration, consider completing a self-assessment. Use the Internet to search for *self-assessment tools for students*. Select one that appeals to you and complete it. What did you find out about yourself?

Critical Thinking

You are in the process of making plans for your career. What type of education or training are you planning to pursue? What factors influenced your decision?

Selecting a Career

As you begin your search for a career, evaluate your goals and objectives. What type of job is best suited for you? There are many career research resources to help you evaluate which careers would make the most of your talents, skills, and interests.

- *Career aptitude tests.* A **career aptitude test** is an exam that analyzes personal interests, strengths, and weaknesses. Career counselors often give career aptitude tests as the first step in choosing a career.

- *Internet research.* Researching various professions, employment trends, industries, and prospective employers provides insight to careers that may interest you.

- *Career handbooks.* The US Bureau of Labor Statistics publishes the *Occupational Outlook Handbook* and the *Career Guide to Industries*. These handbooks describe the training and education needed for various jobs, and can help you research careers.

Career aptitude tests are often the first step in choosing a career.

dboystudio/Shutterstock.com

- *Organizations.* Many professional and educational organizations provide career and employment resources. One example of an organization is the States' Career Clusters Initiative (SCCI). This organization offers information to prepare for any of the 16 career pathways. You can gain valuable information by reading requirements for these career pathways.
- *Networking.* Talking with people you know can help you evaluate career opportunities, and may lead to potential jobs.

Preparing for a Career

There are many steps you will take as you plan for future employment. Education, on-the-job work experience, career and technical student organizations, and professional organizations can help you prepare for and find the right job for you.

Education

Most retail careers require a college education. However, for an entry-level position, a high school diploma may get you in the door. Jobs higher on the career ladder often require additional formal education. **Formal education** is the education received in a school, college, or university. Some positions require an associate or two-year degree. Others require a bachelor or four-year degree.

Work Experience

One way to prepare for a retail career is to obtain a part-time job now and gain actual work experience. There are many sources available to help find job leads.

A good way to find a job is through networking. *Networking* means talking with people you know and making new contacts. Networking with family and friends can sometimes produce job opportunities.

Family and friends might have connections with retailers looking for employees. The more contacts you make, the greater your opportunities for finding a job lead. Be persistent until you find a position that works for you.

School counselors can be good networking connections. They may have contacts at local retail businesses with current job openings. Also, many employers contact local schools to recruit part-time workers.

Classified advertisements in the newspaper and job postings on the Internet are both good ways to find local openings. Both newspaper ads and Internet job postings are updated regularly. Take the time to look through the open positions often.

Career and Technical Student Organizations (CTSOs)

Career and technical student organizations (CTSOs) are national student organizations with local school chapters that are related to career and technical education (CTE) courses. CTSO programs are tied to different course areas. Depending on the course area, internships and other cooperative work experiences may be a part of the CTSO experience. Participation in CTSOs helps prepare high school graduates for the next step, whether that step is postsecondary education or entering a chosen field of work.

FYI

Seasonal employment opportunities are a great way to get your foot in the door of a retail business. Even though seasonal employment is short-term, retailers often ask successful seasonal employees to accept permanent positions.

mangostock/Shutterstock.com

Many local CTSO chapters support community service activities and offer volunteer opportunities to members.

Social Media

Sharing Images

With more than 100 million active users, photo sharing and messaging services, like Instagram and Snapchat, are important social media tools. Photo sharing and messaging services allow members to upload, edit, and share images, with other members. Businesses should consider these tools as another opportunity to connect with existing and potential customers. Sharing images of a new product could be part of a retailer's launch plan.

CTSO Goals

The goal of CTSOs is to help students acquire knowledge and skills in different career and technical areas, as well as related leadership skills and work experience. These organizations help student members become competent, successful members of the workforce. Instructor-advisors organize and lead the local CTSO chapters in their schools. The CTSO advisors help students run the organization and identify the best programs that meet the goals of the educational area.

Support for local CTSO chapters is often coordinated through each state's education department. Local chapters elect officers and establish a program of work. The program may include a variety of activities, including working in the industry, community service, school projects, and competitive events. Student achievement in certain areas, such as leadership or patriotism, is recognized with certificates or public acknowledgment through award ceremonies.

CTSO Opportunities

CTSOs offer a wide variety of activities that can be adapted for almost any school and classroom situation. Competitive events are a main feature of most CTSOs. Competing in various events enables students to show how well they have mastered learning specific content. Events also measure the use of decision-making, problem-solving, and leadership skills. Students may also receive recognition awards and, in some cases, scholarships, if they win at state- and national-level competitions. Members can develop career and leadership skills even if they do not participate in or win CTSO competitions. Simply preparing for the events develops the related skills.

Participating in the many CTSO programs and activities offered can promote a lifelong interest in community service and professional development. Each local chapter typically provides opportunities for members to learn valuable skills for the workplace. In addition to competitive events, other opportunities may include:

- completing a school or community project related to the field of study
- training in the field
- supporting a local or national philanthropic organization
- attending CTSO state meetings
- participating in leadership conferences

Your participation in a CTSO can help you learn more about a profession. These organizations offer training, mentoring, competitive events, and other activities that give students firsthand experience with the demands of a career.

One student organization that you are probably already familiar with is DECA. DECA is a CTSO for business and marketing students. DECA offers leadership activities to help prepare future business leaders. This organization also provides opportunities for marketing students to participate in multiple competitive events that focus on retail activities. These activities invite students to present real-world solutions for situations that happen every day in the workplace.

Professional Organizations

Some professional organizations provide resources for those interested in a retail career. Students can also find valuable industry information by visiting the websites of retail organizations. Professionals in the business can join these organizations to stay current with industry events. Some organizations also offer retail certifications. **Certification programs** are professional development programs. Successful completion of a retail certification program demonstrates that an individual has proven his or her skills, and is prepared for a retail position.

The National Retail Federation (NRF) offers professional certifications in customer service, retail management, and sales. Candidates pay a fee and complete exams electronically at a testing site. The exams cover knowledge and skills needed by retail employees to excel in the specific certification area. Candidates can prepare for the exam by viewing online demonstrations that offer sample questions and answer keys. The NRF certifications are valid for three years. Once obtained, certification can be renewed without having to retake the exam. More information about each certification offered can be found on the NRF website.

The National Occupational Competency Testing Institute (NOCTI) offers assessments that measure job readiness for a variety of career pathways, including retail. Those interested in retail merchandising or advertising and design careers can complete

Retail Ethics

Confidential Information

It is unethical to share personal information about an employee or job applicant. Information that is on a résumé or discussed during an interview is confidential. Employers may learn sensitive information about those who work for them or applicants seeking employment. It is unethical to share confidential information about employees, and doing so may result in a lawsuit. Depending on the confidentiality of the topic, sharing the information may be considered slanderous.

the Job Ready Assessment either online or on paper. During the assessment, candidates complete a written test on the basic knowledge needed for the specific career. The tests are roughly 200 questions. Candidates also perform tasks that cover important functions of the job as part of the assessment. For example, candidates may have to design an advertisement for the advertising and design assessment. The performance assessment can vary in length, based on the tasks given. More information and sample questions can be found in the Job Ready Assessment Blueprint for these career pathways on the NOCTI website.

Professional Development

Once you begin your career, it is important to continue learning and stay up to date on what is happening in your profession. *Professional development* is training that builds on existing skills and knowledge, and contributes to personal growth and career development. *Professional development classes* are for people who have completed formal education and training.

Some professional development opportunities include seeking industry certification, joining trade associations, attending conferences, and taking classes. Employers often sponsor professional development events for their employees. Some may offer on-site training or reimburse tuition costs.

Conferences and seminars may be available as professional development opportunities.

Monkey Business/Shutterstock.com

Checkpoint 19.2

1. Identify examples of resources you can use to help research careers in retail.
2. Describe the role formal education can play in career preparation.
3. Explain how networking can produce job leads.
4. What is the goal of career and technical student organizations (CTSOs)?
5. How do professional organizations keep students and retail industry professionals informed?

Build Your Vocabulary

As you progress through this course, develop a personal glossary of retailing terms and add it to your portfolio. This will help you build your vocabulary and prepare you for a career. Write a definition for each of the following terms, and add it to your personal retailing glossary.

career aptitude test
formal education
career and technical student organization (CTSO)
certification program

Chapter Summary

Section 19.1 Creating a Career Plan

- A job is the work a person does regularly to earn money. A career is a series of related jobs in the same profession. Studying career clusters can help students learn about careers.
- There are many levels of positions within a given career. The positions are grouped by skill level or education and include entry, career, specialist, supervisory, and executive level positions.
- Creating a career plan includes developing short-term and long-term goals. Well-defined goals follow the SMART goal model.

Section 19.2 Retail Careers

- There are many career research resources to help you evaluate which careers would make the most of your talents, skills, and interests. Career aptitude tests, Internet research, career handbooks, organizations, and networking are good resources.
- Most retail careers require formal education. Obtaining work experience now can help you reach your career goal. Career and technical student organizations will help you learn professional skills. Professional organizations are a good source of industry and career information.
- Once you start your career, continue learning to stay up to date in your profession. Professional development will help contribute to your personal growth and career development.

Review Your Knowledge

1. What are career clusters?
2. Name the career pathways in the marketing career cluster.
3. What are the foundation skills that are necessary for career success?
4. Give an example of a *career-level* position.
5. Identify the five characteristics of SMART goals.
6. How can career handbooks help you evaluate which retail career is right for you?
7. What is formal education?
8. What opportunities do CTSOs offer, in addition to competitive events?
9. Name two professional organizations that offer certification or assessment in retail. What do they offer?
10. Describe why professional development is important.

Apply Your Knowledge

1. Conduct an Internet search for jobs related to a career that you might be interested in pursuing. Note the education and work experience requirements of the position. Evaluate and compare the employment opportunities that match your career goals.

2. A career plan is a list of steps to reach a career goal. Write a draft of a career plan for the next five years that you might consider following. Include your career objectives and the strategies you will use to accomplish your goals. Use SMART goals and be as specific as possible in planning how you will accomplish your goals.

3. It is important to possess certain foundation skills to be employable. Identify which foundation skills listed in this chapter you already possess and which you need to develop. How do you demonstrate those you already have? How can you build the foundation skills you still need?

4. Being hired for a job is just the first step in a successful career. It is important to keep your skills sharp to remain employed and advance in your career. Which of the foundation skills listed in this chapter do you think are most helpful in retaining employment? Explain your answer.

5. SMART goals are specific, measurable, attainable, realistic, and timely. Write down three short-term and three long-term SMART goals. They can be educational or professional goals, but should be related to a career that interests you. Research the requirements for meeting these goals, such as level or area of education or years of experience.

6. Interview someone who works in a retail career. Ask questions to learn about how he or she started in the retail field. What retail positions has this person held throughout his or her career? Has this person participated in professional development opportunities to advance in his or her career?

7. CTSOs build on classroom learning through activities and events. Create a list of the CTSOs that are active in your school. Write several paragraphs explaining how participation in these organizations integrates with career and technical subjects.

8. Interview the advisor of a CTSO chapter in your school. Ask the advisor questions about the community service activities and events of the CTSO. How does participation in a CTSO promote lifelong responsibility for community service and professional development?

9. Conduct an Internet search for *retail certificate programs*. Select one that most closely relates to your retail career choice. Make a list of the requirements and actions needed to pursue the certificate. What did you learn from this exercise?

10. Ask someone you know about a professional organization to which that person belongs. How has involvement in this organization aided in his or her professional development? After your conversation, research the organization and the opportunities it offers.

Check Your Retail IQ

Now that you have finished the chapter, see what you learned about retail by taking the chapter posttest. If you do not have a smartphone, visit the G-W Learning companion website.

G-W Learning mobile site: www.m.g-wlearning.com

G-W Learning companion website: www.g-wlearning.com/marketing/

College and Career Readiness

Career Ready Practices To become career ready, it is necessary to utilize critical-thinking skills in order to solve problems. Describe a problem you needed to solve that was important to your success at work or school. How did you apply critical-thinking skills to arrive at a solution?

Reading Read a magazine, newspaper, or online article about how to fund a college education. Analyze the presentation of the information. Determine the strength and quality of the information used to support the central ideas of the article. Review the conclusions made by the author. Evaluate the logic and balance of the information presented.

Speaking Participate in a collaborative classroom discussion about college and career readiness. Pose questions to participants that connect your ideas to the relevant evidence that has been presented. Use inductive reasoning to formulate an argument regarding college and career readiness. Use deductive reasoning to draw conclusions about your classmates' arguments.

Teamwork

Working with a team, make a list of retail careers that are popular with your age group. Research the average salary for each. Record your information in a table and distribute it to your classmates. Discuss your findings.

College and Career Portfolio

Presenting Your E-Portfolio

You created items for your e-portfolio in earlier activities. Now, you will decide how to present your e-portfolio. The items should already be organized in folders. Review the files you have collected. Select the ones you want to include and remove others. Keep files that contain information for your use only separate from the other documents. Decide how you want to present your portfolio materials. For example, you could create an electronic presentation with slides for each section. The slides could have links to documents, videos, graphics, or sound files. Websites are another option for presenting the material. You could have a main page with links to various sections. Each section page could have links to pages with your documents, videos, graphics, or sound files. Another option is to place the files on a CD. The method you choose should allow the viewer to easily navigate and find items.

1. Create the slide show, web pages, or other medium for presenting your e-portfolio.
2. View the completed e-portfolio to check the appearance.

◇DECA Coach

Assigning Responsibilities

Many of DECA's competitive events require teamwork. Teambuilding is a necessary element of teamwork, but another element is *organization*. Each member of the team needs to clearly understand his or her responsibilities early in the process.

Different types of teams require different organizational strategies. When working in a team of two or three, each person on the team should have a well-defined role. For example, it may be decided that one member will be responsible for keying a paper, another is responsible for enforcing due dates, and the third may be responsible for drafting the presentation. There are many things to do, and each team member needs to be assigned responsibilities.

However, several of DECA's competitive events extend well beyond teams of two or three. While only one to three members write and present the project, DECA's Chapter Team Events are projects designed for the entire chapter. Each project needs a project manager or leader. While the project manager may not be able to do it all, he or she needs to have good organizational skills, the ability to lead fellow members, and be able to delegate responsibilities to others in the chapter. Some large chapters have 100 members or more. Understanding what needs to be completed early in the process is critical to success.

Instead of assigning each individual specific tasks, try creating committees and assigning broad responsibilities to each committee. Each committee may designate a leader who reports directly to the project manager. Making sure that everyone in the chapter is active is a key to Chapter Team Event success.

Visit www.deca.org to learn more information about DECA.

G-W Learning Mobile Site

Visit the G-W Learning mobile site to complete the chapter pretest and posttest, and to practice vocabulary using e-flash cards. If you do not have a smartphone, visit the G-W Learning companion website to access these features.

G-W Learning mobile site: www.m.g-wlearning.com

G-W Learning companion website: www.g-wlearning.com/marketing/

Chapter 20
Job Applications and Interviews

There are many exciting career opportunities in retail. To obtain a position, you must convince a potential employer that you are the best person for the job. The first step is to create a résumé. The cover letter submitted with your résumé introduces your qualifications. If the employer thinks you are a good match for the job, you will be invited for an interview.

The employment process typically includes completing a job application. The employer then verifies the information you provided and checks your background. The process can take a long time, but may end with a job offer.

Case Study

Amazon

Amazon is a diverse company that employs more than 88,000 people around the world. There are career opportunities in many different departments, including North America and International Retail, Seller Services, E-Commerce Platform, Worldwide Operations and Customer Service, Finance and Administration, and Human Resources.

Like many large companies, Amazon has an online application process. Applicants create a Careers account with Amazon, which is separate from an Amazon customer account. Users upload and store their résumé, cover letter, and contact information to their Careers account. This allows users to apply for Amazon jobs without reentering their application data each time. Also, personalized job notifications are e-mailed to Careers account users when new positions become available.

The online application system allows Amazon to manage the hundreds, sometimes thousands, of applications they receive for open positions.

College and Career Readiness

Reading Prep

Before reading this chapter, preview the section heads and key terms lists. Make a list of questions that you have before reading the chapter. Search for answers to your questions as you continue reading the chapter.

Check Your Retail IQ

Before you begin the chapter, see what you already know about retail by taking the chapter pretest. If you do not have a smartphone, visit the G-W Learning companion website.

G-W Learning mobile site: www.m.g-wlearning.com

G-W Learning companion website: www.g-wlearning.com/marketing/

Sections

Andrey_Popov/Shutterstock.com

Section 20.1 Professional Résumés

Objectives

After completing this section, you will be able to:
- **Create** an effective résumé.
- **Write** a persuasive cover message.
- **Describe** ways a résumé may be submitted to a potential employer.

Key Terms

résumé	reference
career objective	cover message
chronological résumé	

Web Connect

Conduct an Internet search for the phrase *sample résumés for retail jobs*. Review two or three of the samples you find. Which résumé do you think made the better impression?

Critical Thinking

The retail industry is constantly changing and new jobs are created every day. What types of new retail careers do you think may be available in ten years that do not exist today?

Writing a Résumé

When you begin looking for your first retail job, you must sell your talents and skills to a potential employer. You must persuade the retailer that your skills and experience match the qualifications of the job you are seeking. A **résumé** is a document that profiles a person's career goals, education, and work history. Think of a résumé as a snapshot that shows who you are and why you would be an asset as an employee.

A résumé is the first impression that potential employers will have of you. It must be well written and error free. Keep in mind that the goal of a professional résumé is not to get a job, but to get an interview.

A general rule of thumb is that a résumé should be one page. Résumés have standard parts that employers expect to see. A résumé is illustrated in Figure 20-1.

Name and Personal Information

The top of the résumé page should present your name, address, telephone number, and e-mail address. Use an e-mail address that is your real name, or at least a portion of it. E-mails with nicknames or screen names do not make a professional impression. Before you begin applying for jobs through e-mail, set up an e-mail address that you will use only for professional communication.

Career Objective

A **career objective** is a summary of the type of retail job for which you are looking. An example of an objective is, "To gain retail industry experience as a sales associate while earning my business degree."

FYI

Résumé is pronounced "rez-uh-may."

Robert Jefferies

123 Eastwood Terrace

Saratoga Springs, NY 60123

123-555-9715

rjefferies@e-mail.edu

OBJECTIVE

To obtain a customer service representative position to apply my strong people skills, organizational skills, and educational background and help customers find the information and products they seek.

EXPERIENCE

September 2013 to Present: Customer Service Assistant

Saratoga Springs City Hall, Saratoga Springs, NY

- Assist clients as they enter the office and over the phone.
- Perform filing, data management, and drafting and editing short office communications.
- Assist with all other office administrative duties.

September 2012 to September 2013: Office Assistant

Hunter High School, Saratoga Springs, NY

- Inputting data, running office errands, providing internship and alumni updates.
- Scheduling appointments and assisting students register and find information.

EDUCATION

Hunter High School, Saratoga Springs, NY

Expected graduation date: May 2015

Relevant coursework: Bookkeeping, Public Speaking, Psychology, Job Skills, and Practical Math

HONORS

- Hunter High School Honor Roll, 8 quarters
- Outstanding French Student, 2012
- Volunteer of the Year, 2011

ACTIVITIES

- National Honor Society (2012 to present)
- French Club (2011 to present)
- Cross Country (2011 to present)

Figure 20-1 A résumé provides a potential employer with a snapshot of your educational background and work experience. This is an example of a chronological résumé.

Retail Ethics

Applications and Résumés

When applying for a job, to a college, or for a volunteer position, it is important to be truthful in your application and on your résumé. Fabricating experience or education is unethical and could cost you the opportunity to be a part of that organization. Always tell the truth about your skills, experience, and education. Do not embellish. Play up your strengths without creating the illusion of being someone you are not. Present your information in a positive light, but be honest.

Work Experience

The work experience section of a résumé includes details about your work history. The information in this section is typically the main focus of the employer's attention.

As you begin composing this section, list your current or most recent employer first. List previous employers in reverse chronological order to the earliest job you held. This format is known as a chronological résumé. A **chronological résumé** lists information in reverse chronological order, with the most recent employer listed first.

For each work experience entry, include the company name, your job title, and the duration of time you worked there. List the responsibilities and details about the position you held. Do not list the addresses or telephone numbers of previous employers. You will provide this contact information on a job application form.

Volunteer work may also be listed as work experience. Employers are especially interested in community-oriented applicants who do volunteer work. Be certain to list any volunteer activities and the length of time you have participated in the activities.

Education

List the name of your high school and where it is located. Indicate the year in which you will graduate. Briefly describe any courses you have taken that are relevant to the job for which you are applying. List any certifications you have earned, special courses or training programs completed, and any other educational achievements related to the job you are seeking.

Honors and Activities

Employers look for well-rounded individuals. Include information on your résumé that shows your involvement in activities outside of work or school. List applicable honors, awards, or publications with the corresponding year in which each occurred. If you have been a leader in an organization, note that experience. If you are a member of career and technical student organization (CTSO), include the name of the organization and number of years you have been a member.

References

A **reference** is a person who knows you well and can comment on your qualifications, work ethic, personal qualities, and other work-related aspects of your character. Your references should be three or four people for whom you have worked and one person who knows you socially. Do not list relatives. Get permission from the people you intend to use as references. Your *list of references* should present each person's name, title, and contact information.

It is customary for references to be provided only on request. So, your list of references should be separate from your résumé. To be prepared, bring copies of your list of references to the job interview. Employers who require references in advance usually indicate this in the job advertisement. Otherwise, you will be told during the interview process when references are needed.

Cover Message

A **cover message** is a letter or e-mail sent with a résumé to introduce yourself and summarize the reason you are applying for the job. This is a sales message written to persuade the retailer to offer you an interview. The cover message should focus the potential employer's attention on the aspects of your background, skills, and work experience that match the job you are seeking. An example of a cover message is shown in Figure 20-2.

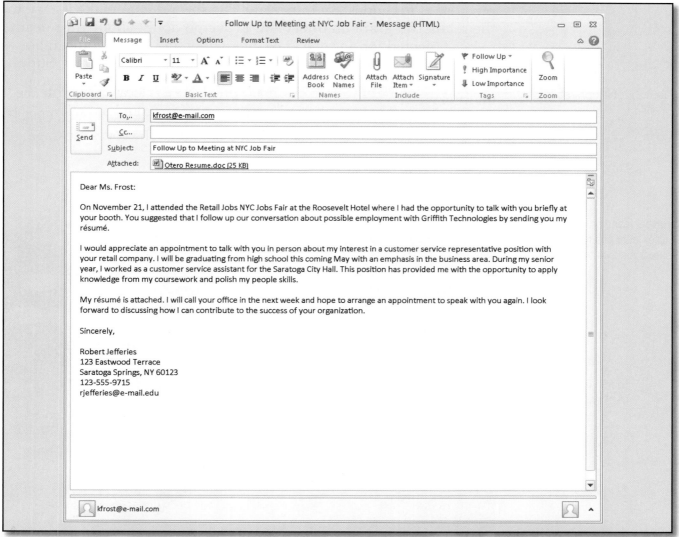

Goodheart-Willcox Publisher

Figure 20-2 A cover message should focus attention on the most relevant points of your résumé.

The cover message should provide a summary that highlights your particular qualifications for the job. The message should also explain how you became aware of the position or why you have sent your résumé. If you are responding to an advertisement, mention the position title and where you found the ad. If you are sending a general letter of application, be specific in explaining how you identified the company and why you are interested in working there.

In the body of the cover message, address the traits and skills that the employer seeks, as explained in the job description. Explain why you are qualified and how your skills and experience make you the best candidate for the job.

Writing a cover message is an important part of the résumé writing process. It sets the tone for the résumé that follows. Use a positive tone, but do not be boastful. Express confidence in your ability to adapt your training and skills to meet the employer's needs. You should also show genuine interest in the business.

The conclusion of the cover message has two purposes. One purpose is to request an interview. The second is to make it easy for the retailer to grant an interview. Leave no doubt about your desire to be contacted for an interview. State how and when you can be reached, or how and when you will make follow-up contact. Supply the potential employer with the information necessary to arrange an interview.

Make sure the presentation of the cover message is perfect. Check for correct grammar, punctuation, and spelling. The cover message must be completely error free.

Have a friend proofread your cover letter and résumé to be sure it is accurate and error free.

ARENA Creative/Shutterstock.com

Submitting a Résumé

You may also choose to post your résumé on social networking sites, such as LinkedIn and Facebook. Be sure to view anything you post through the eyes of a potential employer.

The traditional way to submit a résumé is by mail or in person. However, most people submit résumés online. To do this, you may need to send your résumé as an e-mail attachment or upload it to a website. In some cases, you will need to copy and paste your résumé into an online application form. Be aware that this process usually strips out formatting, such as tabs, indentations, and bold type. You may need to make adjustments to the layout of your résumé after pasting it into an online application form.

Employers may use management software to screen the résumés submitted electronically. These software programs look for keywords in résumé and cover letter files that are related to the open position. These keywords are often used in the job posting. For example, keywords for a retail salesperson position may include *customer service, training, stock, displays, sales goals,* and *team.* Be sure to include the appropriate keywords in your résumé and cover letter to increase your chance of being offered an interview.

Always take a hard copy of your résumé with you to an interview. It should be printed on good-quality white or off-white paper. Colored and patterned paper should not be used for résumés.

Checkpoint 20.1

1. What are the standard parts included on a résumé?
2. How is a list of references prepared?
3. What is the purpose of a cover message?
4. There are two purposes to the conclusion of a cover message. What are they?
5. How are résumés typically submitted to potential employers?

Build Your Vocabulary

As you progress through this course, develop a personal glossary of retailing terms and add it to your portfolio. This will help you build your vocabulary and prepare you for a career. Write a definition for each of the following terms, and add it to your personal retailing glossary.

résumé

career objective

chronological résumé

reference

cover message

Section 20.2 Interviewing

Objectives

After completing this section, you will be able to:
- **Discuss** how to prepare for a job interview.
- **Describe** the employment process.

Key Terms

job interview
hypothetical question
behavioral question
job application

employment
verification
background check

Web Connect

You have learned about selling in a retail environment. Now it is time to sell yourself as a potential employee. Conduct an Internet search for the phrase *selling yourself in a job interview*. Select and read several articles. What did you learn from your research? How could this information help you sell your talents and skills to a potential employer?

Critical Thinking

When applying for a position, it is important to learn information about the company with which you may be interviewing. Make a list of the various ways you could find facts about a company and its background.

Job Interview

A **job interview** is the employer's opportunity to review your résumé and ask questions to see if you are qualified for the position. This is your opportunity to sell yourself in person. Your answers to interview questions are important in the employer's decision-making process.

The first step in preparing for a job interview is to learn as much as you can about the job and the company. There are several ways to do this. If the company has a website, thoroughly browse the site. Pay special attention to the *About Us* section for an overview of the company. Look for press releases, annual reports, and information on products or services offered by the company.

While a company website can be a valuable source of information, do not limit your research to just the company site. Use your network of friends and relatives to find people who are familiar with the retailer. Get as much information as you can from them.

Call the company's human resources department. Indicate that you are interested in employment opportunities at the company and would like to know more about working for the company. The human resources department often has materials designed specifically for potential employees.

Interview Questions

Interview questions are intended to assess your skills and abilities, and explore your personality. Your answers to interview questions help determine whether you will fit in with the company team and the manager's leadership style. Interviewers also want to assess your critical thinking skills. They may ask you to cite specific examples of projects you have completed or problems you have solved.

Questions Likely to Be Asked

Spend some time trying to anticipate questions the interviewer is likely to ask you. The following are ten common interview questions.

- What makes you a good employee?
- What are your strengths?
- What are your weaknesses?
- Tell me something about yourself.
- Describe the experience you have that relates to this position.
- What type of position interests you?
- What do you plan to be doing five years from now?
- In what type of work environment do you function well?
- Why do you want to work for this organization?
- Are you willing to work overtime?

Write down your answers to these questions and practice them in front of a mirror or with a friend or relative. Practice until you can give your planned responses naturally and without reading them off the page. The more prepared you are, the more relaxed, organized, competent, and professional you will appear to the interviewer.

Practicing answers to potential interview questions can increase your confidence for the interview.

Hypothetical Questions

Interviewers may also ask hypothetical questions. **Hypothetical questions** are questions that require you to imagine a situation and describe how you would act. Frequent topics of hypothetical questions relate to working with and getting along with coworkers. For example, "What would you

Bronwyn Photo/Shutterstock.com

Interviewers consider your body language and composure, as well as what you say.

william casey/Shutterstock.com

do if you were waiting on a customer and a coworker was constantly interrupting you?" You cannot prepare specific answers to these questions, so you need to rely on your ability to think on your feet.

For these types of questions, the interviewer is aware that you are being put on the spot. In addition to what you say, he or she considers other aspects of your answer as well. Body language is first and foremost. Work with a friend or relative to practice making eye contact and speaking with confidence. Avoid fidgeting and looking at the ceiling while thinking of your answer. Instead, look at the interviewer and calmly take a moment to compose your thoughts. Keep your answer brief. If your answer runs on too long, you risk losing your train of thought. Try to relate the question to something that is familiar to you and answer honestly. Do not try to figure out what the interviewer wants you to say. Showing that you can remain poised and project confidence carries a lot of weight, even if your answer is not ideal.

Behavioral Questions

Interviewers may ask behavioral questions. **Behavioral questions** are questions that draw on your previous experiences and decisions. Your answer to these types of questions indicate past behavior, which may be used to predict future behavior and success in a position. The following are some examples of behavioral questions.

- Tell me about a situation where you needed to persuade your supervisor to make a change in a process or procedure.

- Tell me about a time when you needed to assume a position of the leader of a group. What were the challenges and how did you help the group meet its goals?

- Describe a time when you missed the opportunity to provide the best service possible. How would you have changed your approach for a more successful outcome?

- Describe a situation where you needed to be creative in order to help a customer with a problem.

- Describe a situation when you made a mistake. Tell me how you corrected the mistake and what measures you put in place to ensure it did not happen again.

Exploring Retail Careers

Regional Sales Manager

For companies that do business nationally or internationally, coordination of sales efforts is important to keep sales running smoothly and efficiently. These companies often divide their sales territories into regions and employ regional sales managers to direct the sales activities in each region. The regional managers then work together under a national or international sales manager to coordinate the company's sales activities. Other typical job titles for a regional sales manager include *sales supervisor*, *general manager*, and *district sales manager*. The following are some examples of tasks that regional sales managers perform.

- Oversee the activities of local sales managers in their region
- Direct the hiring and training of staff, including local sales managers in their region
- Control sales and service programs in their region
- Project sales and monitor profitability
- Resolve customer complaints, as needed

Regional sales managers may need to travel frequently, depending on the size of their region. They must be able to manage employees and offer them advice on both selling techniques and product demonstration. This requires knowledge of sales principles, as well as excellent knowledge of the products being sold. The ability to think critically to solve problems is also helpful. In addition, regional sales managers should have a background in economics and understand accounting principles. Most jobs in this field require a bachelor degree, as well as considerable experience or on-the-job training.

Again, you cannot prepare specific answers to these questions. Remain poised, answer honestly, and keep your answers focused on the question.

Questions to Ask

Write down any questions you have about the job, salary, benefits, and company policies. Keep in mind that the questions you ask reveal details about your personality. Asking questions can make a good impression. Questions show that you are interested and aware. Good questions cover the duties and responsibilities of the position, to whom you will report, what a typical day is like, and how many people are in the department.

Be aware of how you word questions. Some questions are not appropriate until after you have been offered the job. In the early stages of the interview process, your questions should demonstrate that you would be a valuable employee and are interested in learning about the company.

The following are some questions you may want to ask.

- What are the specific duties of this position?
- To whom will I report?

- What is company policy or criteria for employee promotions?
- Do you have a policy for providing on-the-job training?
- What are the working hours?
- When do you expect to make your hiring decision?
- What is the anticipated start date?

Usually, the interviewer will tell you what the company expects to pay for the position. Sometimes, however, an interviewer asks what salary you want or expect. Prepare for questions about salary by researching the industry. If you are unsure, you can simply tell the interviewer that the salary is negotiable.

Dressing for an Interview

An interview is a meeting in which you and the employer discuss the job and your skills. Interviews are usually in person, but initial interviews are sometimes conducted by phone. A face-to-face interview is typically the first time you are seen by a company representative. First impressions are important, so dress appropriately, be well groomed, and be on time. Your appearance communicates certain qualities about you to the interviewer. When dressing for an interview, consider what you wish to communicate about yourself.

The easiest rule to follow is to dress in a way that shows you understand the work environment and know the appropriate attire. It is better to dress more conservatively than to dress in more trendy clothing. Employers understand that interviewees want to put their best foot forward. Dressing more conservatively than needed is not likely to be viewed as a disadvantage. However, dressing too casual, too trendy, or wearing inappropriate clothing is likely to cost you the job.

Many companies conduct phone interviews before inviting a job candidate for a face-to-face interview.

Dress appropriately to make the best first impression during a face-to-face interview.

michaeljung/Shutterstock.com

After the Interview

Evaluate your performance as soon as you can after the interview. Every job interview is an opportunity to practice. If you discover that you are not interested in the job, do not feel your time was wasted. Make a list of the things you feel you did right and things you would do differently next time. Asking yourself the following questions can help in evaluating your performance.

- Was I adequately prepared with knowledge about the company and the position?
- Did I remember to bring copies of my résumé, a list of references, work samples, and any other requested documents to the interview?
- Was I on time for the interview?
- Did I talk too much or too little?
- Did I honestly and completely answer the interviewer's questions?
- Did I dress appropriately?
- Did I display nervous behavior, such as fidgeting, giggling, or forgetting things I wanted to say?
- Did I come across as composed and confident?
- Which questions could I have handled better?

After a job interview, follow up is important to keep your name in front of the employer. Immediately after the interview, write a short *thank-you message* to the person who interviewed you. See Figure 20-3 for an example. The purpose of this message is to thank the interviewer and indicate your interest in the job. Either a hand-written letter or an e-mail to the interviewer is appropriate. When you send a thank-you message, you will stand out as someone with good manners and genuine interest in the position. A thank-you message is an easy way to keep your name active during the selection process. Keep the message brief and to the point. You want to remind the interviewer of your enthusiasm for the position.

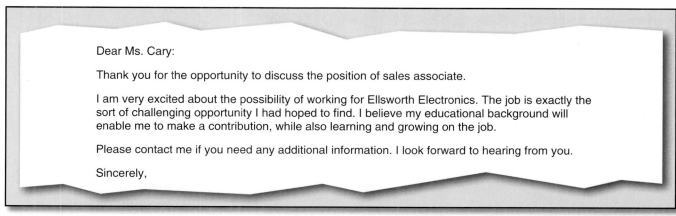

Dear Ms. Cary:

Thank you for the opportunity to discuss the position of sales associate.

I am very excited about the possibility of working for Ellsworth Electronics. The job is exactly the sort of challenging opportunity I had hoped to find. I believe my educational background will enable me to make a contribution, while also learning and growing on the job.

Please contact me if you need any additional information. I look forward to hearing from you.

Sincerely,

Goodheart-Willcox Publisher

Figure 20-3 Sending a short thank-you message can help you stand out among all the applicants being considered for the job.

Social Media

Follow the Competition

Perhaps one of the most important things to consider when using social media is that the competition is using it, too. A business should know how its competitors are using social media, just like print and broadcast advertising efforts. The first step is to *like* your competitors on Facebook, monitor their LinkedIn postings, follow them on Twitter and Pinterest, and subscribe to their blogs. With this information, a retailer can tailor its social media efforts to meet or beat the competition.

Employment decisions can take a long time. Some companies notify all applicants when a decision has been made, but some do not. If you have not heard anything after a week or two, it is appropriate to send an e-mail to follow up and ask for an update on the position.

Employment Process

The employment process can take a substantial amount of time. In addition to the interview, there are other tasks that candidates must complete. There are also tasks that the employer completes to make sure a candidate is fit for the position.

At some point in the employment process, you will complete a job application. A **job application** is a form with spaces for your contact information, education, and work experience. Some companies require this in advance of an interview. In other cases, the job application is completed after the interview process.

Some employers use printed forms and others accept applications online. A typical scenario is for an applicant to go online to a company's employment page, select the job description, review it, and proceed to apply online. The applicant is often asked to upload a résumé at the end of the online form.

A job application should be completed neatly with all of the requested information included.

chanpipat/Shutterstock.com

When you complete an application form, you will need all of your personal data, including information about your citizenship status and the names and locations of past employers. If you are going to complete an application in an employer's office, be sure to bring all of this information with you. Like your résumé, an employment application needs to be free of spelling, grammar, and word-usage errors. Carefully check the form before submitting it. Also, use your best handwriting.

The employer will complete an employment verification using the information on your application or résumé. **Employment verification** is a process through which the information you provided about your employment history is checked to verify that it is correct. Employers typically verify only the dates of employment, position title, and other objective data. Most employers will not provide subjective information about their employees, such as whether or not the employer considered you a good worker.

Another important part of the employment process is a background check. A **background check** is a look into personal data about you. This information is available from government records and other sources, including public information on the Internet. The employer should disclose to you that a background check will be conducted and may ask for your permission. Sometimes employers also run a check of your credit. You must give permission for them to conduct a credit check on you.

Many employers use Internet search engines, such as Google, to search for your name. Employers may also check social networking websites, such as Facebook and LinkedIn. Be aware of this before posting any personal information or photos. These checks might work to your advantage or against you, depending on what the employer finds. It is up to you to ensure that the image you project on social networking sites is not embarrassing or, worse, preventing you from achieving your career goals.

If you are hired for a position, the employer will require that you complete a *Form I-9* to verify your US citizenship status. You will also complete a *W-4 Employee's Withholding Allowance Certificate*. This form is used by the employer to withhold the appropriate amount of taxes from your paycheck.

NRF Tip

NRF provides its members with e-newsletters and other publications, such as its monthly *STORES* magazine. These publications reflect the latest news and information trending in retail.

Checkpoint 20.2

1. Explain the purpose of a job interview for both the employer and the applicant.
2. What are three ways to gain information about a job and a company before the interview?
3. What is the purpose of hypothetical interview questions?
4. Why is it important for an applicant to ask questions during an interview?
5. Describe some of the forms applicants will complete during the employment process.

Build Your Vocabulary

As you progress through this course, develop a personal glossary of retailing terms and add it to your portfolio. This will help you build your vocabulary and prepare you for a career. Write a definition for each of the following terms, and add it to your personal retailing glossary.

job interview	job application
hypothetical question	employment verification
behavioral question	background check

Chapter Summary

Section 20.1 Résumé

- A résumé presents a profile of your career goals, education, and work history. The purpose of a résumé is to persuade the employer that your skills and experience match the qualifications of the job you are seeking.
- A cover message is a letter or e-mail sent with a résumé to introduce yourself and summarize the reason you are applying for the job. This is a sales message written about your background, skills, and work experience that match the job you are seeking.
- The traditional way to submit a résumé is by mail or hand delivery. Most people submit their résumé online by uploading it to an online application form or attaching it to an e-mail message.

Section 20.2 Interviewing

- A job interview is an employer's opportunity to ask questions to see if you are qualified for the position for which you applied. Properly preparing for an interview will increase your chance of success.
- The employment process includes tasks for both the applicant and the employer. The applicant may need to fill out forms, such as a job application and a citizenship verification form. Employers may verify employment history and conduct a background check on potential employees.

Review Your Knowledge

1. What is the purpose of a résumé?
2. What personal information should be included on a résumé?
3. What is a chronological résumé?
4. What should be included in a cover message?
5. Describe how to prepare a hard copy of your résumé to bring to an interview.
6. How can you prepare for the questions a potential employer is likely to ask during an interview?
7. Why is it important to dress appropriately for an interview?
8. Describe the process of evaluating your performance after an interview.
9. What is the purpose of a thank-you message?
10. What information will you need on-hand to complete a job application form?

Apply Your Knowledge

1. Using the Internet, find a retail job for which you would be interested in applying. Prepare a résumé to apply for this position. Use examples in this chapter as a guide.

2. Using the résumé you completed in the last activity, create a cover letter that will accompany your résumé. Your cover letter should explain how you became aware of the position and detail why you are qualified and how your skills and experience make you the best candidate for the job.

3. For the position you selected in the first activity, create a list of five questions you might ask during the interview. Be aware of how you word questions to make the best impression.

4. Assume you have been offered an interview. Come to class dressed as if you were going to the interview. Explain to your class why your appearance is appropriate for the interview and the position. What impression might your attire have on the interviewer?

5. Completing job applications takes practice. Search the Internet for *retail job applications*. Print an application that accompanies a retail job posting. Use a pen to practice completing the application as neatly as possible, without making mistakes.

6. Assume you are preparing for an interview. Write an answer for each of the following potential interview questions.
   • What makes you a good employee?
   • What are your strengths?
   • What are your weaknesses?

7. Select an area of the United States in which you would like to live, other than your hometown. Research employers in that area and identify one for which you would like to work. Write a two-page summary of the company, including the service or product it sells, the location and history of the company, and the function you see yourself performing in the company.

8. List different ways you can submit your résumé. Write a brief paragraph describing each method. Select the method you think is the best way to submit your résumé and explain why.

9. You have recently interviewed for the position of assistant manager at a local retailer. Write a thank-you message to the person that interviewed you.

10. Research employment laws concerning background checks and what an employer is and is not allowed to do. Write a summary of your findings. Be sure to include information regarding federal, state, and local employment laws, if applicable.

Check Your Retail IQ

Now that you have finished the chapter, see what you learned about retail by taking the chapter posttest. If you do not have a smartphone, visit the G-W Learning companion website.

G-W Learning mobile site: www.m.g-wlearning.com

G-W Learning companion website: www.g-wlearning.com/marketing/

College and Career Readiness

Career Ready Practices The Internet can provide opportunities to enhance your career search and increase your productivity. There is much information available on making the job application process efficient. Research this topic and list five things you can do to improve your skills in completing a job application.

Reading Do an Internet search for *personal branding*. Read one of the articles you find. Determine the central ideas the author explored about the importance of branding yourself when looking for a position. Summarize the key supporting details and ideas.

Writing Using independent research, write a report in which you describe and analyze the use of aptitude tests, such as SAT, ACT, ACCUPLACER, and ASVAB. Why do these tests play such an important role in the post-high school plans of students? Cite specific evidence to support your understanding of this issue.

Teamwork

Working with a teammate, take turns interviewing each other. Rotate being the interviewer and the interviewee. After you have played both roles, summarize your performance. Were you a better interviewer or interviewee?

College and Career Portfolio

Storing Your E-Portfolio

You have probably used the Internet as a resource while creating your portfolio. The Internet also provides ways to help you present and store materials for an e-portfolio. Perhaps you created a website to present your e-portfolio. You could create a personal website to host the files. However, another option is using a website that specializes in e-portfolios. Some sites charge a fee to help you develop and host your e-portfolio. However, free sites are also available. Free sites may be sponsored by a school or some other organization. Some sites offer a basic account for free and charge for an account with more services. These sites typically have tutorials, templates, and forms that make placing your materials in an attractive e-portfolio easy. Be sure you read and understand the user agreement for any site on which you place your materials.

1. Search the Internet using the term *free e-portfolio*. Review sites to learn about the portfolio tools and resources offered for free by at least two websites.
2. Write a short summary of each site that includes the website name, web address, sponsoring organization, and tools or resources offered on the site.

◇DECA Coach

Testing

While DECA's competitive events vary from event to event, more than half of them require each competitor to take an occupationally specific exam. Competitors must take a written exam based on the content surrounding that particular event.

Competitors have more control over what takes place in the written exam than any other aspect of competition. During prepared events, judges ask questions that require competitors to be quick on their feet and respond appropriately and immediately to the unexpected. However, there are no surprises with exams. During an exam, there are no new scenarios to analyze and solve during preparation and presentation time.

Preparation is the key to success on an exam, just like other aspects of competition. You know you will be asked content-based questions and will have to answer them. While there is no substitution for learning the material in your classes, you can prepare for tests through practice, practice, and more practice. Ask your advisor to provide sample exams. Practicing the exams will strengthen your abilities and enhance your knowledge. Each time you miss a question during a practice exam, discuss it with your advisor and make each incorrect response a learning opportunity. Make sure that you understand the new concept. Not only will you increase your odds of winning through good test scores, but you will develop a lifelong bank of knowledge.

Visit www.deca.org to learn more information about DECA.

G-W Learning Mobile Site

Visit the G-W Learning mobile site to complete the chapter pretest and posttest, and to practice vocabulary using e-flash cards. If you do not have a smartphone, visit the G-W Learning companion website to access these features.

G-W Learning mobile site: www.m.g-wlearning.com

G-W Learning companion website: www.g-wlearning.com/marketing/

Math Skills Handbook

Table of Contents

Getting Started

Math skills are needed in everyday life. You will need to be able to estimate your purchases at a grocery store, calculate sales tax, or divide a recipe in half. This section is designed to help develop your math proficiency for better understanding of the concepts presented in the textbook. Using the information presented in the Math Skills Handbook will help you understand basic math concepts and their application to the real world.

Using a Calculator

There are many different types of calculators. Some are simple and only perform basic math operations. Become familiar with the keys and operating instructions of your calculator so calculations can be made quickly and correctly.

Shown below is a scientific calculator that comes standard with the Windows 8 operating system. To display this version, select the **View** pull-down menu and click **Scientific** in the menu.

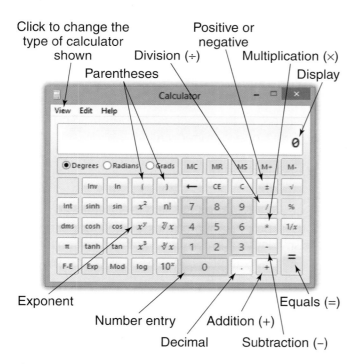

Click to change the type of calculator shown

Parentheses

Division (÷)

Positive or negative

Multiplication (×)

Display

Exponent

Number entry

Decimal

Addition (+)

Subtraction (−)

Equals (=)

Solving Word Problems

Word problems are exercises in which the problem is set up in text, rather than presented in mathematical notation. Many word problems tell a story. You must identify the elements of the math problem and solve it.

There are many strategies for solving word problems. Some common strategies include making a list or table; working backward; guessing, checking, and revising; and substituting simpler numbers to solve the problem.

Strategy	How to Apply
List or table	Identify information in the problem and organize it into a table to identify patterns.
Work backward	When an end result is provided, work backward from that to find the requested information.
Guess, check, revise	Start with a reasonable guess at the answer, check to see if it is correct, and revise the guess as needed until the solution is found.
Substitute simpler information	Use different numbers to simplify the problem and solve it, then solve the problem using the provided numbers.

Number Sense

Number sense is an ability to use and understand numbers to make judgments and solve problems. Someone with good number sense also understands when his or her computations are reasonable in the context of a problem.

Example
Suppose you want to add three basketball scores: 35, 21, and 18.
- First, add $30 + 20 + 10 = 60$.
- Then, add $5 + 1 + 8 = 14$.
- Finally, combine these two sums to find the answer: $60 + 14 = 74$.

Example
Suppose your brother is 72 inches tall and you want to convert this measurement from inches to feet. Suppose you use a calculator to divide 72 by 12 (number of inches in a foot) and the answer is displayed as 864. You recognize immediately that your brother cannot be 864 feet tall and realize you must have miscalculated. In this case, you incorrectly entered a multiplication operation instead of a division operation. The correct answer is 6.

Numbers and Quantity

Numbers are more than just items in a series. Each number has a distinct value relative to all other numbers. They are used to perform mathematical operations from the simplest addition to finding square roots. There are whole numbers, fractions, decimals, exponents, and square roots.

Whole Numbers

A whole number, or integer, is any positive number or zero that has no fractional part. It can be a single digit from 0 to 9, or may contain multiple digits, such as 38.

Place Value

A digit's position in a number determines its *place value.* The digit, or numeral, in the place farthest to the right before the decimal point is in the *ones position.* The next digit to the left is in the *tens position,* followed by next digit in the *hundreds position.* As you continue to move left, the place values increase to thousands, ten thousands, and so forth.

Example

Suppose you win the lottery and receive a check for $23,152,679. Your total prize would be *twenty-three million, one hundred fifty-two thousand, six hundred seventy-nine dollars.*

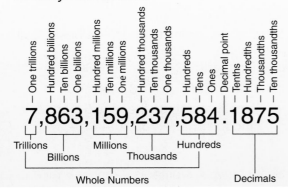

Addition

Addition is the process of combining two or more numbers. The result is called the *sum.*

Example

A plumber installs six faucets on his first job and three faucets on his second job. How many faucets does he install in total?

$$6 + 3 = 9$$

Subtraction

Subtraction is the process of finding the *difference* between two numbers.

Example

A plumber installs six faucets on her first job and three faucets on her second job. How many more faucets did she install on the first job than the second? Subtract 3 from 6 to find the answer.

$$6 - 3 = 3$$

Multiplication

Multiplication is a method of adding a number to itself a given number of times. The multiplied numbers are called *factors,* and the result is called the *product.*

Example

Suppose you are installing computers and need to purchase four adaptors. If the adaptors are $6 each, what is the total cost of the adaptors? The answer can be found by adding $6 four times:

$$\$6 + \$6 + \$6 + \$6 = \$24$$

However, the same answer is found more quickly by multiplying $6 times 4.

$$\$6 \times 4 = \$24$$

Division

Division is the process of determining how many times one number, called the *divisor,* goes into another number, called the *dividend.* The result is called the *quotient.*

Example

Suppose you are installing computers and buy a box of adaptors for $24. There are four adaptors in the box. What is the cost of each adaptor? The answer is found by dividing $24 by 4:

$$\$24 \div 4 = \$6$$

Decimals

A decimal is a kind of fraction with a denominator that is either ten, one hundred, one thousand, or some power of ten. Every decimal has three parts: a whole number (sometimes zero), followed by a decimal point, and one or more whole numbers.

Place Value

The numbers to the right of the decimal point indicate the amount of the fraction. The first place to the right of a decimal point is the tenths place. The second place to the right of the decimal point is the hundredths place. As you continue to the right, the place values move to the thousandths place, the ten thousandths place, and so on.

Example

A machinist is required to produce an airplane part to a very precise measurement of 36.876 inches. This measurement is *thirty-six and eight-hundred seventy six thousandths* inches.

36.876

Addition

To add decimals, place each number in a vertical list and align the decimal points. Then add the numbers in each column starting with the column on the right and working to the left. The decimal point in the answer drops down into the same location.

Example

A landscaper spreads 4.3 pounds of fertilizer in the front yard of a house and 1.2 pounds in the backyard. How many pounds of fertilizer did the landscaper spread in total?

$$\begin{array}{r} 4.3 \\ + \ 1.2 \\ \hline 5.5 \end{array}$$

Subtraction

To subtract decimals, place each number in a vertical list and align the decimal points. Then subtract the numbers in each column, starting with the column on the right and working to the left. The decimal point in the answer drops down into the same location.

Example

A landscaper spreads 4.3 pounds of fertilizer in the front yard of a house and 1.2 pounds in the backyard. How many more pounds were spread in the front yard than in the backyard?

$$\begin{array}{r} 4.3 \\ - \ 1.2 \\ \hline 3.1 \end{array}$$

Multiplication

To multiply decimals, place the numbers in a vertical list. Then multiply each digit of the top number by the right-hand bottom number. Multiply each digit of the top number by the bottom number in the tens position. Place the result on a second line and add a zero to the end of the number. Add the total number of decimal places in both numbers you are multiplying. This will be the number of decimal places in your answer.

Example

An artist orders 13 brushes priced at $3.20 each. What is the total cost of the order? The answer can be found by multiplying $3.20 by 13.

$$\begin{array}{r} \$3.20 \\ \times \quad 13 \\ \hline 960 \\ + \ 3200 \\ \hline 41.60 \end{array}$$

Division

To divide decimals, the dividend is placed under the division symbol, the divisor is placed to the left of the division symbol, and the quotient is placed above the division symbol. Start from the *left* of the dividend and determine how many times the divisor goes into the first number. Continue this until the quotient is found. Add the dollar sign to the final answer.

$$\begin{array}{r} 3.20 \\ 3\overline{)9.60} \end{array}$$

9↓	Product of 3 × 3
06	Bring down the 6
6↓	Product of 2 × 3
0	No remainder

Example

An artist buys a package of three brushes for $9.60. What is the cost of each brush? The quotient is found by dividing $9.60 by 3.

$$\begin{array}{r} 3.20 \\ 3\overline{)9.60} \\ -9 \downarrow \\ \hline 06 \downarrow \\ \hline 00 \end{array}$$

Rounding

When a number is rounded, some of the digits are changed, removed, or changed to zero so the number is easier to work with. Rounding is often used when precise calculations or measurements are not needed. For example, if you are calculating millions of dollars, it might not be important to know the amount down to the dollar or cent. Instead, you might *round* the amount to the nearest ten thousand or even hundred thousand dollars. Also, when working with decimals, the final answer might have several more decimal places than needed.

To round a number, follow these steps. First, underline the digit in the place to which you are rounding. Second, if the digit to the *right* of this place is 5 or greater, add 1 to the underlined digit. If the digit to the right is less than 5, do not change the underlined digit. Third, change all the digits to right of the underlined digit to zero. In the case of decimals, the digits to the right of the underlined digit are removed.

Example

A company's utility expense last year was $32,678.53. The owner of the company is preparing a budget for next year and wants to round this amount to the nearest 1,000.

Step 1: Underline the digit in the 10,000 place.

$$\$3\underline{2},678$$

Step 2: The digit to the right of 2 is greater than 5, so add 1.

$$2 + 1 = 3$$

Step 3: Change the digits to the right of the underlined digit to zero.

$$\$33,000$$

Fractions

A fraction is a part of a whole. It is made up by a numerator that is divided by a denominator.

$$\frac{\text{numerator}}{\text{denominator}}$$

The *numerator* specifies the number of these equal parts that are in the fraction. The *denominator* shows how many equal parts make up the whole.

Proper

In a *proper fraction,* the numerator is less than the denominator.

Example

A lumber yard worker cuts a sheet of plywood into four equal pieces and sells three of them to a carpenter. The carpenter now has 3/4 of the original sheet. The lumber yard has 1/4 of the sheet remaining.

Improper

An *improper fraction* is a fraction where the numerator is equal to or greater than the denominator.

Example

A chef uses a chili recipe which calls for 1/2 cup of chili sauce. However, the chef makes an extra-large batch that will serve three times as many people and uses three of the 1/2 cup measures. The improper fraction in this example is 3/2 cups of chili sauce.

Mixed

A mixed number contains a whole number and a fraction. It is another way of writing an improper fraction.

Example

A chef uses a chili recipe that calls for 1/2 cup of chili sauce. However, the chef makes an extra-large batch that will serve three times as many people and uses three of the 1/2 cup measures. The improper fraction in this example is 3/2 cups of chili sauce. This can be converted to a mixed number by dividing the numerator by the denominator: The remainder is 1, which is 1 over 2. So, the mixed number is 1 1/2 cups.

$$2\overline{)3} \quad \begin{array}{r} 1 \\ \hline 3 \\ -2 \\ \hline 1 \end{array}$$

Reducing

Fractions are reduced to make them easier to work with. Reducing a fraction means writing it with smaller numbers, in *lowest terms*. Reducing a fraction does not change its value.

To find the lowest terms, determine the largest number that *evenly* divides both the numerator and denominator so there is no remainder. Then use this number to divide both the numerator and denominator.

Example

The owner of hair salon asks ten customers if they were satisfied with the service they recently received. Eight customers said they were satisfied, so the fraction of satisfied customers is 8/10. The largest number that evenly divides both the numerator and denominator is 2. The fraction is reduced to its lowest terms as follows.

$$\frac{8}{10} = \frac{8 \div 2}{10 \div 2} = \frac{4}{5}$$

Addition

To add fractions, the numerators are combined and the denominator stays the same. However, fractions can only be added when they have a *common denominator*. The *least common denominator* is the smallest number to which each denominator can be converted.

Example

A snack food company makes a bag of trail mix by combining 3/8 pound of nuts with 1/8 pound of dried fruit. What is the total weight of each bag? The fractions have common denominators, so the total weight is determined by adding the fractions.

$$\frac{3}{8} + \frac{1}{8} = \frac{4}{8}$$

This answer can be reduced from 4/8 to 1/2.

Example

Suppose the company combines 1/4 pound of nuts with 1/8 cup of dried fruit. To add these fractions, the denominators must be made equal. In this case, the least common denominator is 8 because

$4 \times 2 = 8$. Convert 1/4 to its equivalent of 2/8 by multiplying both numerator and denominator by 2. Then the fractions can be added as follows.

$$\frac{2}{8} + \frac{1}{8} = \frac{3}{8}$$

This answer cannot be reduced because 3 and 8 have no common factors.

Subtraction

To subtract fractions, the second numerator is subtracted from the first numerator. The denominators stay the same. However, fractions can only be subtracted when they have a *common denominator.*

Example

A snack food company makes a bag of trail mix by combining 3/8 pound of nuts with 1/8 pound of dried fruit. How much more do the nuts weigh than the dried fruit? The fractions have common denominators, so the difference can be determined by subtracting the fractions.

$$\frac{3}{8} - \frac{1}{8} = \frac{2}{8}$$

This answer can be reduced from 2/8 to 1/4.

Example

Suppose the company combines 1/4 pound of nuts with 1/8 cup of dried fruit. How much more do the nuts weigh than the dried fruit? To subtract these fractions, the denominators must be made equal. The least common denominator is 8, so convert 1/4 to its equivalent of 2/8. Then the fractions can be subtracted as follows.

$$\frac{2}{8} - \frac{1}{8} = \frac{1}{8}$$

This answer cannot be reduced.

Multiplication

Common denominators are not necessary to multiply fractions. Multiply all of the numerators and multiply all of the denominators. Reduce the resulting fraction as needed.

Example

A lab technician makes a saline solution by mixing 3/4 cup of salt with one gallon of water. How much salt should the technician mix if only 1/2 gallon of water is used? Multiply 3/4 by 1/2:

$$\frac{3}{4} \times \frac{1}{2} = \frac{3}{8}$$

Division

To divide one fraction by a second fraction, multiply the first fraction by the reciprocal of the second fraction. The *reciprocal* of a fraction is created by switching the numerator and denominator.

Example

A cabinet maker has 3/4 gallon of wood stain. Each cabinet requires 1/8 gallon of stain to finish. How many cabinets can be finished? To find the answer, divide 3/4 by 1/8, which means multiplying 3/4 by the reciprocal of 1/8.

$$\frac{3}{4} \div \frac{1}{8} = \frac{3}{4} \times \frac{8}{1} = \frac{24}{4} = 6$$

Negative Numbers

Negative numbers are those less than zero. They are written with a minus sign in front of the number.

Example

The number $-34,687,295$ is read as *negative thirty-four million, six hundred eighty-seven thousand, two hundred ninety-five.*

Addition

Adding a negative number is the same as subtracting a positive number.

Example

A football player gains nine yards on his first running play (+9) and loses four yards (−4) on his second play. The two plays combined result in a five yard gain.

$$9 + (-4) = 9 - 4 = 5$$

Suppose this player loses five yards on his first running play (−5) and loses four yards (−4) on his second play. The two plays combined result in a nine yard loss.

$$-5 + (-4) = -5 - 4 = -9$$

Subtraction

Subtracting a negative number is the same as adding a positive number.

Example

Suppose you receive a $100 traffic ticket. This will result in a −$100 change to your cash balance. However, you explain the circumstance to a traffic court judge, and she reduces the fine by $60. The effect is to subtract −$60 from −$100 change to your cash balance. The final result is a −$40 change.

$$-\$100 - (-\$60) = -\$100 + \$60 = -\$40$$

Multiplication

Multiplication of an odd number of negative numbers results in a *negative* product. Multiplication of an even number of negative numbers results in a *positive* product.

Example

If you lose two pounds per week, this will result in a −2 pound weekly change in your weight. After five weeks, there will be a −10 pound change to your weight.

$$5 \times (-2) = -10$$

Suppose you have been losing two pounds per week. Five weeks ago (−5) your weight was 10 pounds higher.

$$(-5) \times (-2) = 10$$

Division

Division of an odd number of negative numbers results in a *negative* quotient. Division of an even number of negative numbers results in a *positive* quotient.

Example

Suppose you lost 10 pounds, which is a −10 pound change in your weight. How many pounds on average did you lose each week if it took five weeks to lose the weight? Divide −10 by 5 to find the answer.

$$-10 \div 5 = -2$$

Suppose you lost 10 pounds. How many weeks did this take if you lost two pounds each week? Divide −10 by −2 to find the answer.

$$-10 \div -2 = 5$$

Percentages

A percentage (%) means a part of 100. It is the same as a fraction or decimal.

Representing Percentages as Decimals

To change a percentage to a decimal, move the decimal point two places to the left. For example, 1% is the same as 1/100 or 0.01; 10% is the same as 10/100 or 0.10; and 100% is the same as 100/100 or 1.0.

Example

A high school cafeteria estimates that 30% of the students prefer sesame seeds on hamburger buns. To convert this percentage to a decimal, move the decimal point two places to the left.

$$30\% = 0.30$$

Representing Fractions as Percentages

To change a fraction to a percentage, first convert the fraction to a decimal by dividing the numerator by the denominator. Then convert the decimal to a percentage by moving the decimal point two places to the right.

Example

A high school cafeteria conducts a survey and finds that three of every ten students prefer sesame seeds on hamburger buns. To change this fraction to a percentage, divide 3 by 10, and move the decimal two places to the right.

$$3 \div 10 = 0.30 = 30\%$$

Calculating a Percentage

To calculate the percentage of a number, change the percentage to a decimal and multiply by the number.

Example

A car dealer sold ten cars last week, of which 70% were sold to women. How many cars did women buy? Change 70% to a decimal by dividing 70 by 100, which equals 0.70. Then multiply by the total number (10).

$$0.70 \times 10 = 7$$

To determine what percentage one number is of another, divide the first number by the second. Then convert the quotient into a percentage by moving the decimal point two places to the right.

Example

A car dealer sold 10 cars last week, of which seven were sold to women. What percentage of the cars were purchased by women? Divide 7 by 10 and then convert to a percentage.

$$7 \div 10 = 0.70$$

$$0.70 = 70\%$$

Ratio

A ratio compares two numbers through division. Ratios are often expressed as a fraction, but can also be written with a colon (:) or the word *to*.

Example

A drugstore's cost for a bottle of vitamins is $2.00, which it sells for $3.00. The ratio of the selling price to the cost can be expressed as follows.

$$\frac{\$3.00}{\$2.00} = \frac{3}{2}$$

$$\$3.00:\$2.00 = 3:2$$

$$\$3.00 \text{ to } \$2.00 = 3 \text{ to } 2$$

Measurement

The official system of measurement in the United States for length, volume, and weight is the US Customary system of measurement. The metric system of measurement is used by most other countries.

US Customary Measurement

The following are the most commonly used units of length in the US Customary system of measurement.

- 1 inch
- 1 foot = 12 inches
- 1 yard = 3 feet
- 1 mile = 5,280 feet

Example

An interior designer measurers the length and width of a room when ordering new floor tiles. The length is measured at 12 feet 4 inches (12′ 4″). The width is measured at 8 feet 7 inches (8′ 7″).

Example

Taxi cab fares are usually determined by measuring distance in miles. A recent cab rate in Chicago was $3.25 for the first 1/9 mile or less, and $0.20 for each additional 1/9 mile.

Metric Conversion

The metric system of measurement is convenient to use because units can be converted by multiplying or dividing by multiples of 10. The following are the commonly used units of length in the metric system of measurement.

- 1 millimeter
- 1 centimeter = 10 millimeters
- 1 meter = 100 centimeters
- 1 kilometer = 1,000 meters

The following are conversions from the US Customary system to the metric system.

- 1 inch = 25.4 millimeters = 2.54 centimeters
- 1 foot = 30.48 centimeters = 0.3048 meters
- 1 yard = 0.9144 meters
- 1 mile = 1.6093 kilometers

Example

A salesperson from the United States is traveling abroad and needs to drive 100 kilometers to meet a customer. How many miles is this trip? Divide 100 kilometers by 1.6093 and round to the hundredth place.

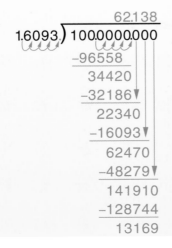

Estimating

Estimating is finding an *approximate* answer and often involves using rounded numbers. It is often quicker to add rounded numbers, for example, than it is to add the precise numbers.

Example

Estimate the total miles a delivery truck will travel along the following three segments of a route.

- Detroit to Chicago: 278 miles
- Chicago to St. Louis: 297 miles
- St. Louis to Wichita: 436 miles

The mileage can be estimated by rounding each segment to the nearest 100 miles.

- Detroit to Chicago: 300 miles
- Chicago to St. Louis: 300 miles
- St. Louis to Wichita: 400 miles

Add the rounded segments to estimate the total miles.

$$300 + 300 + 400 = 1,000 \text{ miles}$$

Accuracy and Precision

Accuracy and precision mean slightly different things. *Accuracy* is the closeness of a measured value to its actual or true value. *Precision* is how close measured values are to each other.

Example

A machine is designed to fill jars with 16 ounces of peanut butter. The machine is considered accurate if the actual amount of peanut butter in a jar is within 0.05 ounces of the target, which is a range of 15.95 to 16.05 ounces. A machine operator tests a jar and measures the weight to be 16.01 ounces. The machine is accurate.

Suppose a machine operator tests 10 jars of peanut butter and finds the weight of each jar to be 15.4 ounces. The machine is considered precise because it fills every jar with exactly the same amount. However, it is not accurate because the amount differs too much from the target.

Algebra

An *equation* is a mathematical statement that has an equal sign (=). An *algebraic* equation is an equation that includes at least one variable. A *variable* is an unknown quantity.

Solving Equations with Variables

Solving an algebraic equation means finding the value of the variable that will make the equation a true statement. To solve a simple equation, perform inverse operations on both sides and isolate the variable.

Example
A computer consultant has sales of $1,000. After deducting $600 in expenses, her profit equals $400. This is expressed with the following equation.

$$\text{sales} - \text{expenses} = \text{profit}$$
$$\$1,000 - \$600 = \$400$$

Example
A computer consultant has expenses of $600 and $400 in profit. What are her sales? An equation can be written in which sales are the unknown quantity, or variable.

$$\text{sales} - \text{expenses} = \text{profit}$$
$$\text{sales} - \$600 = \$400$$

Example
To find the value for sales, perform inverse operations on both sides and isolate the variable.

$$
\begin{array}{rcr}
\text{sales} \;-\; \$600 & = & \$400 \\
+\; \$600 & + & 600 \\
\hline
\text{sales} & = & \$1,000
\end{array}
$$

Order of Operations

The order of operations is a set of rules stating which operations in an equation are performed first. The order of operations is often stated using the acronym *PEMDAS*. PEMDAS stands for parentheses, exponents, multiplication and division, and addition and subtraction. This means anything inside parentheses is computed first. Exponents are computed next. Then, any multiplication and division operations are computed. Finally, any

addition and subtraction operations are computed to find the final answer to the problem. The equation is solved from left to right by applying PEMDAS.

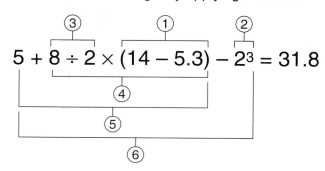

$$5 + 8 \div 2 \times (14 - 5.3) - 2^3 = 31.8$$

Recursive Formulas

A *recursive formula* is used to determine the next term of a sequence, using one or more of the preceding terms. The terms of a sequence are often expressed with a variable and subscript. For example, a sequence might be written as a_1, a_2, a_3, a_4, a_5, and so on. The subscript is essentially the place in line for each term. A recursive formula has two parts. The first is a starting point or seed value (a_1). The second is an equation for another number in the sequence (a_n). The second part of the formula is a function of the prior term (a_{n-1}).

Example
Suppose you buy a car for $10,000. Assume the car declines in value 10% each year. In the second year, the car will be worth 90% of $10,000, which is $9,000. The following year it will be worth 90% of $9,000, which is $8,100. What will the car be worth in the fifth year? Use the following recursive equation to find the answer.

$$a_n = a_{n-1} \times 0.90$$

$$\text{where } a_1 = \$10,000$$

$$a_n = \text{value of car in the } n^{th} \text{ year}$$

Year	Value of Car
$n = 1$	$a_1 = \$10,000$
$n = 2$	$a_2 = a_{2-1} \times 0.90 = a_1 \times 0.90 = \$10,000 \times 0.90 = \$9,000$
$n = 3$	$a_3 = a_{3-1} \times 0.90 = a_2 \times 0.90 = \$9,000 \times 0.90 = \$8,100$
$n = 4$	$a_4 = a_{4-1} \times 0.90 = a_3 \times 0.90 = \$8,100 \times 0.90 = \$7,290$
$n = 5$	$a_5 = a_{5-1} \times 0.90 = a_4 \times 0.90 = \$7,290 \times 0.90 = \$6,561$

Geometry

Geometry is a field of mathematics that deals with shapes, such as circles and polygons. A *polygon* is any shape whose sides are straight. Every polygon has three or more sides.

Parallelograms

A *parallelogram* is a four-sided figure with two pairs of parallel sides. A *rectangle* is a type of parallelogram with four right angles. A *square* is a special type of parallelogram with four right angles (90 degrees) and four equal sides.

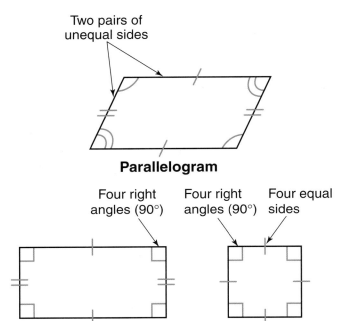

Parallelogram

Rectangle   **Square**

Example
Real-life examples of squares include ceramic floor and wall tiles, and each side of a die. Real-life examples of a rectangle include a football field, pool table, and most doors.

Triangles

A three-sided polygon is called a *triangle.* The following are four types of triangles, which are classified according to their sides and angles.

- *Equilateral:* Three equal sides and three equal angles.
- *Isosceles:* Two equal sides and two equal angles.
- *Scalene:* Three unequal sides and three unequal angles.
- *Right:* One right angle; may be isosceles or scalene.

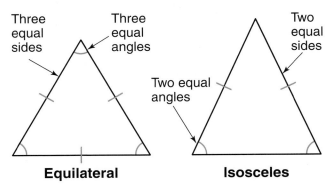

Equilateral   **Isosceles**

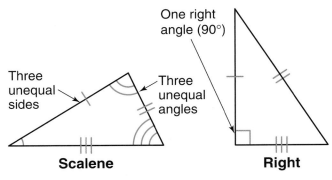

Scalene   **Right**

Example
Real-life examples of equilateral triangles are the sides of a classical Egyptian pyramid.

Circles and Half Circles

A *circle* is a figure in which every point is the same distance from the center. The distance from the center to a point on the circle is called the *radius.* The distance across the circle through the center is the *diameter.* A half circle is formed by dividing a whole circle along the diameter.

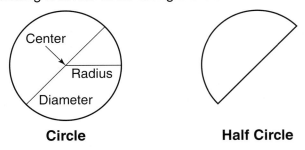

Circle   **Half Circle**

Example
Real life examples of circles include wheels of all sizes.

Perimeter

A *perimeter* is a measure of length around a figure. Add the length of each side to measure the perimeter of any figure whose sides are all line segments, such as a parallelogram or triangle. The perimeter of a circle is called the *circumference*. To measure the perimeter, multiply the diameter by pi (π). Pi is approximately equal to 3.14. The following formulas can be used to calculate the perimeters of various figures.

Figure	Perimeter
parallelogram	2 × width + 2 × length
square	4 × side
rectangle	2 × width + 2 × length
triangle	side + side + side
circle	π × diameter

Example

A professional basketball court is a rectangle 94 feet long and 50 feet wide. The perimeter of the court is calculated as follows.

2 × 94 feet + 2 × 50 feet = 288 feet

Example

A tractor tire has a 43 inch diameter. The circumference of the tire is calculated as follows.

43 inches × 3.14 = 135 inches

Area

Area is a measure of the amount of surface within the perimeter of a flat figure. Area is measured in square units, such as square inches, square feet, or square miles. The areas of the following figures are calculated using the corresponding formulas.

Figure	Area
parallelogram	base × height
square	side × side
rectangle	length × width
triangle	1/2 × base × height
circle	π × radius^2 = π × radius × radius

Example

An interior designer needs to order decorative tiles to fill the following spaces. Measure the area of each space in square feet.

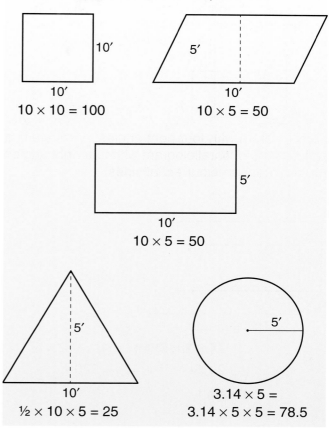

10 × 10 = 100

10 × 5 = 50

10 × 5 = 50

½ × 10 × 5 = 25

3.14 × 5 = 3.14 × 5 × 5 = 78.5

Surface Area

Surface area is the total area of the surface of a figure occupying three-dimensional space, such as a cube or prism. A *cube* is a solid figure that has six identical squares faces. A *prism* has bases or ends which have the same size and shape and are parallel to each other, and each of whose sides is a parallelogram. The following are the formulas to find the surface area of a cube and a prism.

Object	Surface Area
cube	6 × side × side
prism	2 × [(length × width) + (width × height) + (length × height)]

Example

A manufacturer of cardboard boxes wants to determine how much cardboard is needed to make the following size boxes. Calculate the surface area of each in square inches.

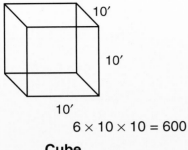

$$6 \times 10 \times 10 = 600$$

Cube

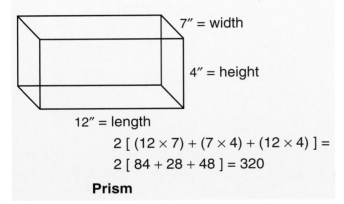

12" = length

$$2\,[\,(12 \times 7) + (7 \times 4) + (12 \times 4)\,] =$$
$$2\,[\,84 + 28 + 48\,] = 320$$

Prism

Volume

Volume is the three-dimensional space occupied by a figure and is measured in cubic units, such as cubic inches or cubic feet. The volumes of the following figures are calculated using the corresponding formulas.

Solid Figure	Volume
cube	side^3 = side × side × side
prism	length × width × height
cylinder	π × radius^2 × height = π × radius × radius × height
sphere	4/3 × π × radius^3 = 4/3 × π × radius × radius × radius

Example

Find the volume of packing material needed to fill the following boxes. Measure the volume of each in cubic inches.

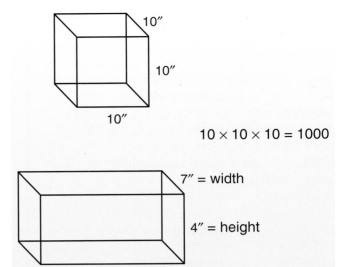

$$10 \times 10 \times 10 = 1000$$

7" = width

4" = height

12" = length

$$12 \times 7 \times 4 = 336$$

Example

Find the volume of grain that will fill the following cylindrical silo. Measure the volume in cubic feet.

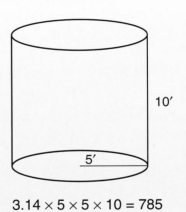

$$3.14 \times 5 \times 5 \times 10 = 785$$

Example

A manufacturer of pool toys wants to stuff soft material into a ball with a 3 inch radius. Find the cubic inches of material that will fit into the ball.

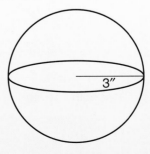

$$\frac{4}{3} \times 3.14 \times 3 \times 3 \times 3 = 113$$

Data Analysis and Statistics

Graphs are used to illustrate data in a picture-like format. It is often easier to understand data when they are shown in a graphical form instead of a numerical form in a table. Common types of graphs are bar graphs, line graphs, and circle graphs.

A *bar graph* organizes information along a vertical axis and horizontal axis. The vertical axis runs up and down one side; the horizontal axis runs along the bottom.

A *line graph* also organizes information on vertical and horizontal axes; however, data are graphed as a continuous line rather than a set of bars. Line graphs are often used to show trends over a period of time.

A *circle graph* looks like a divided circle and shows how a whole object is cut up into parts. Circle graphs are also called *pie charts* and are often used to illustrate percentages.

Example

A business shows the following balances in its cash account for the months of March through July. These data are illustrated below in bar and line graphs.

Month	Account Balance	Month	Account Balance
March	$450	June	$800
April	$625	July	$900
May	$550		

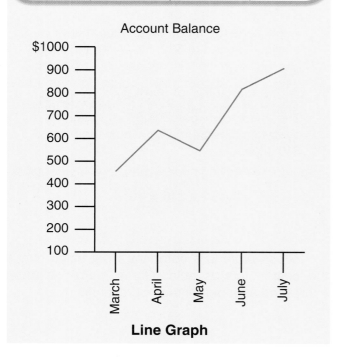

Line Graph

Example

A business lists the percentage of its expenses in the following categories. These data are displayed in the following circle graph.

Expenses	Percentage
Cost of goods	25
Salaries	25
Rent	21
Utilities	17
Advertising	12

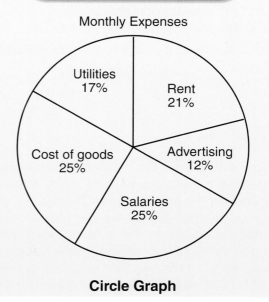

Circle Graph

Math Models for Business and Retail

Math skills used in business and retail are the same math skills required in everyday life. The ability to add, subtract, multiply, and divide different types of numbers is very important. However, this type of math is often focused on prices, taxes, profits, and losses.

Markup

Markup is a retailing term for the amount by which price exceeds the cost. One way to express markup is in dollars. Another way to express markup is percentage. The *markup percentage* is the amount of the markup as a percentage of the cost.

Example

A retailer pays $4 for a pair of athletic socks and prices them for sale at $7. The dollar markup is $3.

selling price − cost = dollar markup

$$\$7 - \$4 = \$3$$

Example

A pair of athletic socks, which cost $4, is priced at $7. The dollar markup is $3. To find the markup percentage, divide $3 by $4. The markup percentage is 75%.

markup dollars ÷ cost = markup percentage

$$\$3 \div \$4 = 0.75 = 75\%$$

Percentage Markup to Determine Selling Price

The selling price of an item can be determined if you know the markup percentage and the cost. First, convert the markup percentage to a decimal. Next multiply the cost by the decimal. Then, add the markup dollars to the cost to determine the selling price. Another way to find the selling price is to convert the markup percentage to a decimal and add 1.0. Then multiply this amount by the cost.

Example

A pair of athletic socks costs $4, which the retailer marks up by 75%. Find the selling price.
1. Convert the markup percentage to a decimal.

$$75\% = 0.75$$

2. Multiply the cost by the markup.

cost × markup = dollar markup

$$\$4 \times 0.75 = \$3$$

3. Add the $3 markup to the $4 cost to find the selling price. The selling price is $7.

$$\$4 + \$3 = \$7$$

Example

A pair of athletic socks costs $4, which the retailer marks up by 75%. Find the selling price.
1. Convert the 75% markup percentage to 0.75 and add 1.0.

$$0.75 + 1.0 = 1.75.$$

2. Multiply 1.75 by the $4 cost to find the selling price.

$$\$4 \times 1.75 = \$7$$

Markdown

A *markdown* is the amount by which the selling price of an item is reduced. Sometimes a markdown is also called a *discount*. To find the amount of a markdown, subtract the new or discounted price from the original price. A markdown can also be expressed as a percentage of the original price. Sometimes this is called a *percentage discount.*

Example

A package of meat at a supermarket is originally priced at $10. However, the meat has not sold and is nearing its expiration date. The supermarket wants to sell it quickly, so it reduces the price to $6. This is a markdown of $4.

selling price − discounted price = dollar markdown

$$\$10 - \$6 = \$4$$

Example

A package of meat at a supermarket is originally priced at $10. However, the meat has not sold and is nearing its expiration date. The supermarket wants to sell it quickly, so it marks down the price by $4. The markdown percentage is determined by dividing the $4 markdown by the original $10 price.

markdown ÷ selling price = markdown percentage

$$\$4 \div \$10 = 40\%$$

Gross Profit

Gross profit is a company's net sales minus the cost of goods sold. *Gross margin* is often expressed as a percentage of revenue.

Example

A wristband manufacturer generated net sales of $100,000 last year. The cost of goods sold for the wristbands was $30,000. The net sales of $100,000 minus the $30,000 cost of goods sold leaves a gross profit $70,000.

net sales − cost of goods sold = gross profit

$$\$100,000 - \$30,000 = \$70,000$$

Example

The gross profit of $70,000 divided by the net sales of $100,000 is 0.70, or 70%.

gross profit ÷ net sales = gross margin percentage

$$\$70,000 \div \$100,000 = 0.70 = 70\%$$

Net Income or Loss

Net income or loss is a company's revenue after total expenses are deducted from gross profit. Total expenses include marketing, administration, interest, and taxes. A company earns a *net income* when gross profit exceeds expenses. A *net loss* is incurred when expenses exceed gross profit.

Example

A wristband manufacturer had a gross profit of $70,000. In addition, expenses for marketing, administration, interest, and taxes were $50,000. Net profit is calculated by subtracting the total expenses of $50,000 from the gross profit of $70,000. The net profit was $20,000.

gross profit on sales − total expenses = net income or loss

$$\$70,000 - \$50,000 = \$20,000$$

Break-Even Point

A *break-even point* is the number of units a company must sell to cover its costs and expenses and earn a zero profit. Use the following formula to find a company's break-even point.

total costs ÷ selling price = break-even point

Sales Tax

Sales tax is a tax collected on the selling price of a good or service. The sales tax rate is usually expressed as a percentage of the selling price. Sales tax is calculated by multiplying the sale price by the tax rate.

Example

Suppose you buy a T-shirt for $10.00. How much is the sales tax if the tax rate is 5%? Convert 5% to a decimal (.05) and multiply it by the sale price.

sale price × sales tax rate percentage = sales tax

$$\$10 \times 0.05 = \$0.50$$

Return on Investment

Return on investment (ROI) is a calculation of a company's net profit as a percentage of the owner's investment. One way to determine ROI is to divide net profit by the owner's investment.

Example

Suppose you start a dry-cleaning business with a $100,000 investment, and you earn a $20,000 net profit during the first year. Divide $20,000 by $100,000, which equals a 20% return on your investment.

net income ÷ owner's investment = return on investment (ROI)

$$\$20,000 \div \$100,000 = 0.20 = 20\%$$

Glossary

A

above the fold. Placing online content on a web page so it can be seen without scrolling down the page. (13)

actionable research. Research intended to improve the retailer's practices; how to fix a problem. (4)

adjourning. Stage five of team development when the team's work is finished and their efforts to meet a common goal come to an end. (16)

adjustment. A discount on the purchase price of an item; usually given on the sale of damaged or defective merchandise. (10)

AIDA. Four-stage buying process model; attention, interest, desire, and action. (10)

anchor store. Large retail store that attracts many consumers to a shopping mall. (2)

approach. The first in-person contact a sales associate makes with a potential customer; first step in the sales process. Also known as the *greeting*. (10)

asymmetrical balance. When the pieces of a display are equally distributed but not mirrored; also known as *informal balance*. (12)

asynchronous service. When a customer asks a question and the response comes at a later time or date. (11)

attitude. Person's perspective and feelings about something; way a person looks at the world and responds to events. (5, 11)

attitude research. Designed to find out how consumers think or feel about aspects of a business; also called *opinion research*. (4)

automated e-mail. Computer-generated response to a customer e-mail. (11)

B

background check. A look into the personal data about an applicant. The information is available from government records and other sources, including public information on the Internet. (20)

bait and switch. Practice of advertising a product, usually at a very low price, so customers will come into the store. When customers arrive, the featured product is sold out and another product is substituted. (17)

balance. Way items are placed around an imaginary centerline. (12)

bandwidth. Measure of the amount of data that can be transmitted via the Internet in a certain amount of time. (14)

base price. Price at which a retailer expects to sell the product. (8)

behavioral intention. Likelihood of engaging in a certain behavior. (4)

behavioral question. Question that draws on an applicant's previous experiences and decisions. (20)

behavioral segmentation. Divides the market by the relationship between customers and a product or service. (5)

benefit. How a product feature fulfills a need. (10) Noncash payments to employees, such as insurance and paid time off. (17)

big box store. Large specialty discount store. (2)

blog. A website in a journal format created by a person or organization; short for *web log*. (9)

boutique. Highly-specialized retail store that caters to consumers seeking unique items and a high level of customer service. (2)

brand. The name, term, or design that consumers relate to a business or product. (12)

break-even point. Point at which revenue from sales equals the costs. (8)

brick-and-mortar. Store that has a physical location to display and sell merchandise and services. (2)

buffer stock. Additional stock kept above the minimum required to meet anticipated needs. (6)

burglary. Occurs when a person breaks into a business to steal merchandise, money, valuable equipment, or take confidential information. (18)

business risk. Possibility of loss or injury that might occur while operating a business. (18)

business-to-consumer (B2C). Retailer that sells to consumers. (1)

buying motive. Reason people buy what they buy. (5)

buying signals. Clues that a customer is ready to buy. (10)

buying status. Describes the timing of when a customer will buy a product or service. (5)

buzz marketing. See *viral marketing*.

C

call center. Remote facility that is typically operated by third-party customer support organizations. (11)

career. Series of related jobs in the same profession. (19)

career and technical student organization (CTSO). National student organization that is related to career and technical education (CTE) courses. (19)

career aptitude test. An exam that analyzes personal interests, strengths, and weaknesses. (19)

career clusters. 16 groups of occupational and career specialties that share common knowledge and skills. (19)

career objective. Brief statement that explains an individual's career goals to an employer. (20)

career pathways. Subgroups of the career clusters that reflect occupations requiring similar knowledge and skills. (19)

career plan. List of steps to reach a career goal. (19)

cascading style sheets (CSS). Type of style language used to easily format the layout and design of a web page. (14)

cash transaction. A purchase for which a customer pays with cash. (10)

central business district (CBD). Central location for retail, business, and transportation activities in a city or town; often referred to as downtown. (2)

centralized visual merchandising. Practice of developing merchandise displays at the home office. (12)

certificate program. Type of professional development program. (19)

chain of command. Organization's structure of decision-making responsibilities, from the highest to the lowest level of authority. (15)

chain store. Two or more retail stores owned by the same person or company. (2)

channel. How the message is transmitted. (9)

channel of distribution. Path that goods take through the supply chain from the producer to the consumer. (1)

chronological résumé. Type of résumé that lists information in reverse chronological order, with the most recent employer listed first. (20)

closeout. End-of-season merchandise sold at reduced prices. (6)

code. Set of instructions for a computer directing it to perform certain activities. (14)

collaboration. Working with others to achieve a common goal. (16)

communication. Process of sending and receiving messages that convey information, ideas, feelings, and beliefs. (9)

communication process. Series of actions on the part of the sender and the receiver of the message. (9)

comparison shopper. Person who visits several competing stores and notes competitors' prices. (8)

compensation. Employee's wage or salary. (17)

competition. Act or process of trying to win something, such as a customer's business. (1)

competition-based pricing. Pricing strategy primarily based on what competitors charge. (8)

competitive intelligence. Data collected to analyze a particular retail industry. (4)

confidentiality agreement. Document stating that an employee will not share any company information with those outside the company. (17)

consensus. All members of a team support an idea. (16)

consumer. Person who buys *and* uses products or services; also called *end user*. (1)

consumer behavior. Includes all the actions people take to satisfy their needs and wants, which includes what they buy. (5)

consumer credit. Credit given to individual consumers by a retail business. (11)

Consumer Product Safety Commission (CPSC). Federal organization charged with protecting consumers from purchasing products that pose a risk of injury or death. (17)

contractor. Outside expert hired to complete a task. (14)

controllable risk. Risk that cannot be avoided, but can be minimized by purchasing insurance or implementing a risk plan. (18)

controlling. Monitoring the progress a team has made in meeting its goals. (15)

copyright. Type of intellectual property registration that grants exclusive rights to copy, license, sell, or distribute material. (17)

corporate gift service. Connects a store consultant with a corporate representative to make gift selections. (11)

corporate social responsibility (CSR). When a business is not only concerned with its own profits, but also acts with the welfare and interests of society in mind. (1)

corporation. Business that is recognized as a separate legal entity from its owners. (2)

cost-based pricing. Pricing strategy that uses the cost of the product to set the selling price. (8)

cover message. Formal written communication that accompanies a résumé or a job application to introduce the applicant and express interest in a position. (20)

credit card transaction. A purchase for which the customer pays with a credit card. (10)

culture. Way a group collectively thinks, feels, and acts. (5)

customer. Person or group that makes a purchase. (1)

customer loyalty. Continued and regular patronage of a business even when there are other places to purchase the same or similar products. (11)

customer profile. Detailed description of a retailer's customer, based on demographic, geographic, psychographic, and behavioral data. (5)

customer relationship management (CRM) system. Software used to track contact information and other data for current and potential customers. (10)

customer service flowchart. Graphic map of possible questions and answers that directs call center representatives though the process of questioning a customer. (11)

customer service. Ability to provide a product or service in the way it has been promised. (11)

cyberbullying. Harassing or threatening an individual through the Internet. (17)

D

data. Pieces of information obtained through research. (4)

data analysis. Process of studying raw data and organizing the information into meaningful graphs or charts. (4).

data mining. Searching through large amounts of data to find useful information; usually done by special software. (4)

debit card transaction. A purchase for which the customer uses a bank card to transfer money from a bank account to the retailer to pay for the merchandise. (10)

deceptive pricing. Pricing an item to intentionally deceive the customer. (17)

decisive. Ability to make decisions quickly and effectively. (16)

decline. Stage of the product life cycle when retailers see a drop in sales as the product gradually loses customer appeal. (6)

decoding. Translating the message into terms that the receiver can understand. (9)

delegate. Assign other people tasks to complete. (16)

demand. Amount of merchandise required to satisfy customers' buying needs. (1, 8)

demand-based pricing. Pricing strategy based on what customers are willing to pay; also known as *value-based pricing*. (8)

demographic segmentation. Divides the market by customers' personal traits. (5)

demographics. Personal traits such as age, gender, education, employment, income, family status, and ethnicity. (5)

dependability. Ability to be reliable and trustworthy. (10)

diary. Written record of a person's own experiences, thoughts, or observations. (4)

digital display. Images and text strategically placed on a web page to draw visitors' attention to specific promotional products, sales, or other special events. (13)

digital marketing. See *electronic promotion*.

direct mail. Any piece of marketing communication sent to potential customers through the US Postal Service; also known as *junk mail*. (3)

discount pricing. Reduction of the normal selling price of a product. (8)

display. Presentation of merchandise designed to attract customers so they will notice and examine the merchandise. (12)

distribution center. Warehouse that receives merchandise from multiple vendors and distributes the merchandise to multiple store locations. (7)

domain registrar (DR). Company that verifies, sells, and registers URLs. (14)

dress code. Set of rules or guidelines about the acceptable clothing in a certain place. (10)

dynamic HTML (DHTML). Code language that combines HTML, JavaScript, and CSS to create vibrant visual effects on a web page. (14)

E

e-tailing. Sale of products or services through the Internet. (3)

early adopter. Person who wants to be the first to own the newest products and is willing to pay more to do so. (8)

economic benefits. Gains that can be measured in financial terms. (1)

economic risk. Situation that occurs when the economy suffers due to negative business conditions either in the United States or someplace in the world. (18)

electronic data interchange (EDI). Standard transfer of electronic data for business transactions between organizations. (7)

electronic promotion. Any promotion that uses the Internet, e-mail, or other digital technology; also known as *digital marketing*. (9)

embezzlement. Type of fraud that occurs when somebody entrusted with confidential company information, financial records, money, or other valuables takes it for personal gain. (18)

emotional buying motive. Motive that appeals to the way a customer thinks or feels. (5)

employment verification. Process through which the information an applicant provided about employment history is checked to verify that it is correct. (20)

encoding. Process of turning the idea for a message into symbols that are communicated to others. (9)

end user. See *consumer*.

Equal Employment Opportunity Commission (EEOC). Federal agency that enforces federal laws that state it is illegal to discriminate against people in the workplace based on race, color, religion, sex, national origin, age, disability, or genetic information. (17)

ergonomics. Science concerned with designing and arranging things people use so they can interact efficiently and safely. (11)

ethics. Rules of behavior based on ideas about what is right and wrong. (16)

even pricing. Pricing strategy in which a product's price ends with an even number. (8)

evoked set. Includes the choices that a consumer is aware of and thinks highly of during the search process. (5)

extensible markup language (XML). Code language that allows advanced web page features and can be viewed by most web browsers. (14)

F

factory outlet. Retail store in which excess or unsold merchandise is sold at a discount directly to the public by the manufacturers, designers, or specialty stores. (2)

falling hazard. Source of potential injuries from slipping or falling. (18)

false advertising. Overstating the features and benefits of products or services, or making false claims about them. (17)

feature. Physical characteristic of a product. (10)

feature-benefit selling. Sales method in which the major selling features of a product and how they can benefit the customer are shown. Also known as *solution selling*. (10)

feedback. Receiver's response to a message. (9)

file transfer protocol (FTP). Computer software that provides tools to transfer files from a computer to the Internet. (14)

finance. Activity involved in controlling and managing money and other business assets. (1)

firewall. Software that prevents unwelcomed Internet access to data stored on a computer. (18)

fixed expense. Business expense that does not change and is not affected by the number of products sold. (8)

Flash®. Program based on ActionScript code that can create dynamic animated and video elements on a web page. (14)

flexible. Ability to adapt to circumstances as they change. (16)

FOB. Shipping terms that mean the manufacturer owns the merchandise until it is received by the retailer; stands for *free on board*. (6)

focus group. Group of six to nine people with whom an interview is conducted. (4)

food court. Area inside of a shopping mall where a number of fast-food restaurants are located. (2)

food truck. Mobile kitchens that prepare and sell different foods. (3)

formal balance. See *symmetrical balance*.

formal education. Education received in a school, college, or university. (19)

forming. Stage one of team development that occurs when a group of people come together and are in the introduction stage of the team. (16)

frames. Web page layout tool that allows more than one web page to be displayed within a single browser window. (14)

franchise. Legal agreement granting the right to sell a company's goods or services in a particular geographic area. (2)

franchisee. People who buy the rights to use the brand, learn the franchisor's trade secrets, and open their own businesses. (2)

franchisor. Parent company that owns the chain and the brand of a franchise. (2)

fraud. Cheating or deceiving a business out of money or property. (18)

free-enterprise economic system. Allows businesses to compete with limited government intervention; also called a *free market*. (1)

free market. See *free enterprise economic system*.

freeware. Fully functional software that can be used forever without purchasing it. (17)

functionality. The quality of having a practical use. (13)

functions of management. Business management activities of planning, organizing, staffing, leading, and controlling. (15)

G

geographic segmentation. Divides consumers based on where they live. (5)

gift registry. In-store wish list completed by the customer so that potential gift-givers can see what the person would like to receive. (11)

goal. Something a person wants to achieve in a specified time period. (19)

goal setting. Process of deciding what a person wants to achieve. (19)

goods. Tangible products that can be touched, such as food and clothing. (1)

gross domestic product (GDP). Market value of all goods and services produced within a country during a given period of time; one measure of a country's economic health. (1)

growth. Stage of the product life cycle when there is evidence that sales of the product are increasing. (6)

H

harmony. When all of the elements of a display blend to form a unified picture. (12)

hearing. Physical process of sound waves reaching a person's ears, which sends signals to the brain. (9)

home page. First page a person sees when visiting an online store that acts as a gateway to the rest of the pages and content on the site; also called an *index page* or *landing page*. (13)

home-shopping television. Television that is devoted solely to retail sales. (3)

HTML. Fundamental code language for web pages; stands for *hypertext markup language*. (14)

human resources. Managing employees and looking out for their general well-being. (1)

human resources management. Facilitating and managing employees in an organization. (15)

human risk. Situation caused by human actions. (18)

hyperlink. Element on a web page that visitors can click to connect to another location. Also called *link*. (13)

hypermarket. See *supercenter*.

hypertext markup language. See *HTML*.

hypothetical question. Question that requires an applicant to imagine a situation and describe how he or she would act. (20)

I

identity theft. Stealing someone's personal information to get money or make purchases. (3)

image cruncher. Web authoring tool that reduces the file size of images so they open and download faster. (14)

income statement. Documents that show a business' revenue and expense during a specific period of time. (15)

independent store. Small retail business with one location and is privately owned and operated. (2)

index page. See *home page*.

indexing. Search engine process of associating web pages or websites with particular keywords and phrases. (14)

infomercial. Paid television commercials placed in television program time slots. (3)

informal balance. See *asymmetrical balance*.

information technology (IT). All forms of technology used to create, store, exchange, and analyze various types of digital information. (1)

infringement. Use of intellectual property without permission. (17)

installment loan. Loan paid in regular payments, usually with interest, until the loan is paid in full. (11)

institutional display. Display created to promote the store image rather than a product. (12)

institutional promotion. Promoting an organization or company rather than its products. (9)

insurance. Financial product that offers protection against a specific type of loss. (18)

Integrated marketing communications (IMC). A promotional strategy that combines all forms of marketing communication in a coordinated way. (9)

intellectual property. Something that comes from a person's mind such as an idea, invention, or process. (17)

intermediary. Positioned between the manufacturer and the consumer in the supply chain; also called *middleman*. (1)

internal record. Data and information generated and stored by a business about current traits and activities of customers. (4)

interpersonal skills. Group of skills that enable a person to interact with others in a positive way. (16)

interview. Meeting or conversation where one or more persons question or evaluate another person. (4)

introduction. Stage of the product life cycle when a limited number of customers buy the product. (6)

inventory management. Involves ordering merchandise, receiving it into stock on arrival, and paying the vendor. (7)

invoice. Vendor bill requesting payment for goods shipped or services provided. (7)

J

Java. Code language that allows web designers to build entire web pages, or to build separate small programs to be inserted into web pages. (14)

Java applets. Small programs created using Java that act as additional features inserted into HTML web pages. (14)

JavaScript. Pieces of code that can be inserted into web pages to perform many different functions, such as password protection, games, navigation bars, and animated features. (14)

job. Work a person does regularly to earn money. (19)

job application. Form with spaces for an applicant's contact information, education, and work experience. (20)

job interview. Employer's opportunity to review a résumé and to ask questions to see if an applicant is qualified for the position. (20)

junk mail. See *direct mail.*

K

keystone pricing. Method of determining the base price of a product in which the total cost of the product is simply doubled. (8)

keyword. Search term describing the desired online content. (14)

kiosk. Very small structures with one or more open sides to display and sell a limited number of goods. (2)

L

labor union. Group of wage earners and or salaried employees that join together to negotiate with management regarding workplace laws. (17)

landing page. See *home page.*

lead time. Total time it takes from placing an order until it is received. (6)

leadership. Ability of a person to guide others to a goal. (16)

leading. Giving the team clear and concise directions. (15)

leased department. Space within a larger store that is leased to a smaller store, boutique, or designer. (2)

liability. Legal and financial responsibility. (2)

lifting hazard. Source of potential injury from improperly lifting or carrying items. (18)

Likert scale. Rating scale used in marketing research to measure attitudes. (4)

limited liability company (LLC). Form of business ownership that limits the personal liability of owners and can provide tax benefits. (2)

link. See *hyperlink.*

list price. The established price expected to be paid for a product; usually stated on a label, tag, sticker, or other type of price display. (8)

listening. Intellectual process that combines hearing with evaluation. (9)

long-term goal. Goal that will take a longer period of time to achieve—usually more than one year. (19)

loss prevention. Using a plan designed to prevent loss of company assets. (7)

M

m-commerce. Online sales that take place though smartphones or other mobile devices instead of computers; short for *mobile commerce.* (3)

malware. Computer program designed to damage or disrupt a computer or network. (18)

management. Process of controlling and making decisions about a business. (15)

manager. Person responsible for carrying out the goals of the business. (15)

manual tag system. Method of counting inventory that tracks sales using price tags that are removed when the products are sold. (7)

manufacturer. Business or person that makes products. (1)

manufacturer retail store. Retail store that only sells the products from one manufacturer. (2)

manufacturer's suggested retail price (MSRP). List price for merchandise as recommended by the manufacturer. (6)

market. Group of people who want a product and are able to buy it. (5)

market intelligence. See *market research.*

market research. Gathering statistics on a specific market's size, makeup, and buying trends; also called *market intelligence.* (4)

market risk. Potential that the target market for products or services is much less than originally thought. (18)

market segment. Group of individuals in the market who share common traits, characteristics, or interests. (5)

market segmentation. Dividing large markets into smaller groups. (5)

market week. An event where designers or manufacturers display and sell their latest products. (6)

marketing mix. Marketing strategy that considers the four *P*s of marketing—product, price, promotion, and place. (5)

marketing research. Gathering information on how to promote, sell, and distribute a product or service. (4)

marking. Recording the selling price on each item that will be sold to customers. (7)

marquee. Overhanging structure containing a signboard located at the entrance to the store. (12)

mass market. Entire group of people who might buy a product or service. (5)

material-storage hazard. Source of potential injury caused by the improper storage of merchandise or equipment. (18)

maturity. Stage of the product life cycle when the most customers buy the product. (6)

merchandise. Goods purchased with the intent of reselling to customers. (6)

merchandise assortment. Number of items within the product line. (6)

merchandise greeting. Greeting that includes a comment about a product or in-store event. (10)

merchandise plan. Tool that is used to define the goals and budgets for purchasing. (6)

merchandise planning. Process of deciding which products will appeal to the target audience. (6)

merchandising. Selecting and buying products to be resold to customers. (1)

meta tags. Specific types of metadata associated with a web page. (14)

metadata. Hidden data within a site that provide information about the content of certain items. (14)

middleman. See *intermediary*.

mobile applications. Software applications developed specifically for portable digital devices, such as smartphones and tablet computers; also called *mobile apps*. (3)

mobile apps. See *mobile applications*.

model stock. Optimum amount of merchandise needed on hand from each category to meet customer demands. (6)

motive. Reason a person acts in a certain way. (5)

multichannel retailer. Retailer that uses two or more retail channels to sell products. (3)

N

NAICS. North American Industry Classification System; a governmental system developed by the United States, Canada, and Mexico used to classify businesses and collect economic statistics. (1)

natural risk. Situation caused by nature. (18)

nav bar. See *navigation bar*.

navigation bar. Primary tool customers use to locate products and services on an e-tail site; also called *nav bar*. (13)

navigation label. Titles placed on the navigation bar buttons. (13)

negotiating. Mutual discussion and planning of the terms of a transaction or agreement. (6)

netiquette. Social and professional guidelines for online communications. (17)

nonprice competition. Competitive advantage based on factors other than price. (8)

nonselling tasks. Duties performed by sales associates while not in direct contact with customers. (10)

nonverbal communication. Actions that send messages. (9)

norming. Stage three of team development when teams eventually come together on their ideas and reach a consensus. (16)

O

Occupational Safety and Health Administration (OSHA). Federal agency that enforces safety and health regulations in the workplace. (17)

odd pricing. Pricing strategy in which a product's price ends with an odd number, usually just lower than an even dollar amount. (8)

off-price retailer. Retailer that sells brand-name merchandise at big discounts. (2)

off-site purchasing. Any type of sale that takes place in a location other than a brick-and-mortar store. (3)

one-way labeled scale. Rating scale that measures a topic's importance to the participants. (4)

open-to-buy. Amount of money that is available to purchase new merchandise after all other purchases have been deducted. (6)

operating expenses. Ongoing expenses that keep a business functioning. (8)

operations. Day-to-day activities necessary to keep a business up and running. (1)

opinion research. See *attitude research*.

opt-in marketing. See *permission marketing*.

organic SEO. Process of creating a website so that it will be ranked high in search engine indexes. (14)

organizational chart. Diagram of employee positions that shows how the positions interact within the chain of command. (15)

organizing. Coordinating the efforts of a team to reach its goals. (15)

orphaned page. Web page that does not have an obvious way for a visitor to move around the site. (13)

outsourcing. To contract with an expert to perform specific work. (14)

P

pace. Refers to how quickly information is being covered. (9)

packing slip. Form that lists the contents of a shipped box or container. (7)

partnership. Relationship between two or more people who join to create a business. (2)

patent. Type of intellectual property registration that grants a person or company the right to be the sole producer of a product for a defined period of time. (17)

patronage buying motive. Motive based on loyalty and suggests that a customer prefers to buy a particular brand or from a particular store. (5)

peer pressure. Social influence, mild or strong, exerted on an individual by his or her peers. (5)

people skills. Ability to get along with others, to resolve issues with others, and communicate effectively with people. (10)

performing. Stage four of team development when the team is functioning at its best. (16)

periodic inventory control system. Method of counting inventory that involves taking a physical count of merchandise at regular periods. (7)

permission marketing. The practice of receiving permission to send people company information through e-mail, text messaging, and other means; also known as *opt-in marketing*. (9)

perpetual inventory control system. Method of counting inventory that shows the quantity of items on hand at all times. (7)

personal selling. Direct contact between a salesperson and a customer for the purpose of persuading the customer to make a purchase. (10)

personal shopper. Helps select products for individual customers based on the customer's personal preferences; also called *store consultant*. (11)

personnel. People who work for the retail business. (5)

persuasion. Using logic to change a belief or get people to take a certain action. (9)

philanthropy. Action that contributes to the improvement of the welfare of others. (1)

phishing. Using fraudulent e-mails and copies of valid websites to trick people into providing private, confidential, and personal data; pronounced *fishing*. (18)

piracy. Illegal copying or downloading of software, files, or other protected material. (17)

place. All of the activities in getting the product to the customer; also called *distribution*. (5)

plagiarism. Claiming another person's material as your own. (17)

planned retail purchases. Amount of merchandise that is planned for delivery during a given period. (6)

planned stock. Dollar amount of merchandise required to meet sales goals. (6)

planning. Deciding on the actions that will guide the store in reaching its goals. (15)

plug-in. Browser software applications that read and interpret the technology. (13)

point-of-purchase display. Special display usually found near a cash register where goods are purchased. (12)

point-of-sale software. Electronically records each sale when it happens by scanning product bar codes. (7)

pop-up menu. Navigation bar that displays a submenu when a site visitor places the cursor over or clicks on a navigational button or link. (13)

pre-approach. Tasks sales associates complete before coming in contact with customers. (10)

predatory pricing. Setting prices low to drive other companies out of business. (17)

premium. Amount paid for insurance. (18)

presentation. See *visual merchandising*.

prestige pricing. Setting product prices high to convey quality and status. (8)

price. Amount of money requested or exchanged for a product or service. (5, 8)

price ceiling. Maximum prices for certain products or services that are set by the government. (17)

price competition. Occurs when a lower price is the main reason for customers to buy from one retailer over another. (8)

price discrimination. Selling the same product at different prices to different customers based on customers' personal characteristics. (17)

price fixing. When two or more retailers get together and agree upon a set price for similar products. (17)

price floor. Minimum prices for certain products or services that are set by the government. (17)

price gouging. Practice of raising prices at times of emergency or great need. (17)

price lining. Setting various prices for the same type of product to indicate different levels of quality. (8)

pricing objective. Goal defined in the business plan for the overall pricing policies of the company. (8)

primary data. Data collected directly by researchers. (4)

problem-solving skills. Group of skills that give a person the ability to identify a problem and take steps to solve it. (16)

process. Series of actions that lead to an end, such as a sale or a return. (5)

product. Anything that can be bought or sold. (6)

product life cycle. Customers' acceptance and buying levels of a product. (6)

product management. Process of managing a product across its complete life cycle. (6)

product mix. Range of all products sold by a retailer. (5)

product obsolescence. Occurs when customers no longer want to buy a product. (18)

product promotion. Promoting specific products or services. (9)

product research. Research conducted to gather consumer opinions about both new and existing products. (4)

professional development. Training that builds on the skills and knowledge that contribute to personal growth and career development. (16)

profit. Amount by which revenue from sales exceeds the costs of making and selling a product. (1)

promotion. All of the communication techniques sellers use to inform or motivate people to buy their products. (1)

promotional display. Display created to help sell merchandise. (12)

promotional mix. Combination of personal selling, sales promotion, advertising, and public relations used in a retailer's promotional efforts. (5)

promotional pricing. Reducing the price of a product for a short period of time. (8)

prop. Object used in a display to support the theme or to physically support the merchandise. (12)

proportion. Refers to the size and space relationship of all items in a display; also known as *scale*. (12)

proprietary information. Confidential information a company needs to keep private; also known as *trade secrets*. (17)

psychographic segmentation. Divides consumers based on personal lifestyle preferences or choices. (5)

psychological influence. Influence that comes from within a person. (5)

psychological pricing. Pricing technique that creates an image of a product to entice customers to buy. (8)

public relations (PR). Activities that promote goodwill between the company and the public. (9)

puffery. Claims that cannot be measured. (17)

punctuality. Being on time. (10)

purchase order. Form a buyer sends to a vendor to officially place an order. (7)

purchasing management. Ordering the necessary goods, receiving them into stock on arrival, and paying the vendor for the order. (6)

Q

qualitative data. Provides insight into what people are thinking. (4)

quality control. Actions involved in checking goods as they are received to ensure the quality meets expectation. (7)

quantitative data. Provides facts and figures. (4)

quick response (QR) codes. Bar codes that, when scanned with a mobile device, connect the user to a website or other digital information. (9)

R

radio frequency identification (RFID). System that uses computer chips attached to inventory items and radio frequency receivers to track inventory. (7)

rational buying motive. Motive based on practical reasoning, such as price, quality, or durability. (5)

readability. Describes how clear and easy something is to read. (13)

recall. When a retailer or manufacturer requests that customers return a product for a refund or replacement. (17)

receiver. Person who physically receives the message from the sender. (9)

receiving record. Form on which all merchandise received is listed as it comes into the business. (7)

recruiting. Process of finding suitable people and getting them to join a company. (15)

reference group. Other people whose values, beliefs, behaviors, and opinions are used by an individual as a basis for decision making. (5)

reference. Person who knows a person well and can comment on his or her qualifications, work ethic, personal qualities, and work-related aspects of the person's character. (20)

referral. Names of people, as provided by satisfied customers, who might buy the retailer's products. (10)

research process. Set of defined steps through which marketing data are collected, analyzed, and used. (4)

research proposal. Written outline detailing the research process to address the defined problem. (4)

respect. Feeling that someone or something is good, valuable, and important. (16)

résumé. Document that profiles a person's career goals, education, and work history. (20)

retail. Business of exchanging of goods and services for personal, family, or household use. (1)

retail buyer. Person who selects and purchases merchandise for resale. (6)

retail channel. Pathways through which goods or services can be sold. (3)

retail mix. Marketing strategy that considers personnel, presentation, and process in addition to the marketing mix. (5)

retailer. Business that offers goods to or provides services for individual consumers. (1)

revenue. Amount of money a company generates from sales during a specific period. (1)

rhythm. When all elements of a display help to move the eye smoothly from one item to another. (12)

risk management. Process of identifying, assessing, and reducing different kinds of risks. (18)

robbery. Theft involving another person, often using force or the threat of violence. (18)

S

sales process. Series of steps sales associates take to help the customers make satisfying buying decisions. (10)

sales promotion. A marketing method that encourages customers to take immediate action, usually to buy products or services. (9)

sales return. Merchandise that is brought back to the retailer for a refund or credit. (10)

sample. Subset of the targeted population. (4)

sans serif font. Type fonts that do not have serifs on letters. (13)

scale. A response format that allows researchers to assign numeric value to responses. (4) For the visual merchandising definition, see *proportion*.

search engine. Computer program that online visitors use to look for information on the Internet. (14)

search engine optimization (SEO). Process of getting a website ranked higher on the results pages when an Internet search is conducted. (14)

secondary data. Information, data, and statistics that have already been compiled. (4)

self-actualization. Need to fulfill one's own potential through reaching personal goals and contributing to the well-being of others. (5)

selling price. Price a customer actually pays for a product after discounts and coupons. (8)

selling tasks. Duties performed by sales associates when they are in direct contact with customers. (10)

semantic differential scale. Rating scale that contains a range of opposite responses. (4)

sender. Person who has a message to communicate. (9)

serif font. Type fonts that have short lines near the top and bottom of the long parts of some letters. (13)

service greeting. Greeting that immediately offers assistance to the customer. (10)

service mix. Range of all services sold by the retailer. (5)

service retailer. Business that provides services for a price. (2)

services. Activities performed for the benefit of others, usually for a fee, such as repairing a car or giving a manicure. (1)

shareware. Software that can be installed and used at no cost, but usually has a notice screen, time-delayed startup, or fewer features. (17)

shoplifter. Person posing as a customer who takes goods from the store without paying for them. (18)

shopping bot. Online search tool that compares prices for an item on different websites. (3)

shopping cart. Software application that helps online customers select and place items in the cart, pay, and get a receipt for their purchase. (13)

short-term goal. Goal that can be achieved in less than one year. (19)

site map. Overview of the pages within a website, often in the form of an outline. (14)

site usability. Describes how effective a website is for visitors. (13)

situational influence. Influence that comes from various factors in the general marketing environment. (5)

skill. Ability to do something well. (16)

SMART goal. Goal that is specific, measureable, attainable, realistic, and timely. (19)

social greeting. Greeting that acknowledges the customer's presence in the store. (10)

social influence. Influence that comes from the society in which a person lives and is acquired from the people around him or her. (5)

sole proprietorship. Business owned by one person. (2)

solution selling. See *feature-benefit selling*.

sourcing. Process of finding and analyzing potential suppliers of products to be purchased for resale. (17)

spam. Any electronic message sent in bulk to people who did not give a company permission to e-mail them. (17)

specialty store. Retailer that sells a limited product line, but offers a wide variety of options within the product line, in addition to other related items. (2)

splash page. Web page that appears before the website home page. (13)

staffing. Process of hiring people and matching them to the best position for their talents. (15)

standard of living. Level of material comfort as measured by the goods, services, and luxuries available to people; quality of life. (1)

stickiness. Describes how long visitors stay on a website. (13)

stock shrinkage. Difference between perpetual inventory and the actual physical inventory. (7)

stock turnover. Number of times merchandise is sold in a given period of time. (7)

stockholders. People who invest money in a company through buying stock, or a part ownership. (2)

store consultant. See *personal shopper*.

store image. Perception or impression created by the location, design, and décor of a retail business. (12)

store layout. Floor plan that shows how the space in a store is used. (12)

store manager. Person in charge of the overall well-being of a retail store. (15)

storefront. Exterior signs and logos, marquee, display windows, entrances, outdoor lighting, landscaping, and the building itself. (12)

storming. Stage two of team development that occurs when team members become less patient with the team process, as well as with one another, and start to experience conflict. (16)

storyboard. Series of drawings that helps a web designer see what the website should look like. (14)

street vendor. Retailer who sets up a portable store outdoors on a sidewalk, in a parking lot, or in an open-air market. (3)

style. Visual elements in HTML that are displayed on completed web pages. (14)

substitute selling. Offering a different product that still meets the customer's needs. (10)

suggestion selling. Offering items that work with the product a customer just purchased. (10)

supercenter. Very large discount department store that also sells a complete line of grocery products; also called a *hypermarket*. (2)

supervise. Make sure employees perform their jobs. (15)

supply. Amount of product retailers are willing to offer, or the overall quantity of merchandise available. (1, 8)

supply chain. Businesses, people, and activities involved in creating products and delivering them to end users. (1)

supply chain management. Process of coordinating the manufacturers, wholesalers, agents, and retailers to get products into the hands of the consumers. (1)

surveillance. Closely observing activity within a store to detect and prevent crimes. (18)

survey. Set of questions asked to a group of people to determine how that group thinks, feels, or acts. (4)

symmetrical balance. The placement of identical items on either side of an imaginary centerline on a display; also known as *formal balance*. (12)

synchronous service. When a customer asks a question and receives a response to his or her question in real time. (11)

T

tables. Web page layout tool used to display data in rows and columns, keeping the elements neatly aligned for easy reading. (14)

target market. Specific group of customers to which retailers aim to sell their products and services. (5)

team. Two or more people working together to reach a goal. (16)

teamwork. Action of people who come together for the purpose of a common goal. (16)

template. Page that contains all of the elements common to every page on a website. (14)

test marketing. Placing a new product in selected stores to test customer response in actual selling conditions. (4)

thumbnail. See *thumbnail image*.

thumbnail image. Small product image that has a very small file size; also called *thumbnail*. (13)

time management. Ability to organize time and work assignments to increase personal efficiency. (16)

tone. Impression of the overall content of the message. (9)

town center. Open-air shopping center with many retailers. (2)

trade discount. The amount that a vendor reduces the list price or manufacturer's suggested retail price (MSRP). (6)

trade publication. Publication, usually a magazine, that is geared toward people who work in a specific industry. (6)

trade secrets. See *proprietary information*.

trademark. Type of intellectual property registration that protects taglines, slogans, names, symbols, and any unique method to identify a product or company. (17)

traditional retailer. Store-based retailer that uses the five senses (sight, touch, taste, smell, and hearing) to enhance the shopping experience. (2)

traits. Behavioral and emotional characteristics that make each individual unique. (16)

transmission. Act of sending a message. (9)

trend research. Research that shows what has happened in the past as an indicator of the future. (6)

trustworthy. Worthy of people's confidence. (16)

U

uncontrollable risk. Situation that cannot be predicted or covered by purchasing insurance. (18)

uniform resource locator (URL). Unique Internet address of a document, web page, or website. (14)

uninsurable risk. Risk that an insurance company will not cover. (18)

unit pricing. Practice of pricing of goods based on a standard unit of measure, such as an ounce or a pound. (8)

upsell. Suggesting a product of higher quality or quantity, normally at a higher price. (10)

usage rate. How often customers use or buy a product or service. (5)

utility. Attribute that makes a business or product capable of satisfying a need or want; defines how or why something is useful. (1)

V

value. Relative worth of a product. (8)

value-based pricing. See *demand-based pricing*.

values. Beliefs about what is good or appropriate. (5)

variable expense. Business expense that changes based on the activities of the business. (8)

vending machine. Coin-, bill-, or credit-card machines used to sell small products. (3)

vendor. Person or business that sells something. (3) Company from which a buyer purchases merchandise. (6)

verbal communication. Speaking. (9)

viral marketing. Information about products that customers or viewers are compelled to pass along to others; also known as *buzz marketing*. (9)

visual merchandiser. Person in charge of carrying out the plan for helping develop the store image. (12)

visual merchandising. Way merchandise is presented in a store; also called *presentation*. (5) Process of creating floor plans and displays to attract customer attention and encourage purchases. (12)

volume pricing. Lowering the per-unit price of a product when a higher number of units are purchased at one time. (8)

W

warehouse club. Retailer that only sells merchandise in bulk. (2)

web authoring software. Computer software used to build a website; also called *web design software*. (14)

web browser. Software program used to view websites. (14)

web design software. See *web authoring software*.

web host. Company that provides a place for a business to post its website onto the Internet. (14)

web-influenced sale. Purchase made in a brick-and-mortar store where buyers first researched the products or services on the Internet. (3)

web widget. Add-on program that runs when a visitor opens a web page. (14)

webmaster. Person responsible for maintaining and updating a website once it has been published. (14)

wholesaler. Purchases goods in large quantities directly from manufacturers. (1)

wish list. Function of a checkout system that saves selected items in a customer's shopping cart for a future purchase. (13)

word-of-mouth publicity. When people talk casually about their experiences with a product, service, or business. (5)

written communication. Transmitting information using written symbols, either printed or handwritten. (9)

WYSIWYG. Web authoring software that automatically converts content and design elements into code; stands for *what you see is what you get*. (14)

Index